HTML/XML

IN THE SAME SERIES...

C/C++ New Reference

Windows 98 New Reference

Java 2 New Reference

HTML/XML

Oliver Pott

Prentice
Hall

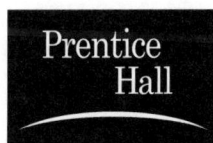

An imprint of PEARSON EDUCATION

PEARSON EDUCATION LIMITED

Head Office:
Edinburgh Gate
Harlow CM20 2JE
Tel: +44 (0)1279 623623
Fax: +44 (0)1279 431059

London Office:
128 Long Acre
London WC2E 9AN
Tel: +44 (0)20 7447 2000
Fax: +44 (0)20 7240 5771

—————————

First published in Great Britain in 2001
© Pearson Education Limited 2001

First published in 1999 as HTML/XML: *Referenz & Praxis*
by Markt & Technik Verlag GmbH
Martin-Kollar-Straße 10–12
D-81829 Munich
GERMANY

ISBN 0-13-032143-5

British Library Cataloguing in Publication Data
A CIP catalogue record for this book can be obtained from the British Library.

10 9 8 7 6 5 4 3 2 1

Translated and typeset by Cybertechnics, Sheffield.
Printed and bound in Great Britain by Biddles Ltd, Guildford & King's Lynn.

The publishers' policy is to use paper manufactured from sustainable forests.

Contents

Contents

Contents

How to use this book

HTML/XML New Reference is divided into two major sections: Reference and Practice. In the reference section all the entries are identified by easily recognisable symbols.

Key

☺   SMIL

W3C HTML 4.0 ✓   World Wide Web Consortium/HTML 4.0

<html attribute>   html attribute

CASCADING STYLE SHEETS   Cascading style sheets

XSL   XSL

XML   XML

ℯ   Microsoft Internet Explorer

N   Netscape Navigator

Reference

<!--Comments-->

Inserting comments in documents

Description

This syntax is used to insert comments in HTML documents. These comments are particularly helpful for later updates and alterations and to make the source code open. Comments are not displayed by the Browser and are invisible to visitors to the site.

Application

Insert a comment in the document in an arbitrary place. The text is enclosed between two tags, one at the beginning and one at the end. The complete text, which falls between the comment syntax, is ignored by the browser.

Example

```
<B>
<!-- This is the current shell of the tag -->
There is no news today.
<!-- End of current shell -->

<!-- Comments...
... should contain several lines -- >

<script language="JavaScript">
<!--

... This is the program code ...

//-->
</script>
```

Scripts enclosed in an HTML document are normally put in comment parenthesis. A browser which doesn't understand JavaScript will ignore these lines.

A

☺

Defining hyperlinks

Description

Using this SMIL element you can create hyperlinks in the same way as when using an HTML command.

Application

Hyperlinks are used to connect different media clips with each other using a shortcut. Instead of text, the link or anchor is included into the A container.

Parameters

HREF

With HREF, the command is given the destination address of the hyperlink, exactly as in HTML.

ID

This identifies the document. Through ID, other elements in this area can be accessed.

Show

The Show attribute specifies how the linked document should be shown. Three values are used for this:

new

Opens the clip in the browser while the RealPlayer continues in the background.

pause

Opens the clip in the browser and interrupts the RealPlayer.

replace

Opens the clip in the RealPlayer and replaces the current clip which may be running.

Example

```
<a id="identifier"
    show = "replace"
    href = "URL" >
</a>

<a href="http://www.microsoft.com/index.htm" show="new">
     <video src="video.rm" />
</a>
```

A

Determining links

W3C HTML 4.0 ✔

Description

Links between documents are defined with this elementary tag. You can add hyperlinks to other Web sites using this tag.

Application

The A tag (abbreviation for "anchor") requires the mandatory instruction of the HREF attribute. Through this attribute, the browser is provided with the destination address when the hyperlink is selected.

HTML 4.0 standard

ACCESSKEY, CHARSET, CLASS, COORDS, DIR, HREF, HREFLANG, ID, LANG, NAME, REF, REL, SHAPE, STYLE, TABINDEX, TITLE, TYPE

Start tag: required; End tag: required.

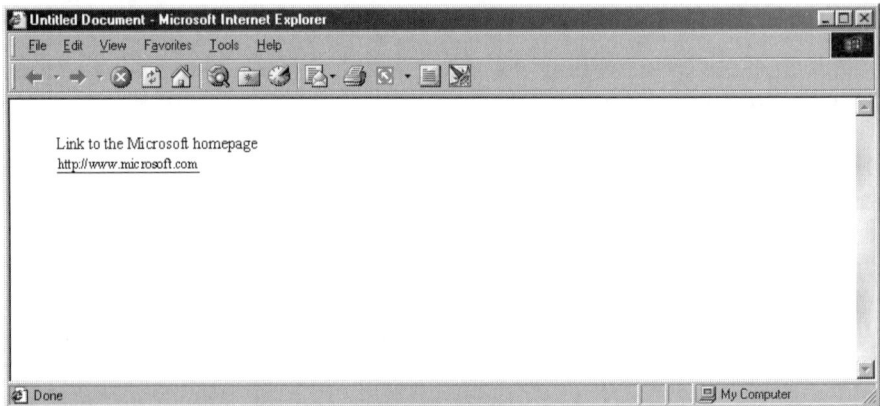

As a rule, hyperlinks are represented in blue and appear underlined in the browser.

Attributes

ACCESSKEY

The ACCESSKEY attribute gives the option of accessing an element through the keyboard. A keyboard shortcut allows you to load a document connected to the key shortcut by pressing the corresponding button. Therefore the ACCESSKEY ="A" command means that, after pressing the "A" key, the element is activated by the user.

CLASS

Through the CLASS attribute, the element can be assigned to a group (class). Enter one of the free selectable class name as a value. These groupings then provide easy access to all related elements. You can therefore easily change all properties of the elements of a class with the help of cascading style sheets or other languages, or select a value.

CHARSET

This attribute is used to determine the character encoding for data connected by the link. If the character set is not indicated explicitly, the browser will determine the character set to be used.

DIR

This attribute is necessary to determine the text direction. This attribute can have the values:

LTR

This value determines the text direction from left to right (and is short for "left-to-right"). This direction is predefined in the browser.

RTL

If the text must run contrary to the standard direction, from the right to the left margin of the screen, then choose the RTL value (short for "right-to-left").

ID

ID identifies the document. Using ID, a specific element can be accessed with the help of a script language to select or modify its value.

TYPE

Specifies the MIME type of the linked document. In this way, the browser is instructed to start a special display module for the content type and to show the document. For example "text/plain" for normal text or "application/msword" for a MS Word document.

HREF

With the HREF attribute, the linked element to which the anchor refers is indicated. You can use the common notation for Internet addresses (URL). The anchor can refer to an arbitrary Web site.

HREFLANG

This attribute indicates the language of the linked document. This is particularly important in search engines for identification purposes. Use the language codes according to ISO 639, for example "en" for English or "en-us" for American English.

NAME

Through the NAME attribute, an element can be assigned a name. These names should be unique for clarity purposes, which means that names are used only once in the document. This command is comparable with the ID attribute.

ONCLICK

This event takes place if you single-click on an element with the mouse. A given script is executed by this action.

5

ONDBLCLICK

This event takes place if you double-click on an element with the mouse. A given script is executed by this action.

ONFOCUS

The ONFOCUS event is triggered when the element is focused on, that is when the user goes on to this field with a mouse click or keyboard stroke and makes it the active element.

ONKEYDOWN

This event takes place if you are in an element and a key is pressed and held down. This action executes a specific script.

ONKEYPRESS

This event takes place if you are in an element and a key is pressed and released. This action executes a specific script.

ONKEYUP

This event takes place if you are in an element and a key that was pressed is released. This action executes a specific script.

ONMOUSEDOWN

This event takes place if you are in an element and a mouse button is clicked and held down. A given script is executed by this action.

ONMOUSEMOVE

This event takes place if you move the cursor over an object with the mouse. A given script is executed by this action.

ONMOUSEOUT

This event takes place if the mouse moves the cursor off an element. This action executes a given script.

ONMOUSEOVER

This event takes place if the mouse moves the cursor directly over the element (object). A given script is executed by this action.

ONMOUSEUP

This event takes place if you are in an element and a mouse button that was clicked and held down is released. A given script is executed by this action.

REL

With this attribute, you can affix link types for the linked document. You can therefore define a reference to a glossary or the index, for example. These commands allow the browser to help with navigation.

ALTERNATE

Indicates an alternative version of the document, a version in a different language or a shortened text version, for example.

APPENDIX

Refers to a document serving as an appendix to the Web site.

BOOKMARK

Indicates a special page which can be saved as a bookmark in your browser.

CHAPTER

Refers to the chapter of which the current document is part.

CONTENTS
> Points out a table of contents in which all pages are clearly listed.

COPYRIGHT
> In this page, you will find details about the originator of the document on this site.

GLOSSARY
> In this page, you will find a glossary which explains important concepts.

HELP
> Refers to a help page that helps with the navigation and use of the site.

INDEX
> Refers to an index that contains all the keywords in the Web site.

NEXT
> Indicates the following page in the current document.

PREV
> Indicates the previous document in the site.

SECTION
> Refers to the primary section that is part of the current document.

START
> Indicates the origin or start page of the Web site.

STYLESHEET
> Refers to an external style sheet that holds the current document format details.

SUBSECTION
> Refers to a sub-section within the document.

REV

Similar to REL, this attribute indicates the link back to the previous document. This attribute is rarely used. It does not indicate the jump destination, but the jump source, unlike a normal hyperlink.

ALTERNATE
> Indicates an alternative version of the document; a version in a different language or a shortened text version, for example.

APPENDIX
> Refers to an appendix to the Web site.

BOOKMARK
> Indicates a special page, which can be saved as a bookmark into your browser.

CHAPTER
> Refers to the chapter of which the current document is a part.

CONTENTS
> Points out a table of contents in which all pages are clearly listed.

COPYRIGHT
> In this page, you will find details about the originator of the document on this site.

GLOSSARY
> In this page, you will find a glossary which explains important concepts.

HELP
> Refers to a help page that helps with the navigation and use of the site.

INDEX
> Refers to an index that contains all the keywords in the Web site.

NEXT
> Indicates the following page in the current document.

PREV
> Indicates the previous document in this site.

SECTION
> Refers to the section that is part of the current document.

START
> Indicates the origin or start page of the Web site.

STYLESHEET
> Refers to an external style sheet that holds the current document format details.

SUBSECTION
> Refers to a sub-section in the document.

SHAPE
> The SHAPE attribute defines the area which should represent a link. The following commands are valid:

DEFAULT
> Specifies the entire area

RECT
> Defines a rectangular area; x1 = left upper corner, pixel at the link, y1 = left upper corner, above pixel, x2 = lower right corner, left pixel, y2 = lower right corner, above pixel

CIRCLE
> Defines a circular area; x = centre, left pixel, y = centre, above pixel, R = radius in pixels

POLY
> Defines a polygonal area; x1-xn, x = pixel of a corner on the left, y1-yn, y = pixels of an upper corner

> The chosen form is important for the interpretation of the commands that are executed under COORDS.

COORDS
> Absolute co-ordinates of squares can be defined within a graphic using this attribute. The form of co-ordinate details depends on the region form defined in SHAPE.

STYLE
> The STYLE attribute can be used to change style settings, in particular the appearance of the element. As the value of the attribute, apply the corresponding options of a style sheet language (usually CSS).

TABINDEX
> This attribute assigns the tab command to an element using positive or negative integers. Elements provided with this attribute can be selected one after the other with the Tab key. This operation helps users who do not use the mouse.

TARGET
> The TARGET attribute is used to fix the name of a window in which a link is opened. This attribute is used if several windows are open or should be opened with a new window using a link.

TITLE
> You should give the user further information about the used element by defining a meaningful title with the help of the TITLE command. Navigation on your Web site is made easier for users who are dependent on voice response.

Example

```
<A HREF="http://www.w3c.org">
Link to World Wide Web Consortium
</a>

<a HREF="mailto:name@domain.com">
Please write to me!
</A>
```

With the term "mailto:" you can automatically start connected email programs by clicking the browser link. The given address is inserted into the receiver field.

Events

```
ONBLUR,   ONCLICK,   ONDBLCLICK,   ONFOCUS,   ONKEYDOWN,   ONKEYPRESS,
ONKEYUP,   ONMOUSEDOWN,   ONMOUSEMOVE,   ONMOUSEOUT,   ONMOUSEOVER,
ONMOUSEUP
```

XML definition

```
<! ENTITY % Shape "(rect|circle|poly|default)">
<!ENTITY % Coords "CDATA>

<! ELEMENT A - - (%inline;)* -(A)>
<!ATTLIST A
% attrs;
      charset          % Charset;      # IMPLIED
      type             % ContentType;  # IMPLIED
      name             CDATA           # IMPLIED
      href             % URI;          # IMPLIED
      hreflang         % LanguageCode; # IMPLIED
      rel              % LinkTtype;    # IMPLIED
      rev              % LinkType;     # IMPLIED
      accesskey        % Character;    # IMPLIED
```

```
shape          % Shape;       # IMPLIED
coords         %Coords;       # IMPLIED
tabindex       NUMBER         # IMPLIED
onfocus        % Script;      # IMPLIED
onblur         % Script;      # IMPLIED>
```

Related commands

```
AREA
BASE
LINK
```

ABBR   <html attribute>

Short description for table cell

Description

This attribute allows a short description to be defined for both a table cell and a table header. If this attribute is not submitted, the first character of the content will automatically be used as the default setting.

Application

Complete the corresponding command with this attribute using the short description as the value. The use of this attribute is optional.

Values

You can give any string to this attribute as the value. If possible, this character string should not start or end with a space. The processing browser may filter these out.

Example

```
<td abbr="Sales 1999">2.500.000 </td>
<th abbr="Sales"></th>
```

Accompanying elements

TD
TH

ABBR
Abbreviations

Description
Abbreviations are indicated with this command. The content of these abbreviations, which are components of other concepts, as in acronyms, are formatted in different ways by the browser.

Application
The ABBR command can be used to identify concepts, such as UFO, FAQ, WWW, URL or HTTP. It is used in first line programs to analyse the contents of a document.

HTML 4.0 standard
CLASS, DIR, ID, LANG STYLE, TITLE

Start tag: required; End tag: required.

Attributes
CLASS

    Through the attribute CLASS, the element can be assigned to a group (class). Enter one of the free selectable class name as a value. These groupings then provides easy access to all related elements. You can therefore easily change all properties of the elements of a class with the help of cascading style sheets or other languages, or select a value.

DIR

    This attribute is necessary to determine the text direction. This attribute can have the values:

    LTR

        This value determines the text direction from left to right (and is short for "left-to-right"). This direction is predefined in the browser.

    RTL

        If the text must run contrary to the standard direction, from the right to the left margin of the screen, then choose the RTL value (short for "right-to-left").

ID

    This identifies the document. Using ID, a specific element can be accessed with the help of a script language, to select or modify its values.

LANG

    This attribute indicates the language of the linked document. This is particularly important in search engines for identification purposes. Use the language codes according to ISO 639, for example "en" for English or "en-us" for American English.

ONCLICK

This event takes place if you single-click on an element with the mouse. A given script is executed by this action.

ONDBLCLICK

This event takes place if you double-click on an element with the mouse. A given script is executed by this action.

ONKEYDOWN

This event takes place if you are in an element and a key is pressed and held down. This action executes a specific script.

ONKEYPRESS

This event takes place if you are in an element and a key pressed and released. This action executes a specific script.

ONKEYUP

This event takes place if you are in an element and a key that was pressed is released. This action executes a specific script.

ONMOUSEDOWN

This event takes place if you are in an element and a mouse button is clicked and held down. A given script is executed by this action.

ONMOUSEMOVE

This event takes place if you move the cursor over an object with the mouse. A given script is executed by this action.

ONMOUSEOUT

This event takes place if the mouse moves the cursor off an element. This action excecutes a given script.

ONMOUSEOVER

This event takes place if the mouse moves the cursor directly over the element (object). A given script is executed by this action.

ONMOUSEUP

This event takes place if you are in an element and a mouse button that was clicked and held down is released. A given script is executed by this action.

STYLE

The attribute STYLE can be used to change style settings, in particular the appearance of an element. As the value of the attribute, you apply the corresponding options of a style sheet language (usually CSS).

TITLE

You should gives the user further information about the used element defining a meaningful title with the help of the TITLE command. The navigation on your Web site is made easier for users who are dependent on voice responces.

Example

```
etc.
</ABBR>
and so on
```

Events

ONCLICK, ONDBLCLICK, ONKEYDOWN, ONKEYPRESS, ONKEYUP, ONMOUSEDOWN, ONMOUSEMOVE, ONMOUSEOUT, ONMOUSEOVER, ONMOUSEUP

Related commands

ACRONYM
ADDRESS
CITE
CODE
DFN
EM
KBD
SAMP
STRONG
VAR

ACCEPT   <html attribute>

Indicating a valid data format in the transmission

Description

This attribute can be used to filter out incompatible files when the user selects data, for example.

Application

This attribute indicates a list of valid content types separated by commas which the server can process directly. The use of this attribute is optional.

Values

The values valid for the attribute ACCEPT are content types. Special data formats are indicated with these values; a Microsoft Word document or an Adobe PDF document, for example. Use the definitions to define data format which you can find under the keyword MIME types. Several values can be separated by a comma.

Example

```
<input accept="image/gif">
<input accept="text/html">
<input accept="text/css">
```

Related elements

INPUT

ACCEPT-CHARSET   <html attribute>

Defining valid character sets for form fields

Description

You can define character sets valid for input in form fields with the help of this attribute.

Application

Give one or more names to the attribute by separated commas or spaces for character sets. The CHARSET parameter indicates a method to convert a byte sequence into a character string. The use of this attribute is optional.

Values

Under the keyword **Character Sets** you will find all the codes and names with which you can determine character sets. Give this attribute to a single character set or to a list of several valid character sets.

Example

```
<form accept-charset="ISO-8859-1">
<form accept-charset="ISO-8859-1, ISO-8859-2">
```

Related elements

FORM

ACCESSKEY   <html attribute>

Setting a key for the operation

Description

With the help of this attribute you can indicate hotkeys for an element. When the user presses this key, the corresponding element automatically becomes the active element.

Application

The attribute ACCESSKEY makes access to an element possible via the keyboard shortcuts. The command ACCESSKEY ="A" leads to the activation of the element after the user presses "A". The use of this attribute is optional, but it is necessary to make HTML documents usable without a mouse.

Values

You can give a single valid character in the ISO 10646 character set as the value to this attribute.

Example

```
<input name="Name" accesskey="v">
<input name="Surname" accesskey="n">
<input name="Address" accesskey="s">
```

Related elements

A
AREA
BUTTON
INPUT
LABEL
LEGEND
TEXTAREA

ACRONYM

W3C HTML 4.0 ✔

Abbreviations

Description

Abbreviations and acronyms are indicated with this command. The contents of these abbreviations, which are components of other concepts, are formatted in another way.

Application

The command ACRONYM is used to identify concepts, such as FAQ, WWW, URL or HTTP. It can be used like the command ABBR.

HTML-4.0-Standard

CLASS, DIR, ID, LANG STYLE, TITLE

Start tag: required; End tag: required.

Attribute

CLASS

Through the attribute CLASS, an element can be assigned to a group (class). Enter one of the free selectable class names as a value. These groupings then provides easy access to all related elements. You can therefore easily change all properties of the elements of a class with the help of cascading style sheets or other languages, or select a value.

DIR

This attribute is necessary to determine the text direction. This attribute can have the values:

LTR

This value determines the text direction from left to right (and is short for "left-to-right"). This direction is predefined in the browser.

RTL

If the text must run contrary to the standard direction from the right to the left margin of the screen, then choose the value RTL (short for "right-to-left").

ID

ID identifies the document. Using ID, a specific element can be accessed with the help of a script language, to select or modify its values.

LANG

This attribute indicates the language of the linked document. This is particularly important in search engines for identification purposes. Use the language codes according to ISO 639, for example "en" for English or "en-us" for American English.

ONCLICK

This event takes place if you single-click on an element with the mouse. A given script is executed by this action.

ONDBLCLICK

This event takes place if you double-click on an element with the mouse. A given script is executed by this action.

ONKEYDOWN

This event takes place if you are in an element and a key is pressed and held down. This action executes a specific script.

ONKEYPRESS

This event takes place if you are in an element and a key pressed and released. This action executes a specific script.

ONKEYUP

This event takes place if you are in an element and a key that was pressed is released. This action executes a specific script.

ONMOUSEDOWN

This event takes place if you are in an element and a mouse button is clicked and held down. A given script is executed by this action.

ONMOUSEMOVE
> This event takes place if you move the mouse cursor over an object. A given script is executed by this action.

ONMOUSEOUT
> This event takes place if the mouse moves the cursor off an element. This action excecutes a given script.

ONMOUSEOVER
> This event takes place if the mouse moves the cursor directly over the element (object). A given script is executed by this action.

ONMOUSEUP
> This event takes place if you are in an element and a mouse button that was clicked and held down is released. A given script is executed by this action.

STYLE
> The attribute STYLE can be used to change style settings, in particular the appearance of an element. As the value of the attribute, you apply the corresponding options of a style sheet language (usually CSS).

TITLE
> You should give the user further information about the used element defining a meaningful title with the help of the TITLE command. The navigation on your Web site is made easier for users who are dependent on voice responces.

Example

```
<ACRONYM>
FAQ
</ACRONYM>
Frequently asked Questions
```

Events

ONCLICK, ONDBLCLICK, ONKEYDOWN, ONKEYPRESS, ONKEYUP, ONMOUSEDOWN, ONMOUSEMOVE, ONMOUSEOUT, ONMOUSEOVER, ONMOUSEUP

Related commands

ACRONYM
ADDRESS
CITE
CODE
DFN
EM
KBD
SAMP
STRONG
VAR

ACTION **<html attribute>**

Transmitting form data

Description
This attribute refers to scripts or programs which process user input.

Application
Make sure that the instruction of this attribute is specified, otherwise no interaction can be set up with the server. This attribute refers to a CGI script of the server which usually reprocesses and evaluates data entered.

Values
A valid value for this attribute is the URI (Uniform Resource Identifier). The construction of a URI is as follows:

```
[protocol]: // [Domain]/[Directory]/[File]
```

Possible protocols used are the following:

ftp	File Transfer Protocol
http	Hypertext Transfer Protocol
gopher	Gopher Protocol
mailto	Electronic Mail Address
news	USENET News
nntp	USENET News (NNTP access)
telnet	Reference to interactive sessions
wais	Wide Area Information Server
file	Host-specific file names
prospero	Prospero Directory Service

Example
```
<form action="http://www.online-shop.co.uk/purchase command.cgi">
<form action="mailto:purchase command@online-shop.co.uk">>
```

Accompanying element
FORM

ADDRESS

Specifying addresses

Description

This command is used to specify addresses, particularly in documents. With this tag it is possible to create contact information which allows the user to contact the author of a document.

Application

With the element ADDRESS an HTML programmer gives the user contact information about themselves. Therefore, this element is primarily meaningful in connection with email references.

HTML 4.0 standard

CLASS, DIR, ID, LANG, TITLE

Start tag: required; End tag: required.

Attributes

CLASS

Through the attribute CLASS, the element can be assigned to a group (class). Enter one of the free selectable class name as a value. These groupings then provides easy access to all related elements. You can therefore easily change all properties of the elements of a class with the help of cascading style sheets or other languages, or select a value.

DIR

This attribute is necessary to determine the text direction. This attribute can have the values:

LTR

This value determines the text direction from left to right (and is short for "left-to-right"). This direction is predefined in the browser.

RTL

If the text must run contrary to the standard direction from the right to the left margin of the screen, then choose the value RTL (short for "right-to-left").

ID

ID identifies a document. Using ID, a specific element can be accessed with the help of a script language, to select or modify its values.

LANG

This attribute indicates the language of the linked document. This is particularly important in search engines for identification purposes. Use the language codes according to ISO 639, for example "en" for English or "en-us" for American English.

ONCLICK

This event takes place if you single-click on an element with the mouse. A given script is executed by this action.

ONDBLCLICK

This event takes place if you double-click on an element with the mouse. A given script is executed by this action.

ONKEYDOWN

This event takes place if you are in an element and a key is pressed and held down. This action executes a specific script.

ONKEYPRESS

This event takes place if you are in an element and a key is pressed and released. This action executes a specific script.

ONKEYUP

This event takes place if you are in an element and a key that was pressed is released. This action executes a specific script.

ONMOUSEDOWN

This event takes place if you are in an element and a mouse button is clicked and held down. A given script is executed by this action.

ONMOUSEMOVE

This event takes place if you move the mouse cursor over an object. A given script is executed by this action.

ONMOUSEOUT

This event takes place if the mouse moves the cursor off an element. This action excecutes a given script.

ONMOUSEOVER

This event takes place if the mouse moves the cursor directly over the element (object). A given script is executed by this action.

ONMOUSEUP

This event takes place if you are in an element and a mouse button that was clicked and held down is released. A given script is executed by this action.

STYLE

The attribute STYLE can be used to change style settings, in particular the appearance of an element. As the value of the attribute, you apply the corresponding options of a style sheet language (usually CSS).

TITLE

You should give the user further information about the element used defining a meaningful title with the help of the TITLE command. The navigation on your Web site is made easier for users who are dependent on voice responses.

Example

```
<ADDRESS>
<A HREF="http://www.pott-it.de/">Oliver Pott</a>
</ADDRESS>
```

The above is an example of an address element, in this case the address of the author of this book.

Events

ONBLUR, ONCLICK, ONDBLCLICK, ONFOCUS, ONKEYDOWN, ONKEYPRESS, ONKEYUP, ONMOUSEDOWN, ONMOUSEMOVE, ONMOUSEOUT, ONMOUSEOVER, ONMOUSEUP

XML definition

```
<!ELEMENT ADDRESS>
<!ATTLIST ADDRESS
% attrs; >
```

Related elements

ACRONYM
ADDRESS
CITE
CODE
DFN
EM
KBD
SAMP
STRONG
VAR

ALIGN   \<html attribute\>

Aligning an element

Description

With this attribute elements can be aligned on the page. In connection with some commands, however, ALIGN also causes the alignment within the primary object. The use of this attribute is optional.

Application

You should apply the ALIGN attribute and give one of the descriptions mentioned below as the value.

Values

For each command in which you use this attribute there are different validity ranges for the given value. We have listed the single elements and possible values as follows:

CAPTION
   TOP
      With ALIGN=TOP you can produce a table header aligned centred.
   BOTTOM
      With ALIGN=BOTTOM you create a table footer aligned centred.
   LEFT
      With ALIGN=LEFT you create a table header aligned centred.
   RIGHT
      With ALIGN=RIGHT you create a table footer aligned right.
APPLET, IFRAME, IMG, INPUT, OBJECT
   TOP
      With ALIGN=TOP the text of the entry field is aligned at the top of the element.
   BOTTOM
      With ALIGN=BOTTOM the text of the entry field is aligned at the bottom of the element.
   MIDDLE
      With ALIGN=MIDDLE the text following the entry field is centred.
   LEFT
      With ALIGN=LEFT the object is left aligned.
   RIGHT
      With ALIGN=RIGHT the object is right aligned.
LEGEND
   TOP
      The legend is placed above the group. This is a default value.
   BOTTOM
      The legend is placed at the bottom of the group.
   LEFT
      Left-justified alignment of the legend within the group.
   RIGHT
      Right-justified alignment of the legend within the group.
TABLE
   LEFT
      Left-justified alignment of a table.
   RIGHT
      Right-justified alignment of a table.
   CENTER
      Centred alignment of a table.
HR
   LEFT
      The horizontal dividing line is aligned left-justified.

RIGHT

The horizontal dividing line is aligned right-justified.

CENTER

The horizontal dividing line is centred. If the attribute ALIGN is missing, then the value CENTER is accepted as the default setting.

DIV, H1, H2, H3, H4, H5, H6, P

CENTER

Centred alignment of a section.

LEFT

Left alignment of a section.

RIGHT

Right alignment of a section.

JUSTIFY

Provides an alignment of the text to both sides (justified typesetting).

COL, COLGROUP, TBODY, TD, TFOOT, TH, THEAD, TR

LEFT

Left alignment of data within a table. Default setting.

RIGHT

Right alignment of data within a table.

CENTER

Centred alignment of data within a table. Default setting for table headers.

JUSTIFY

Creates justified text in a table.

CHAR

Aligns text within a table around a specific character with the attribute CHAR.

Example

```
hr align="center">
<caption align="bottom">Heading </caption>

<td align="justify">Table content justified </td>
<div align="right">Flush right alignment </div>
```

Accompanying elements

APPLET

CAPTION

COL

COLGROUP

DIV

H1

H2

H3

H4

H5

H6
HR
IFRAME
IMG
INPUT
LEGEND
OBJECT
P
TABLE
TBODY
TD
TFOOT
TH
THEAD
TR

alignment

Horizontal alignment

Description

Aligning a text paragraph in accordance with the given setting.

Parameter

left
    Alignment is to the left.
center
    Alignment is centred.
right
    Alignment is to the right.
justify
    Alignment is justified.

Example

```
<style type="text/css">
h1, h2 { alignment: right}
h3, h4 { alignment: justify}
</style>

<div style="alignment: justify " >
</div>
```

ALINK   <html attribute>

Specifying the colour of an active hyperlink

Description
With this attribute, the colour of the hyperlinks activated by a user may be specified.

Application
Besides the 16 defined colours, up to 256 colours can be represented here with the determined hexadecimal numbers. This command is not supported by HTML version 4.0. The use of this attribute is optional.

Values
Either give a colour value in RGB syntax or a valid colour name to the attribute. For the RGB value, indicate the colour values of the colours red, green and blue in hexadecimal notation: #RRGGBB (i.e. #008000 for green). Alternatively, predefined colour names can be used. (i.e. YELLOW). Under the **Color Palette** keyword you will find a complete list of all standard colours. These are the 16 most frequently used primary colours:

```
BLACK    = #000000  SILVER   = #C0C0C0
GRAY     = #808080  WHITE    = #FFFFFF
MAROON   = #800000  RED      = #FF0000
PURPLE   = #800080  FUCHSIA  = #FF00FF
GREEN    = #008000  LIME     = #00FF00
OLIVE    = #808000  YELLOW   = #FFFF00
NAVY     = #000080  BLUE     = #0000FF
TEAL     = #008080  AQUA     = #00FFFF
```

Example
```
<body alink="black">
<body vlink="red">
<body link="#00FFFF">
```

Accompanying elements
BODY

ALT

<html attribute>

Instruction for an alternative representation

Description

Using this attribute you can indicate an alternative representation for graphic objects in text form. If a browser cannot represent this element or is dependent on language reproduction, then the given text is used as an alternative.

Application

The use of this attribute is optional yet recommended, particularly to support non graphic-compatible browsers and people who are dependent on a language reproduction or Braille keyboard.

Values

You can give any string to this attribute as a value. If possible, this character string should not start or end with blank characters, as the processing browser may filter these out.

Example

```
<img src="tree.jpg" alt="Image of a tree in the grass">
```

Accompanying elements
APPLET
AREA
IMG
INPUT

ANCHOR ☺

Defining hot spots

Description

This command enables you to provide a media clip with a hot spot.

Parameter

begin
    Indicates time output. You can use the description h, min, s or ms as units.

coords
> Through coords you determine the coordinates of the referring sensitive area.

end
> Indicates the end of the group. This value refers relatively to the begin attribute. You can use the description h, min, s or ms as units.

href
> With href you give the command of the destination address of the hyperlink, exactly as in HTML.

id
> This identifies a document. Through id you can access other elements in this area.

show
> The show attribute displays how the connected document will be displayed. Three values are available for this attribute:
>
> new
>> Opens the clip in the browser while the RealPlayer continues in the background.
>
> pause
>> Opens the clip in the browser and stops the RealPlayer.
>
> replace
>> Opens the clip in the RealPlayer and replaces the current clip.

Example

```
<anchor id="identifier"
      show = "replace"
      href = "URL"
      skip-content = "false"
      coords = "100.200.150.250"
      begin = "10 s"
      ends = "2 h"/>

<video src="vido.rm">
<anchor
      href = "index.htm"
      show = "pause"
      coords ="10,20,30,40" />
</video>
```

any

All descendants of a target element

Description

This command can be used to consider all descendants of the target element.

Example

```
</element type="document">
     <any>
           <target element/>
     </any>
     </element>
```

APP

Embedding references in HotJava

Description

With the app command references are defined as HotJava according to the Sun syntax (*app = applet = application snippet*). In practice, this command is redundant. Embedding with the APPLET command is adequate. By the introduction of the OBJECT element in HTML 4.0 even the APPLET tag is no longer required.

Application

The APP command is applied only in exceptions, because this command, which was developed by Sun, has a special syntax. APP has no ending tag.

HTML 4.0 standard

This command does not belong to the official HTML definition.

Attributes

CLASS

The attribute describes the object class according to the Sun syntax. It is therefore used for the file names of an executable APPLET file. Typical for this type is that the otherwise required extension .class is missing.

SRC
> This is an optional instruction which is only significant if the source code of a Java applet is needed by the Java Interpreter (*src = source*). You should use this instruction only if it is explicitly requested in the documentation of a Java applet.

Example
```
<app class="Button" src="button.java">
```

Related commands
APPLET

OBJECT

APPLET

W3C HTML 4.0 ✓

Embedding Java programs

Description
With this command it is possible to embed Java applets into available HTML pages or source codes. Since the introduction of the version HTML 4.0 the command OBJECT is used instead of the APPLET tag.

Application
The APPLET command is used to embed Java applets into HTML documents. Java applets are small programs which are carried out in browser windows. This command disappeared from the HotJava syntax in HTML 3.2. In HTML 4.0 it has been replaced by OBJECT.

HTML 4.0 standard
ALIGN, ALT, ARCHIVE, CLASS, CLASS, CODE, CODEBASE, DIR, HEIGHT, HSPACE, ID, ID, LANG, NAME, OBJECT, STYLE, STYLE, TITLE, TITLE, VSPACE, WIDTH

The use of this command is not supported in the current HTML version and it has been replaced by other commands.

Attributes
ALIGN
> Attribute which is used to determine the alignment of an APPLET window within the main window.

ALT
>It is required if an APPLET should not be executed. In this case, the text contained in the attribute is reported to the user.

ARCHIVE
>(Use: APPLET archive = URI) Contains a list of URIs separated by commas. These URIs refer to elements such as classes or other files which could require a Java applet to execute a preload.

CLASS
>With this attribute you assign the applet to a class or a group of classes. The use of classes is helpful if elements need to be changed. The alteration then affects every element belonging to a class.

CODE
>The CODE attribute determines the class of an applet. This attribute can contain references to the complete path of an applet. If several classes are needed for an applet, the search for these classes takes place in the CODEBASE attribute.

CODEBASE
>The CODEBASE attribute is responsible for delivering a file path. This path is used by an applet if relative address references should appear when processing an object. The APPLET command only uses a subdirectory of the corresponding document directories for the CODEBASE=URI attribute.

HEIGHT
>Attribute to determine the height of a window.

HSPACE
>Attribute to determine the amount of free horizontal space in an APPLET window.

ID
>ID identifies a document. Using ID, a single element can be accessed with the help of a script language, to select or modify its value.

NAME
>Using this attribute a name can be assigned to a Java applet which ensures a clear identification compared to other applets.

OBJECT
>This attribute is used to execute an APPLET class code depending on the path of a CODEBASE attribute. Remember that an applet executes only the method start () but not the method init ().

STYLE
>The attribute STYLE can be used to change style settings, in particular the appearance of an element. As the value of the attribute, you apply the corresponding options of a style sheet language (usually CSS).

TITLE
>You should give the user further information about the element used, defining a meaningful title with the help of the TITLE command. Navigation in your Web site is made easier for users who are dependent on voice response.

VSPACE
>   Attribute to determine the vacant vertical space within an APPLET window.

WIDTH
>   Attribute to determine the width of a window.

Example

```
<applet code="AnimText.class"
    width = 150 height = 100 hspace = 500 >
    <param name="text" value="Animierter Text">
    <param name="type" value="wave">
    <param name="bgcolor" value="yellow">
    <param name="fgcolor" value="red">
    <param name="style" value="bold">
    <param name="min" value="10">
    <param name="max" value="40">
</applet>
```

Related commands

APP
OBJECT

apply

Using style sheets

Description

Applies the given style sheets to the target element.

Parameter

All style sheet definitions.

Example

```
<apply font-style="bold"/>
    <apply font-size="12pt"/>
```

Archives   <html attribute>

Specifying data archives as an object source

Description

This attribute indicates the data source of archives which refer to the object. It contains the data source which is better designated with the attributes CLASSID and DATA. Object classes can be searched from ZIP archives.

Application

Indicates the archive file as a value of the URI. The use of this attribute is optional.

Values

There are different validity ranges for the given result every time you use this attribute for a command. Below is a list of the commands and their possible values:

APPLET
> (Use: APPLET archive = URI) This URI contains a list separated by commas. These URIs refer to elements such as class or other files which could require a Java applet to execute a preload.

OBJECT
> A valid value for this attribute is the URI (Uniform Resource Identifier). The construction of a URI corresponds or the following scheme:
>
> [protocol]: // [Domain]/[Directory]/[File]
>
> The following values are possible instructions for the protocol used:

ftp	File Transfer Protocol
http	Hypertext Transfer Protocol
gopher	Gopher Protocol
mailto	Electronic Mail Address
news	USENET News
nntp	USENET News (NNTP access)
telnet	Reference to interactive sessions
wais	Wide Area Information Server
file	Host-specific file names
prospero	Prospero Directory Service

Example

```
object code="action.class"
    width = 100 height = 50 hspace = 50
    archives = "http://www.domain.co.uk/classes.zip" >
```

Accompanying elements

APPLET

OBJECT

AREA

Definition of areas in a reference-sensitive graphic

Description

With this command, single areas of an image map are defined, which stand out as they are reference-sensitive.

Application

The command AREA is used to represent maps, for example. These maps are represented as reference-sensitive graphics in which users can have details expanded on with a mouse click.

HTML 4.0 standard

ACCESSKEY, ALT, CLASS, COORDS, DIR, HREF, ID, LANG, NOHREF, SHAPE, STYLE, TABINDEX, TITLE

Start tag: required; end tag: not allowed.

With the help of image maps such reference-sensitive maps can be created by clicking on the address.

Attributes

ALT

Gives an alternative description to the graphic to support pure Text browsers. In this way the elements of the reference-sensitive graphic can be accessed far more easily.

ACCESSKEY

The attribute ACCESSKEY enables access to an element through the keyboard using a keyboard shortcut. In this way the command ACCESSKEY="A" means that when the user presses the "A" key the element is activated.

CLASS

Through the CLASS attribute, the element can be assigned to a group (class). Enter one of the free selectable class name as a value. These groupings then provide easy access to all related elements. You can therefore easily change all properties of the elements of a class with the help of cascading style sheets or other languages, or select a value.

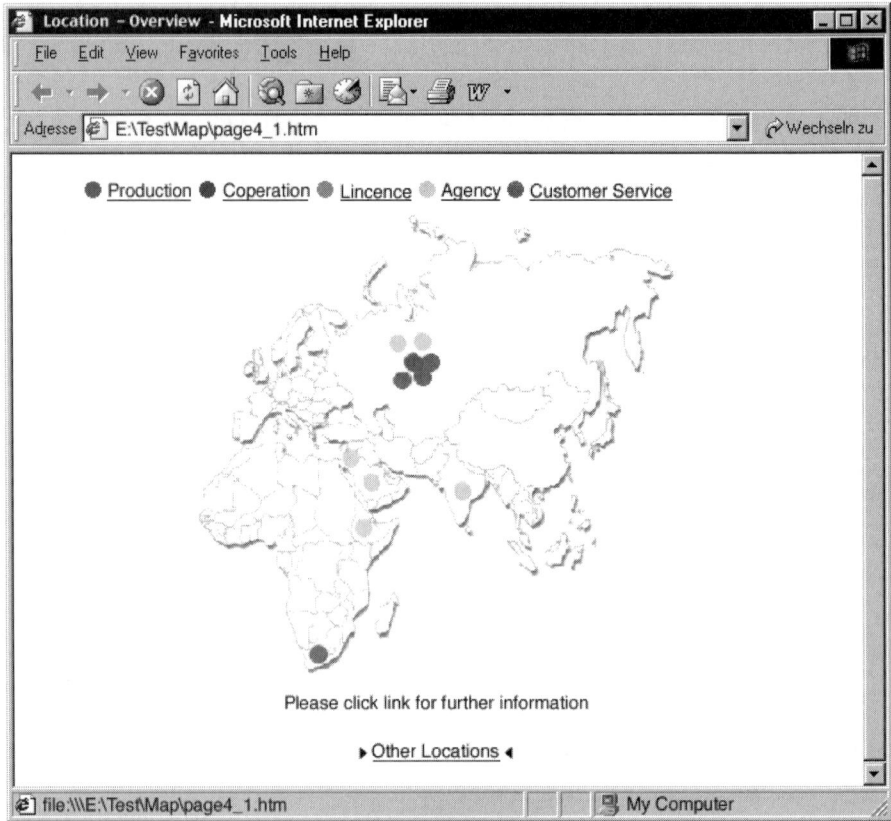

```
Location – Overview - Microsoft Internet Explorer
File  Edit  View  Favorites  Tools  Help
Adresse  E:\Test\Map\page4_1.htm                           Wechseln zu

● Production ● Coperation ● Lincence ● Agency ● Customer Service



Please click link for further information

▶ Other Locations ◀

file:\\\E:\Test\Map\page4_1.htm                    My Computer
```

With image maps, reference-sensitive maps can be created, where the address is displayed by clicking on a place

COORDS

   With this attribute absolute coordinates of areas within a graphic are defined. The shape of the coordinate command depends on the area shape defined with SHAPE.

DIR

   This attribute is necessary to determine the text direction. This attribute can have the values:

   LTR

      This value determines the text direction from left to right (and is short for "left-to-right"). This direction is predefined in the browser.

   RTL

      If the text must run contrary to the standard direction, from the right to the left margin of the screen, then choose the RTL value (short for "right-to-left").

ID

   This identifies a document. Using ID, a specific element can be accessed with the help of a script language, to select or modify its value.

HREF

The HREF attribute gives a reference to the linked target, for example a file activated by clicking on a sensitive area.

HREFLANG

This attribute indicates the language of the target document. This is particularly important in search engines for identification purposes. Use the language codes according to ISO 639, for example "en" for English or "en-us" for American English.

LANG

This attribute indicates the language of the linked document. This is particularly important in search engines for identification purposes. Use the language codes according to ISO 639, for example "en" for English or "en-us" for American English.

NOHREF

If this attribute is used for a clickable region there is no reference to other documents.

ONCLICK

This event takes place if you single-click on an element with the mouse. A given script is executed by this action.

ONDBLCLICK

This event takes place if you double-click on an element with the mouse. A given script is executed by this action.

ONKEYDOWN

This event takes place if you are in an element and a key is pressed and held down. This action executes a specific script.

ONKEYPRESS

This event takes place if you are in an element and a key is pressed and released. This action executes a specific script.

ONKEYUP

This event takes place if you are in an element and a key that was pressed is released. This action executes a specific script.

ONMOUSEDOWN

This event takes place if you are in an element and a mouse button is clicked and held down. A given script is executed by this action.

ONMOUSEMOVE

This event takes place if you move the cursor over an object with the mouse. A given script is executed by this action.

ONMOUSEOUT

This event takes place if the mouse moves the cursor off an element. This action excecutes a given script.

ONMOUSEOVER

This event takes place if the mouse moves the cursor directly over the element (object). A given script is executed by this action.

ONMOUSEUP

This event takes place if you are in the described element and a mouse button that was clicked and held down is released. A given script is executed by this action.

SHAPE

With the attribute SHAPE the shape of a selectable region can be checked in an AREA element. The following instructions are valid:

DEFAULT

Complete area.

RECT

Rectangle; x1 = left top corner, left pixel, y1 = left top corner, above pixel, x2 = right bottom corner, left pixel, y2 = right bottom corner, above pixel.

CIRCLE

Circle; x = centre, left pixel, y = centre, above pixel, R = radius in pixels.

POLY

Polygon; x1-xn, x = pixel in a left corner, y1-yn, y = pixels in a top corner. The chosen shape is important to interpret the coordinate instruction which is executed under COORDS.

STYLE

The attribute STYLE can be used to change style settings, in particular the appearance of an element. As the value of the attribute, you apply the corresponding options of a style sheet language (usually CSS).

TABINDEX

This attribute assigns a command position to an element by using positive or negative integers. Elements which are provided with this attribute can be selected with the tab key one after the other. This makes the operation easier particularly for people who do not use a mouse.

TARGET

The TARGET attribute is used to fix the name of a window in which the link is opened. This attribute is used if several windows are open or if you want to open a new window with another link.

TITLE

You should give the user further information about the used element defining a meaningful title with the help of the TITLE command. The navigation on your Web site is made easier for users who are dependent on voice responses.

Example

```
<<map name="Testimage">
<area shape=rect coords="1,1,249,49" href="#anchor">
<area shape=rect coords="1,51,149,299" href="file.htm">
<area shape=rect coords="251,1,399,399" href="file.htm">
<area shape=rect coords="151,51,249,299"
href = "http://www.nix.co.uk/" >
<area shape=rect coords="1,301,249,399" nohref>
</map>
```

```
<img src="hypgraph.gif" usemap="#Testimage" bcommand=0>
```

Events

ONBLUR,   ONCLICK,   ONDBLCLICK,   ONFOCUS,   ONKEYDOWN,   ONKEYPRESS,
ONKEYUP,   ONMOUSEDOWN,   ONMOUSEMOVE,   ONMOUSEOUT,   ONMOUSEOVER,
ONMOUSEUP

Related commands

MAP

ATTLIST

Defining attributes of an element

Description

Elements can contain further options through attributes, so they can contain many HTML tag attributes which determine the alignment of the element, for example.

Application

A general attribute declaration consists of the keyword ATTLIST, the element name to which the attribute shall be assigned, the name of the attribute and the value type.

Example

```
<! ATTLIST align (left|center|right) "left">

<!ATTLIST book title CDATA # IMPLIED
              author CDATA # IMPLIED >

<?xml version = "1.0" ?>
<list>
<book     title = " Zen Buddhism"
              author = "Masaaki Imai" >
</book>
</list>
```

attribute

Supplementing search patterns with attributes

Description

The search pattern of a construction rule compares the attributes of an element.

Application

Not only the name of the element can be indicated in the pattern, but also an attribute used in the element.

Parameter

`name`
   Describes the name of the attribute used in the markup.
`value`
   Describes the value of the attribute used.
`has-value`
   It will frequently be necessary to check whether a value is used for an attribute. Instead of "`value`" the keyword "`has-value`" is used. Valid values to check the contents are "`yes`" (a value is available) and "`no`" (no value is available).

Example

```
<attribute name="attribute" value="value"/>
<attribute name="attribute" has-value="no">
    <attribute name="attribute" has-value="yes">

<target-element type="description">
    <!-- no value for "group" is available -->
<attribute name="group" has-value="no">
</target-element>

<target-element type="description">
    <!-- there exists a value for "group" -->
<attribute name="group" has-value="yes">
</target-element>
```

AXIS <html attribute>

Categorizing table axes

Description

You can assign an element to a group of table elements which have similar contents with this attribute. The organisation of these table elements is executed according to a hierarchy.

Application

As a value of this attribute you can indicate a specific designation of the connection between the single cells. This simplifies the automatic analysis of a table by a computer or speech synthesizers. The use of this attribute is optional.

Values

You can give an arbitrary string to this attribute as a value. If possible, this character string should not start or end with blank characters as the processing browser may filter these out.

A table axis can be assigned to a category as follows:

Example

```
<th id="a1" axis="Quarter">1 </th>
<th id="a2" axis="Turnover">May </th>
<th id="a3" axis="Profit">After control </th>
```

Accompanying elements

TD
TH

B

W3C HTML 4.0 ✓

Representation of text in bold type

Description
With this command text is shown in bold type.

Application
The B command (abbreviation for "bold") is used when parts of text need to be highlighted. Bold text is different from italic text, which is indicated with the "I-tag".

HTML 4.0 standard
CLASS, DIR, ID, LANG, STYLE, TITLE

Start tag: required; end tag: required.

Attributes
CLASS

> Through the CLASS attribute, the element can be assigned to a group (class). Enter one of the free selectable class name as a value. These groupings then provide easy access to all related elements. You can therefore easily change all properties of the elements of a class with the help of cascading style sheets or other languages, or select a value.

DIR

> This attribute is necessary to determine the text direction. This attribute can have the values:
>
> LTR
>> This value determines the text direction from left to right (and is short for "left-to-right"). This direction is the default in the browser.
>
> RTL
>> If the text must run contrary to the standard direction from the right to the left margin of the screen, then choose the value RTL (short for "right-to-left").

ID

> ID identifies the document. Using ID, a specific element can be accessed with the help of a script language to select or modify its values.

LANG

> This attribute indicates the language of the linked document. This is particularly important in search engines for identification purposes. Use the language codes according to ISO 639, for example "en" for English or "en-us" for American English.

ONCLICK

This event takes place if you single-click on an element with the mouse. A given script is executed by this action.

ONDBLCLICK

This event takes place if you double-click on an element with the mouse. A given script is executed by this action.

ONKEYDOWN

This event takes place if you are in an element and a key is pressed and held down. This action executes a specific script.

ONKEYPRESS

This event takes place if you are in an element and a key is pressed and released. This action executes a specific script.

ONKEYUP

This event takes place if you are in an element and a key that was pressed is released. This action executes a specific script.

ONMOUSEDOWN

This event takes place if you are in an element and a mouse button is clicked and held down. A given script is executed by this action.

ONMOUSEMOVE

This event takes place if you move the cursor over an object with the mouse. A given script is executed by this action.

ONMOUSEOUT

This event takes place if the mouse moves the cursor off an element. This action excecutes a given script.

ONMOUSEOVER

This event takes place if the mouse moves the cursor directly over the element (object). A given script is executed by this action.

ONMOUSEUP

This event takes place if you are in an element and a mouse button that was clicked and held down is released. A given script is executed by this action.

STYLE

The attribute STYLE can be used to change style settings, in particular the appearance of an element. As the value of the attribute, you apply the corresponding options of a style sheet language (usually CSS).

TITLE

You should give the user further information about the used element defining a meaningful title with the help of the TITLE command. The navigation on your Web site is made easier for users who are dependent on voice responses.

Example

```
<b>this line is distributed in boldface font style</b>
Single <b> words</b>can be highlighted
```

Events

ONBLUR, ONCLICK, ONDBLCLICK, ONFOCUS, ONKEYDOWN, ONKEYPRESS, ONKEYUP, ONMOUSEDOWN, ONMOUSEMOVE, ONMOUSEOUT, ONMOUSEOVER, ONMOUSEUP

Related commands

BIG
I
LISTING
PLAINTEXT
PRE
S
SMALL
STRIKE
TT
U
XMP

Background   \<html attribute\>

Indicating background graphics

Description

This attribute is used to embed a graphic display background.

Application

If you want to embed a background, you must submit the necessary graphic to the URI. This command is not supported by HTML version 4.0. You can use style sheets instead for the same purpose. The use of this attribute is optional.

Values

A valid value for this attribute is the URI (Uniform Resource Identifier). The construction of a URI is as follows:

[protocol]: // [Domain]/[Directory]/[File]

Possible instruction for the used protocol are the following values:

ftp	File Transfer Protocol
http	Hypertext Transfer Protocol
gopher	Gopher Protocol

mailto	Electronic Mail Address
news	USENET News
nntp	USENET News (NNTP access)
telnet	Reference to interactive sessions
wais	Wide Area Information Server
file	Host-specific file names
prospero	Prospero Directory Service

Example

```
body background="tile.gif">
<body bgcolor="black" background="black.gif">
```

Accompanying elements
BODY

background-attachment

CASCADING STYLE SHEETS

Creating a watermark effect for your background

Description

In larger documents the background usually moves when you scroll the text. The watermark effect avoids this and the background remains on the screen whether or not the content is moved.

Parameter

```
fixed
```
Background picture remains as watermark.
```
scroll
```
Background picture moves with the text.

Example

```
<style type="text/css">
body  { background-attachment: fixed}
</style>

<div style="background-attachment: scroll " >
</div>
```

background-color

Fixing background colour

Description

The background colour of an element can be changed in this way.

Parameter

`color`

> The colour can either be set with a keyword (i. e. `"red"`) or with a composite RGB value (i. e. `"rgb (0.0.255) "`).

Example

```
<style type="text/css">
h1, h2 { background-color: yellow}
h3, h4 { background-color: #0090989}
</style>

<div style="background-color: blue">
</div>
```

background-image

Defines a background picture

Description

With this command a background graphic can be defined.

Parameter

`url`

> Indicates the source of a GIF or JPEG graphic file.

Example

```
<style type="text/css">
h1, h2 { background-image: back.gif}
h3, h4 { background-image: http://www.dom.co.uk/img/back.jpg}
</style>

<div style="background-image: back.jpg">
</div>
```

background-position

Defining the position of the background graphic

Description

With this command the position of a background graphic can be defined.

Parameter

As the parameter you indicate two values which represent the distance to the top-left edge of the screen. Otherwise you can use the following values:

bottom
> Alignment to the bottom of the screen.

center
> Alignment in the centre of the screen (horizontal).

left
> Alignment to the left margin of the screen.

middle
> Alignment in the centre of the screen (vertical).

right
> Alignment to the right margin of the screen.

top
> Alignment to the top of the screen.

Example

```
<style type="text/css">
h1, h2 { background-position: right}
h3, h4 { background-position: left}
</style>

<div style=" background-position: centre " >
</div>
```

background-repeat

Changing the tile effect of the background

Description

A background graphic is usually distributed over the whole screen automatically as a tile. Using this attribute this setting may be changed.

Parameter

`no-repeat`
> The repetition of the graphic is deactivated and it is shown as a single picture.

`repeat`
> The graphic is distributed over the screen by default.

`repeat-x`
> The graphic is repeated only horizontally.

`repeat-y`
> The graphic is repeated only vertically.

Example

```
<style type="text/css">
h1, h2 { alignment: right}
h3, h4 { alignment: justify}
</style>

<div style="alignment: justify">
</div>
```

BASE

W3C HTML 4.0 ✔

Setting an absolute URI

Description

With this command you can indicate an absolute URI or URL to be used as a reference if a browser is given a relative URI.

Application

The command BASE is required to determine the base URI of a document. Within this document, references to other documents can be determined. The BASE element must be in the document header before the first appearance of a relative URI.

HTML 4.0 standard

`HREF, TARGET`

Start tag: required; end tag: not allowed.

Attributes

`HREF`
> The base file is determined with the HREF attribute. Out of this base file it is possible to cancel all relative links within the document.

TARGET
This attribute determines the name of the window in which the link will be opened. This window must be defined before a frame-set with the corresponding frame window. The frame window must have a name assigned with the additional instruction NAME=.

Example

```
<<head>
<base href="http://www.w3c.org/index.htm">
... other details in the file head ...
</head>

<head>
<base target="LinkWindow">
... other instructions in the file head ...
</head>
```

The use of an absolute base address makes a later allocation of a relative URL to an Internet address easier for visitors to your site who have saved the address on their hard disk, but this makes working on the project more difficult since the browser will try to access the Internet address locally. Use a BASE address only to conclude a project.

XML definition

```
<! ELEMENT BASE>
<!ATTLIST BASE
href      % URI;  # REQUIRED>
```

Related commands

A
LINK

BASEFONT

Determining the standard font size

Description

This command defines a standard font for a document header. In HTML version 4.0 this command is not supported.

Application

The command BASEFONT determines the standard font. The FONT command, on the other hand, is used only for a definite range of text.

HTML 4.0 standard

CLASS, COLOR, DIR, FACE, ID, LANG, SIZE, STYLE, TITLE

The use of this command is no longer recommended in the current HTML version and has been replaced by other commands.

Start tag: required; end tag: not allowed.

Attributes

CLASS

Through the CLASS attribute, the element can be assigned to a group (class). Enter one of the free selectable class name as a value. These groupings then provide easy access to all related elements. You can easily change all properties of the elements of a class with the help of cascading style sheets or other languages, or select a value.

COLOR

The colour of the text to be represented is set with this attribute. Besides the 16 specific keywords, up to 256 colours can be represented, indicated by fixed hexadecimal numbers. These settings are usually created with style sheets in HTML 4.0.

DIR

This attribute is necessary to determine the text direction. This attribute can have the values:

LTR

This value determines the text direction from left to right (and is short for "left-to-right"). This is the default direction in the browser.

RTL

If the text must run contrary to the standard direction from the right to the left margin of the screen, then choose the value RTL (short for "right-to-left").

FACE

With the FACE attribute the font in which a Web site should be displayed is defined. It is important to list the different fonts separated by commas. Always make sure that the client has at least one of the fonts used. The browser establishes whether the given fonts are available and can be displayed.

ID

ID identifies the document. Using ID, a specific element can be accessed with the help of a script language to select or modify its values.

LANG

This attribute indicates the language of the linked document. This is particularly important in search engines for identification purposes. Use the language codes according to ISO 639, for example "en" for English or "en-us" for American English.

SIZE

The SIZE attribute is used to determine the font size. The value available for the size command ranges from 1 to 7. If this number is not explicitly determined, documents are represented in font size 3 by default.

STYLE

The STYLE attribute can be used to change style settings, in particular the appearance of an element. As the value of the attribute, you apply the corresponding options of a style sheet language (usually CSS).

TITLE

You should give the user further information about the element used by defining a meaningful title with the help of the TITLE command. The navigation on your Web site is made easier for users who are dependent on voice responses.

Example

```
<basefont color=blue>
I am blue, only <font color=#000000> not  here </font>
Now blue again
Representation of the text in color

<basefont face="Arial">
I  am a font and my name is Arial, only
<font face="Courier">I am Courier here</font>
and now Arial again
```

Related command

FONT

BDO

Determining the text direction

Description

Browsers usually work with a bidirectional text flow. However, there may be cases in which only one text direction (monodirection) is required (BDO = abbreviation for "bidirectional override").

Application

The BDO command determines the text direction of a document. If a text is to be represented in Arabic, for example, the bidirectional algorithm can be changed using this command.

HTML 4.0 standard

ID, CLASS, DIR, LANG, STYLE, TITLE

Start tag: required; ending tag: required.

Attributes

CLASS

Through the CLASS attribute, the element can be assigned to a group (class). Enter one of the free selectable class name as a value. These groupings then provide easy access to all related elements. You can easily change all properties of the elements in a class with the help of cascading style sheets or other languages, or select a value.

DIR

This attribute is necessary to determine the text direction. This attribute can have the values:

LTR

This value determines the text direction from left to right (and is short for "left-to-right"). This is the default direction in the browser.

RTL

If the text must run contrary to the standard direction from the right to the left margin of the screen, then choose the value RTL (short for "right-to-left").

ID

ID identifies a document. Using ID, a specific element can be accessed with the help of a script language, to select or modify its values.

LANG

This attribute indicates the language of the linked document. This is particularly important in search engines for identification purposes. Use the language codes according to ISO 639, for example "en" for English or "en-us" for American English.

STYLE

The STYLE attribute can be used to change style settings, in particular the appearance of an element. As the value of the attribute, you apply the corresponding options of a style sheet language (usually CSS).

TITLE
You should give the user further information about the element used by defining a meaningful title with the help of the TITLE command. The navigation on your Web site is made easier for users who are dependent on voice responses.

Example

```
<BDO DIR=RTL>sträwkcüR</bdo>
Show in normal reading direction "backwards"
<BDO DIR=LTR>the standard setting is</BDO>
```

BGCOLOR   <html attribute>
Indicating background colour

Description
This attribute determines the colour of the background.

Application
Besides the 16 defined colour keywords, up to 256 colours can be represented. This command is not supported by HTML version 4.0. The use of this attribute is optional.

Values
Give either a colour value in RGB syntax or a valid colour name to the attribute. For the RGB value, indicate the colour values of the colours red, green and blue in hexadecimal notation: #RRGGBB (i.e. #008000 for green). Alternatively, predefined colour names can be used. (i.e. YELLOW). Under the **Color Palette** keyword you will find a complete list of all standard colours. These are the 16 most frequently used primary colours:

```
BLACK     = #000000  SILVER   = #COCOCO
GRAY      = #808080  WHITE    = #FFFFFF
MAROON    = #800000  RED      = #FF0000
PURPLE    = #800080  FUCHSIA  = #FF00FF
GREEN     = #008000  LIME     = #00FF00
OLIVE     = #808000  YELLOW   = #FFFF00
NAVY      = #000080  BLUE     = #0000FF
TEAL      = #008080  AQUA     = #00FFFF
```

Example
```
body bgcolor="blue">
```

```
<body bgcolor="#FFFF00">
```

Accompanying elements

BODY
TABLE
TD
TH
TR

BGSOUND

Embedding background sound

Description

This command introduced by Microsoft enables background music to be played on accessing a Web site.

Application

The BGSOUND command is required to play background music when accessing a Web site. The files to be embedded must be in .WAV, .AU or in .MID format.

This command is not part of the official W3C HTML declaration. To embed a background sound with any browser, use EMBED or OBJECT. The BGSOUND command is placed in the head of the document.

HTML 4.0 standard

The command is not part of the official HTML standard.

Attributes

LOOP
   This attribute determines how frequently the sound should be played. You can use a natural number for n. To repeat the sound in a loop you must assign either the value −1 to n or insert LOOP=INFINITE.
SRC
   With this attribute the source is defined with its URI.

Example

```
<head>
<bgsound src="file.mid" loop=-1>
</head>
<body>
```

Related commands
EMBED
OBJECT

BIG

Displaying text in a larger font size

Description
With this command a larger size of text can be represented. Three steps are available to enlarge the text.

Application
The BIG command sets text which needs to be displayed with a larger font size in the container between <big> and </big>. These containers can be interleaved. Unlike the instruction of a font size, for example through style sheets, this command extends the appearance of the text relative to the standard font size used.

HTML 4.0 standard
CLASS, DIR, ID, LANG, STYLE, TITLE

Start tag: required; end tag: required.

Different types of text in the browser

Attributes

CLASS

Through the CLASS attribute, the element can be assigned to a group (class). Enter one of the free selectable class names as a value. These groupings then provide easy access to all related elements. You can easily change all properties of the elements of a class with the help of cascading style sheets or other languages, or select a value.

DIR

This attribute is necessary to determine the text direction. This attribute can have the values:

LTR

This value determines the text direction from left to right (and is short for "left-to-right"). This is the default direction in the browser.

RTL

If the text must run contrary to the standard direction from the right to the left margin of the screen, then choose the RTL value (short for "right-to-left").

ID

ID identifies a document. Using ID, a specific element can be accessed with the help of a script language, to select or modify its values.

LANG

This attribute indicates the language of the linked document. This is particularly important in search engines for identification purposes. Use the language codes according to ISO 639, for example "en" for English or "en-us" for American English.

ONCLICK

This event takes place if you single-click on an element with the mouse. A given script is executed by this action.

ONDBLCLICK

This event takes place if you double-click on an element with the mouse. A given script is executed by this action.

ONKEYDOWN

This event takes place if you are in an element and a key is pressed and held down. This action executes a specific script.

ONKEYPRESS

This event takes place if you are in an element and a key is pressed and released. This action executes a specific script.

ONKEYUP

This event takes place if you are in an element and a key that was pressed is released. This action executes a specific script.

ONMOUSEDOWN

This event takes place if you are in an element and a mouse button is clicked and held down. A given script is executed by this action.

ONMOUSEMOVE
This event takes place if you move the cursor over an object with the mouse. A given script is executed by this action.

ONMOUSEOUT
This event takes place if the mouse moves the cursor off an element. This action excecutes a given script.

ONMOUSEOVER
This event takes place if the mouse moves the cursor directly over the element (object). A given script is executed by this action.

ONMOUSEUP
This event takes place if you are in an element and a mouse button that was clicked and held down is released. A given script is executed by this action.

TITLE
You should give the user further information about the element used by defining a meaningful title with the help of the TITLE command. Navigation on your Web site is made easier for users who are dependent on voice responses.

Example

```
This was a <BIG>big</BIG> mistake!
```

Events

ONBLUR, ONCLICK, ONDBLCLICK, ONFOCUS, ONKEYDOWN, ONKEYPRESS, ONKEYUP, ONMOUSEDOWN, ONMOUSEMOVE, ONMOUSEOUT, ONMOUSEOVER, ONMOUSEUP

Related commands

B
LISTING
PLAINTEXT
PRE
S
SMALL
STRIKE
TT
U
XMP

Blank space

Defining blank space

Description

Blank space is the most basic component of a document. It is however a very important component in the overall scheme of the document.

There are four invisible but important elements included in the definition of empty space, which are:

– blank space

– carriage return

– space bar

– tab key

Application

The treatment of blank space in XML is as ruthless as in HTML. Wherever more than one blank space occurs, this is automatically removed and then the text is passed to the parser. Occasionally you may need to maintain blank spaces that have been inserted for a purpose. Such intended blank space is described as significant blank space.

To inform the parser whether blank spaces are significant or not, declare a new attribute of the type:

```
xml:space
```

The attribute can accept the values `"default"` and `"preserve"`. The default value, shown in the above example, can be obtained through the keyword `"default"`. If significant blank space needs to be retained, choose `"preserve"`.

Example

```
<!ATTLIST paragraph xml:space (default|preserve) "preserve">
```

The following example shows a situation where blank spaces within the <text>-markup remain unchanged.

```
<!ATTLIST text xml:space (default|preserve) "preserve">
<?xml version = "1.0" ?>
<text xml:space="preserve">
        Word

    Word
        Word
        Word
```

```
</text>
```

BLINK

N

Displaying blinking text

Description
This command creates blinking text.

Application

The BLINK command makes text or parts of a text appear to blink (flicker) at regular intervals. This form of representation is mainly used to focus the attention on a specific part of a Web document.

This command is not provided in the official HTML definition and was introduced by Netscape. The use of this command should therefore be avoided, if possible.

HTML 4.0 standard

The command is not part of the official HTML standard.

Example

```
Now follows <BLINK> blinking text </BLINK>
```

Related commands

B
I
S
SMALL
STRIKE
SUP
TT
U

BLOCKQUOTE

W3C HTML 4.0 ✓

Designates text as a quotation

Description

With this command, quotations are marked by speech marks. If the original quotation is to be made available on the World Wide Web, it makes sense to provide a hyperlink to the quotation.

Application

The command BLOCKQUOTE is used to identify items from other media. These quotations are sometimes represented in italics. For shorter quotations you should use the CITE command.

HTML 4.0 standard

CITE, CLASS, DIR, ID, LANG, STYLE, TITLE

Start tag: required; end tag: required.

Attributes

CLASS

Through the CLASS attribute, the element can be assigned to a group (class). Enter one of the free selectable class name as a value. These groupings then provide easy access to all related elements. You can easily change all properties of the elements of a class with the help of cascading style sheets or other languages, or select a value.

DIR

This attribute is necessary to determine the text direction. This attribute can have the values:

LTR

This value determines the text direction from left to right (and is short for "left-to-right"). This is the default direction in the browser.

RTL

If the text must run contrary to the standard direction from the right to the left margin of the screen, then choose the RTL value (short for "right-to-left").

ID

ID identifies a document. Using ID, a specific element can be accessed with the help of a script language, to select or modify its values.

LANG

This attribute indicates the language of the linked document. This is particularly important in search engines for identification purposes. Use the language codes according to ISO 639, for example "en" for English or "en-us" for American English.

ONCLICK
> This event takes place if you single-click on a particular element with the mouse. A given script is executed by this action.

ONDBLCLICK
> This event takes place if you double-click on an element with the mouse. A given script is executed by this action.

ONKEYDOWN
> This event takes place if you are in an element and a key is pressed and held down. This action executes a specific script.

ONKEYPRESS
> This event takes place if you are in an element and a key is pressed and released. This action executes a specific script.

ONKEYUP
> This event takes place if you are in an element and a key that was pressed is released. This action executes a specific script.

ONMOUSEDOWN
> This event takes place if you are in an element and a mouse button is clicked and held down. A given script is executed by this action.

ONMOUSEMOVE
> This event takes place if you move the cursor over an object with the mouse. A given script is executed by this action.

ONMOUSEOUT
> This event takes place if the mouse moves the cursor off an element. This action excecutes a given script.

ONMOUSEOVER
> This event takes place if the mouse moves the cursor directly over the element (object). A given script is executed by this action.

ONMOUSEUP
> This event takes place if you are in an element and a mouse button that was clicked and held down is released. A given script is executed by this action.

STYLE
> The STYLE attribute can be used to change style settings, in particular the appearance of the element. As the value of the attribute, you apply the corresponding options of a style sheet language (usually CSS).

TITLE
> You should give the user further information about the element used defining a meaningful title with the help of the TITLE command. Navigation on your Web site is made easier for users who are dependent on voice responses.

Example

```
<blockquote>
This is a completely quoted text!
</blockquote>
```

Events

ONCLICK, ONDBLCLICK, ONKEYDOWN, ONKEYPRESS, ONKEYUP, ONMOUSEDOWN, ONMOUSEMOVE, ONMOUSEOUT, ONMOUSEOVER, ONMOUSEUP

XML definition

```
<!ELEMENT BLOCKQUOTE - - (%block;|SCRIPT)+
<!ATTLIST BLOCKQUOTE
% attrs;
cite        % URI;  # IMPLIED>
```

Related commands

ACRONYM
CODE
DFN
EM
KBD
SAMP
STRONG

BODY

Determining the body content of a SMIL document

Description

The BODY command defines the content of the SMIL document.

Application

The contents of the document are enclosed within the BODY tags.

Example

```
<smil>
<body>
</body>
</smil>
```

BODY

W3C HTML 4.0 ✔

Selecting the main part of an HTML document

Description

With this command, all visible components of a Web site are represented. It defines the "body text" of a document. An HTML document can also contain a file head declared with HEAD.

Application

The BODY command is required for every range of an HTML document apart from the document head. The area between the opening and closing command is described as a container.

HTML 4.0 standard

ALINK, BACKGROUND, CLASS, DIR, ID, LANG, LINK, STYLE, TEXT, TITLE, VLINK

Start tag: optional; end tag: optional.

Attributes

ALINK

   This attribute determines the colour of the link which is activated by a user. Besides the16 defined colour keywords up to 256 colours can be represented. This command is not supported by HTML 4.0.

BACKGROUND

   This attribute is used to embed a display background. If you want to embed a background in this way, you must assign the URI to the required graphic. This command is not supported by HTML 4.0. Instead, you can use style sheets.

BGCOLOR

   This attribute is used to define a background colour instead of a graphic in the background. It should again be noted at this point that besides the 16 defined colour keywords, up to 256 colours can be represented by hexadecimal numbers. This command is not supported by HTML 4.0.

CLASS

   Through the CLASS attribute, the element can be assigned to a group (class). Enter one of the free selectable class name as a value. These groupings then provide easy access to all related elements. You can easily change all properties of the elements of a class with the help of cascading style sheets or other languages, or select a value.

DIR

   This attribute is necessary to determine the text direction. This attribute can have the values:

LTR

> This value determines the text direction from left to right (and is short for "left-to-right"). This is the default direction in the browser.

RTL

> If the text must run contrary to the standard direction from the right to the left margin of the screen, then choose the RTL value (short for "right-to-left").

ID

> ID identifies a document. Using ID, a specific element can be accessed with the help of a script language, to select or modify its values.

LANG

> This attribute indicates the language of the linked document. This is particularly important in search engines for identification purposes. Use the language codes according to ISO 639, for example "en" for English or "en-us" for American English.

LEFTMARGIN

> This attribute is an element introduced by Microsoft. It is used to determine the left margin for the BODY. The default values for the left margin are modified with this command. If you give this attribute the value 0, this means that the margin is exactly on the left edge of the screen.

LINK

> With this attribute, the colour of the links is determined in an HTML document. This command is discouraged by HTML 4.0.

ONCLICK

> This event takes place if you single-click on a particular element with the mouse. A given script is executed by this action.

ONDBLCLICK

> This event takes place if you double-click on an element with the mouse. A given script is executed by this action.

ONKEYDOWN

> This event takes place if you are in an element and a key is pressed and held down. This action executes a specific script.

ONKEYPRESS

> This event takes place if you are in an element and a key is pressed and released. This action executes a specific script.

ONKEYUP

> This event takes place if you are in an element and a key that was pressed is released. This action executes a specific script.

ONMOUSEDOWN

> This event takes place if you are in an element and a mouse button is clicked and held down. A given script is executed by this action.

ONMOUSEMOVE

> This event takes place if you move the cursor over an object with the mouse. A given script is executed by this action.

ONMOUSEOUT

This event takes place if the mouse moves the cursor off an element. This action excecutes a given script.

ONMOUSEOVER

This event takes place if the mouse moves the cursor directly over the element (object). A given script is executed by this action.

ONMOUSEUP

This event takes place if you are in an element and a mouse button that was clicked and held down is released. A given script is executed by this action.

ONLOAD

This event takes place if a browser has completely uploaded an HTML document. On a FRAMESET document, this means that a script is executed if all required frames have been loaded.

ONUNLOAD

This event takes place if a browser has completely downloaded an HTML document. On a FRAMESET document, this means that a script is executed if all required frames have been unloaded.

STYLE

The STYLE attribute can be used to change style settings, particularly the appearance of the element. As the value of the attribute, you apply the corresponding options of a style sheet language (usually CSS).

TEXT

This attribute is used to determine text colour in an HTML document. This command is not supported by HTML 4.0.

TOPMARGIN

This attribute is an element introduced by Microsoft. It is used to determine the top margin of the complete BODY. Default values to determine a top edge margin are overridden with this command. If you give this attribute the value 0, this means that the margin is exactly on the top edge of the screen.

VLINK

With this attribute the colour of the links which have already been activated by a user are determined. It should be noted that besides the 16 defined colour keywords, up to 256 colors can be represented by given hexadecimal numbers. This command is not supported by HTML 4.0.

TITLE

You should give the user further information about the element used by defining a meaningful title with the help of the TITLE command. Navigation on your Web site is made easier for users who are dependent on voice responses.

Example

```
<html>
<head>
<title>Title text </title>
</head>
```

63

```
<body background="back.gif">
Text, links, graphics etc..
</body>
</html>
```

Events
ONCLICK, ONDBLCLICK, ONKEYDOWN, ONKEYPRESS, ONKEYUP, ONMOUSEDOWN,
ONMOUSEMOVE, ONMOUSEOUT, ONMOUSEOVER, ONMOUSEUP

XML definition
```
<! ELEMENT BODY O O (%block;|SCRIPT)+ +(INS|DEL)>
 <!ATTLIST BODY
% attrs;

onload % script;  # IMPLIED
onunload % script;  # IMPLIED>
```

Related commands
HEAD

BORDER   <html attribute>
Setting frame borders

Description
With the help of the BORDER attribute you can set the border of a frame surrounding an object.

Application
Set the frame board to the attribute. If you want to prevent the frame of a graphic defined as a hyperlink from being shown, set "0" as the frame strength value. The use of this attribute is optional.

Values
The value of this attribute indicates a size in pixels or per cent. Valid values for pixels are positive integer numbers (integer values). The input of ="100" corresponds to the size of 100 pixels, for example. An instruction in per cent corresponds to the per cent area of available horizontal or vertical window borders in the browser. An input of ="30%" corresponds to a border of 30 per cent.

Example

```
<table border>
<table border="3">
<table border="5%">
<a href="link.htm">
<img border="0">
</a>
```

Accompanying elements

IMG
OBJECT
TABLE

border-color

Determining border colour

Description

The border colour can be changed with this command.

Parameter

Indicates the desired colour of the line as a hexadecimal value or as a name.

Example

```
<style type="text/css">
h1, h2 { border-colour: red}
h3, h4 { border-colour: #000000}
</style>

<div style="border-color: blue">
</div>
```

border-style

Determining frame type

Description

Determines the border style of the frame.

Parameter

dashed	dashed border
dotted	dotted border
double	double border
groove	border with 3D effect
inset	border with 3D effect
none	no border
outset	border with 3D effect
ridge	border with 3D effect
solid	solid border

Example

```
<style type="text/css">
h1, h2 { border-style: dotted }
h3, h4 { border-style: solid }
</style>

<div style="border-style: none">
</div>
```

BR

W3C HTML 4.0 ✓

Forcing a line break

Description

With this command manual line breaks can be forced.

Application

The BR command (abbreviation for "break") is used to create line breaks manually. As a rule, browser software provides the line break. No end tag follows this command.

HTML 4.0 standard

ID, CLASS, STYLE, TITLE

Start tag: required; end tag: not allowed.

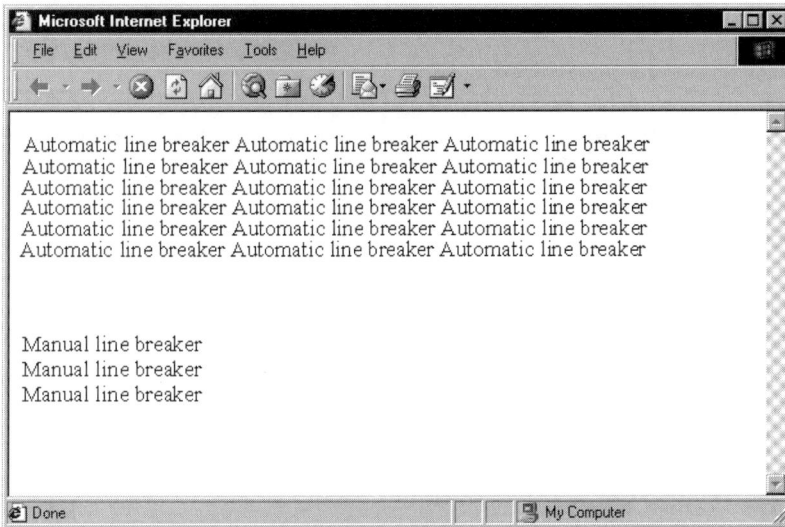

A manual line break can be created with the help of the BR element.

Attributes

CLASS

Through the CLASS attribute, the element can be assigned to a group (class). Enter one of the free selectable class name as a value. These groupings then provide easy access to all related elements. You can easily change all properties of the elements in a class with the help of cascading style sheets or other languages, or select a value.

CLEAR

With this attribute a browser is induced to set up a line break only if there is no HTML object aligned in the specified direction. It this way, it is possible to embed pictures into a text. Four possible values can be given to this attribute:

LEFT

With CLEAR=LEFT it is essential that the next blank space be in the left window margin.

RIGHT

With CLEAR=RIGHT it is essential that the next blank space be in the right window margin.

ALL

A line break is set up where there is a blank space either to the left or to the right window margin.

NONE

Default; a line break immediately takes place after the input of the BR command.

ID

> ID identifies the document. Using ID, a specific element can be accessed with the help of a script language, to select or modify its values.

STYLE

> The STYLE attribute can be used to change style settings, in particular the appearance of the elements. As the value of the attribute, you apply the corresponding options of a style sheet language (usually CSS).

TITLE

> You should give the user further information about the element used by defining a meaningful title with the help of the TITLE command. Navigation on your Web site is made easier for users who are dependent on voice responses.

Example

```
The line ends here .<br>
A new line starts here.
```

XML definition

```
<! ELEMENT BR>
<! ATTLIST BR %coreattrs;>
```

BUTTON

W3C HTML 4.0 ✓

Producing user-defined buttons

Description

With this command it is possible to create user-defined buttons ("Push-buttons") in an HTML document.

Application

The BUTTON command is used if events are to take place by pressing a key, or by clicking with the mouse. The command enables the production of several entry fields.

HTML 4.0 standard

```
ACCESSKEY, CLASS, DIR, DISABLED, ID, LANG, NAME, STYLE, TABINDEX,
TITLE, TYPE, VALUE
```

Start tag: required; end tag: required.

Attributes

ACCESSKEY

The ACCESSKEY attribute enables access to an element via a keyboard shortcut. So the ACCESSKEY="A" instruction means that after pressing the "A" key, the element is activated.

CLASS

Through the CLASS attribute, the element can be assigned to a group (class). Enter one of the free selectable class name as a value. These groupings then provide easy access to all related elements. You can easily change all properties of the elements of a class with the help of cascading style sheets or other languages, or select a value.

DIR

This attribute is necessary to determine the text direction. This attribute can have the values:

LTR

This value determines the text direction from left to right (and is short for "left-to-right"). This is the default direction in the browser.

RTL

If the text must run contrary to the standard direction from the right to the left margin of the screen, then choose the RTL value (short for "right-to-left").

DISABLED

With this attribute it is possible to deactivate keys.

ID

ID identifies the document. Using ID, a specific element can be accessed with the help of a script language, to select or modify its values.

LANG

This attribute indicates the language of the linked document. This is particularly important in search engines for identification purposes. Use the language codes according to ISO 639, for example "en" for English or "en-us" for American English.

NAME

Through the NAME attribute a name can be assigned to the element. It should be clear that names can be used only once in the document. This command is comparable with the ID attribute.

ONCLICK

This event takes place if you single-click on a particular element with the mouse. A given script is executed by this action.

ONDBLCLICK

This event takes place if you double-click on an element with the mouse. A given script is executed by this action.

ONKEYDOWN

This event takes place if you are in an element and a key is pressed and held down. This action executes a specific script.

ONKEYPRESS

This event takes place if you are in an element and a key is pressed and released. This action executes a specific script.

ONKEYUP

This event takes place if you are in an element and a key that was pressed is released. This action executes a specific script.

ONMOUSEDOWN

This event takes place if you are in an element and a mouse button is clicked and held down. A given script is executed by this action.

ONMOUSEMOVE

This event takes place if you move the cursor over an object with the mouse. A given script is executed by this action.

ONMOUSEOUT

This event takes place if the mouse moves the cursor off an element. This action excecutes a given script.

ONMOUSEOVER

This event takes place if the mouse moves the cursor directly over the element (object). A given script is executed by this action.

ONMOUSEUP

This event takes place if you are in an element and a mouse button that was clicked and held down is released. A given script is executed by this action.

STYLE

The STYLE attribute can be used to change style settings, in particular the appearance of the element. As the value of the attribute, you apply the corresponding options of a style sheet language (usually CSS).

TABINDEX

This attribute assigns the tabbing order to an element using positive or negative integers. Elements provided with this attribute can be selected with the Tab key one after the other. This operation helps users who do not use the mouse.

TITLE

You should give the user further information about the element used by defining a meaningful title with the help of the TITLE command. Navigation on your Web site is made easier for users who are dependent on voice responses.

TYPE

This attribute determines the type or the purpose of the button.

SUBMIT

With TYPE=SUBMIT it is possible to produce an entry field. With the help of this entry field a user can mail a form. Within a form there are usually several mail buttons. You should be careful in this procedure to assign a name to every button with the NAME attribute.

RESET

With TYPE=RESET it is possible to produce an entry field in which executed inputs are deleted. The default values to the presettings are reset on the exit values.

BUTTON

With TYPE=BUTTON a button is produced which, if clicked, starts a script. This option makes it possible to interact with the visitor without evaluation of the data on the server.

VALUE

This attribute assigns a value to a button. This value will be submitted to the server if the button is selected.

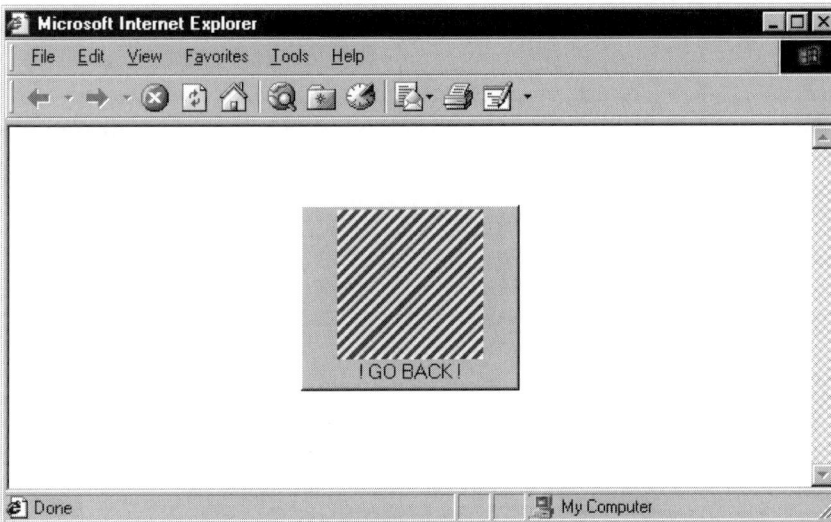

Button with graphic embedding

Example

```
<button name="I'm a button. Select me".
" type = "button"  value= go back" onClick = "history.back ()" >

<img src="click.gif" alt="clickimage">!GO BACK!</button>
```

Events

ONFOCUS, ONKEYDOWN, ONKEYPRESSED, ONKEYUP, ONMOUSEDOWN, ONMOUSEMOVE, ONMOUSEOUT, ONMOUSEOVER, ONMOUSEUP

XML definition

```
<! ELEMENT BUTTON (%flow;)* -(A|%formctrl;|FORM|FIELDSET)>
<!ATTLIST BUTTON
% attrs;
name        CDATA       #IMPLIED
value       CDATA       #IMPLIED
type        (button|submit|reset) #IMPLIED
tabindex    NUMBER      #IMPLIED
```

```
accesskey      %Character;    #IMPLIED
onfocus        %script;       #IMPLIED
onblur         %script;       #IMPLIED
% reserved; >
```

Related commands

FORM

INPUT

CAPTION

Adding text to tables

Description

Create headers and footers of tables with this command.

Application

The CAPTION command is needed to provide tables with headers or footers. When you use this command, you should make sure that this element appears only once in the position provided for it within a table definition. This position is immediately after the opening command TABLE. However, the instruction of a table header is only an optional part of a table.

HTML 4.0 standard

CLASS, DIR, ID, LANG, STYLE, TITLE

Start tag: required; end tag: required.

Attribute

ALIGN

With this attribute you determine whether the text formatted with the CAPTION command is a table header or a table footer. Text which is marked with this command is normally centred and in bold.

TOP

With ALIGN=TOP you produce a table header which is centre-aligned.

BOTTOM

With ALIGN=BOTTOM you produce a table footer which is centre-aligned.

LEFT

With ALIGN=LEFT you produce a table header which is on the top left margin of the table.

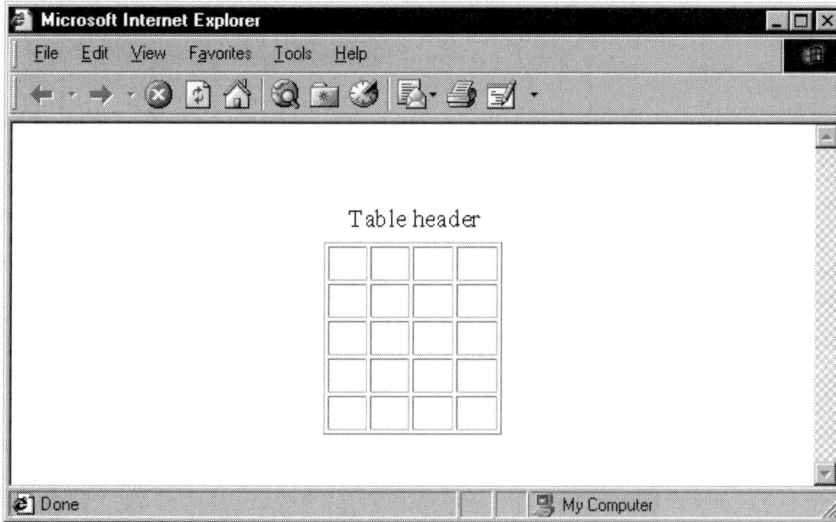

Table with table header

RIGHT

 With ALIGN=RIGHT you produce a table footer which is on the right top margin of the table.

CLASS

 Through the CLASS attribute, the element can be assigned to a group (class). Enter one of the free selectable class name as a value. These groupings then provide easy access to all related elements. You can easily change all properties of the elements of a class with the help of cascading style sheets or other languages, or select a value.

DIR

 This attribute is necessary to determine the text direction. This attribute can have the values:

 LTR

 This value determines the text direction from left to right (and is short for "left-to-right"). This is the default direction in the browser.

 RTL

 If the text must run contrary to the standard direction from the right to the left margin of the screen, then choose the RTL value (short for "right-to-left").

ID

 ID identifies the document. Using ID, a specific element can be accessed with the help of a script language, to select or modify its values.

LANG

This attribute indicates the language of the linked document. This is particularly important in search engines for identification purposes. Use the language codes according to ISO 639, for example "en" for English or "en-us" for American English.

ONCLICK

This event takes place if you single-click on an element with the mouse. A given script is executed by this action.

ONDBLCLICK

This event takes place if you double-click on an element with the mouse. A given script is executed by this action.

ONKEYDOWN

This event takes place if you are in an element and a key is pressed and held down. This action executes a specific script.

ONKEYPRESS

This event takes place if you are in an element and a key is pressed and released. This action executes a specific script.

ONKEYUP

This event takes place if you are in an element and a key that was pressed is released. This action executes a specific script.

ONMOUSEDOWN

This event takes place if you are in an element and a mouse button is clicked and held down. A given script is executed by this action.

ONMOUSEMOVE

This event takes place if you move the cursor over an object with the mouse. A given script is executed by this action.

ONMOUSEOUT

This event takes place if the mouse moves the cursor off an element. This action excecutes a given script.

ONMOUSEOVER

This event takes place if the mouse moves the cursor directly over the element (object). A given script is executed by this action.

ONMOUSEUP

This event takes place if you are in an element and a mouse button that was clicked and held down is released. A given script is executed by this action.

STYLE

The STYLE attribute is used to determine specific properties in the representation of an element. The setting of the style used is defined by cascading style sheets.

TITLE

Through this attribute, information is assigned to highlighted elements. This information is displayed in the pop-up window in many browsers, if the mouse cursor is on the element.

Example

```
<table border>
<caption align=top>Table heading </caption>
<tr>
<td>Data </td>
<td>Data </td>
</tr>
</table>
```

Events

ONCLICK, ONDBLCLICK, ONKEYDOWN, ONKEYPRESSED, ONKEYUP, ONMOUSEDOWN, ONMOUSEMOVE, ONMOUSEOUT, ONMOUSEOVER, ONMOUSEUP

XML definition

```
<! ELEMENT CAPTION - - (%inline;)*>
<! ATTLIST CAPTION %attrs;>
```

Related commands

TABLE
TD
TH
TR

CDATA

Leading characters directly to the parser

Description

Character data, embedded in CDATA section, are executed without being evaluated by the parser.

Application

Markup commands within a CDATA section remain without function.

The CDATA (character data) section within a document instructs the parser not to evaluate this text and to ignore markup commands and entities. This form is used, if, for example, you would like to integrate source code into the site and have it displayed.

Example

```
<![CDATA
```

```
[
<description>
</description>
]]>
```

CDATA

Passing on data without further processing

Description

The enclosed character set goes into the target document without further processing by the parser.

Example

```
<![CDATA
[
...
]]>
```

CELLPADDING   <html attribute>

Indicating separation between cells

Description

With this attribute the free area between cells in a table is determined in pixels or as a percentage.

Application

Gives the desired separation as a value to the attribute. The use of this attribute is optional.

Values

The value of this attribute indicates a size in pixels or per cent. Valid values for pixels are positive integer numbers (integer values). The input of ="100" corresponds to the size of 100 pixels, for example. An instruction in percentage corresponds to the per cent area of available horizontal or vertical window borders in the browser. An input of ="30%" corresponds to a border of 30 per cent.

Example

```
<table cellpadding="199">
<table cellpadding="3%">
```

Accompanying elements

TABLE

CELLSPACING   <html attribute>
Spacing between cell margin and cell content

Description

With this attribute the free area between the cell margin and the cell contents is determined in pixels or as a percentage.

Application

You should give the required separation as a value to the attribute. The use of this attribute is optional.

Values

The value of this attribute indicates a size in pixels or per cent. Valid values for pixels are positive integer numbers (integer values). The input of ="100" corresponds to the size of 100 pixels, for example. An instruction in percentage corresponds to the per cent area of available horizontal or vertical window borders in the Browser. An input of ="30%" corresponds to a border of 30 per cent.

Example

```
<table cellspacing="100">
<table cellspacing="1%">
```

Accompanying elements

TABLE

CENTER

W3C HTML 4.0 ✓

Centering paragraphs

Description

With this command, paragraphs in an HTML document can be centred.

Application

The CENTER command is applied if sections of an HTML document should be displayed as centred. Elements which can be centred include text, graphics, headers and tables.

HTML 4.0 recommends you to use the command DIV instead with the attribute ALIGN.

HTML 4.0 standard

The use of this command is no longer recommended in the current HTML version and has been replaced by other commands.

Start tag: required; end tag: required.

Example

```
<center>
Centred text
</center>
<DIV ALIGN=CENTER>
The use of ALIGN is recommended in HTML 4.0.
</div>
```

Related commands

HR

CHAR   <html attribute>

Aligning contents with a character

Description

Alignment of data within a table to characters fixed with the CHAR attribute.

Application

This attribute is used to align numbers with a comma or decimal point. The use of this attribute is optional.

Values

As a value you can give a single valid character in the ISO 10646 character set to this attribute.

Example

```
<td align="char" char=",">
100.000 <br>
999.9 <br>
989898.9987687687 <br>
</td>
```

Accompanying elements

COL
COLGROUP
TBODY
TD
FOOT
TH
THEAD
TR

CHAROFF   <html attribute>

Determining character space in alignment with CHAR

Description

This attribute defines the character space for the first character which was formatted with the CHAR attribute.

Application

Indicates the space for the first character in a line relative to the margin. Use of this attribute is optional.

Value

The value of this attribute indicates a size in pixels or per cent. Valid values for pixels are positive integer numbers (integer values). The input of ="100" corresponds to the size of 100 pixels, for example. An instruction in percentage corresponds to the per cent area of available horizontal or vertical window borders in the Browser. An input of ="30%" corresponds to a border of 30 per cent.

Example

```
<td align="char" char="," charoff="10">
DM 10.000
DM 1.500
DM 350
DM 1.000.000
</td>
```

Accompanying elements

COL
COLGROUP
TBODY
TD
TFOOT
TH
THEAD
TR

CHARSET   \<html attribute>

Indicating the character set for linked data

Description

This attribute is used to determine the character set for linked data.

Application

You should indicate the character set for the required font. If the font is not explicitly specified, the browser should determine the font used. The use of this attribute is optional.

Values

Under the keyword **Character sets** you will find all codes and descriptions with which you can set fonts. Give a single character set to the attribute.

Example

```
<a charset="iso-8859-1">
<link charset="iso-8859-1">
<script charset="iso-8859-1">
```

Accompanying elements

A
LINK
SCRIPT

CHECKED   <html attribute>
Activating dialog fields as preselections

Description

With the CheckBox and RadioButton dialog types the CHECKED attribute is used to activate an options display as a preselection. This cannot be used with other input types.

Application

You cannot submit any value to this attribute; you should use only the name of the attribute. By using this attribute with RadioButton only, an element of the group can be activated. The use of this attribute is optional.

Values

To activate this option, simply use the name of the attribute. You do not need to submit any value to this attribute. If the attribute is not used, then the option remains deactivated. It does not differentiate between the use of upper and lower case for initial letters.

Example

```
<input type="checkbox" checked>
<input name="Infos" value="Telephon" type="radio" checked>
<input name="Infos" value="Telefax" type="radio">
<input name="Infos" value="Post" type="radio">
```

Accompanying elements

INPUT

children

Using an element in an action message

Description

Specifies where the element which agrees with the pattern of the construction rule should be used in the action message.

This command is an empty element and is therefore used in the form < children/>.

Example

```
<xsl>
<rule>
    <target element/>
    <p>
        <children/>
    </p>
</rule>
</xsl>
```

CITE   <html attribute>

Indicating the source of a citation

Description

With this attribute you can indicate the source document for the quotation used.

Application

You should indicate a valid Internet address as the source of a quotation. The use of this attribute is optional.

Values

A valid value for this attribute is a URI (Uniform Resource Identifier). The construction of a URI is as follows:

```
[protocol]: // [Domain]/[Directory]/[File]
```

Possible instructions for the used protocol are the following values:

ftp	File Transfer Protocol
http	Hypertext Transfer Protocol
gopher	Gopher Protocol
mailto	Electronic Mail Address
news	USENET News
nntp	USENET News (NNTP-access)
telnet	Reference to interactive sessions
wais	Wide Area Information Server
file	Host-specific file names
prospero	Prospero Directory Service

Example

```
<blockquote cite="http://www.microsoft.com">
Quotation by Bill Gates ...
</blockquote>
```

Accompanying elements

BLOCKQUOTA

Q

CITE

Indicating quotations

Description

Quotations are labelled with this command. If the original quotation cited is to be accessed on the World Wide Web, it makes sense to provide the quotation cited with a hyperlink. Using CITE, the source of the quotation is reported in the first line, together with the originator or the title of the text from which the quotation was taken.

Application

The CITE command is used to identify concepts from other media. These quotations are usually represented in italics. As a rule, longer quotations are represented with the BLOCKQUOTA command.

HTML 4.0 standard

CLASS, DIR, ID, LANG, STYLE, TITLE

Start tag: required; end tag: required.

Attributes

CLASS

Through the CLASS attribute, the element can be assigned to a group (class). Enter one of the free selectable class name as a value. These groupings then provide easy access to all related elements. You can easily change all properties of the elements of a class with the help of cascading style sheets or other languages, or select a value.

DIR

This attribute is necessary to determine the text direction. This attribute can have the values:

LTR

This value determines the text direction from left to right (and is short for "left-to-right"). This is the default direction in the browser.

RTL

If the text must run contrary to the standard direction from the right to the left margin of the screen, then choose the RTL value (short for "right-to-left").

ID

ID identifies the document. Using ID, a specific element can be accessed with the help of a script language, to select or modify its values.

LANG

This attribute indicates the language of the linked document. This is particularly important in search engines for identification purposes. Use the language codes according to ISO 639, for example "en" for English or "en-us" for American English.

ONCLICK

This event takes place if you single-click on an element with the mouse. A given script is executed by this action.

ONDBLCLICK

This event takes place if you double-click on an element with the mouse. A given script is executed by this action.

ONKEYDOWN

This event takes place if you are in an element and a key is pressed and held down. This action executes a specific script.

ONKEYPRESS

This event takes place if you are in an element and a key is pressed and released. This action executes a specific script.

ONKEYUP

This event takes place if you are in an element and a key that was pressed is released. This action executes a specific script.

ONMOUSEDOWN

This event takes place if you are in an element and a mouse button is clicked and held down. A given script is executed by this action.

ONMOUSEMOVE
> This event takes place if you move the cursor over an object with the mouse. A given script is executed by this action.

ONMOUSEOUT
> This event takes place if the mouse moves the cursor off an element. This action excecutes a given script.

ONMOUSEOVER
> This event takes place if the mouse moves the cursor directly over the element (object). A given script is executed by this action.

ONMOUSEUP
> This event takes place if you are in an element and a mouse button that was clicked and held down is released. A given script is executed by this action.

STYLE
> The STYLE attribute can be used to change style settings, in particular the appearance of the element. You apply the corresponding options of a style sheet language (usually CSS) as the value of the attribute.

TITLE
> You should give the user further information about the element used by defining a meaningful title with the help of the TITLE command. Navigation on your Web site is made easier for users who are dependent on voice responses.

Example

```
<cite>John Osborne </cite> said:

<blockquote>
"The computer is the logical development of man:
Intelligence   without   morals".
</blockquote>

<q>"Genius is industriousness" <q>
<cite>Goethe </cite>
```

Events

ONCLICK, ONDBLCLICK, ONKEYDOWN, ONKEYPRESSED, ONKEYUP, ONMOUSEDOWN, ONMOUSEMOVE, ONMOUSEOUT, ONMOUSEOVER, ONMOUSEUP

Related commands

ABBR
ACRONYM
BLOCKQUOTE
Q
CODE
DFN
EM

KBD
SAMP
STRONG
VAR

CLASS   <html attribute>
Class assignment of elements

Description

With the CLASS attribute the element can be assigned to a group (class). These groupings then provide easy access to all accompanying elements. In this way, it is easy to change the properties of all elements or to select values with the help of cascading style sheets or other languages.

Application

You should indicate one free class name as a value. The use of this attribute is optional.

Values

You can give any string to this attribute as a value. Therefore, this character string should not start or end with spaces, if possible, as the processing browser may filter them out.

Example

```
<p id="Paragraph1" class="short decription">Text ... </p>
<p id="Paragraph2" class="Content">Text ... </p>
<p id="Paragraph3"
class ="Conclusion" > Text ... </p>

<p id="Paragraph4" class="Short decription">Text ... </p>
<p id="Paragraph5" class="Content">Text ... </p>
<p id="Paragraph6" class="Conclusion">Text ... </p>
```

Accompanying elements

A	FORM	P
ABBR	FRAME	PRE
ACRONYM	FRAMESET	Q
ADDRESS	H1	S
APPLET	H2	SAMP
AREA	H3	SELECT
B	H4	SMALL
BDO	H5	SPAN
BIG	H6	STRIKE
BLOCKQUOTE	HR	STRONG
BODY	I	SUB
BR	IFRAME	SUP
BUTTON	IMG	TABLE
CAPTION	INPUT	TBODY
CENTER	INS	TD
CITE	ISINDEX	TEXTAREA
CODE	KBD	TFOOT
COL	LABEL	TH
COLGROUP	LEGEND	THEAD
DD	LI\hLINK	TR
DEL	MAP	TT
DFN	MENU	U
DIR	NOFRAMES	UL
DIV	NOSCRIPT	VAR
DL	OBJECT	
DT	OL	
EM	OPTGROUP	
FIELDSET	OPTION	
FONT		

CLASSID   \<html attribute\>

Indicating the source of a class implementation of an object

Description

This attribute is used to refer to the program file (classid = class identifier).

Application

Make sure that this command is in quotation marks. The command can also be used for the DATA attribute. It consists of the following solid string: java: – the name of the .class file must then follow (also the executable Java Program file). The use of this attribute is optional.

Values

A valid value for this attribute is a URI (Uniform Resource Identifier). The structure of a URI is as follows:

```
[protocol]: // [domain]/[directory]/[file]
```

Possible instructions for the used protocol are the following values:

ftp	File Transfer Protocol
http	Hypertext Transfer Protocol
gopher	Gopher Protocol
mailto	Electronic Mail Address
news	USENET News
nntp	USENET News (NNTP-access)
telnet	Reference to interactive sessions
wais	Wide Area Information Server
file	Host-specific file names
prospero	Prospero Directory Service

Example

```
<object classid="http://www.source.co.uk/java/anim.class">
<object
    classid="java:action"
    codebase=". . /java/"
    codetype = "application/java-vm" >
```

Accompanying elements

OBJECT

CLEAR   <html attribute>

Forcing line breaks

Description

With this attribute a browser will set up a line break only if there is no HTML object aligned in the required direction.

Application

It is possible to embed pictures into a text using this attribute. The following four possible values can be submitted to this attribute. The use of this attribute is optional.

Values

LEFT

With CLEAR=LEFT it is essential that the next blank space should be in the left margin of the window.

RIGHT

With CLEAR=RIGHT it is essential that the next blank space should be in the right margin of the window.

ALL

A line break is set up at the next place in which there is a blank space either to the left or to the right margin of the window.

NONE

Default value; a line break is placed immediately after the input of the BR command.

Example

```
<br>
<br clear="left">
<br clear="all">
```

Accompanying element

BR

clip

CASCADING
STYLE SHEETS

Reducing display area

Description

With this command you can make only a specific part of an element visible. If the element is larger than the chosen display area, it is resized according to the available display area.

Parameter

This command can have four numeric values, which are the value for the top, right, bottom and left positions. Moreover, the keyword auto can still be used instead of a numeric value. The corresponding area is then automatically determined depending on the size of the element.

Example

```
<style type="text/css">
h1, h2 { clip:rect (10 x 10 x 10 x 10) }
h3, h4 { clip:rect (auto x 10 x auto x 10) }
</style>

<div style="clip:rect (10 x 10 x 10 x 10)">
</div>
```

CODE   <html attribute>

Determining the class of a Java applet

Description

The class of an applet is determined with the CODE attribute. References to the complete path of an applet can be contained in this attribute. If several classes are required for an applet, the search for these classes takes place with the CODEBASE attribute.

Application

You should indicate either the name of the Class file, which contains the compiled applet subclass, or the path which leads directly to the Class file. The use of this attribute is no longer recommended; use instead the OBJECT element with CODEBASE.

Values

You can apply any string to this attribute as a value. This character string should not start or end with spaces, if possible, as the processing browser may filter these out.

Example

```
<applet code="anim.class" width="100" height="100">
</applet>
<object codetype="application/java"
     "classid = java for anim.class: "
     width = "100"
     height = "100">
```

Accompanying element
APPLET

CODE

Indicating fragments of computer codes

Description

This command determines fragments of computer codes or other highlighted text. The representation is displayed in a proportional script (see figure below). This is important for program listings (fragments of computer codes) so that these source codes retain their clarity.

Application

The CODE command is used to identify program listings (codes), program objects or program elements. It is better to retain this kind of formatting although it seems more complicated than other formattings, using the commands STYLES or TT, for example. The CODE element can serve as marking for searching source codes in future browser versions.

HTML 4.0 standard

CLASS, DIR, ID, LANG, STYLE, TITLE

Start tag: required; end tag: required.

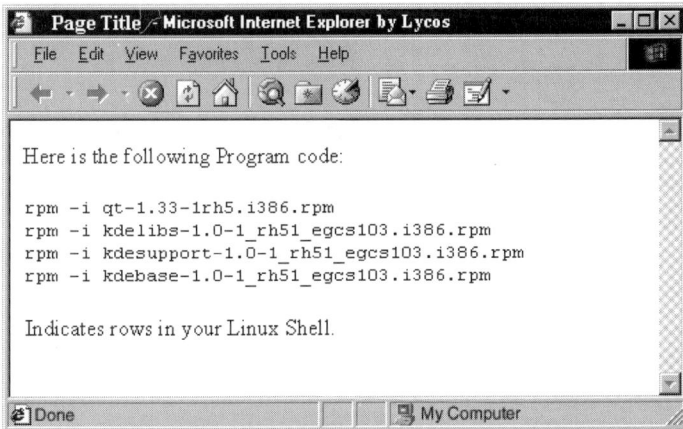

The program code appears as proportional script

Attributes

CLASS

Through the CLASS attribute, the element can be assigned to a group (class). Enter one of the free selectable class name as a value. These groupings then provide easy access to all related elements. You can easily change all properties of the elements of a class with the help of cascading style sheets or other languages, or select a value.

DIR

This attribute is necessary to determine the text direction. This attribute can have the values:

LTR

This value determines the text direction from left to right (and is short for "left-to-right"). This is the default direction in the browser.

RTL

If the text must run contrary to the standard direction from the right to the left margin of the screen, then choose the RTL value (short for "right-to-left").

ID

ID identifies the document. Using ID, a specific element can be accessed with the help of a script language, to select or modify its values.

LANG

This attribute indicates the language of the linked document. This is particularly important in search engines for identification purposes. Use the language codes according to ISO 639, for example "en" for English or "en-us" for American English.

ONCLICK

This event takes place if you single-click on an element with the mouse. A given script is executed by this action.

ONDBLCLICK

This event takes place if you double-click on an element with the mouse. A given script is executed by this action.

ONKEYDOWN

This event takes place if you are in an element and a key is pressed and held down. This action executes a specific script.

ONKEYPRESS

This event takes place if you are in an element and a key is pressed and released. This action executes a specific script.

ONKEYUP

This event takes place if you are in an element and a key that was pressed is released. This action executes a specific script.

ONMOUSEDOWN

This event takes place if you are in an element and a mouse button is clicked and held down. A given script is executed by this action.

ONMOUSEMOVE
>This event takes place if you move the cursor over an object with the mouse. A given script is executed by this action.

ONMOUSEOUT
>This event takes place if the mouse moves the cursor off an element. This action excecutes a given script.

ONMOUSEOVER
>This event takes place if the mouse moves the cursor directly over the element (object). A given script is executed by this action.

ONMOUSEUP
>This event takes place if you are in an element and a mouse button that was clicked and held down is released. A given script is executed by this action.

STYLE
>The STYLE attribute can be used to change style settings, in particular the apperance of the element. As the value of the attribute, you apply the corresponding options of a style sheet language (usually CSS).

TITLE
>You should give the user further information about the element used by defining a meaningful title with the help of the TITLE command. Navigation on your Web site is made easier for users who are dependent on voice responses.

Example

```
<code>
rpm-I qt 1.33-1 rh5.i386.rpm
rpm-I kdelibs 1.0-1_ rh51_egcs103.i386.rpm
rpm-I kdesupport 1.0-1_ rh51_egcs103.i386.rpm
rpm-I kdebase 1.0-1_ rh51_egcs103.i386.rpm
</code>
```

Events

ONCLICK, ONDBLCLICK, ONKEYDOWN, ONKEYPRESSED, ONKEYUP, ONMOUSEDOWN, ONMOUSEMOVE, ONMOUSEOUT, ONMOUSEOVER, ONMOUSEUP

Related commands

ACRONYM
CITE
DFN
EM
KBD
SAMP
STRONG
VAR

CODEBASE   \<html attribute\>

Indicating the data source for an applet

Description

The CODEBASE attribute is responsible for delivering a file path. This path is used by an applet if relative address references appear at the processing of an object.

Application

The APPLET command is used for the CODEBASE=URI attribute only in sub-folders of the document directory. All attributes appearing in the CLASSID, DATA and ARCHIVES attributes are changed from CODEBASE with the help of the absolute path. The use of this attribute is optional.

Values

A valid value for this attribute is the URI (Uniform Resource Identifier). The construction of a URI is as follows:

```
[protocol]: // [domain]/[directory]/[file]
```

Possible instructions for the used protocol are the following Values:

ftp	File Transfer Protocol
http	Hypertext Transfer Protocol
gopher	Gopher Protocol
mailto	Electronic Mail Address
news	USENET News
nntp	USENET News (NNTP-access)
telnet	Reference to interactive sessions
wais	Wide Area Information Server
file	Host-specific file names
prospero	Prospero Directory Service

Example

```
<object
    classid="java:action"
    codebase=". . /java/"
    code type="application/java vm">
```

Accompanying elements

APPLET
OBJECT

CODETYPE   **\<html attribute\>**

Defining media type

Description

With the help of this attribute we can define the Internet media type of the corresponding object.

Application

You should give a valid (active) media type by choosing MIME type as a value to determine the format in which the object is saved.

Values

Valid values for the CODETYPE attribute are content types. Special data formats are marked with these; a Microsoft Word document or an Adobe PDF document, for example. Use the definitions to name the data format which you can find in the keyword MIME types.

Example

```
<object codetype="video/mpeg">
<object codetype="image/gif">
<object
     classid="java:action"
     codebase=". . /java/"
     code type="application/java vm">
```

Accompanying element

OBJECT

COL

Defining columns in a table

Description

Use this command to define columns in a table.

Application

The COL command is used to define the height and width of columns in a table. This command, first introduced in HTML 4.0, informs the browser about the size of the table when loading the table contents. The use of the command is optional, but it optimises the browser output speed.

The COL command is always used within a COLGROUP container.

HTML 4.0 standard

ALIGN, CHAR, CHAROFF, CLASS, DIR, ID, LANG, SPAN, STYLE, TITLE, VALIGN, WIDTH

Start tag: required; end tag : not allowed.

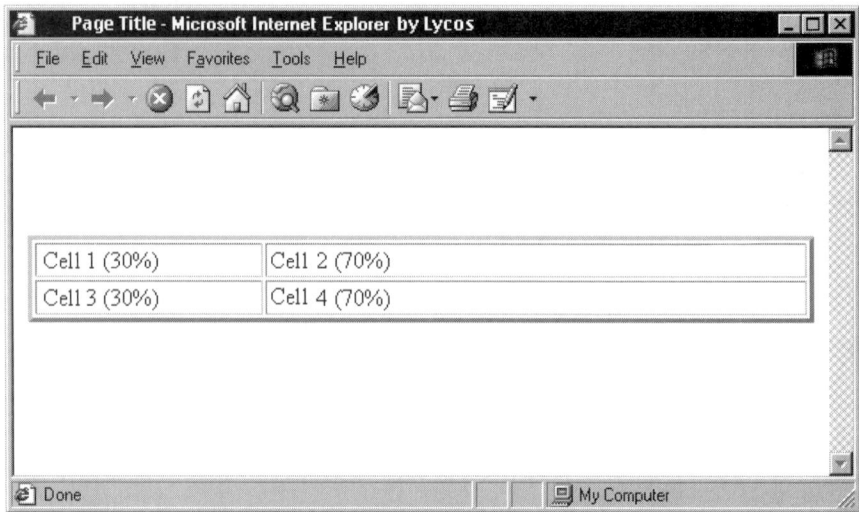

With COL you can determine the column width in a table

Attributes

ALIGN

This attribute is responsible for determining the alignment of data within a table column.

LEFT

Left alignment of data within a table. Default setting.

RIGHT

Right alignment of data within a table.

CENTER

Centred alignment of data within a table. Default setting for table headers.

JUSTIFY

Justifies the text in a table.

CHAR

Alignment of the data on a character set with the CHAR attribute.

CLASS

Through the CLASS attribute, the element can be assigned to a group (class). Enter one of the free selectable class name as a value. These groupings then provide easy access to all related elements. You can easily change all properties of the elements of a class with the help of cascading style sheets or other languages, or select a value.

CHAR

You can use this attribute to determine a character from a valid character set with which data in the table are aligned. Be careful to distinguish between upper and lower case letters in this attribute. The predefined character for the alignment is the decimal point. Depending on the language (LANG) used this can be a comma or a full stop.

CHAROFF

This attribute defines the separation to the first character which was formatted with the CHAR attribute.

DIR

This attribute is necessary to determine the text direction. This attribute can have the values:

LTR

This value determines the text direction from left to right (and is short for "left-to-right"). This is the default direction is in the browser.

RTL

If the text must run contrary to the standard direction from the right to the left margin of the screen, then choose the RTL value (short for "right-to-left").

ID

ID attribute identifies the document. Using ID, a specific element can be accessed with the help of a script language, to select or modify its values.

LANG

This attribute indicates the language of the linked document. This is particularly important in search engines for identification purposes. Use the language codes according to ISO 639, for example "en" for English or "en-us" for American English.

ONCLICK

This event takes place if you single-click on an element with the mouse. A given script is executed by this action.

ONDBLCLICK

This event takes place if you double-click on an element with the mouse. A given script is executed by this action.

ONKEYDOWN

This event takes place if you are in an element and a key is pressed and held down. This action executes a specific script.

ONKEYPRESS

This event takes place if you are in an element and a key is pressed and released. This action executes a specific script.

ONKEYUP

This event takes place if you are in an element and a key that was pressed is released. This action executes a specific script.

ONMOUSEDOWN

This event takes place if you are in an element and a mouse button is clicked and held down. A given script is executed by this action.

ONMOUSEMOVE

This event takes place if you move the cursor over an object with the mouse. A given script is executed by this action.

ONMOUSEOUT

This event takes place if the mouse moves the cursor off an element. This action excecutes a given script.

ONMOUSEOVER

This event takes place if the mouse moves the cursor directly over the element (object). A given script is executed by this action.

ONMOUSEUP

This event takes place if you are in an element and a mouse button that was clicked and held down is released. A given script is executed by this action.

SPAN

You can determine the number of columns of a table with this attribute. Valid values for this attribute are positive integers.

STYLE

The STYLE attribute is used to determine specific properties of an element. The style settings used are defined by cascading style sheets.

TITLE

You should give the user further information about the element used by defining a meaningful title with the help of the TITLE command. Navigation on your Web site is made easier for users who are dependent on voice responses.

VALIGN

With this attribute the vertical alignment of text within a table can be determined. If this element is not used, all text is automatically centre aligned.

TOP

Highlighted text is aligned at the top.

BOTTOM

Highlighted text is aligned at the bottom.

MIDDLE

Highlighted text is aligned in the centre.

BASELINE

The text, which is next to the highlighted text, is aligned along a baseline used by the two texts.

WIDTH

This attribute is used to determine the column width. With the input WIDTH="*0" you can set a column to an optimal width. Other valid values can be integers for the number of pixels per column or a percentage of the screen width.

Pixel

By defining a number value, you get a column width which corresponds exactly to the given value in pixels.

Per cent

It is also possible to give a percentage of the column width. Simply add a per cent symbol to the number.

Proportional

By adding an asterisk you will obtain a proportional instruction concerning the column width.

Example

```
<table>
    <colgroup>
    <col width="100">
    <col width="200">
    <col width="150">
    </colgroup>
```

...

```
<table>
    <colgroup>
    <col width="1*">
    <col width="3*">
    </colgroup>
```

This example produces a table in which the first column takes up $\frac{1}{4}$ of the entire width and the second column $\frac{3}{4}$ to give the complete width (1*+ 3* = 4).

```
<table border="3" width="100%">
    <colgroup>
    <col width="30%">
    <col width="70%">
    </colgroup>
    <tr>
        <td>Cell 1 (30%) </td>
        <td>Cell 2 (70%) </td>
    </tr>
    <tr>
        <td>Cell 3 (30%) </td>
        <td>Cell 4 (70%) </td>
    </tr>
</table>
```

Events

ONCLICK, ONDBLCLICK, ONKEYDOWN, ONKEYPRESSED, ONKEYUP, ONMOUSEDOWN, ONMOUSEMOVE, ONMOUSEOUT, ONMOUSEOVER, ONMOUSEUP

XML Definition

```
<!ELEMENT COL - O EMPTY>
<!ATTLIST COL
% of attrs;
span        NUMBER 1
width       % MultiLength; # IMPLIED
% cellhalign;
% cellvalign;>
```

Related commands

COLGROUP
TABLE

COLGROUP

Defining a column group

Description

It is possible to define groups of columns with this command.

Application

The COLGROUP command is used to determine combination or groupings of table columns. In grouping, these elements can be assigned the same style pattern, for example. This feature is important to compile overviews for different products.

HTML 4.0 standard

ALIGN, CHAR, CHAROFF, CLASS, DIR, ID, LANG, SPAN, STYLE, TITLE, VALIGN, WIDTH

Start tag: required; end tag: optional.

Attributes

ALIGN

This attribute is responsible for determining the alignment of data within a table column.

LEFT

Left alignment of data within a table. Default setting.

RIGHT

Right alignment of data within a table.

CENTER

Data centred within a table. Default setting for table headers.

JUSTIFY

Justifies text in a table.

CHAR

Alignment of the data on a character set with the CHAR attribute.

CLASS

Through the CLASS attribute, the element can be assigned to a group (class). Enter one of the free selectable class name as a value. These groupings then provide easy access to all related elements. You can easily change all properties of the elements of a class with the help of cascading style sheets or other languages, or select a value.

CHAR

With this attribute you can determine a character from a valid character set with which data situated in the table are aligned. Be careful to distinguish between upper and lower case letters in this attribute. The predefined character for the alignment is the decimal point. Depending on the language (LANG) used these can be a comma or a full stop.

CHAROFF

This attribute defines the separation to the first character which was formatted with the CHAR attribute.

DIR

This attribute is necessary to determine the text direction. This attribute can have the values:

LTR

This value determines the text direction from left to right (and is short for "left-to-right"). This is the default direction in the browser.

RTL

If the text must run contrary to the standard direction from the right to the left margin of the screen, then choose the RTL value (short for "right-to-left").

ID

ID identifies the document. Using ID, a specific element can be accessed with the help of a script language, to select or modify its values.

LANG

This attribute indicates the language of the linked document. This is particularly important in search engines for identification purposes. Use the language codes according to ISO 639, for example "en" for English or "en-us" for American English.

ONCLICK

This event takes place if you single-click on an element with the mouse. A given script is executed by this action.

ONDBLCLICK

This event takes place if you double-click on an element with the mouse. A given script is executed by this action.

ONKEYDOWN

This event takes place if you are in an element and a key is pressed and held down. This action executes a specific script.

ONKEYPRESS

This event takes place if you are in an element and a key is pressed and released. This action executes a specific script.

ONKEYUP

This event takes place if you are in an element and a key that was pressed is released. This action executes a specific script.

ONMOUSEDOWN

This event takes place if you are in an element and a mouse button is clicked and held down. A given script is executed by this action.

ONMOUSEMOVE

This event takes place if you move the cursor over an object with the mouse. A given script is executed by this action.

ONMOUSEOUT

This event takes place if the mouse moves the cursor off an element. This action excecutes a given script.

ONMOUSEOVER

This event takes place if the mouse moves the cursor directly over the element (object). A given script is executed by this action.

ONMOUSEUP

This event takes place if you are in an element and a mouse button that was clicked and held down is released. A given script is executed by this action.

SPAN

You can set the number of columns of a table with this attribute. Positive integers are the only valid values for this attribute.

STYLE

The STYLE attribute is used to determine specific properties in the representation of an element. The style settings used are defined by cascading style sheets.

TITLE

You should give the user further information about the element used by defining a meaningful title with the help of the TITLE command. Navigation on your Web site is made easier for users who are dependent on voice responses.

VALIGN

With this attribute the vertical alignment of text within a table can be set. If this element is not used, all text is automatically centre-aligned.

TOP
>Highlighted text is aligned at the top.

BOTTOM
>Highlighted text is aligned at the bottom.

MIDDLE
>Highlighted text is aligned in the centre.

BASELINE
>The text, which is available next to the highlighted text, is aligned along a baseline used by the two texts.

WIDTH
>This attribute is used to determine the column width. With the input WIDTH="*0" you can set a column to an optimal width. Other valid values can be integers for the number of pixels per column or a percentage of the screen width.

Pixel
>By defining a number value, you get a column width which corresponds exactly to the given value in pixels.

Per cent
>It is also possible to give a percentage of the column width. Simply add a per cent symbol to the number.

Proportional
>By adding an asterisk you will obtain a proportional instruction concerning the column width.

Example

```
<colgroup span="10" width="20">
</colgroup>

<colgroup>
        <col width="20">
        <col width="20">
        <col width="20">
        <col width="20">
        <col width="20">
        <col width="20">
        <col width="20">
        <col width="20">
        <col width="20">
        <col width="20">
</colgroup>
```

With the above examples the same result is reached in both cases. The COLGROUP options make work easier in many cases.

Events

ONCLICK, ONDBLCLICK, ONKEYDOWN, ONKEYPRESSED, ONKEYUP, ONMOUSEDOWN, ONMOUSEMOVE, ONMOUSEOUT, ONMOUSEOVER, ONMOUSEUP

XML Definition

```
<!ELEMENT COLGROUP - O (col)*>
<!ATTLIST COLGROUP
% of attrs;
span          NUMBER 1
width         %MultiLength; #IMPLIED
%cellhalign;
%cellvalign;>
```

Related commands

COL
TABLE

color

CASCADING STYLE SHEETS

Setting the colour of an element

Description

Bring a little colour into your life. With color you can change the colour of the elements included in a text.

Parameter

The colour can either be set as a keyword (for example "red") or as a composite RGB value ("rgb(0,0,255)"), for example. The RGB value indicates the single colour ratios of the colours red, green and blue and from this produces a composite colour. Valid values for the three ratios are numbers between 0 and 255.

Example

```
<style type="text/css">
h1, h2 {color: red}
h3, h4 {color: #000000}
</style>

<div style="color: green">
</div>
```

COLOR <html attribute>

Determining text colour

Description

With this attribute you can set the colour of a text section defined with FONT.

Application

Give a valid colour value to the COLOR attribute. The use of this attribute is optional.

Values

Give either a colour value in RGB syntax or a valid colour name to the attribute. For the RGB value, indicate the colour values of the colours red, green and blue in hexadecimal notation: #RRGGBB (i.e. #008000 for green). Alternatively, predefined colour names can be used. (i.e. YELLOW). Under the **Color Palette** keyword you will find a complete list of all standard colours. These are the 16 most frequently used primary colours:

```
BLACK    = #000000  SILVER  = #C0C0C0
GRAY     = #808080  WHITE   = #FFFFFF
MAROON   = #800000  RED     = #FF0000
PURPLE   = #800080  FUCHSIA = #FF00FF
GREEN    = #008000  LIME    = #00FF00
OLIVE    = #808000  YELLOW  = #FFFF00
NAVY     = #000080  BLUE    = #0000FF
TEAL     = #008080  AQUA    = #00FFFF
```

Example

```
<font face="Arial" color="blue">
Now continue in blue  ...
</font>
<font color="#000000">
... and now become black!
</font>
```

Accompanying elements

BASEFONT
FONT

COLS <html attribute>

Determining number and width of columns

Description

This attribute is used to set the column width of a frame or to determine the number of a text entry field in a column. The value for the frame width can be defined in pixels or per cent related to the width of the screen.

Application

You should indicate the single values for the column width of the frame or text field separated by commas.

Values

For each command where you can use this attribute there are different validity ranges for the given value. Below is a list of the commands and their possible values:

FRAMESET

You can indicate the size in pixels, per cent or relative length. To give a size in pixels, submit an integer value to the attribute, and every pixel corresponds to a microdot in the chosen resolution. The instruction in per cent is executed using a number from 1 to 100 and an affixed percent sign (="50%"). The instruction of a relative length is as an integer with affixed asterisk (="1*").

The browser first distributes the vertical or horizontal place according to the pixel statement, then it processes the per cent statement and the remaining area is then distributed according to relative numbers. If it is left with a width of 100 pixels, for example, then the instruction of ="2*,3*" corresponds to a width of 40 and 60 pixels.

TEXTAREA

This attribute determines the number of the columns. The only valid values for this attribute are integer numbers. The number must contain at least one of the numbers from 0 to 9 (="9").

Example

```
<frameset cols="40%,60%">
<frame src="reference.htm" name="Reference">
<frame src="title.htm" name="Data">
</frameset>

<frameset cols="100, *">
<frame src="reference.htm" name="Reference">
```

```
<frame src="title.htm" name="Data">
</frameset>

<textarea cols="80" rows="3">
Your comment ...
</textarea>
```

Accompanying elements
FRAMESET
TEXTAREA

COLSPAN   <html attribute>

Producing cells through several columns

Description
This attribute determines the number of columns required for a cell.

Application
As a rule, if only one column is required, then the value need not be indicated. But if you want to extend a cell over three columns, then indicate COLSPAN="3".

The use of this attribute is optional.

Values
Valid values for this attribute are integer numbers. The number must contain at least one of the numbers between 0 and 9 (="9").

Example
```
<table>
<tr>
     <td>Cell 1 </td>
     <td>Cell 2 </td>
     <tr>
<td colspan="2">Cell 3 </td>
     </tr>
</table>
```

Accompanying elements
TD
TH

Comments

Inserting comments in XML documents

Description

Comments can be inserted within a document and in any place in the Document Type Definition.

Application

Comments must always be outside the markup commands. A parser does not interpret and display comments. Within a comment the character string "--" may not appear. Comments, as in HTML, must be delimited.

Example

```
<address>
<!-- comment -->



</addresss>
```

COMPACT   <html attribute>

Showing lists in a compact form

Description

Provided that this value is set, the browser tries to represent this list in a compact form. The interpretation of this option depends on the bowser used.

Application

The use of this attribute is optional and has no effect on the representation of the lists used in most browsers today.

Values

To activate this option, simply use the name of the attribute. You do not need to provide any value for this attribute. If the attribute is not used, then the option remains deactivated. This attribute is not case-sensitive.

Example

```
<ol compact>
```

```
      <li>First</li>
      <li>Second</li>
      <li>Third</li>
</ol>
<ul compact>
      <li>First</li>
      <li>Second</li>
      <li>Third</li>
</ul>
```

Accompanying elements

DIR
DL
MENU
OL
UL

<u>CONTENT</u>   **\<html attribute>**

Indicating the contents of a META tag

Description
With this attribute you can execute instructions concerning a document's content.

Application
First you must set the information that you want to give with HTTP-EQUIV or NAME (for example KEYWORDS), then indicate the content with CONTENT. Some information can be indicated by commas or separated by spaces. The use of this attribute is required.

Values
You can submit any string to this attribute as a value. If possible, this character string should not start or end with blank characters, as the processing browser may filter these out.

Example
```
<meta name="keywords" lang="en"
      content = "second-hand cars, cars", for >
<meta name="author" content="John Smith">
<meta name="generator" content="Frontpage 2000">
```

Accompanying element
META

COORDS <html attribute>

Giving coordinates for a reference sensitive area

Description

This attribute helps to define the absolute coordinates of areas within a graphic.

Application

The form of the coordinate information depends on the area form determined under SHAPE. Valid values are single lengths or dimensional information separated by commas.

Values

According to the type you have chosen under SHAPE, the information of the single coordinates is executed in various forms:

RECT
  Rectangle; x1=left top edge, left pixel, y1=left top edge, top pixel, x2=right bottom edge, left pixel, y2=right bottom edge, top pixel.
CIRCLE
  Circle; x = centre, left pixel, y = centre, top pixel, R = radius in pixels.
POLY
  Polygon; x1-xn, x=corner pixel from the left, y1-yn, y= corner pixel from the top.

Example

```
<a shape="rect" coords="1, 1, 120, 90">
<a shape="circle" coords="120, 300, 20">
<a shape="poly" coords="78, 67, 122, 324, 123, 90, 15, 10">
```

Accompanying elements

  A
  AREA

Data   <html attribute>

Reference to data related to an object

Description

With this attribute data are referred to the affiliated object.

Application

You indicate through the attribute data the source code of an object which you would like to embed into your HTML document. In addition you may indicate the media type of the object through TYPE.

Values

A valid value for this attribute is the URI (Uniform Resource Identifier). The construction of a URI is as follows:

```
[protocol]: // [Domain]/[Directory]/[File]
```

Possible information for the protocol used are the following values:

ftp	File Transfer Protocol
http	Hypertext Transfer Protocol
gopher	Gopher Protocol
mailto	Electronic Mail Address
news	USENET News
nntp	USENET News (NNTP-access)
telnet	Reference to interactive sessions
wais	Wide Area Information Server
file	Host-specific file names
prospero	Prospero Directory Service

Example

```
<object data="song.wav" type="audio/wav">
<object
    data = "http://www.music.com/song.wav"
    type = "audio/wav">
```

Accompanying element

OBJECT

Data characters

Inserting text in a XML document

Description

Characters in a document which are not markup characters, are data characters.

Application

All characters are accepted within an XML document except for the limitation characters of the markups. Some special characters must be replaced by entities.

Example

```
<ADDRESS>
<SURNAME>Smith </SURNAME>
<NAME>Elena</NAME>
<STREET>142 Murray Rd</STREET>
<POST CODE>S11 7GH</POST CODE>
<PCITY>Sheffield</CITY>
</ADDRESS>
```

Datetime   <html attribute>

Modifying date and time

Description

You can change the date and time using this attribute for the elements INS and DEL. In this way you can view projects which are being developed by several employees.

Application

Indicate the date and time in the appropriate format. The use of this attribute is optional.

Values

With the help of this attribute you can modify the date and time. If you use this attribute, you must ensure that the corresponding information conforms to the ISO 8601 standard.

If you proceed in this way, the entry has the following appearance:

```
JJJ-MMDDThh: mm: ssTZD
```
These entries have the following meaning:

```
JJJJ
```
four-digit date
```
Mm
```
two-digit month detail (03 = March)
```
DD
```
two-digit day date detail (05, 27)
```
T
```
Hyphen according to ISO 8061 between the date and time indication
```
hh
```
two-digit hour information (00 – 23)
```
mm
```
two-digit minute information (00 – 59)
```
ss
```
two-digit second information (00 – 59)
```
TZD
```

Abbreviation for "Time Zone Designator". Description of the time zone. The Z in this abbreviation stands for "Greenwich Mean Time" (GMT). Therefore entries such as +hh:mm or –hh:mm represent local time information, which means before or after the UTC.

Example

```
<ins datetime="1999-06-08T06:00:01+03:00">Inserted </ins>
<del datetime="1999-09-01T02:32:18+00:00">Deleted f </del>
```

Accompanying elements
DEL
INS

DD

Description of definitions

Description
With this command expressions can be defined within definition lists.

Application
The command DD is used to describe a definition concept. Text formatted in this way can be represented as flow text. Within this command, paragraph and text markings may also be used. This command is used for glossaries, for example. Single concepts are listed (with DT) and then defined through the command DD. The list of definitions is determined by the container DL.

HTML 4.0 standard

CLASS, DIR, ID, LANG, STYLE, TITLE

Start tag: required; end tag: optional.

Attributes

CLASS

Through the attribute CLASS the element can be assigned to a group (class). Enter one of the free selectable class names as a value. These groupings then permit you an easy access to all related elements, so you can easily change all the properties the elements in a class with the help of cascading style sheets or other languages, or select a value.

DIR

This attribute is necessary to determine the text direction. This attribute can have two values:

LTR

This value determines the text direction from left to right (and is short for "left-to-right"). This is the default direction in the browser.

RTL

If the text should run contrary to the standard movement from the right to the left margin of the screen, then choose the value RTL (short for "right-to-left").

ID

ID identifies the document. Using ID a specific element can be accessed with the help of a script language to select or change values, for example.

LANG

This attribute indicates the language of the linked document. This is particularly important in search engines for identification purposes. Use the language codes according to ISO 639, for example "en" for English or "en-us" for American English.

ONCLICK

This event takes place if you single-click on an element with the mouse. A given script is executed by this action.

ONDBLCLICK

This event takes place if you double-click on an element with the mouse. A given script is executed by this action.

ONKEYDOWN

This event takes place if you are in an element and a key is pressed and held down. This action executes a specific script.

ONKEYPRESS

This event takes place if you are in an element and a key is simultaneously pressed and released again. This action executes a determinedscript.

ONKEYUP

This event takes place if you are in an element and a key that was pressed is released. This action executes a specific script.

ONMOUSEDOWN

This event takes place if you are in an element and a mouse button is clicked and held down. A given script is executed by this action.

ONMOUSEMOVE

This event takes place if one moves the cursor over an object with the mouse. A given script is executed by this action.

ONMOUSEOUT

This event takes place if a mouse moves the cursor off an element. By this action it is excecuted a given script is executed.

ONMOUSEOVER

This event takes place if the mouse moves the cursor directly over the element (object). A given script is executed by this action.

ONMOUSEUP

This event takes place if you are in an element and a mouse button that was clicked and held down is released. A given script is executed by this action.

STYLE

The attribute STYLE can be used to change style settings, in particular the appearance of the element. As value of the attribute you apply the corresponding options of a style sheet language (usually CSS).

TITLE

Give the user further information about the element used by fixing a meaningful title with the help of the TITLE command. Navigation in your Web site is made particularly easy for users who are dependent on voice response.

Example

```
<dl>
<dt>single expression </dt>
<dd>Definition of this expression </dd>

<dt>Further expression of </dt>
<dd>Definition of the second printout </dd>
</dl>

<dl>
    <dt>LTR </dt>
    <dd>left to right
    <dt>RTL </dt>
    <dd>right to left
</dl>
```

Events

ONCLICK, ONDBLCLICK, ONKEYDOWN, ONKEYPRESSED, ONKEYUP, ONMOUSEDOWN, ONMOUSEMOVE, ONMOUSEOUT, ONMOUSEOVER, ONMOUSEUP

Related commands

DL
DT

Declare <html attribute>

Changing an object into a definition

Description

With this attribute an object is changed into a definition.

Application

This attribute is used if cross references need to be made to a corresponding object or if the object is a parameter of another object.

Values

To activate this option, simply use the name of the attribute. You do not have to submit any value to this attribute. If the attribute is not used, then the option remains deactivated. This attribute is not case-sensitive i.e. it does not distinguish between upper and lower case initial letters.

Example

```
<object declare>
```

Accompanying element

OBJECT

Defer   <html attribute>
Making no changes to page setup by a script

Description
This attribute is used if no changes are to be made by a script in a HTML document, making it possible for the browser to continue to page setup without further changes .

Application
You may put the attribute into the SCRIPT command.

Values
To activate this option, simply use the name of the attribute. You do not have to submit any value to this attribute. If the attribute is not used, then the option remains deactivated. This attribute is not case-sensitive.

Example
```
<script type="JavaScript" defer>
```

Accompanying element
SCRIPT

Define-script   **XSL**
Executing script at runtime

Description
This is the definition of a script which is executed by the parser at translation time. In this way it is possible to trigger the target document dynamically.

Application
As a rule, <define-script> is used in connection with a CDATA section.

Example
```
<define-script>
     <![CDATA
[
...
```

```
]]>
</define-script>
```

DEL
Identifying deleted text

Description
With this command text deleted in a newer version of a document may be identified.

Application
The command DEL is used to make changes recognisable in texts on which several people work, for example. In this case, it is used for texts wich are labelled as deleted and have been replaced by a more current version of a HTML document. A command which causes the opposite effect is INS. These commands are used in many word proccessing programs.

HTML 4.0 standard
CITE, CLASS, DATETIME, DIR, ID, LANG, STYLE, TITLE

Start tag: required; end tag: required.

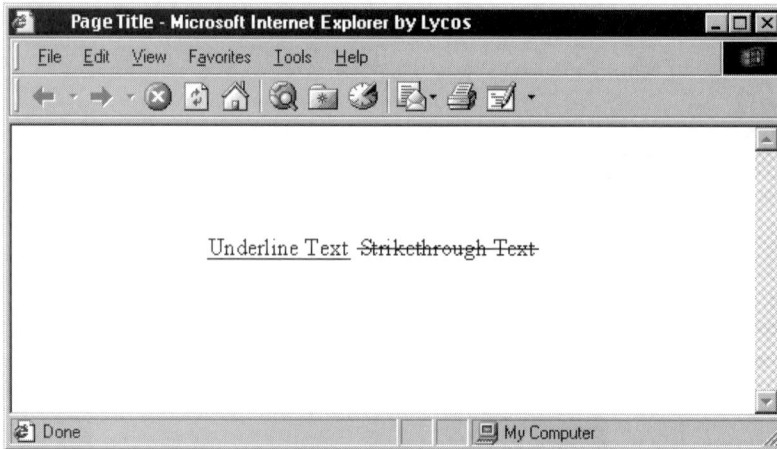

The inserted text is underlined and the deleted sentence crossed out

Attributes

CLASS

Through the attribute CLASS the element can be assigned to a group (class). Enter one of the free selectable class names as a value. These groupings then provide easy access to all related elements, so you can easily change all the properties of the elements of a class with the help of cascading style sheets or other languages, or select a value.

CITE

With this attribute it is possible either to identify documents which refer to the original document, or to execute an instruction to the document to which modifications have been made.

DATETIME

With the help of this attribute you can find out when changes were made to the document. If you use this attribute, you must ensure that the corresponding instructions comply with the ISO 8601 standard.

If you proceed, the entry has the following appearance:

JJJJ-MMDDThh: mm: ssTZD

These entries have the following meaning:

JJJJ

four-digit date

MM

two-digit month instruction (03 = March)

DD

two-digit day date (05, 27)

T

Hyphen between the date and time indication according to ISO 8061

hh

two-digit hour instruction (00 – 23)

mm

two-digit minute instruction (00 – 59)

ss

two-digit second instruction (00 – 59)

TZD

Abbreviation for Time Zone Designator. Name of the time zone. The Z in this abbreviation indicates Greenwich Mean Time (GMT). Either before or after GMT, there are inputs like +hh:mm or -hh:mm for local time indications.

DIR

This attribute is necessary to determine the text direction. This attribute can have the values:

LTR

> This value determines the text direction from left to right (and is short for "left-to-right"). This is the default direction in the browser.

RTL

> If the text should run contrary to the standard movement from the right to the left margin of the screen, then choose the value RTL (short for "right-to-left").

ID

> ID identifies the document. Using ID a specific element can be accessed with the help of a script language to select or change values.

LANG

> This attribute indicates the language of the linked document. This is particularly important in search engines for identification purposes. Use the language codes according to ISO 639, for example "en" for English or "en-us" for American English.

ONCLICK

> This event takes place if you single-click on an element with the mouse. A given script is executed by this action.

ONDBLCLICK

> This event takes place if you double-click on an element with the mouse. A given script is executed by this action.

ONKEYDOWN

> This event takes place if you are in an element and a key is pressed and held down. This action executes a specific script.

ONKEYPRESS

> This event takes place if you are in an element and a key is simultaneously pressed and released again. This action executes a script.

ONKEYUP

> This event takes place if you are in an element and a key that was pressed is released. This action executes a specific script.

ONMOUSEDOWN

> This event takes place if you are in an element and a mouse button is clicked and held down. A given script is executed by this action.

ONMOUSEMOVE

> This event takes place if one moves the cursor over an object with the mouse. A given script is executed by this action.

ONMOUSEOUT

> This event takes place if a mouse moves the cursor off an element. By this action it is excecuted a given script is executed.

ONMOUSEOVER

> This event takes place if the mouse moves the cursor directly over the element (object). A given script is executed by this action.

ONMOUSEUP
> This event takes place if you are in an element and a mouse button that was clicked and held down is released. A given script is executed by this action.

STYLE
> The attribute STYLE can be used to change style settings, in particular the appearance of the element. As value of the attribute you apply the corresponding options of a style sheet language (usually CSS).

TITLE
> Give the user further information about the element used by giving it a meaningful title with the help of the TITLE command. Navigation in your Web site is made particularly easy for users who are dependent on voice response.

Example

```
<del datetime="1999-06-08T06:00:01Z">Flow </del>
<ins>River </ins>

<ins datetime="1999-06-08T06:00:01+03:00">Inserted for </ins>
```

Events

ONCLICK, ONDBLCLICK, ONKEYDOWN, ONKEYPRESSED, ONKEYUP, ONMOUSEDOWN, ONMOUSEMOVE, ONMOUSEOUT, ONMOUSEOVER, ONMOUSEUP

XML definition

```
<! ELEMENT (INS|DEL) - - (%flow;)*>
<!ATTLIST (INS|DEL)
%attrs;

cite       % URI;  # IMPLIED
datetime % Datetime;  # IMPLIED >
```

Related command

INS

DFN

Indicating definitions

Description

Definitions are indicated with this command. The command DFN is a new command which occurred first in the Internet Explorer browser .

Application

The command DFN is used to identify definitions which occur within a text. Browsers that show which can interpret this kind of formatting the command DFN in italics.

HTML 4.0 standard

CLASS, DIR, ID, LANG, STYLE, TITLE

Start tag: required; end tag: required.

Attributes

CLASS

> Through the attribute CLASS the element can be assigned to a group (class). Enter one of the free selectable class name as a value. These groupings then permit you easy access to all related elements so you can easily change properties of the elements of a class with the help of cascading style sheets or other languages, or select a value.

DIR

> This attribute is necessary to determine the text direction. This attribute can have the values:

> LTR

>> This value determines the text direction from left to right (and is short for "left-to-right"). This is the default direction in the browser.

> RTL

>> If the text should run contrary to the standard movement from the right to the left margin of the screen, then choose the value RTL (short for "right-to-left").

ID

> ID identifies the document. Using ID a specific element can be accessed with the help of a script language to select or change values, for example.

LANG

> This attribute indicates the language of the linked document. This is particularly important in search engines for identification. Use the language codes according to ISO 639, for example "en" for English or "en-us" for American English.

ONCLICK

> This event takes place if you single-click on an element with the mouse. A given script is executed by this action.

ONDBLCLICK

> This event takes place if you double-click on an element with the mouse. A given script is executed by this action.

ONKEYDOWN

> This event takes place if you are in an element and a key is pressed and held down. This action executes a specific script.

ONKEYPRESS

This event takes place if you are in an element and a key is simultaneously pressed and released again. This action executes a determined script.

ONKEYUP

This event takes place if you are in an element and a key that was pressed is released. This action executes a specific script.

ONMOUSEDOWN

This event takes place if you are in an element and a mouse button is clicked and held down. A given script is executed by this action.

ONMOUSEMOVE

This event takes place if one moves the cursor over an object with the mouse. A given script is executed by this action.

ONMOUSEOUT

This event takes place if a mouse moves the cursor off an element. By this action it is executed a given script is executed.

ONMOUSEOVER

This event takes place if the mouse moves the cursor directly over the element (object). A given script is executed by this action.

ONMOUSEUP

This event takes place if you are in an element and a mouse button that was clicked and held down is released. A given script is executed by this action.

STYLE

The attribute STYLE is used to determine specific properties in the representation of labelled elements. Style settings are defined by the cascading style sheets.

TITLE

Give the user further information about the element used by giving it a meaningful title with the help of the TITLE command. Navigation in your Web site is made particularly easy for users who are dependent on voice response.

Example

```
<dfn>
HTML is the abbreviation for Hypertext Markup Language. The language
of the Internet.
</dfn>
```

Events

ONCLICK, ONDBLCLICK, ONKEYDOWN, ONKEYPRESS, ONKEYUP, ONMOUSEDOWN, ONMOUSEMOVE, ONMOUSEOUT, ONMOUSEOVER, ONMOUSEUP

Related commands

ACRONYM

CITE

CODE
EM
KBD
Q
SAMP
STRONG
VAR

DIR <html attribute>
Determining text direction

Description
This attribute determines the direction of text.

Application
The use of this attribute is optional. Two values can be applied to this attribute.

Values
LTR
> This value determines the text direction as being from left to right (short for "left-to-right"). This is the default direction in the browser.

RTL
> If the text should run contrary to the standard direction from the right screen margin to the left margin, then choose the value RTL (short for "right-to-left").

Example
```
<div dir="ltr"></div>
<div dir="rtl"></div>
```

Accompanying elements

A	H1	P
ABBR	H2	PRE
ACRONYM	H3	Q
ADDRESS	H4	S
AREA	H5	SAMP
B	H6	SELECT
BIG	HEAD	SMALL
BLOCKQUOTE	HTML	SPAN
BODY	I	STRIKE
BUTTON	IMG	STRONG
CAPTION	INPUT	STYLE
CENTER	INS	SUB
CITE	ISINDEX	SUP
CODE	KBD	TABLE
COL	LABEL	TBODY
COLGROUP	LEGEND	TD
DD	LI	TEXTAREA
DEL	LINK	TFOOT
DFN	MAP	TH
DIR	MENU	THEAD
DIV	META	TITLE
DL	NOFRAMES	TR
DT	NOSCRIPT	TT
EM	OBJECT	U
FIELDSET	OL	UL
FONT	OPTGROUP	VARNTER
FORM	OPTION	

Dir

Indicating directory lists

Description

With this command it is possible to indicate directory lists.

Application

The command DIR occurs to indicate directory lists. Short entries, which can be up to 20 characters long, are contained in these directory lists. The lists are oragnised into columns. This command is not supported in HTML 4.0.

The single list entries within the DIR container are made recognisable with LI.

HTML 4.0 standard

ID, CLASS, LANG, DIR, TITLE, STYLE

The use of this command is not supported by the current HTML version; it has been replaced by other commands.

Start tag: required; end tag: required.

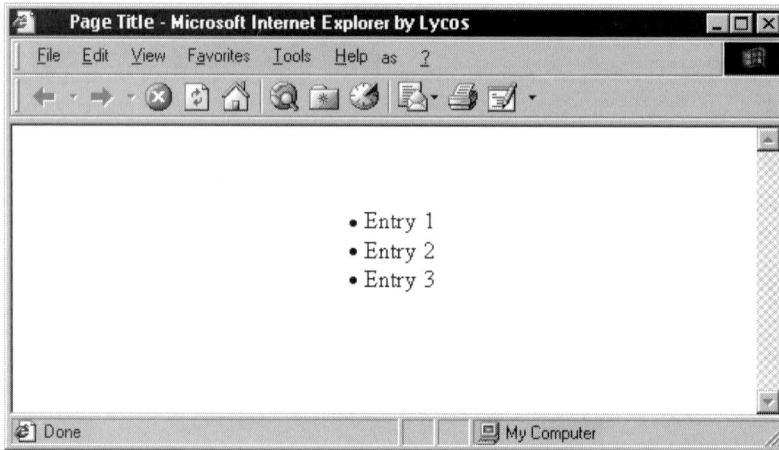

Directory lists are usually represented as above

Attributes

CLASS

Through the attribute CLASS the element can be assigned to a group (class). Enter one of the free selectable class names as a value. These groupings then provide easy access to all related elements so you can change properties of the elements of a class with the help of cascading style sheets or other languages, or select a value.

DIR

This attribute is necessary to determine the text direction. This attribute can have the values:

LTR

> This value determines the text direction from left to right (and is short for "left-to-right"). This is the default direction in the browser.

RTL

> If the text should run contrary to the standard movement from the right to the left margin of the screen, then choose the value RTL (short for "right-to-left").

ID

> ID identifies the document. Using ID it can be accessed to a specific element with the help of a script language to select or change values, for example.

LANG

> This attribute indicates the language of the linked document. This is particularly important in search engines for identification purposes. Use the language codes according to ISO 639, for example "en" for English or "en-us" for American English.

ONCLICK

> This event takes place if you single-click on an element with the mouse. A given script is executed by this actiot.

ONDBLCLICK

> This event takes place if you double-click on an element with the mouse. A given script is executed by this action.

ONKEYDOWN

> This event takes place if you are in an element and a key is pressed and held down. This action executes a specific script.

ONKEYPRESS

> This event takes place if you are in an element and a key is simultaneously pressed and released again. This action executes a determined script.

ONKEYUP

> This event takes place if you are in an element and a key that was pressed is released. This action executes a specific script.

ONMOUSEDOWN

> This event takes place if you are in an element and a mouse button is clicked and held down. A given script is executed by this action.

ONMOUSEMOVE

> This event takes place if one moves the cursor over an object with the mouse. A given script is executed by this action.

ONMOUSEOUT

> This event takes place if a mouse moves the cursor off an element. A given script is executed by this action.

ONMOUSEOVER

> This event takes place if the mouse moves the cursor directly over the element (object). A given script is executed by this action.

ONMOUSEUP

This event takes place if you are in an element and a mouse button that was clicked and held down is released. A given script is executed by this action.

TITLE

Give the user further information about the element used by fixing a meaningful title with the help of the TITLE command. Navigation in your Web site is made particularly easy for users who are dependent on voice response.

Example

```
<dir>
<li>Entry 1 </li>
<li>Entry 2 </li>
<li>Entry 3 </li>
</dir>
```

Events

ONCLICK, ONDBLCLICK, ONKEYDOWN, ONKEYPRESS, ONKEYUP, ONMOUSEDOWN, ONMOUSEMOVE, ONMOUSEOUT, ONMOUSEOVER, ONMOUSEUP

Related commands

MENU

UL

Disable

<html attribute>

Deactivating elements

Description

With this attribute it is possible to deactivate buttons or entry fields in a form.

Application

Through the disable command it is possible to deactivate the use of single elements in a form. Fields are shown in grey and are thus made recognisable as inactive. The use of this attribute is optional.

Values

To activate this option, simply use the name of the attribute. You do not have to submit any value to this attribute. If the attribute is not used, then the option remains deactivated. This attribute is not case-sensitive.

Example

```
<textarea cols="10" rows="3" disable>

<select name="Operating system" size="3" multiple>
<option>Windows    3.11
<option>Windows    95
<option>Windows    98
<option>Windows    NT   4.0
<option disable>Windows 2000
</select>
```

Accompanying elements

BUTTON
INPUT
OPTGROUP
OPTION
SELECT
TEXTAREA

Display

Determining automatic line breaks

Description

The keyword display is used to inform the browser whether an automatic line break is executed on a text element. Usually assignments executed within a text require on a line break, whereas elements such as paragraphs naturally end with a line break.

Parameter

Elements within a text (quotations of indicated sentences, for example) do not usually break into pages. The parameter inline has to be used here. Other elements on which a line break is normally executed (the title, for example) are indicated.

Example

```
<style type="text/css">
h1, h2 { display: inline}
h3, h4 { display: block}
</style>

<div style="display: inline">
```

```
</div>
```

DIV

Structuring text

Description

HTML documents can be structured with this command.

Application

The command DIV serves to structure text just like the command SPAN. This command replaces the absolute CENTER-tag with the corresponding attribute. The command will then be used when paragraphs of an HTML document should be represented centred, or justified right or left.

Elements which can be formatted in this way are text, graphics, headings and tables. DIV is always used if a text section is not already determined by another container which could do the formatting.

HTML 4.0 standard

CLASS, DIR, ID, LANG, STYLE, TITLE

Start tag: required; end tag: required.

Attributes

ALIGN

With this attribute you determine whether you align a paragraph formatted with the command DIV left, right or centred.

CENTER

Alignment of a paragraph on the centre of a page.

LEFT

Left alignment of a paragraph.

RIGHT

Right alignment of a paragraph.

JUSTIFY

Alignment of a paragraph to both sides (justified).

DIR

This attribute is necessary to determine the text direction. This attribute can have the values:

```
┌─────────────────────────────────────────────────────────────────────────┐
│ 🎴  Page Title - Microsoft Internet Explorer by Lycos          _ □ ✕      │
├─────────────────────────────────────────────────────────────────────────┤
│  File   Edit   View   Favorites   Tools   Help                       ▓    │
├─────────────────────────────────────────────────────────────────────────┤
│  ← · → · ⊗ ⌂ ⌂ | ⌕ ⌂ ◉ | ⧉· ⊜ ✐ ·                                         │
├─────────────────────────────────────────────────────────────────────────┤
│                                                                      ▲    │
│                                                                           │
│              FLASH CENTRE [ALIGN="CENTER"]                                │
│                                                                           │
│   FLASH LEFT [ALIGN="LEFT"]                                               │
│                                                                           │
│                                    FLASH RIGHT [ALIGN="RIGHT"]            │
│                                                                           │
│                                                                           │
│   JUSTIFIED     [ALIGN="JUSTIFY"]     Blocksatz     [ALIGN="JUSTIFY"]     Blocksatz │
│   [ALIGN="JUSTIFY"]   Blocksatz   [ALIGN="JUSTIFY"]   Blocksatz   [ALIGN="JUSTIFY"] │
│   Blocksatz     [ALIGN="JUSTIFY"]     Blocksatz     [ALIGN="JUSTIFY"]     Blocksatz │
│   [ALIGN="JUSTIFY"]   Blocksatz   [ALIGN="JUSTIFY"]   Blocksatz   [ALIGN="JUSTIFY"] │
│   Blocksatz [ALIGN="JUSTIFY"] Blocksatz [ALIGN="JUSTIFY"]                  │
│                                                                      ▼    │
├─────────────────────────────────────────────────────────────────────────┤
│ 🎴 Done                                    │   │ 🖳 My Computer          //│
└─────────────────────────────────────────────────────────────────────────┘
```

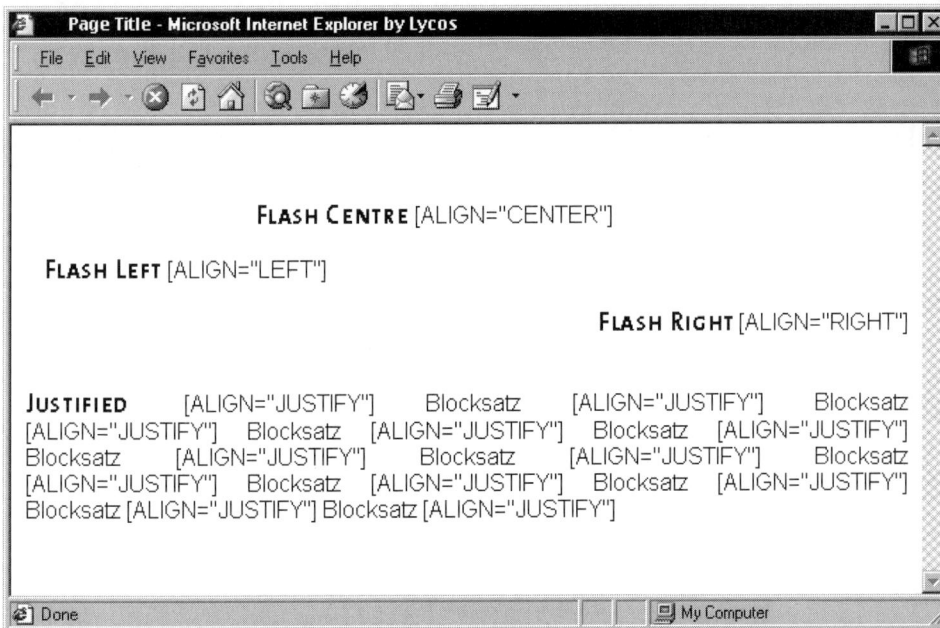

Form fields combined into groups

LTR

> This value determines the text direction from left to right (and is short for "left-to-right"). This is the default direction in the browser.

RTL

> If the text should run contrary to the standard movement from the right to the left margin of the screen, then choose the value RTL (short for "right-to-left").

CLASS

> Through the attribute CLASS the element can be assigned to a group (class). Enter one of the free selectable class name as a value. These groupings then provide easy access to all related elements so you can change all properties of the elements of a class with the help of cascading style sheets or other languages, or select a value.

ID

> ID identifies the document. Using ID a specific element can be accessed with the help of a script language to select or change values, for example.

LANG

> This attribute indicates the language of the linked document. This is particularly important in search engines for identification purposes. Use the language codes according to ISO 639, for example "en" for English or "en-us" for American English.

ONCLICK
This event takes place if you single-click on an element with the mouse. A given script is executed by this action.

ONDBLCLICK
This event takes place if you double-click on an element with the mouse. A given script is executed by this action.

ONKEYDOWN
This event takes place if you are in an element and a key is pressed and held down. This action executes a specific script.

ONKEYPRESS
This event takes place if you are in an element and a key is simultaneously pressed and released again. This action executes a determined script.

ONKEYUP
This event takes place if you are in an element and a key that was pressed is released. This action executes a specific script.

ONMOUSEDOWN
This event takes place if you are in an element and a mouse button is clicked and held down. A given script is executed by this action.

ONMOUSEMOVE
This event takes place if one moves the cursor over an object with the mouse. A given script is executed by this action.

ONMOUSEOUT
This event takes place if a mouse moves the cursor off an element. By this action a given script is executed.

ONMOUSEOVER
This event takes place if the mouse moves the cursor directly over the element (object). A given script is executed by this action.

ONMOUSEUP
This event takes place if you are in an element and a mouse button that was clicked and held down is released. A given script is executed by this action.

STYLE
The attribute STYLE is used to determine specific properties in the representation of labelled elements. Style settings are defined by the cascading style sheets.

TITLE
Give the user further information about the element used by fixing a meaningful title with the help of the TITLE command. Navigation in your Web site is made particularly easy for users who are dependent on voice response.

Example

```
<div align=right>
Flush right text
</div>
```

Events

ONCLICK, ONDBLCLICK, ONKEYDOWN, ONKEYPRESS, ONKEYUP, ONMOUSEDOWN, ONMOUSEMOVE, ONMOUSEOUT, ONMOUSEOVER, ONMOUSEUP

XML definition

```
<! ELEMENT DIV>
<!ATTLIST DIV
% attrs;

% reserved; >
```

Related command

SPAN

DL

Identification of lists of definitions

Description

Texts which represent definitions are identified with this command.

Application

The command DL is used to display the beginning or the end of a lists of definitions within a HTML document. This command is helpful in connection with the necessary commands DT and DD to structure a glossary or a text, for example.

HTML 4.0 standard

CLASS, DIR, ID, LANG, STYLE, TITLE

Start tag: required; end tag: required.

Attributes

CLASS

Through the attribute CLASS the element can be assigned to a group (class). Enter one of the free selectable class name as a value. These groupings then provide easy access to all related elements. so you can change all properties of the elements of a class with the help of cascading style sheets or other languages or select a value.

DIR

This attribute is necessary to determine the text direction. This attribute can have the values:

LTR

This value determines the text direction from the left to the right (and is short for "left-to-right"). This is the default direction in the browser.

RTL

If the text should run contrary to the standard movement from the right to the left margin of the screen, then choose the value RTL (and is short for "right-to-left").

ID

ID identifies the document. Using ID a specific element can be accessed with the help of a script language to select or change values, for example.

LANG

This attribute indicates the language of the linked document. This is particularly important in search engines for identification purposes. Use the language codes according to ISO 639, for example "en" for English or "en-us" for American English.

ONCLICK

This event takes place if you single-click on an element with the mouse. A given script is executed by this action.

ONDBLCLICK

This event takes place if you double-click on an element with the mouse. A given script is executed by this action.

ONKEYDOWN

This event takes place if you are in an element and a key is pressed and held down. This action executes a specific script.

ONKEYPRESS

This event takes place if you are in an element and a key is simultaneously pressed and released again. This action executes a determined script.

ONKEYUP

This event takes place if you are in an element and a key that was pressed is released. This action executes a specific script.

ONMOUSEDOWN

This event takes place if you are in an element and a mouse button is clicked and held down. A given script is executed by this action.

ONMOUSEMOVE

This event takes place if one moves the cursor over an object with the mouse. A given script is executed by this action.

ONMOUSEOUT

This event takes place if a mouse moves the cursor off an element. By this action a given script is executed.

ONMOUSEOVER
> This event takes place if the mouse moves the cursor directly over the element (object). A given script is executed by this action.

ONMOUSEUP
> This event takes place if you are in an element and a mouse button that was clicked and held down is released. A given script is executed by this action.

STYLE
> The attribute STYLE can be used to change style settings, in particular the appearance of the element. You apply the corresponding options of a style sheet language (usually CSS) as value of the attribute.

TITLE
> Give the user further information about the element used by giving it a meaningful title with the help of the TITLE command. Navigation in your Website is made particularly easy for users who are dependent on voice response.

Example

```
<dl>
<dt>single expression of </dt>
<dd>Definition of this expression </dd>
<dt>Other expression </dt>
<dd>Definition of the second expression </dd>
</dl>
```

Events

ONCLICK, ONDBLCLICK, ONKEYDOWN, ONKEYPRESS, ONKEYUP, ONMOUSEDOWN, ONMOUSEMOVE, ONMOUSEOUT, ONMOUSEOVER, ONMOUSEUP

XML definition

```
<! ELEMENT DL - - (DT|DD)+>
<! ATTLIST DL %attrs;>
```

Related commands

DD
DT

Doctype

Assigning DTD to a document

Description

There are two options for assigning a DTD to a XML file. You can assign it in a separate file or alternatively within the document. The parser then does not have to fetch the instructions on the DTD from an external file but can import the XML file directly.

As a rule, a reference to an internal or external Document Type Definition is carried out at the beginning of the document.

Application

External DTD:

```
<!DOCTYPE Address SYSTEM "Adress.dtd">
```

If you want to refer to a publicly accessible DTD definition, then simply use the keyword PUBLIC instead of the keyword SYSTEM and indicate the complete URL path.

```
<!DOCTYPE Address
     PUBLIC "http://www.domain.uk/Addresses.dtd" >
```

Internal DTD:

```
<!DOCTYPE Address [internal DTD-instruction]>
```

Example

```
<!DOCTYPE address
     [
          <! ELEMENT surname (#PCDATA)>
          <! ELEMENT first name (#PCDATA)>
     ]>
```

DT

Identification of terms to be defined (definition term)

Description

Expressions which must be defined more precisely are identified with this command.

Application

The command DT is used to indicate terms within a list of definitions which are described more precisely as follows. The commands DL, DT and DD can be seen as a unit which helps to structure definitions within HTML pages.

HTML 4.0 standard

CLASS, DIR, ID, LANG, STYLE, TITLE

Start tag: required; end tag: optional.

Attributes

CLASS

Through the attribute CLASS the element can be assigned to a group (class). Enter one of the free selectable class name as a value. These groupings then provide easy access to all related elements so you can change all properties of the elements of a class with the help of cascading style sheets or other languages, or select a value.

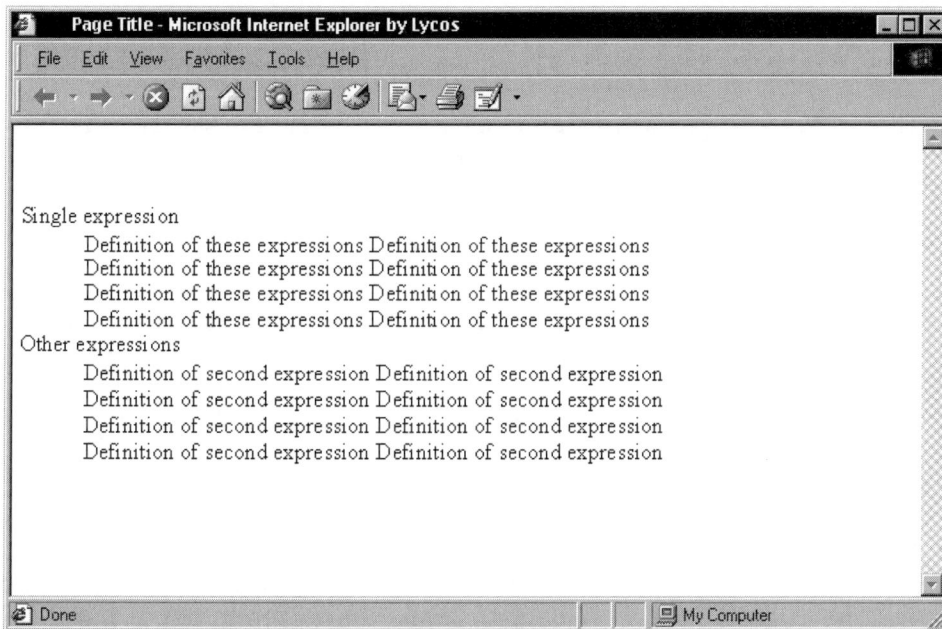

DT is comparable with DL and DD. For example representing a glossary

DIR

This attribute is necessary to determine the text direction. This attribute can have the values:

LTR

This value determines the text direction from left to right (and is short for "left-to-right"). This is the default direction in the browser.

RTL

If the text should run contrary to the standard movement from the right to the left margin of the screen, then choose the value RTL (short for "right-to-left").

ID

ID identifies the document. Using ID a specific element can be accessed with the help of a script language to select or change values, for example.

LANG

This attribute indicates the language of the linked document. This is particularly important in search engines for identification purposes. Use the language codes according to ISO 639, for example "en" for English or "en-us" for American English.

ONCLICK

This event takes place if you single-click on an element with the mouse. A given script is executed by this action.

ONDBLCLICK

This event takes place if you double-click on an element with the mouse. A given script is executed by this action.

ONKEYDOWN

This event takes place if you are in an element and a key is pressed and held down. This action executes a specific script.

ONKEYPRESS

This event takes place if you are in an element and a key is simultaneously pressed and released again. This action executes a determined script.

ONKEYUP

This event takes place if you are in an element and a key that was pressed is released. This action executes a specific script.

ONMOUSEDOWN

This event takes place if you are in an element and a mouse button is clicked and held down. A given script is executed by this action.

ONMOUSEMOVE

This event takes place if one moves the cursor over an object with the mouse. A given script is executed by this action.

ONMOUSEOUT

This event takes place if a mouse moves the cursor off an element. A given script is executed by this action.

ONMOUSEOVER

This event takes place if the mouse moves the cursor directly over the element (object). A given script is executed by this action.

ONMOUSEUP

This event takes place if you are in an element and a mouse button that was clicked and held down is released. A given script is executed by this action.

STYLE

The attribute STYLE can be used to change style settings, in particular the appearance of the element. As a value of the attribute you apply the corresponding options of a style sheet language (usually CSS).

TITLE

Give the user further information about the element used by giving it a meaningful title with the help of the TITLE command. Navigation in your Web site is made particularly easy for users who are dependent on voice response.

Example

```
<dl>
<dt>single expression </dt>
<dd>Definition of this expression </dd>
<dt>Further expression of </dt>
<dd>Definition of the second expression </dd>
</dl>
```

Events

ONCLICK, ONDBLCLICK, ONKEYDOWN, ONKEYPRESS, ONKEYUP, ONMOUSEDOWN, ONMOUSEMOVE, ONMOUSEOUT, ONMOUSEOVER, ONMOUSEUP

XML definition

```
<! ELEMENT DT - O (%inline;)*>
<! ELEMENT DD - O (%flow;)*>
<! ATTLIST (DT|DD) %attrs;>
```

Related commands

DD
DT

DTD

Document Type Definition

Description

Every XML definition can refer to one or several DTDs. Single commands should overlap into the DTDs; in this way the definition which was read first is valid. With this essential feature it is possible to write a document using HTML and to add or to specify commands with the help of another DTD. This makes working with XML easier.

Application

The following keywords classify every entry in the DTD:

`<!ELEMENT ... >`	Definition of a new markup command
`<!ATTLIST ... >`	Definition of attributes
`<!ENTITY ... >`	Definition of entities
`<!NOTATION ... >`	Definition of a data type notation
`<!-- Comment -->`	Inserting a comment

In principle, one distinguishes between logical and physical structures. The commands which are used in DTD are divided into these two groups.

Logical structures can be represented with the `ELEMENT` definition and the corresponding `ATTLIST` declaration. `ENTITY` and `NOTATION` form the physical structures.

Example

```
<?xml version = "1.0"?>
<!-- internal DTD -->
 <!DOCTYPE address [
<! ELEMENT address (name, surname, street, postcode, town)>
        <! ELEMENT name      # PCDATA>
        <! ELEMENT surname   # PCDATA>
        <! ELEMENT street    # PCDATA>
        <!ELEMENT  postcode  # PCDATA>
        <!ELEMENT  town      # PCDATA>
]>
<!-- Begin of the body text -->
<address>
        <name>       Peter          </name>
        <surname>    Meyer           </surname>
        <street>     5 Forest Road </street>
        <post code>  AB10 4CD        </post code>
        <town>       Aberdeen        </town
</address>
```

(internal DTD)

ELEMENT

Defining markup commands

Description

This element is the most important part of a DTD. It determines which markup commands may be used.

Application

The definition of a new tag is started with the keyword ELEMENT, followed by a space.

An element name must start with a letter, but it may contain numbers. Moreover, some additional punctuation marks are permitted (".", "-", "_" and ":"). Otherwise, there are no restrictions on the choice of the element name, or its length. You should not use any element name twice in a DTD.

Colours can actually be used within a valid name, yet the specification nowadays appears as a hyphen, in name areas for example.

This means that the character can be used elsewhere and can be used for something else in future, existing documents then have to be updated.

Example

```
<i>
< article: B 5000 >
<even_longer_element names_are_not_a problem>
```

Element

Definition of a pattern

Description

The simplest definition of a pattern does not take the markup command into account. This consideration often isn't necessary, yet in more complex documents, an additional detail is frequently used in context. For example, a mailing list which distinguishes between private and business addresses.

Application

The detail of an additional context is carried out via the tag <element>. A wider pattern is indicated through the attribute type, and the target element must be found here.

Parameter

type
> Enables the closer delimitation of the pattern by the detail of the super ordered element in which the target element must be found.

Example

```
</element type="element">

<rule>
    <!-- Pattern for private addresses / name -->
    </element type="private">
        <target-element type="name">
    </element>
    <P color="red">
        <children/>
    </P>
</rule>

<rule>
    <!-- Pattern for private addresses / Surname -->
    </lement type="private">
        <target-element type="surname">
    </element>
    <P color="red" font-style="bold">
        <children/>
    </P>
</rule>
```

EM

Indicating highlighted text

Description

Words or sentences which should be emphasised in text are indicated with this command.

Application

The command EM (short for "emphasise") is used if text should stand out from the normal text. A further increase in emphasis can be reached with the command STRONG.

HTML 4.0 standard

CLASS, DIR, ID, LANG, STYLE, TITLE

Start tag: required; end tag: required.

Attributes

CLASS

Through the attribute CLASS the element can be assigned to a group (class). Enter one of the free selectable class name as a value. These groupings then provide easy access to all related elements so you can change properties of the elements of a class with the help of cascading style sheets or other languages, or select a value.

DIR

This attribute is necessary to determine the text direction. This attribute can have the values:

LTR

This value determines the text direction from left to right (and is short for "left-to-right"). This is the default direction in the browser.

RTL

If the text should run contrary to the standard movement from the right to the left margin of the screen, then choose the value RTL (short for "right-to-left").

ID

ID identifies the document. Using ID, a specific element can be accessed with the help of a script language to select or change values, for example.

LANG

This attribute indicates the language of the linked document. This is particularly important in search engines for identification purposes. Use the language codes according to ISO 639, for example "en" for English or "en-us" for American English.

ONCLICK

This event takes place if you single-click on an element with the mouse. A given script is executed by this action.

ONDBLCLICK

This event takes place if you double-click on an element with the mouse. A given script is executed by this action.

ONKEYDOWN

This event takes place if you are in an element and a key is pressed and held down. This action executes a specific script.

ONKEYPRESS

This event takes place if you are in an element and a key is simultaneously pressed and released again. This action executes a determined script.

ONKEYUP

This event takes place if you are in an element and a key that was pressed is released. This action executes a specific script.

ONMOUSEDOWN

This event takes place if you are in an element and a mouse button is clicked and held down. A given script is executed by this action.

ONMOUSEMOVE

This event takes place if one moves the cursor over an object with the mouse. A given script is executed by this action.

ONMOUSEOUT

This event takes place if a mouse moves the cursor off an element. By this action a given script is executed.

ONMOUSEOVER

This event takes place if the mouse moves the cursor directly over the element (object). A given script is executed by this action.

ONMOUSEUP

This event takes place if you are in an element and a mouse button that was clicked and held down is released. A given script is executed by this action.

STYLE

The attribute STYLE is used to determine specific properties labelled elements. Style settings are defined by the cascading style sheets.

TITLE

Give the user further information about the element used by giving it a meaningful title with the help of the TITLE command. Navigation on your Web site is made particularly easy for users who are dependent on voice response.

Example

```
</em>
Result of the type ...
</em>
```

Events

ONCLICK, ONDBLCLICK, ONKEYDOWN, ONKEYPRESS, ONKEYUP, ONMOUSEDOWN, ONMOUSEMOVE, ONMOUSEOUT, ONMOUSEOVER, ONMOUSEUP

Related commands

ACRONYM
CITE
CODE
DFN

KBD
SAMP
STRONG
VAR

Embed

Embedding multimedia files

Description

With this command it is possible to embed various multimedia files into a HTML document.

Application

The command EMBED is used to embed various multimedia files into a HTML document. These files can be video, audio or graphics files, for example. To run such files plug-ins must be installed. These plug-ins then make it possible to play different multimedia files. Current browsers already automatically support the most frequently used formats.

HTML 4.0 standard

The command EMBED was introduced by Netscape and is not provided for in the official HTML definition. Files are better inserted using OBJECT.

Attributes

ALIGN
    This attribute makes it possible to write on top of an embedded object. However, you can also let text flow over the object with this attribute.
    TOP
        This setting aligns the following text flush at the top.
    MIDDLE
        This setting centres the object.
    BOTTOM
        This setting lines the following text flush at the bottom.

LEFT

This setting aligns the object to the left.

RIGHT

This setting aligns an object to the right.

AUTOSTART

When the value of this attribute is set on "true", multimedia files can be played immediately without an account function having to be activated beforehand. This function is no longer documented by Netscape 4.x.

BORDER

If you assign a value bigger than 0 to this attribute, a browser puts a margin around the embedded object.

HEIGHT

This attribute indicates the height of an object to be embedded in pixels.

HIDDEN

If the value of this attribute is "true", the embedded object will not appear on the display. This approach is then used in the first line, if audio files should be played, without a Sound-Player having to be reported simultaneously.

HSPACE

With this attribute the horizontal space round an embedded object is fixed in proportion to its environment within a window.

LOOP

If the value of this attribute is set on "true", an endless repetition of a playable multimedia file can be achieved. This function is not documented or interpreted by Netscape 4.x.

PALETTE

If the value of this attribute is set on "foreground", the corresponding plug-in with the foreground colours of the user's computer can be displayed. If the value of this attribute is set on "background", it displays a corresponding plug-in with the background colours of the user's computer.

PLUGINSPAGE

This attribute holds a URI address on the Internet which contains the installation notes for a plug-in which are necessary to display or play an embedded object.

PLUGINURI

This attribute holds a URI address on the Internet, which sets a plug-in to display or play an embedded object. This is a Java archive (files *.jar). The JAR installation manager (Jim) integrated in Netscape 4.0 will start, and the desired plug-in can then be installed online from this URI address.

SRC

The origin of a multimedia file to be embedded is defined with this attribute.

TYPE

It is possible to indicate the MIME type of an embedded file with this attribute. Ensure that the MIME type is always in quotation marks.

VSPACE
> With this attribute the vertical space round of an embedded object is fixed in proportion to its environment within a window.

WIDTH
> This attribute determines the width in pixels of a displayed object to be embedded. This attribute embeds multimedia files as well as other objects.

Example

```
<embed src="table1.xls">
<embed src="video1.avi" width="200" height="100">
<embed src="file://localhost/d:/windows/progman.hlp">

<embed src="sound.mid" autostart="true" loop="true">
```

Related commands

BGSOUND
OBJECT

ENCTYPE   <html attribute>

Fixing the format of form data

Description

With this attribute you can determine how to code form data. Indicate within the form in which format the users should transmit data.

Application

The standard setting should usually suffice for most applications, which means you will not have to execute any changes.

In some cases it could be important to specify the file format, particularly when combining the element INPUT with the attribute TYPE="FILE".

Values

Valid values for the attribute ENCTYPE are content types. Special data formats are indicated with this attribute, such as a Microsoft Word document or an Adobe PDF document, for example. Use the definitions to describe the data format which you can find under the keyword **MIME types**. Several values can be indicated, separated by commas.

The MIME type `"application/x-www-form-urlencoded"` is the default.

Example

```
<form
action = "http://www.domain.co.uk/action.cgi"
enctype = "multinational share/form-data"
method = "post" >
<input type="file">

<form
action = "http://www.domain.co.uk/action.cgi"
" enctype = "text/html"
method = "post" >
```

Accompanying element

FORM

Eval

Converting functional expressions into text characters

Description

Today we know about automatic page and paragraph numbering from every simple word processing program, but in HTML such functions were either not implemented or only very complex. XSL makes it easy for us to set up such numbering with the help of an `<eval>` section. Numerous built-in functions, which we will explain in the next section, help us to insert automatically generated page numbers, for example.

Application

The `<eval>` element serves primarily to convert functional expressions and variables into text characters. The result of this instruction is a character string. As well as the default functions, user-defined functions can also be set up. However, these must be fixed within the global definition. The `<eval>` element may only execute a single-line function call and will not be used for the definition of functions.

Example

```
<rule>
    <element type="document">
    <target-element type="page"/>
    </element>
    <p><children/> < BR/>
    Page
    <eval>
    formatNumber (childNumber (this) "1")
    </eval>
    </p>
</rule>
```

FACE   <html attribute>
Indicating script

Description
This attribute allows you to use the formatting of a TrueType document installed under Windows in your computer.

Application
Give one or more documents a name separated by commas or spaces with the attribute FACE. Pay attention to the correct notation of the TrueType fonts. This command will not automatically transfer any script fonts; the script types selected by you will only have an effect on the display of your document.

Values
You can give this attribute a value of an arbitrary string. Therefore, this character string if possible should not start or end with spaces. The browser will filter these out if necessary.

If you indicate several font types, try to find the first script next to the browser. If this is not available, it tries to reach the next given font. You should therefore indicate several documents.

The font type "Arial" is rarely available on Macintosh computers, for example. It is always replaced by an almost identical font "Helvetica". You therefore give FACE="Arial, Helvetica" as a value to obtain an optimal result.

Example

```
<font face="Arial" size="+2">
</font>
<basefont face="Arial, Helvetica, Times, Courier">
```

Accompanying elements

BASEFONT

FONT

FIELDSET

Combining form elements

Description

With this command it is possible to combine form elements with the same theme into groups.

Application

The command FIELDSET is used when data in a form need to be combined into a group. Data selected with this element are provided with a frame. This command makes forms clearer.

Moreover, the groupings produced with FIELDSET can be provided with an accompanying field heading using the command LEGEND.

HTML 4.0 standard

CLASS, DIR, ID, LANG, STYLE, TITLE

Start tag: required; end tag: required.

Attributes

ACCESSKEY

The attribute ACCESSKEY enables access to an element via a keyboard shortcut. Press ACCESSKEY="A" and the element will be activated.

CLASS

Through the attribute CLASS the element can be assigned to a group (class). Enter one of the free selectable class name as a value. These groupings then provide easy access to all related elements so you can change all properties of the elements of a class with the help of cascading style sheets or other languages, or select a value.

DIR
> This attribute is necessary to determine the text direction. This attribute can have the values:
>
> LTR
>> This value determines the text direction from left to right (and is short for "left-to-right"). This is the default direction in the browser.
>
> RTL
>> If the text should run contrary to the standard movement from the right to the left margin of the screen, then choose the value RTL (short for "right-to-left").

ID
> ID identifies the document. Using ID it can be accessed to a specific element with the help of a script language to select or change values, for example.

LANG
> This attribute indicates the language of the linked document. This is particularly important in search engines for the identification. Use the language codes according to ISO 639, for example "en" for English or "en-us" for American English.

ONCLICK
> This event takes place if you single-click on an element with the mouse. A given script is executed by this action.

ONDBLCLICK
> This event takes place if you double-click on an element with the mouse. A given script is executed by this action.

ONKEYDOWN
> This event takes place if you are in an element and a key is pressed and held down. This action executes a specific script.

ONKEYPRESS
> This event takes place if you are in an element and a key is simultaneously pressed and released again. This action executes a determined script.

ONKEYUP
> This event takes place if you are in an element and a key that was pressed is released. This action executes a specific script.

ONMOUSEDOWN
> This event takes place if you are in an element and a mouse button is clicked and held down. A given script is executed by this action.

ONMOUSEMOVE
> This event takes place if one moves the cursor over an object with the mouse. A given script is executed by this action.

ONMOUSEOUT
> This event takes place if a mouse moves the cursor off an element. This action executes a given script.

ONMOUSEOVER

This event takes place if the mouse moves the cursor directly over the element (object). A given script is executed by this action.

ONMOUSEUP

This event takes place if you are in an element and a mouse button that was clicked and held down is released. A given script is executed by this action.

STYLE

The attribute STYLE can be used to change style settings, particularly the look of the element. As a value of the attribute you give the corresponding options of a style sheet language (usually of CSS).

TITLE

Give the user further information about the element used by fixing a meaningful title with the help of the TITLE command. Navigation in your site is made easier for users who are dependent on voice response.

Example

```
<form>
<fieldset>
<legend>Address </legend>
<input name="Name" type="text" value="Name"><br>
<input name="Surname" type="text" value="Surname"><br>
</fieldset>
```

Events

ONCLICK, ONDBLCLICK, ONKEYDOWN, ONKEYPRESS, ONKEYUP, ONMOUSEDOWN, ONMOUSEMOVE, ONMOUSEOUT, ONMOUSEOVER, ONMOUSEUP

XML definition

```
<! ELEMENT FIELDSET - - (#PCDATA,LEGEND,(%flow;)*)>
<! ATTLIST FIELDSET %attrs;>
```

Related command

LEGEND

FONT

W3C HTML 4.0 ✓

Determining the standard font size

Description

This command sets a standard font size for a document.

Application

The command FONT sets the standard font. Unlike this the BASEFONT command is already fixed in the header for the complete range of the text.

This command is considered redundant in HTML 4.0. To format text use style sheets instead.

HTML 4.0 standard

CLASS, COLOR, DIR, FACE, ID, LANG, SIZE, STYLE, TITLE

The use of this command is not supported in the current HTML version any more; it has been replaced by other commands.

Start tag: required; end tag: required.

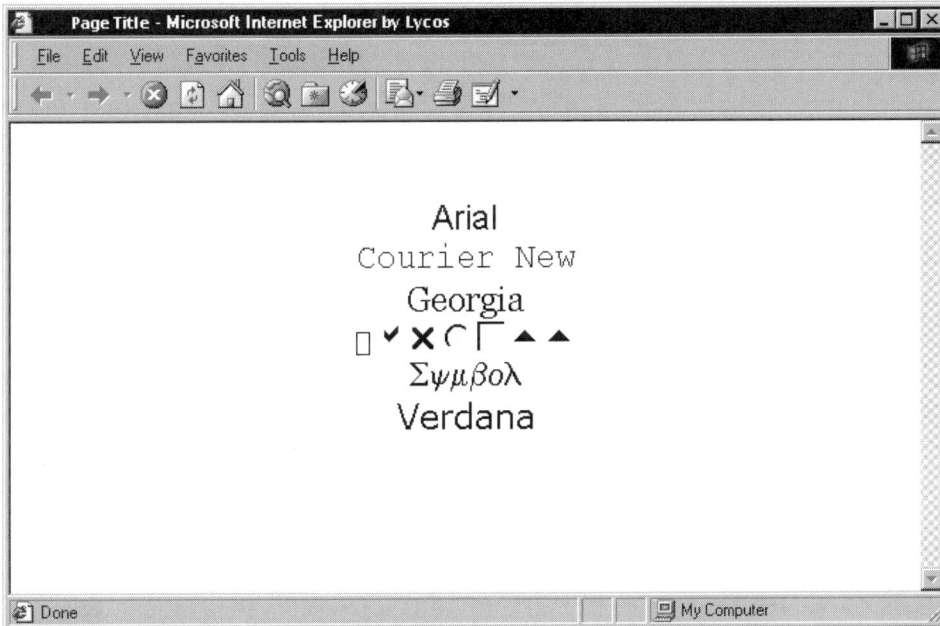

If you use different fonts, these must also be available to the user

Attributes

CLASS

Through the attribute CLASS the element can be assigned to a group (class). Enter one of the selectable class names. These groupings then provide easy access to all related elements so you can change properties of the elements of a

153

class with the help of cascading style sheets or other languages, or select a value.

COLOR

With this attribute you can set the colour of the text. Besides the 16 keywords defined, up to 256 colours can be represented, which are indicated by fixed hexadecimal numbers. These settings are usually created with style sheets in HTML 4.0.

DIR

This attribute is necessary to determine the text direction. This attribute can have the values:

LTR

This value determines the text direction from left to right (and is short for "left-to-right"). This is the default (and is short for "left-to-right") direction in the browser.

RTL

If the text should run contrary to the standard movement from the right to the left margin of the screen, then choose the value RTL (abbreviation for "right-to-left").

ID

ID identifies the document. Using ID a specific element can be accessed with the help of a script language to select or change values, for example.

FACE

The font in which a Web site is represented is determined with the attribute FACE. Therefore, you should be careful that font names are indicated separated by commas. You must ensure that at least one of the given fonts is on the client side to find out. With this detail the browser tries the fonts one after the other, whether the given fonts are available and thus representable.

LANG

This attribute indicates the language of the linked document. This is particularly important in search engines for identification purposes. Use the language codes according to ISO 639, for example "en" for English or "en-us" for American English.

SIZE

The attribute SIZE is used to fix the font size. The values available for the size command are from 1 to 7. If this number is not explicitly determined, documents are represented by default in font size 3. In addition, the value can be indicated with negative or positive signs to reduce or increase the font size in proportion to the standard font size.

STYLE

The attribute STYLE can be used to change style settings, in particular the look of the element. As a value of the attribute you can apply options from a style sheet language (usually CSS).

`TITLE`

Give the user further information about the element used by giving it a meaningful title with the help of the `TITLE` command. Navigation in your Web site is made particularly easy for users who are dependent on voice response.

Example

```
<basefont color=blue>
I am not blue, <font color=#000000> nor here </font>
blue I am again

<basefont face="Arial">
I am only a font and I am called Arial
<font face="Courier" size="+2">I am Courier here</font>
and now Arial again

<font face="Bookman, Arial, Helvetica">
```

Related command

BASEFONT

Font-family

CASCADING STYLE SHEETS

Fixing font family

Description

One can specify the font family to be used with this reference. The correct font in the browser depends on the system used and the fonts installed.

Parameter

`family-name`

Name of the fonts (i.e. Arial, Symbol, Times, Helvetica).

`generic-family`

To produce a more rugged code independently of installed fonts, one can still define a specific font family. If the given font is not installed on the computer, then a similar font may be used. Possible details are: `"serif"`, `"sans-serif"`, `"cursive"`, `"fantasy"` and `"monospace"`.

Example

```
<style type="text/css">
h1, h2 { font-family: Arial}
h3, h4 { font-family: serif}
```

```
</style>

<div style="font-family: Arial, Helvetica,">
</div>
```

Font-size

Fixing font size

Description

An important factor is font size, which can be changed by specifying a new size or by modifying the existing size by a percentage.

Parameter

length

> Defines the absolute size of the font in dot measurement unity. This setting is independent from the used system and the predefined font sizes (i.e. "12 pt").

percentage

> Allows a modification of the font size relative to the predefined standard font (i.e. "150%").

Example

```
<style type="text/css">
h1, h2 { font-size: 12 pt}
h3, h4 { font-size: 120%}
</style>

<div style="font-size: 150%">
</div>
```

Font-stretch

Changing font width

Description

The font's width can be changed by using font-stretch.

Parameter

You can assign the following keywords as parameters. They are listed in ascending order from the most compact (thinnest) to wider fonts:

```
ultra-condensed
extra-condensed
condensed
semi-condensed
normal
semi-expanded
expanded
extra-expanded
ultra-expanded
```

Example

```
<style type="text/css">
h1, h2 { font-strech: expanded}
h3, h4 { font-strech: condensed}
</style>

<div style="font-strech: ultra-condensed" >
</div>
```

Font-style

Choosing normal or italic fonts

Description

Using font-style you can choose between normal or italic font.

Parameter

normal
> The default is the normal font.

italic
> With this you produce an italic font.

Example

```
<style type="text/css">
font h1, h2 give {: italic}
font h3, h4 give {: normal}
</style>

<div style="font-style: italic">
</div>
```

Font-weight

Defining font weight

Description

This parameter gives information about the font thickness, from normal thickness to bold letters.

Parameter

As well as numerical values the following keywords can also be used to determine font thickness:

`normal`
    Normal font thickness (corresponds to a numerical value of "400").

`bold`
    Bold font (corresponds to a numerical value of "700").

`bolder`
    Causes an automatic increase of font weight relative to the standard font used.

`lighter`
    Causes a reduction of the font weight.

    Moreover, font weight can be also indicated as a numerical value from "100" up to "900".

Example

```
<style type="text/css">
h1, h2 { font-weight: 300}
h3, h4 { font-weight: bold}
</style>

<div style="font-weight: bold">
</div>
```

For   <html attribute>

Assigning a name to a form field

Description

With this attribute a label is assigned to a form element with a corresponding ID.

Application

The use of this attribute is optional and does not work on all browsers.

Values

With this attribute a label is assigned to a table element with a corresponding ID. A valid ID must begin with a letter (A-Z, a-z) followed by any number of letters or digits. The following additional characters are permitted: underscore ("_"), hyphen ("-"), colon (":") and period (".").

Example

```
<label for="Place of residence">Place of residence </label>
<input type="text" id="Place of residence">
```

Accompanying element

LABEL

FORM

Indicating forms

Description

With this command you can create interactive forms for Web sites. These forms can contain different control elements.

Application

The command FORM inserts forms into HTML pages. Users can fill in entry fields, select entries or enter text.

HTML 4.0 standard

ACCEPT-CHARSET, ACTION, CLASS, DIR, ENCTYPE, ID, LANG, METHOD, STYLE, TITLE
Start tag: required; end tag: required.

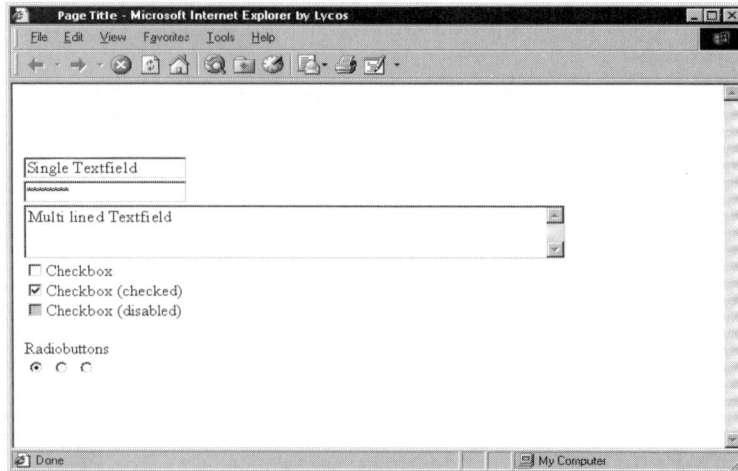

Text fields in a form

Attributes

ACCEPT

This attribute indicates a list of valid types of content separated by commas which the server can process straightforwardly. This attribute can be used to filter out non concurring files when the user selects a file.

ACCEPT-CHARSET

You can define fonts which are valid for input in the respective form fields using this attribute.

ACTION

This attribute refers to scripts or programs which reprocess the inputs received by users. Details of this attribute must be specified, otherwise no interaction can be set up with the server.

CLASS

Through the attribute CLASS the element can be assigned to a group (class). Enter one of the selectable class names. These groupings then provide easy access to all related elements so you can change properties of the elements of a class with the help of cascading style sheets or other languages, or select a value.

DIR

This attribute is necessary to determine the text direction. This attribute can have the values:

LTR

This value determines the text direction from left to right (and is short for left-to-right). This is the default direction in the browser.

RTL
> If the text should run contrary to the standard movement from the right to the left margin of the screen, then choose the value RTL (short for "right-to-left").

ENCTYPE
> This attribute determines the coding method used when assigning data forms.

ID
> ID identifies the document. Using ID a specific element can be accessed with the help of a script language to select or change values, for example.

LANG
> This attribute indicates the language of the linked document. This is particularly important in search engines for identification purposes. Use the language codes according to ISO 639, for example "en" for English or "en-us" for American English.

METHOD
> There are two different transmission modes of data forms to a server.
>
> GET
>> The setting METHOD=GET causes data in a full form to be saved in the QUERY_STRING, the standard environmental variable of a WWW server. The contents of these environmental variables are then selected with the help of CGI-program or a CGI-script.
>
> POST
>> The setting METHOD=POST causes input to be treated as commands. An evaluating program must in this case actively determine the length of the transmitted data. This usually happens in CONTENT_LENGTH with help from the standard environmental variables.

NAME
> With this attribute, a name is given to a form. It is particularly important that the name be used for identification for a later evaluation or access to single elements of the form.

ONCLICK
> This event takes place if you single-click on an element with the mouse. A given script is executed by this action.

ONDBLCLICK
> This event takes place if you double-click on an element with the mouse. A given script is executed by this action.

ONKEYDOWN
> This event takes place if you are in an element and a key is pressed and held down. This action executes a specific script.

ONKEYPRESS
> This event takes place if you are in an element and a key is simultaneously pressed and released again. This action executes a determined script.

ONKEYUP

This event takes place if you are in an element and a key that was pressed is released. This action executes a specific script.

ONMOUSEDOWN

This event takes place if you are in an element and a mouse button is clicked and held down. A given script is executed by this action.

ONMOUSEMOVE

This event takes place if one moves the cursor over an object with the mouse. A given script is executed by this action.

ONMOUSEOUT

This event takes place if a mouse moves the cursor off an element. By this action a given script is executed.

ONMOUSEOVER

This event takes place if the mouse moves the cursor directly over the element (object). A given script is executed by this action.

ONMOUSEUP

This event takes place if you are in an element and a mouse button that was clicked and held down is released. A given script is executed by this action.

ONRESET

Triggered when the data forms are reset (returned in their output condition). Following this the given script goes off.

ONSUBMIT

Triggered when data forms are assigned to a server. Following this the given script goes off.

STYLE

The attribute STYLE can be used to change style settings, in particular the look of the element. As a value of the attribute you can apply options from a style sheet language (usually CSS).

TARGET

The attribute TARGET is used to fix the name of a window in which a link is opened. This attribute is used if several windows are open or if a new window with a link is opened.

TITLE

Give the user further information about the element used by giving a meaningful title with the help of the TITLE command. Navigation in your Web site is made particularly easy for users who are dependent on voice response.

Example

```
<form action="../cgi-bin/evaluate.pl" method=get>
...
Elements of the form
as entry fields, select lists, buttons etc..
...
</form>
```

```
<form>

<input name="single-line text field"
value = "single-line text field" > <br>
<input name="Password" type=password value="Password">

<textarea name="several lines text field""
cols = = 60 rows 3 wrap = virtual > text field of several lines
</textarea> <br>

<input name="Checkbox" type=checkbox
value = "checkbox" > checkbox <br>
<input name="Checkbox" type=checkbox
value = "checkbox" checked > checkbox (checked) <br>
<input name="Checkbox" type=checkbox
value = "checkbox" disabled > checkbox (disabled) <br> <br>

</form>
```

Events

```
ONCLICK, ONDBLCLICK, ONKEYDOWN, ONKEYPRESS, ONKEYUP, ONMOUSEDOWN,
ONMOUSEMOVE, ONMOUSEOUT, ONMOUSEOVER, ONMOUSEUP, ONSUBMIT, ONRESET
```

XML definition

```
<! ELEMENT FORM - - (%block;|SCRIPT)+ -(FORM)>
<!ATTLIST FORM
%attrs;

action % URI;   # REQUIRED
method GET | (post) GET
enctype % ContentType;

"application/x-www form urlencoded "
onsubMit % script;  # IMPLIED
onreset % script;  # IMPLIED
accept-charset % of Charsets;  # IMPLIED >
```

Related commands
BUTTON
INPUT
SELECT
TEXTAREA

FRAME **\<html attribute\>**

Frames to define tables

Description

By default a frame can be drawn around a table with the command BORDER. With the attribute FRAME this frame can be adjusted as you wish.

Application

Through this attribute the specific position of the table frame can be defined. Through the different values provided, you can determine, for example, that the frame runs only outside the table. Assign a frame thickness with BORDER so that this option becomes effective. The use of this attribute is optional.

Values

The following are the values allowed for FRAME:

ABOVE
  Show the frame only at the top of the table.
BELOW
  Show the frame only at the bottom of the table.
BORDER
  The default setting. A frame is set around the entire table.
BOX
  This is the same as FRAME=BORDER using the BORDER detail without using the FRAME attribute.
LHS
  A frame line is produced only at the left of the table (LHS="left hand side").
RHS
  A frame line is produced only at the right of the table (RHS="right hand side").
VOID
  With the detail VOID no frame is displayed. However, if you use the attribute BORDER, then the inner lines of the table are displayed. The outer frame line is not shown (VOID = empty).
VSIDES
  Frame lines are displayed only at the left and right sides of the table (VSIDES= "vertical sides").

Example

```
<table border="3" frame="box">
<table border="2" frame="vsides">
<table borderframe="void">
```

Accompanying element

TABLE

FRAME

W3C HTML 4.0 ✔

Defining sub-windows

Description

With this command windows are defined within already available browser windows.

Application

This command constructs one or several windows within existing browser windows. The content of this is HTML files which are specially represented in windows fixed with the command FRAMESET.

HTML 4.0 standard

CLASS, FRAMEBORDER, ID, LONGDESC, MARGINHEIGHT, MARGINWIDTH, NAME, NORESIZE, SCROLLING, SRC, STYLE, TITLE

Start tag: required; end tag: not allowed.

Attributes

CLASS

Through the attribute CLASS the element can be assigned to a group (class). Enter one of the selectable class names. These groupings then provide easy access to all related elements so you can change properties of the elements of a class with the help of cascading style sheets or other languages, or select a value.

FRAMEBORDER

If this attribute is put on the value 1, a three-dimensional border will be drawn around the window. The window remains without a border if the value is put on 0.

ID

ID identifies the document. Using ID a specific element can be accessed with the help of a script language to select or change values, for example.

LONGDESC

This attribute defines a detailed description of the contents of the frame. This completes the course description which can be indicated with the TITLE attribute.

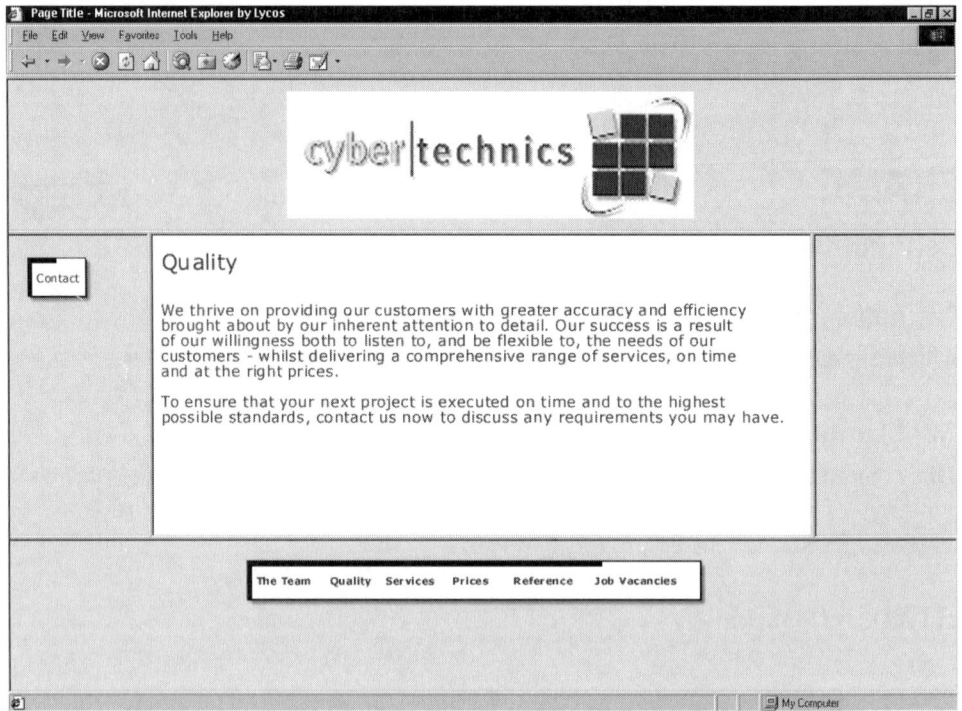

Dividing the screen with frames

MARGINHEIGHT

With the attribute MARGINHEIGHT the distance between the top and bottom margin of the window can be determined.

MARGINWIDTH

The attribute MARGINWIDTH indicates the distance between the left and right margin of a window. The value must be chosen bigger than zero. The presetting of the margin depends on the setting of the browser and cannot be set separately.

NAME

With this attribute the single frame receives a name. This attribute is relatively important in the use of frames because through the instruction of the frame name you determine in which area the page is displayed. Be careful to assign names only once.

NORESIZE

This attribute ensures that the size of a frame window cannot be resized by a user.

SCROLLING

The attribute SCROLLING determines whether the corresponding FRAME should be equipped with a scrolling device. Possible values are:

YES
>   In principle, scrolling devices are always provided in a frame even if they are not necessary.

NO
>   Scrolling devices are not displayed even if necessary. Part of the picture contents may not visible for the visitor.

AUTO
>   This value is set at the same time as the presetting. Provided that the contents of the window exceed the size of the window, a scroll bar is displayed.

SRC
>   With this attribute it is possible to fix the source path (URI). These source paths refer to the contents of one or several frames.

STYLE
>   The attribute STYLE can be used to change style settings, in particular the look of the element. As a value of the attribute you can apply the corresponding options of a style sheet language (usually CSS).

TARGET
>   The attribute TARGET is used to fix the name of a window in which a link is opened. This attribute is used if several windows are open or if a new window with a link is opened.

TITLE
>   Give the user further information about the element used by fixing a meaningful title with the help of the TITLE command. Navigation in your Web site is made particularly easy for users who are dependent on voice response.

Example

```
<html>
<head>
<title>Frame test </title>
</head>
<frameset cols="40%,60%">
<frame src="reference.htm" name="reference">
<frame src="title.htm" name="Data">
</frameset>
</html>

<html>
<head>
<title>Industria corporate group </title>
</head>
<frameset rows="*,35" frameborder=0>
<frame src="start.htm" name="main window" scrolling=auto>
<frame src="menu.htm" name="Menu"
marginwidth = 0 marginheight = 0 scrolling = no noresize >
</frameset>
```

```
</html>
```

Related commands
FRAMESET
IFRAME
NOFRAMES

FRAMEBORDER   <html attribute>
Activating a three-dimensional border around a frame

Description
Through FRAMEBORDER you can fix further properties for the border line of a frame.

Application
With this attribute you can choose between two settings. Further values cannot be submitted. A visible border is either displayed or not between the frame window and the adjacent windows. The use of this attribute is optional.

Values
If this attribute is set at the value 1, a three-dimensional border will be drawn around the window. The window remains without a border if the value is at 0. For the values 0 and 1 you can also use YES or NO alternatively.

Example
```
<frameset cols="20%,80%" border="0" frameborder="0">
<frame src="left.htm">
<frame src="right.htm">
</frameset>

<frameset cols="20%,80%" border="2" frameborder="yes">
<frame src="left.htm">
<frame src="right.htm">
</frameset>
```

Accompanying elements
FRAME
IFRAME

FRAMESET

W3C HTML 4.0 ✔

Structuring of sub-windows

Description

This command defines the structures of windows inside windows already available in the browser.

Application

This command constructs a structure of frames. The number and the size of the frame contained in the frame set are fixed with this command. The single areas are then defined within the FRAMESET container through the command FRAME. Usually, HTML documents with a frame definition don't contain any BODY section, but exclusively contain the FRAMESET definition and eventually the NOFRAMES unit.

HTML 4.0 standard

ID, CLASS, COLS, ROWS, STYLE, TITLE

Start tag: required; end tag: required.

Attributes

BORDER

Submit the desired border weight to this attribute as a value in pixels. A value of zero lets the border disappear. This attribute is not part of the official HTML 4.0 standard, it works only in Netscape browsers.

BORDERCOLOR

This attribute is not an official HTML standard either. With IT you can fix the colour of the border. In the meantime, the command is recognised by all common browsers.

CLASS

Through the attribute CLASS the element can be assigned to a group (class). Enter one of the selectable class names. These groupings then provide easy access to all related elements so you can change all properties of the elements of a class with the help of cascading style sheets or other languages, or select a value.

COLS

This attribute helps to determine the width of columns. The value for the frame width can be executed in pixels or a percentage obtained on the complete width of the screen.

FRAMEBORDER

If this attribute is set at the value 1, a three-dimensional border is drawn around the window. The window remains without a border if the value is set at 0. The values "yes" and "no" can also be used.

FRAMESPACING

This attribute indicates the space in pixels between the single frames.

ID

ID identifies the document. Using ID a specific element can be accessed with the help of a script language to select or change values, for example.

ONLOAD

This event is triggered when a browser has completely loaded a HTML document. Obtained on a FRAMESET document this means that a script is then executed if all necessary frames have been loaded.

ONUNLOAD

This event is triggered when a browser has completely unloaded a HTML document. Obtained on a FRAMESET document this means that a script is then executed if all necessary frames have been downloaded.

ROWS

This attribute helps to determine the rows with the necessary horizontal layout of a frame. The value for the width of the frame can be carried out in pixels or a percentage obtained on the total amount of the screen. The horizontal layout of single rows are separated by commas.

STYLE

The attribute STYLE can be used to change style settings, in particular the look of the element. As a value of the attribute you apply the corresponding options of a style sheet language (usually CSS).

TITLE

Give the user further information about the element used by fixing a meaningful title with the help of the TITLE command. Navigation in your Web site is made particularly easy for users who are dependent on voice response.

Example

```
<html>
<head>
<title>Frame test </title>
</head>
<frameset cols="40%,60%">
<frame src="reference.htm" name="Reference">
<frame src="titel.htm" name="Data">
</frameset>
<body>
Please, call the <a href="title.htm">title page</a>!
</body>
</html>
```

Events

ONLOAD, ONUNLOAD

Related commands
FRAME
IFRAME
NOFRAMES

General entity

Defining special characters and abbreviations

Description
Entities are already familiar to us from HTML. With their help, special characters are defined with the help of abbreviations.

Application

For example, the copyright sign "©" is defined with the entity &copy. In the course of the document the agreed abbreviation can be used instead of the special character. Entities are in this case absolutely necessary since the character set of the text file contains only 128 characters and there are no special characters specific to a country.

Moreover, abbreviations which are automatically replaced by longer and frequent strings can be used. An entity declaration in the DTD is started with the keyword ENTITY.

Be careful with the predefined abbreviations at the definition of entities for the character set. Entities can also be defined as a declaration of abbreviations for characters or strings. Of course, it is up to you whether an entity is really an "abbreviation".

Example

With the following example, the abbreviation "js" is assigned to the complete name:

```
<! ENTITY js "John Smith">
```

You can use this abbreviation within a document simply by using the created name as entity:

```
<?xml version = "1.0" ?>
```
The author of this document is &js;

H1

Hierarchical headings

Description

With this command headings are sub-divided hierarchically by HTML documents.

Application

This command structures HTML documents in relation to the hierarchical order of their headings. Six levels of heading are provided which all have different font sizes. The seventh heading is reached through the containers H1, H2, H3, H4, H5 and H6 in which the real text of the heading is part of the container. Therefore, the most important level is H1.

HTML 4.0 standard

CLASS, DIR, ID, LANG, STYLE, TITLE

Start tag: required; end tag: required.

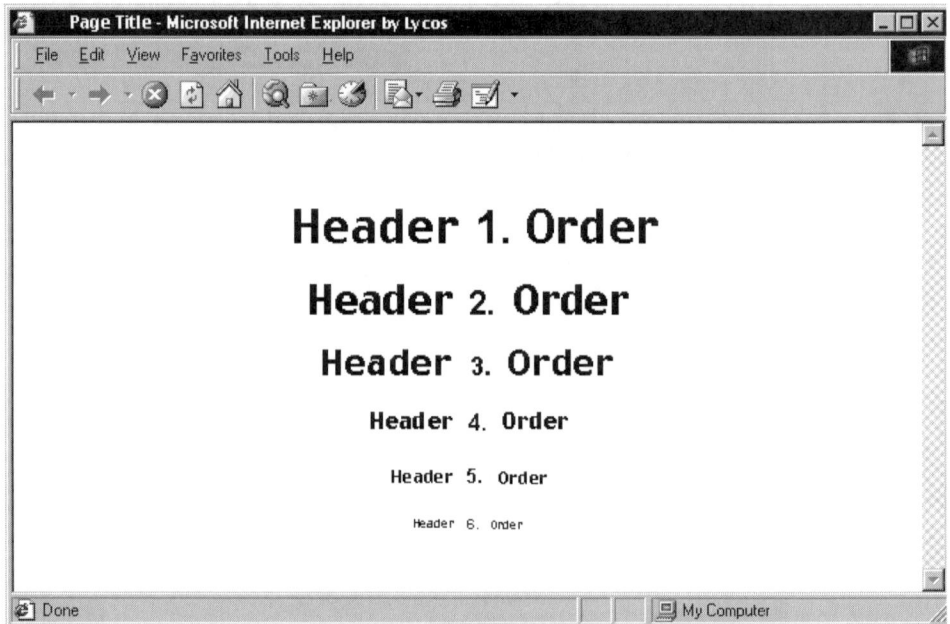

Your document can be subdivided using the different heading levels

Attributes

ALIGN

With this attribute you determine whether you align a paragraph formatted with the command DIV left, right or centred.

CENTER

Alignment of a paragraph centred.

LEFT

Left alignment of a paragraph.

RIGHT

Right alignment of a paragraph.

JUSTIFY

Alignment of the text to both sides (justified).

CLASS

Through the attribute CLASS the element can be assigned to a group (class). Enter one of the selectable class names. These groupings then provide easy access to all related elements so you can change all properties of the elements of a class with the help of cascading style sheets or other languages, or select a value.

DIR

This attribute is necessary to determine the text direction. This attribute can have two values:

LTR

This value determines the text direction from the left to the right. (and is short for "left-to-right") This is the default direction in the browser.

RTL

If the text should run contrary to the standard movement from the right to the left margin of the screen, then choose the value RTL (short for "right-to-left").

ID

ID identifies the document. Using ID it can be accessed to a specific element with the help of a script language to select or change values, for example.

LANG

This attribute indicates the language of the linked document. This is particularly important in search engines for identification purposes. Use the language codes according to ISO 639, for example "en" for English or "en-us" for American English.

ONCLICK

This event takes place if you single-click on an element with the mouse. A given script is executed by this action.

ONDBLCLICK

This event takes place if you double-click on an element with the mouse. A given script is executed by this action.

ONKEYDOWN

This event takes place if you are in an element and a key is pressed and held down. This action executes a specific script.

ONKEYPRESS

This event takes place if you are in an element and a key is simultaneously pressed and released again. This action executes a determined script.

ONKEYUP

This event takes place if you are in an element and a key that was pressed is released. This action executes a specific script.

ONMOUSEDOWN

This event takes place if you are in an element and a mouse button is clicked and held down. A given script is executed by this action.

ONMOUSEMOVE

This event takes place if one moves the cursor over an object with the mouse. A given script is executed by this action.

ONMOUSEOUT

This event takes place if a mouse moves the cursor off an element. A given script is executed by this action.

ONMOUSEOVER

This event takes place if the mouse moves the cursor directly over the element (object). A given script is executed by this action.

ONMOUSEUP

This event takes place if you are in an element and a mouse button that was clicked and held down is released. A given script is executed by this action.

STYLE

The attribute STYLE is used to determine specific properties in labelled elements. Style settings are defined by cascading style sheets.

TITLE

Give the user further information about the element used by fixing a meaningful title with the help of the TITLE command. Navigation in your Web site is made particularly easy for users who are dependent on voice response.

Example

```
<h1>Heading 1st order</h1>
<h2>Heading 2nd order</h2>
<h3>Heading 3rd order</h3>
<h4>Heading 4th order</h4>
<h5>Heading 5th order</h5>
<h6>Heading 6th order</h6>
```

Events

ONCLICK, ONDBLCLICK, ONKEYDOWN, ONKEYPRESS, ONKEYUP, ONMOUSEDOWN, ONMOUSEMOVE, ONMOUSEOUT, ONMOUSEOVER, ONMOUSEUP

Related commands
DIV
P

HEAD ☺

Head information of a SMIL document

Description
In a SMIL document META information can be defined within the document head, for example.

Application
The command HEAD encloses the head information of the document. The commands META, LAYOUT and SWITCH could be used within the head.

Parameter
id

Using ID identifies the document. Using ID this area can be accessed by other elements.

Example
```
smil>
<head id="identifier">
</head>
<!-- head information -->
</head>
<body>
</body>
</smil>
```

HEAD

Information about HTML documents

Description
With this command information for HTML documents is written.

Application

The command HEAD brings up the collection of information and settings which are necessary to characterise a document. This command indicates which heading a HTML document should have, by whom it was created and which hyperlink shortcuts are available.

HTML 4.0 standard

LANG, DIR, PROFILE

Start tag: optional; end tag: optional.

Attributes

DIR

This attribute is necessary to determine the text direction. This attribute can have two values:

LTR

This value determines the text direction from left to right (and is short for "left-to-right"). This direction is the default in the browser.

RTL

If the text should run contrary to the standard movement from the right to the left margin of the screen, then choose the value RTL (short for "right-to-left").

LANG

This attribute indicates the language of the linked document. This is particularly important in search engines for identification purposes. Use the language codes according to ISO 639, for example"en" for English or "en-us" for American English.

PROFILE

The attribute PROFILE describes one or more external files. In these files, separated by spaces, is contained META information on the corresponding files. This attribute is not yet supported by most browsers. The complete function is still in the discussion phase.

Example

```
<head lang="en">
<title>Title text </title>
</head>
<body>

...
```

XML definition

```
<!ENTITY % head.content "TITLE & BASE?">
```

```
<! ELEMENT HEAD 0 0 (%head.content;) +(%head.misc;)>
<!ATTLIST HEAD
% i18n;

profiles % URI;  # IMPLIED>
```

XML definition

```
<! ENTITY % html.content "HEAD, BODY">

<! ELEMENT HTML 0 0 (%html.content;)>
<! ATTLIST HTML %i18n;>
```

Related commands

BODY
HTML
TITLE

HEADERS   <html attribute>

Producing headers between cells and columns

Description

The attribute HEADERS produces a header between the cell content and the column heading. For example the cell contents can be distributed together with the suitable column heading for voice output systems more easily.

Application

ID is the value given to the column heading. The use of this attribute is optional.

Values

With this attribute a header is assigned to a table element with a corresponding ID. A valid ID must begin with a letter (A-Z, a-z) followed by an number of letters or digits. The following additional characters are permitted: hyphen ("-"), underscore("_"), colon (":") and period ("."). Several elements can be indicated separated by commas.

Example

```
<table>
```

```
<tr>
    <th id="Month_1" width="50%">January </td>
    <th id="Month_2" width="50%">February </td>
    </tr>
<tr>
    <td headers="Month_1" width="50%">100.000 GBP </td>
<td headers="Month_2" width="50%">123.000 JBP </td>
    </tr>
</table>
```

Accompanying elements
TD
TH

HEIGHT   <html attribute>
Indicating the height of an element

Description
Attribute to determine the height of a window or object.

Application
Through this attribute you can submit the desired height as a numerical value to the element. If you would like to change the size of an embedded graphic with the help of this attribute and you only want to change the height, the width is automatically adapted in the correct ratio. Values can also be indicated as percentage details relative to the absolute window width.

Values
The value of this attribute indicates a size in pixels or percentage. Valid values for pixels are positive integer numbers. The input of ="100" corresponds for example to a size of 100 pixels. A percentage detail corresponds to the percent quota of horizontal or vertical window width available in the browser. An input of = "30%" corresponds to a width of 30 per cent.

Example
```
<img src="image.gif" height="10%">
<img src="image.gif" height="200" width="300">
<img src="image.gif" height="10%" width="100">
```

```
<td height="120">
</td>
```

Accompanying elements
APPLET
IFRAME
IMG
ONJECT
TD
TH

HR

Horizontal separation of sections

Description
With this command, sections within a HTML document are graphically separated from each other by a horizontal line.

Application
The command HR separates sections of a HTML text from each other. This separation is carried out by inserting a horizontal line. This command was one of the first graphic elements available in HTML. Currently, this command is only rarely used. It is used primarily for long HTML documents..

HTML 4.0 standard
ALIGN, ID, CLASS, NOSHADE, SIZE, STYLE, TITLE, WIDTH

Start tag: required; end tag: forbidden.

Attributes
ALIGN
   This attribute determines the alignment of the horizontal line.
   LEFT
      The horizontal separating line will be aligned left.
   RIGHT
      The horizontal separating line will be aligned right.
   CENTER
      The horizontal separating line is centred. If the attribute ALIGN is missing, then the value CENTER is accepted as presetting.

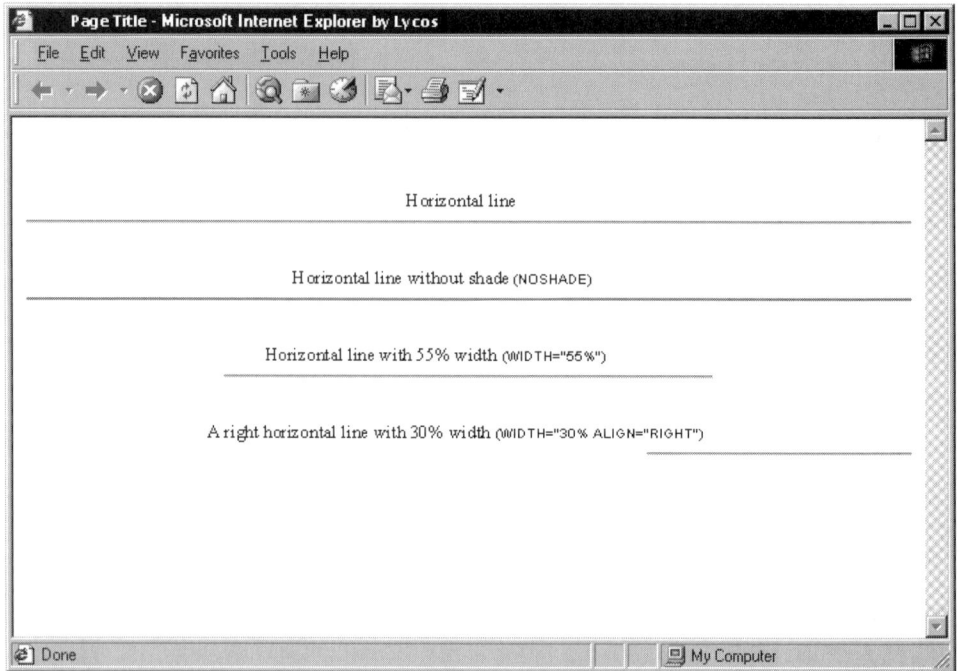

Horizontal separating lines with different attributes

CLASS

Through the attribute CLASS the element can be assigned to a group (class). Enter one of the selectable class names. These groupings then provide easy access to all related elements so you can change all properties of the elements of a class with the help of cascading style sheets or other languages, or select a value.

COLOR

With this attribute the colour of the separating bars to be represented is determined. Besides the 16 colour keywords defined, up to 256 colours can be represented, indicated by hexadecimal numbers. These settings are usually executed with the style sheet in HTML 4.0.

ID

ID the identifies the document. Using ID a specific element can be accessed with the help of a script language to select or change values, for example.

NOSHADE

If you use this attribute, separating lines are represented between the single sections without 3D effects.

ONCLICK

This event takes place if you single-click on an element with the mouse. A given script is executed by this action.

ONDBLCLICK
: This event takes place if you double-click on an element with the mouse. A given script is executed by this action.

ONKEYDOWN
: This event takes place if you are in an element and a key is pressed and held down. This action executes a specific script.

ONKEYPRESS
: This event takes place if you are in an element and a key is simultaneously pressed and released again. This action executes a determined script.

ONKEYUP
: This event takes place if you are in an element and a key that was pressed is released. This action executes a specific script.

ONMOUSEDOWN
: This event takes place if you are in an element and a mouse button is clicked and held down. A given script is executed by this action.

ONMOUSEMOVE
: This event takes place if one moves the cursor over an object with the mouse. A given script is executed by this action.

ONMOUSEOUT
: This event takes place if a mouse moves the cursor off an element. By this action given script is executed.

ONMOUSEOVER
: This event takes place if the mouse moves the cursor directly over the element (object). A given script is executed by this action.

ONMOUSEUP
: This event takes place if you are in an element and a mouse button that was clicked and held down is released. A given script is executed by this action.

SIZE
: With this attribute it is possible to indicate the height of the separating line in pixels.

STYLE
: The STYLE attribute can be used to change style settings, in particular the look of the element. As a value of the attribute you apply the corresponding options of a style sheet language (usually CSS).

WIDTH
: This attribute determines the character width in pixels. With this detail it is possible for the browser to choose a font which guarantees that the complete text will be shown.

TITLE
: Give the user further information about the element used by fixing a meaningful title with the help of the TITLE command. Navigation in your Web site is made particularly easy for users who are dependent on voice response.

Example

```
This section comes to an end now.
<hr size="5" width="65%" align="right" noshade>
A new section begins here.

<hr>
<hr noshade>
<hr width="55%">
<hr align="right" width="30%">
```

Events

ONCLICK, ONDBLCLICK, ONKEYDOWN, ONKEYPRESS, ONKEYUP, ONMOUSEDOWN, ONMOUSEMOVE, ONMOUSEOUT, ONMOUSEOVER, ONMOUSEUP

XML definition

```
<! ELEMENT HR>
<!ATTLIST HR
%coreattrs;
% events; >
```

Related command

BR

HREF   <html attribute>

Defining references

Description

The target element to which the anchor refers is indicated with the attribute HREF. Otherwise, you can use the common notation for Internet addresses (URI). The anchor can refer to any Web site.

Application

The use of this attribute is required for the functioning of the accompanying commands.

Values

A valid value for this attribute is the URI (Uniform Resource Identifier). The construction of a URI is as follows:

```
[protocol]: // [Domain]/[Directory]/[File]
```

Possible details for the used protocol are the following values:

ftp	File Transfer Protocol
http	Hypertext Transfer Protocol
gopher	Gopher Protocol
mailto	Electronic Mail Address
news	USENET News
nntp	USENET News (NNTP-access)
telnet	Reference to interactive sessions
wais	Wide Area Information Server
file	Host-specific file names
prospero	Prospero Directory Service

Example

```
<a href="page2.htm">Next</a>
<a href="http://www.microsoft.co.uk">Microsoft</a>
<a href="mailto:elena@goldcom.co.uk"> write me </a>
<a href="ftp://www.download.com/public/archive/windows/">
```

Accompanying elements

A
AREA
BASE
LINK

HREFLANG   <html attribute>

Indicating the language of a target document

Description

This attribute indicates the language of the target document. This is particularly important for identification purposes in search engines. You can already find out from the source document in which language the document to be linked is written, for example.

Application

Use the language codes according to the ISO 639, where "en" stands for English or "en-us" stands for American English, for example. The use of this attribute is optional.

Values

Submit a language code to this attribute as a value. It gives precise information about the language used in a document. The language code consists of two parts, so besides the language used (English or American English) dialects can also be determined. This second detail is optional, though. Language codes are fixed in ISO 639, which you can find under the keyword **ISO 639**. Valid values for the used language are:

FR	French	DE	German
IT	Italian	ES	Spanish
EN	English	NL	Dutch

In addition, besides the use of the language code (="EN" for English, for example) a country detail can be indicated (="DE-CH" means German as spoken in Switzerland, for example). You will find the complete overview of the country codes under the keyword **ISO 3166**.

DE	Germany	US	USA
UK	Great Britain	NL	Netherlands

Example

```
<a href="english.htm" hreflang="en">
<a href="german1.htm hreflang="de-ch">
<a href="german2.htm hreflang="de-de">
```

Accompanying elements

A

LINK

HSPACE   <html attribute>

Indicating horizontal separation

Description

With this attribute the horizontal separation of an embedded object is fixed in proportion to its environment within a window.

Application

Enter a horizontal separation of the object to the surrounding text on the left and on the right. The use of this attribute is optional.

Values

The value of this attribute indicates a size in pixels, and therefore in microdots. Valid values are positive integer numbers. Inputing = "100" corresponds to a size of 100 pixels, for example.

Example

```
<object
    data = "video.avi"
    width = "100"
    height = "100"
    hspace = 25
    vspace = 25>
</object>
```

Accompanying elements

APPLET
IMG
OBJECT

HTML

Basic markups for an HTML document

Description

Every HTML document consists of basic commands which give the necessary structure to the document.

Application

A HTML document consists of the enclosing HTML tags. A document head is still defined with HEAD followed by the text body with BODY. Though, the use of the HTML element is optional. You can produce valid HTML documents without this command.

HTML 4.0 standard

DIR, LANG

Start tag: optional; end tag: optional.

Attributes

DIR

> This attribute is necessary to determine the text direction. This attribute can have the values:
>
> LTR
>
> > This value determines the text direction from the left to the right (and is short for left-to-right"). This is the default direction in the browser.
> >
> RTL
>
> > If the text should run contrary to the standard movement from the right to the left margin of the screen, then choose the value RTL (short for "right-to-left").

LANG

> This attribute indicates the language of the linked document. This is particularly important in search engines for identification purposes. Use the language codes according to ISO 639, for example "en" for English or "en-us" for American English.

VERSION

> The HTML version used can be indicated through the attribute VERSION. This attribute is not used in version HTML 4.0 any more. It has been replaced by a corresponding detail in the element DOCTYPE.

Example

```
<html>
<head>
<title>The title of the page </title>
</head>
<body>
The real text body or the contents of the document follow here.
</body>
</html>
```

Related commands

BODY
HEAD
TITLE

HTTP-EQUIV   <html attribute>
Indicating meta information

Description
With the help of the attribute HTTP-EQUIV you decide which meta information to transmit with the command META.

Application
With the command META at least the use of the attribute HTTP-EQUIV is expected, alternatively the attribute NAME can be used.

Values
You can submit one of the following values to the attribute HTTP-EQUIV. Besides the listed values, other names can also be used because a clear determination of the valid concepts is not defined in HTML 4.0. Nevertheless, you should limit yourself to the common and known names to reach the desired functions.

An official definition of the possible values is not provided by the W3C. The following content types are common and can be used:

CONTENT-LANGUAGE
Indicates the language of the HTML document. Use the usual definitions of a language in HTML as value for CONTENT ("en" for English, "en-uk" for English/Great Britain, for example).

CONTENT-SCRIPT-TYPE
To use document script language you have to indicate the predefined language with this value ("text/vbscript" or "text/javascript", for example).

CONTENT-STYLE-TYPE
Indicates the standard style LANGUAGE. Use "text/css" for style sheets, for example.

CONTENT-TYPE
Through CONTENT-TYPE you can indicate the predefined character set. For example: "text/html; charset = iso-8859-1" for the Western European character set.

EXPIRES
EXPIRES can inform you when your page will be downloaded. If the page is stored intermediately in a proxy cache, then this loads your page again from the Net according to the period of time set.

PRAGMA
Submit the value "no-cache" with CONTENT to prevent your pages from being stored indefinitely in the cache memory.

REFRESH

With REFRESH another HTML document can be loaded automatically into the browser after a given waiting time in seconds. The current document can naturally be transmitted once more, for example in live pictures by video camera. Indicate the number in seconds followed by the URL of the document to be loaded: CONTENT="10; URL=seite2.html".

Example

```
<meta http-equiv="content-type"
    content = " HTML write/; charset = " iso 8859-1>
<meta http-equiv="expires"
    content = "Thu, 24 Jun 1999 12:00:00 GMT",>
```

Accompanying element

META

I

Representation of text in italic font

Description

With this command text can be shown in italic. The term "I" is derived from the initial letter of "Italic".

Application

The command I (abbreviation for "italic") changes text from roman font to italic font.

HTML 4.0 standard

CLASS, DIR, ID, LANG, STYLE, TITLE

Start tag: required; end tag: required.

Attributes

CLASS

Through the attribute CLASS the element can be assigned to a group (class). Enter one of the free class names. These groupings then provide easy access to all related element so you can change all properties of the elements of a class with the help of cascading style sheets or other languages, or select a value.

DIR

This attribute is necessary to determine the text direction. This attribute can have two values:

LTR

This value determines the text direction from the left to the right (and is short for "left-to-right"). This is the default direction in the browser.

RTL

If the text should run contrary to the standard movement from the right to the left margin of the screen, then choose the value RTL (short for "right-to-left").

ID

ID identifies the document. Using ID a specific element can be accessed with the help of a script language to select or change values, for example.

LANG

This attribute indicates the language of the linked document. This is particularly important in search engines for identification purposes. Use the language codes according to ISO 639, for example "en" for English or "en-us" for American English.

ONCLICK

This event takes place if you single-click on an element with the mouse. A given script is executed by this action.

ONDBLCLICK

This event takes place if you double-click on an element with the mouse. A given script is executed by this action.

ONKEYDOWN

This event takes place if you are in an element and a key is pressed and held down. This action executes a specific script.

ONKEYPRESS

This event takes place if you are in an element and a key is simultaneously pressed and released again. This action executes a determined script.

ONKEYUP

This event takes place if you are in an element and a key that was pressed is released. This action executes a specific script.

ONMOUSEDOWN

This event takes place if you are in an element and a mouse button is clicked and held down. A given script is executed by this action.

ONMOUSEMOVE

This event takes place if one moves the cursor over an object with the mouse. A given script is executed by this action.

ONMOUSEOUT

This event takes place if a mouse moves the cursor off an element. By doing this a given script is executed.

ONMOUSEOVER

> This event takes place if the mouse moves the cursor directly over the element (object). A given script is executed by this action.

ONMOUSEUP

> This event takes place if you are in an element and a mouse button that was clicked and held down is released. A given script is executed by this action.

STYLE

> The attribute STYLE is used to determine specific properties in labelled elements. Style settings are defined by cascading style sheets.

TITLE

> Give the user further information about the used element by fixing a meaningful title with the help of the TITLE command. Navigation in your Web site is made particularly easy for users who are dependent on voice response.

Example

```
This is an <i>italic</i> document!
And now in <b>bold</b>
Naturally they can be used together:
<b><i>bold and italic</i></b>
```

Events

ONCLICK, ONDBLCLICK, ONKEYDOWN, ONKEYPRESS, ONKEYUP, ONMOUSEDOWN, ONMOUSEMOVE, ONMOUSEOUT, ONMOUSEOVER, ONMOUSEUP

Related commands

B
BIG
LISTING
PLAINTEXT
PRE
S
SMALL
STRIKE
TT
U
XMP

ID **\<html attribute\>**

Assigning clear name

Description
Through the ID attribute, the element will provide a definite identification of the document. Using ID a specific element can be accessed with the help of a script language to select or change values, for example.

Application
Assign a name or a definition to an element which occurs only once in the complete document. The use of this attribute is optional; however, it is frequently used to access an element by JavaScript or to produce connections between table cells, for example.

Values
With this attribute a label is assigned to an element with a corresponding ID. A valid ID must begin with a letter (A-Z, a-z), followed by any number of letters or digits. The following additional characters are allowed: underscore ("_"), hyphen ("-"), colon (": ") and period (".").

Example
```
<div id="Absatz_1></div>
<div id="A1.2"></div>
<div id="a-z.d.3-67"></div>
```

Related commands

A	H1	P
ABBR	H2	PRE
ACRONYM	H3	Q
ADDRESS	H4	S
AREA	H5	SAMP
B	H6	SELECT
BIG	HEAD	SMALL
BLOCKQUOTE	HTML	SPAN
BODY	I	STRIKE
BUTTON	IMG	STRONG
CAPTION	INPUT	STYLE
CENTER	INS	SUB
CITE	ISINDEX	SUP
CODE	KBD	TABLE
COL	LABEL	TBODY
COLGROUP	LEGEND	TD
DD	LI	TEXTAREA
DEL	LINK	TFOOT
DFN	MAP	TH
DIR	MENU	THEAD
DIV	META	TITLE
DL	NOFRAMES	TR
DT	NOSCRIPT	TT
EM	OBJECT	U
FIELDSET	OL	UL
FONT	OPTGROUP	VARNTER
FORM	OPTION	

IFRAME

Defining independent sub-windows

Description

Independent windows within windows already available in the browser are defined using this command. Unlike frames, embedded frames (IFRAME) are not screen windows but simply regions of a window. Embedded frames are like images and graphics integrated into the site.

Application

This command enables an embedded frame to be constructed within existing browser windows. Many of the attributes of this inline frame are also applicable in the conventional frame. Other HTML documents can be shown within the defined area as in a frame. The size of embedded frames cannot be changed by the user.

Until now, although the command IFRAME is officially defined in HTML 4.0, it is only supported by Microsoft Internet Explorer.

HTML 4.0 standard

ALIGN, CLASS, FRAMEBORDER, HEIGHT, ID, LONGDESC, MARGINHEIGHT, MARGINWIDTH, NAME, SCROLLING, SRC, STYLE, TITLE, WIDTH

Start tag: required; end tag: required.

Attributes

ALIGN

> With this attribute you set the IFRAME within the browser window.
>
> TOP
>> ALIGN=TOP ensures that surrounding text is aligned with the top of a window.
>
> BOTTOM
>> ALIGN=BOTTOM ensures that the surrounding text is aligned with the bottom of a window.
>
> MIDDLE
>> ALIGN=MIDDLE ensures that the surrounding text is aligned in the centre of a window.
>
> LEFT
>> ALIGN=LEFT aligns the window left.
>
> RIGHT
>> ALIGN=RIGHT aligns the window right.
>
> CENTER
>> ALIGN=CENTER aligns the window in the centre.

CLASS

> Through the attribute CLASS the element can be assigned to a group (class). Enter one of the selectable class name. These groupings then provide easy access to all related elements so you can change all properties of the elements of a class with the help of cascading style sheets or other languages or select a value.

FRAMEBORDER

> If this attribute is set to the value 1, it draws a three-dimensional border around the window. The window remains without a border if it is set to the value 0.

HEIGHT

> With this attribute the width of a window can be set in pixels.

HSPACE

With this attribute the horizontal separation (left and right) of a text in an embedded frame can be determined. This attribute is only interpreted by Internet Explorer and is not provided by the official HTML standard.

ID

ID identifies the document. Using ID a specific element can be accessed with the help of a script language to select or change values, for example.

LONGDESC

This attribute defines a detailed description of the frame content. This completes the long description which can be indicated through the TITLE attribute.

MARGINHEIGHT

With the help of the attribute MARGINHEIGHT the margin height of the window can be set.

MARGINWIDTH

With the help of the attribute MARGINWIDTH the margin width of the window can be set.

NAME

Through the attribute NAME the element can be assigned a name. You should ensure that a name is used only once in a document. This command can be related to the attribute ID.

SCROLLING

With the help of SCROLLING you can set whether or not the corresponding FRAME should be equipped with a scroll bar. Possible values are YES, NO and AUTO.

SRC

With this attribute it is possible to fix the source path. These source paths refer to the content of one or several frames.

STYLE

The attribute STYLE can be used to change style settings, in particular the look of the element. As a value of the attribute you apply the corresponding options of a style sheet language (usually CSS).

TARGET

The attribute TARGET is used to fix the name of a window in which a link is opened. This attribute is used if several windows are open or a new window with a link is opened.

TITLE

Give the user further information about the element used by fixing a meaningful title with the help of the TITLE command. Navigation in your Web site is made particularly easy for users who are dependent on voice response.

VSPACE

With this attribute you can determine the vertical separation (top and bottom) of the text in an embedded frame. This attribute is only interpreted by Internet Explorer and is not provided by the official HTML standard.

WIDTH
> With this attribute the width of the embedded frames is set in pixels.

Example

```
<iframe src="info.html" scrolling="auto" frameborder="1">
This text is displayed
if the browser doesn't know the command
</iframe>
```

Related commands

FRAMESET
FRAME
NOFRAMES
OBJECT

ILAYER

Defining inline layers

Description

With this command you can place inline layer regions within a HTML file.

Application

The command ILAYER is used within layers when inline layers should be represented. They have all the properties found in a normal layer.

HTML 4.0 standard

This command is not part of the official HTML standard and, just like the command LAYER, is only evaluated by the Netscape browser. Replace the numerous possibilities offered by layer with style sheets.

Attributes

ABOVE
> If you put layers one above the other, you can set using ABOVE which layer should be on top. Use the name of the layer lying below it as a value. You must indicate any layers whose names you have already defined.

ALIGN
> This attribute fixes where in a document an inline layer is embedded, and how text is built up in or next to a graphic. The fixed values orientate themselves using the normal position of the inline-layer.

LEFT

    With ALIGN=LEFT an inline layer is aligned left.

RIGHT

    With ALIGN=RIGHT an inline layer is aligned right.

TOP

    With ALIGN=TOP you can align an inline layer is with the top edge of a window.

BOTTOM

    With ALIGN=BOTTOM you can align an inline layer with the bottom of a window.

MIDDLE

    With ALIGN=MIDDLE you can align an inline layer in the middle of a window.

BACKGROUND

A background image can be indicated for every layer, in much the same way as you can indicate a graphic for the background using the BODY command.

BELOW

If you put several layers one on top of the other, you can fix the order of the layers using BELOW. You must indicate all layers you have previously defined.

BGCOLOR

As with BACKGROUND, with this attribute you can fix a background. However, only a single colour can be indicated according to the HTML standard.

CLASS

Through the attribute CLASS you assign an element to a group (class). Enter one of the selectable class names. These groupings then provide easy access to all related elements so you can change properties of the elements of a class with the help of cascading style sheets or other languages, or select a value.

CLIP

With CLIP you can crop the range of layers. If you indicate four values, then these are interpreted as the coordinates of an overflowed section. On the contrary, if you submit only two values then these are treated as the height and width of a rectangle.

HEIGHT

This attribute defines the height of the selected area.

ID

ID identifies the document. Using ID a specific element can be accessed with the help of a script language to select or change values, for example.

LEFT

Through LEFT you can determine the correct position of the layer measured in pixels from the left margin.

NAME

A name can be assigned to an element through the attribute NAME. You should ensure that this name occurs only once in the document. This command is like the attribute ID.

PAGEX
> Through PAGEX you determine the correct position of the layer measured in pixels from the left margin of the window (as in TOP).

PAGEY
> Through PAGEY you determine the correct position of the layer measured in pixels from the top margin of the window (as in TOP).

SRC
> As in a frame, you can display the contents of another HTML document inside a layer. Give the URI of the other file through SRC.

TOP
> Through TOP you can determine the correct position of the layer measured in pixels from the top of the document.

VISIBILITY
> Single layers can be displayed and deleted. This is only necessary if you want to change the visibility of the layers afterwards with JavaScript. Three values can be submitted for this attribute:
>
> HIDE
>> Hides the given layer.
>
> SHOW
>> Shows the layer. This value is the default value.
>
> INHERIT
>> The layer is shown only if its sub-layer is also visible. This value is only used with interleaved layers.
>
> WIDTH
>> Fix the correct width of the layer with this attribute.
>
> Z-INDEX
>> The position of the interleaved layers can be organised with the help of the attributes ABOVE and BELOW. Using index numbers is simpler, however through the attribute Z-INDEX. Layers with higher index numbers cover layers with lower numbers.

Example

```
Here there is
<ilayer left="50" top="100">Layer text </ilayer>
```

Related command

LAYER

IMG ☺

Including an image in a document

Description

This command (also IMAGE) allows you to display a graphic in a restricted area of the window.

Attributes

abstract
Create a short description for the group with this attribute.

author
Give the name of the author for this media grouping.

begin
Indicates the reproduction time. You can use h, min, s or ms as units.

copyright
Gives information about the originator and the copyright can be submitted as a value of this attribute.

dur
Indicates the complete duration of the group. You can use h, min, s or ms as units.

end
Indicates the end of the group. This value is the opposite of the attribute begin. You can use h, min, s or ms as units.

id
Through ID the element will provide a clear identification for the document. Using ID it can be accessed from other elements in this region.

repeat
The complete group will repeat a given number of times.

src
Indicates the source of the media clip or graphic. Give a valid URL as the value.

title
Gives the complete group a title with a short description of the content.

Example

```
<img id="identifier"
    src="URL"
    alt="string"
    region="identifier"
    title="string"
    abstract="string"
    author="string"
    copyright="string"
    longdesc="string"
    type="string"
    begin="clock-value"
```

```
end="clock-value"
dur="clock-value"
repeat="integer"
fill="remove|freeze"
system-bitrate="integer"
system-captions="on|off"
system-language="comma-separated-list"
system-overdub-or-caption="caption|overdub"

system-required="string"
system-screen-depth="integer"
system-screen-size="integerXinteger" />
```

IMG

Embedding pictures

Description
With this command it is possible to embed graphics and pictures into a HTML document.

Application
The command IMG is used to embed inline images into an HTML document. Images were the first visual objects which could be represented on Web sites. These images have not only an informative or decorative purpose but are frequently used as buttons. There is no end tag after the IMG tag.

HTML 4.0 standard
ALT, CLASS, DIR, HEIGHT, ID, ISMAP, LANG, LONGDESC, SRC, STYLE, TITLE, USEMAP, WIDTH

Start tag: required; end tag: not allowed.

Attributes
ALIGN

Determine how text is built up in or next to an image with this attribute.

LEFT

Aligns the complete graphic left on the page. The text following the graphic flows around the graphic to the right.

RIGHT

Aligns the complete graphic right on the page. The text following the graphic flows round.

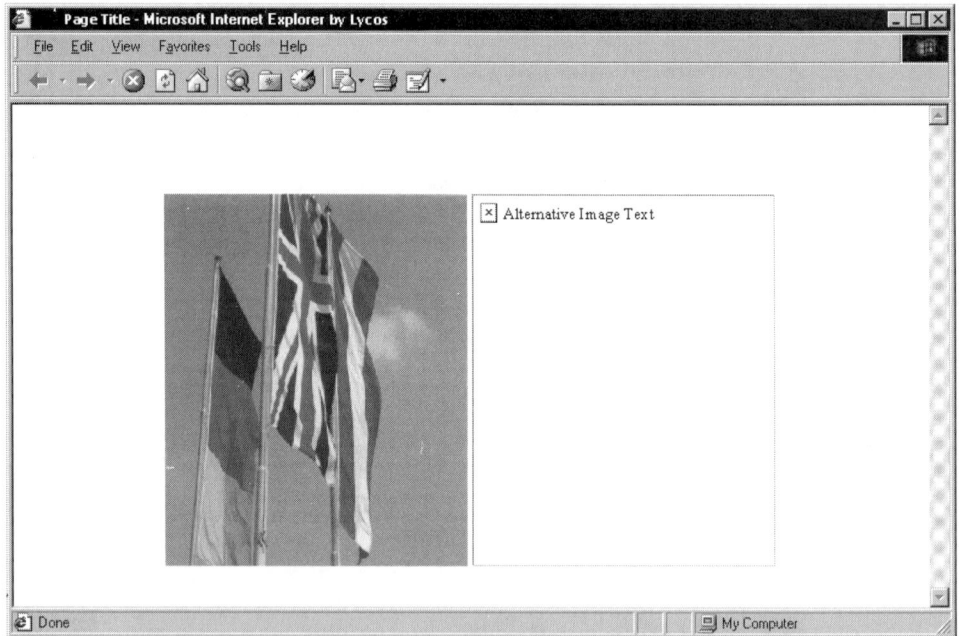

If a picture cannot be shown, then text is shown as an alternative

TOP

    ALIGN=TOP means that text is aligned next to the graphic at the top of the screen.

BOTTOM

    ALIGN=BOTTOM means that text is aligned next to the graphic at the bottom of the screen.

MIDDLE

    ALIGN=MIDDLE means that text is aligned next to the graphic.

ABSMIDDLE

    Aligns the text with the top edge centred on the graphic. This value is not defined in HTML 4.0 and is evaluated only with the Netscape browser.

ABSBOTTOM

    Aligns the text with the bottom edge below the graphic. This value is not defined in HTML 4.0 and is evaluated only with the Netscape browser.

BASELINE

    Corresponds to the value BOTTOM. This value is not defined in HTML 4.0 and is evaluated only with the Netscape browser.

TEXTTOP

    Aligns the available text with the top edge up to the graphic. This value is not defined in HTML 4.0 and is evaluated only with the Netscape browser.

ALT

    This attribute contains alternative text to be used if a browser is unable to show a graphic. This text should then replace the graphic. The use of this attribute is recommended in HTML 4.0. Users, particularly those who use text-oriented browsers, can evaluate the information of your site.

BORDER

If you assign a value of more than 0 to this attribute, a browser sets a margin around the graphic. If the picture is highlighted as a hyperlink, a frame is always set by default to make the graphic recognisable as such. If you want to avoid this, insert the value BORDER="0".

CLASS

Through the attribute CLASS the element can be assigned to a group (class). Enter one of the selectable class names. These groupings then provides easy access to all related elements so you can change the properties of the elements of a class with the help of cascading style sheets or other languages, or select a value.

CONTROLS

This attribute is used if you want to embed and play video clips. The attribute CONTROL provides a list of commands to control a video. This attribute is not part of the official language and is only interpreted by Explorer.

DIR

This attribute is necessary to determine the text direction. This attribute can have the values:

LTR

This value determines the text direction from left to right (and is short for "left-to-right"). This is the default direction in the browser.

RTL

If the text should run contrary to the standard movement from the right to the left margin of the screen, then choose the value RTL (short for "right-to-left").

DYNSRC

This attribute refers to a video clip which will be represented in a window. This attribute is not part of the official language and is only interpreted by Explorer.

HEIGHT

With this attribute you can indicate the height of a graphic in pixels.

HSPACE

This attribute fixes the horizontal free area around a graphic in pixels.

ID

ID provides identification for the document. Using ID a specific element can be accessed with the help of a script language to select or change values, for example.

ISMAP

With this attribute you show that you want to branch an image to an imagemap program on the server. A browser can send the coordinates of an image to a server, which can then determine the necessary branching using this information.

LANG

This attribute indicates the language of the linked document. This is particularly important in search engines for identification purposes. Use the language codes according to ISO 639, for example "en" for English or "en-us" for American English.

LONGDESC

This attribute defines a detailed description of the contents of the frame. This completes the long description which can be indicated through the TITLE attribute.

LOOP

You can fix the number of loops of a video clip with this attribute. 1 or infinite causes infinite repetitions of the clip. This attribute is not part of the official language and is interpreted only by Explorer.

LOWSRC

With this attribute it is possible to indicate a second graphic which is displayed before the actual image, but only with a Netscape browser. With LOWSRC you get a preview of the original image in lower quality. This preview is transferred and displayed to the user faster due to the lower file size. If the larger arrives later, this is displayed in the same place.

NAME

Through the attribute NAME a name can be assigned to an element. Ensure that a used name occurs only once in a document. This command is comparable to the attribute ID.

ONCLICK

This event takes place if you single-click on an element with the mouse. A given script is executed by this action.

ONDBLCLICK

This event takes place if you double-click on an element with the mouse. A given script is executed by this action.

ONKEYDOWN

This event takes place if you are in an element and a key is pressed and held down. This action executes a specific script.

ONKEYPRESS

This event takes place if you are in an element and a key is simultaneously pressed and released again. This action executes a determined script.

ONKEYUP

This event takes place if you are in an element and a key that was pressed is released. This action executes a specific script.

ONMOUSEDOWN

This event takes place if you are in an element and a mouse button is clicked and held down. A given script is executed by this action.

ONMOUSEMOVE

This event takes place if one moves the cursor over an object with the mouse. A given script is executed by this action.

ONMOUSEOUT
   This event takes place if a mouse moves the cursor off an element. By this action a given script is executed.

ONMOUSEUP
   This event takes place if you are in an element and a mouse button that was clicked and held down is released. A given script is executed by this action.

SRC
   An absolute or relative address is assigned to an image using SRC.

START
   With this attribute you can determine when a video clip is played (which was indicated with the command DYNSRC). This attribute is not part of the official language and is only interpreted by Explorer.

MOUSEOVER
   This event takes place if the mouse moves the cursor directly over the element (object). A given script is executed by this action.

FILEOPEN
   A video will start immediately after it is transferred to a user's computer.

STYLE
   The attribute STYLE can be used to change style settings, in particular the look of an element. As a value of the attribute you submit the corresponding options of a style sheet language (usually CSS).

TITLE
   Through this attribute highlighted elements show additional information. This information is displayed in a pop up menu in many browsers, if the mouse pointer is on the element.

USEMAP
   This attribute is used for client-side imagemaps. Here information is written about the imagemap.

VSPACE
   This attribute fixes the vertical free area around an image in pixels.

WIDTH
   Use this attribute to give the height of an image in pixels.

Example

```
<img src="image.gif" alt="alternative description">
<img src="graphic.jpg" width="200" height="158">
<img src="original.gif" lowsrc="sw.gif">

<a href="http://www.mut.com">
<img src="logo.jpg" border="0">
</a>

<img src="logo.jpg" width="100">
```

Events

ONCLICK, ONDBLCLICK, ONKEYDOWN, ONKEYPRESS, ONKEYUP, ONMOUSEDOWN, ONMOUSEMOVE, ONMOUSEOUT, ONMOUSEOVER, ONMOUSEUP

XML definition

```
<!ENTITY % Length "CDATA " >
<! ENTITY % MultiLength "CDATA">
<! ENTITY % MultiLengths "CDATA">
<!ENTITY % Pixels "CDATA " >

<! ELEMENT IMG>
 <!ATTLIST IMG
% attrs;
src             % URI;          # REQUIRED
old             % text;         # REQUIRED
longdesc        % URI;          # IMPLIED
height          % Length;       # IMPLIED
width           % Length;       # IMPLIED
usemap          % URI;          # IMPLIED >
```

Related command

OBJECT

import

Importing a style sheet

Description

You can integrate additional XSL files within a XSL style sheet by reference. In this way it is possible to divide bigger projects into single modules. Reusing ready XSL documents is made easier. These do not have to be brought together in a file using "copy and paste" but can be included by a command.

Parameter

href

Imports a style sheet into another XSL style sheet. Indicates the source of the style sheet.

Example

```
<import href="customers.xsl"/>
```

INPUT

Defining control elements

Description

With this simple command you can insert user inputs.

Application

The command INPUT is used to fix control elements. The type of control element is determined with the attribute TYPE. The command is used in forms within the FORM container.

HTML 4.0 standard

ACCEPT, ACCESSKEY, ALT, CHECKED, CLASS, DIR, DISABLED, ID, LANG, MAX-LENGTH, NAME, READONLY, SIZE, SRC, STYLE, TABINDEX, TITLE, TYPE, USEMAP, VALUE

Start tag: required; end tag: not allowed.

Attributes

ACCEPT

    With this attribute you can define the fonts which are valid for the input in the respective form fields.

ACCESSKEY

    The attribute ACCESSKEY enables access to an element through a keyboard shortcut. So, the instruction ACCESSKEY="A" means that when the user presses the "A" key the element is activated.

ALIGN

    Through ALIGN you fix the alignment of the dialog element.

    TOP

        With ALIGN=TOP the text of the entry field is aligned with the top of the element.

    BOTTOM

        With ALIGN=BOTTOM the text of the entry field is aligned at the bottom of the element.

    MIDDLE

        With ALIGN=MIDDLE the text of the entry field is aligned to the middle of the element.

    LEFT

        With ALIGN=LEFT the object is aligned to the left.

    RIGHT

        With ALIGN=RIGHT the object is aligned to the right.

ALT

ALT

This attribute contains alternative text in case a browser cannot show an object. This text should give details about the entry field. This attribute gains meaning particularly in the input type IMAGE.

CHECKED

The attribute CHECKED activates an options display for preselection in check boxes and radio buttons.

CLASS

Through the attribute CLASS the element can be assigned to a group (class). Enter one of the selectable class names. These groupings then provide easy access to all related elements so you can change the properties of the elements of a class with the help of cascading style sheets or other languages, or select a value.

DIR

This attribute is necessary to determine the text direction. This attribute can have the values:

LTR

This value determines the text direction from left to right (and is short for "left-to-right"). This is the default direction in the browser.

RTL

If the text should run contrary to the standard movement from the right to the left margin of the screen, then choose the value RTL (short for "right-to-left").

DISABLED

The use of this attribute deactivates the related button and prevents any input.

ID

Through the attribute ID the element will provide identification for the document. Using ID a specific element can be accessed with the help of a script language to select or change values, for example.

LANG

This attribute indicates the language of the linked document. This is particularly important in search engines for identification purposes. Use the language codes according to ISO 639, for example "en" for English or "en-us" for American English.

MAXLENGTH

The maximum number of characters a user may enter into an entry field created by TYPE=TEXT is determined with the attribute MAXLENGTH. The length of the field which is shown on the window is fixed through SIZE. This also evaluates the input type PASSWORD, whereas other fields have the value left without meaning.

NAME

With the attribute TYPE the type of input is determined. Every input must have a name assigned with the attribute NAME. The related data are usually transmitted in connection with the name when mailing the form.

ONBLUR

The event ONBLUR is triggered when an input element loses focus. The user has moved to the next field with a mouse click or keyboard. This event can call a script which checks and reprocesses the entered values.

ONCHANGE

This event takes place if the contents of the entry field are changed. By this action a given script is executed.

ONCLICK

This event takes place if you single-click on an element with the mouse. A given script is executed by this action.

ONDBLCLICK

This event takes place if you double-click on an element with the mouse. A given script is executed by this action.

ONKEYDOWN

This event takes place if you are in an element and a key is pressed and held down. This action executes a specific script.

ONKEYPRESS

This event takes place if you are in an element and a key is simultaneously pressed and released again. This action executes a determined script.

ONKEYUP

This event takes place if you are in an element and a key that was pressed is released. This action executes a specific script.

ONMOUSEDOWN

This event takes place if you are in an element and a mouse button is clicked and held down. A given script is executed by this action.

ONMOUSEMOVE

This event takes place if one moves the cursor over an object with the mouse. A given script is executed by this action.

ONMOUSEOUT

This event takes place if a mouse moves the cursor off an element. By this action a given script is executed.

ONMOUSEOVER

This event takes place if the mouse moves the cursor directly over the element (object). A given script is executed by this action.

ONMOUSEUP

This event takes place if you are in an element and a mouse button that was clicked and held down is released. A given script is executed by this action

ONFOCUS

The ONFOCUS event is triggered when the current element receives focus, i.e. when the user goes on this field with a mouse click or the keyboard and the element is activated.

ONSELECT

This event is active when the user selects the text in the entry field.

READONLY

This attribute labels an entry field as readable only. Other changes, like writing in the entry field, are not allowed.

SIZE

This attribute indicates the size of an entry field. If the given value exceeds the area to be represented, the entered text can be scrollable.

SRC

Provided that the control type is IMAGE, you must indicate the image location through the attribute SRC. Give the image a URI. This is then used as a graphic button.

STYLE

The attribute STYLE can be used to change style settings, particularly the appearance of an element. As a value of the attribute you submit the corresponding options of a style sheet language (usually of CSS).

TABINDEX

This attribute assigns an order position to an element by using positive or negative integers. Elements provided with this attribute can be selected one after the other with the tab key.

TYPE

With this attribute you fix the kind of control element you want to use. The following control types are available:

BUTTON

Creates a simple Windows style button . Through this button various actions can be started, a script, for example. You produce graphic buttons with the option IMAGE.

CHECKBOX

Produces a check box. This control check box gives the user the chance to choose an option by "checking" the field. For every check box two states exist, selected and not selected.

FILE

This control type allows the user to select a file, so that its content can be transmitted with the form.

HIDDEN

This value produces a hidden dialog field. The entry field is not displayed on the screen. It transmits additional information to the server which the user does not have to enter. The value of the field can be indicated with VALUE.

IMAGE

With IMAGE you can create a graphic button. The image shown must be indicated through SRC. The coordinates, by which the user has selected the graphic, are transmitted to the server as an input result.

PASSWORD

Produces a simple single-line entry field. The entered letters are not shown but are replaced by asterisks. In this way passwords or other sensitive data cannot be read from the screen. However, this option should not lull the user into a false sense of security. Data in the field will be transferred to the server unencrypted.

RADIO

A radio button allows the user to select one option from several. Radio buttons, are combined in a group according to their same name. Only one radio button can be selected within a group.

RESET

If the Reset button is activated by the user, then all data in the form are deleted.

SUBMIT

This option produces a button. If the Submit button is activated by the visitor, then all data in the form are transmitted to the server by the browser.

TEXT

Produces a simple single-line entry field.

USEMAP

This attribute is used for client-side imagemaps. Here information is written about the imagemap.

VALUE

With TYPE=CHECKBOX options can be created which can be selected by the user. The attribute TYPE describes the type of input. All options of a group of inputs should be assigned with the same name using the attribute NAME. The attribute VALUE should be different for every input.

Example

```
<input type=text name="Name" size="30" maxlength="60">

<input type=radio name="Operating system" value="Linux">
<input type=radio name="Operating system" value="Windows 95">
<input type=radio name="Operating system" value="Windows 98">
<input type=radio name="Operating system" value="Windows NT">

<input type=checkbox name="Program" value="MS Word">
<input type=checkbox name="Program" value="MS Excel">
<input type=checkbox name="Program" value="MS Access">
<input type=checkbox name="Program" value="MS Outlook">

<input type=image src="click.gif">
```

```
<input type=hidden name="Form version" value="12.08.99">
```

Events

ONBLUR, ONCHANGE, ONCLICK, ONDBLCLICK, ONFOCUS, ONKEYDOWN, ONKEY-
PRESS, ONKEYUP, ONMOUSEDOWN, ONMOUSEMOVE, ONMOUSEOUT, ONMOUSEOVER,
ONMOUSEUP, ONSELECT

XML definition

```
<!ENTITY % InputType
"(TEXT), | PASSWORD | CHECKBOX| RADIO | SUBMIT | RESET | FILE | HID-
DEN | IMAGE | BUTTON) " >

<! ELEMENT INPUT>
 <!ATTLIST INPUT
%  attrs;

type           % inputType;      Text
name           CDATA             # IMPLIED
value          CDATA             # IMPLIED
checked        (checked)         # IMPLIED
disabled       (disabled)        # IMPLIED
readonly       (readonly)        # IMPLIED
size           CDATA             # IMPLIED
maxlength      NUMBER            # IMPLIED
src            % URI;            # IMPLIED
alt            CDATA             # IMPLIED
usemap         % URI;            # IMPLIED
tabindex       NUMBER            # IMPLIED
accesskey      % Character;      # IMPLIED
onfocus        % Script;         # IMPLIED
onblur         % script;         # IMPLIED
onselect       % Script;         # IMPLIED
onchange       % Script;         # IMPLIED
accept         % ContentTypes;   # IMPLIED
% reserved;>
```

Related command

FORM

INS

Selecting inserted text

Description

With this command the text inserted in a newer version of a document is selected.

Application

The command INS is used to recognise changes in a text on which several persons work, for example. In this case it identifies text which should be selected in a more current version of a HTML document. The opposite command is DEL. This function is already familiar from different word processing programs.

HTML 4.0 standard

CITE, CLASS, DATETIME, DIR, ID, LANG, STYLE, TITLE

Start tag: required; end tag: required.

Attributes

CITE

   With this attribute it is possible to indicate documents which either refer to the original document or execute an instruction to the document, in which the changes applied are explained.

DATETIME

   With the help of this attribute the exact date and time of changes carried out can be set up. If you use this attribute, the corresponding details must comply with the ISO 8601 standard.

   If you proceed in this way, the entry appears as follows:

JJJ-MMDDThh:mm:ssTZD

   These entries have the following meaning:

   JJJJ

      four-digit year

   MM

      two-digit month (03=March)

   DD

      two-digit day date (05, 27)

   T

      Hyphen between the date and time indication according to ISO 8061

   hh

      two-digit hour (00 – 23)

   mm

      two-digit minute (00 – 59)

SS
> two-digit second (00 – 59)

TZD
> Abbreviation for "Time Zone Designator". Name of the time zone. The Z in this abbreviation stands for "Geenwich Mean Time" (GMT). Therefore, entries like =hh:mm or -hh:mm represent the local time, which indicate either before or after the GMT.

LANG
> This attribute indicates the language of the linked document. This is particularly important in search engines for identification purposes. Use the language codes according to ISO 639, for example "en" for English or "en-us" for American English.

Example

```
<del datetime="1999-06-08T06:00:01Z">flow </del>
<ins>flow </ins>

<ins datetime="1999-06-08T06:00:01+03:00">Inserted </ins>
```

XML definition

```
<! ELEMENT (INS|DEL) - - (%flow;)*>
<!ATTLIST (INS|DEL)
%  attrs;

cite       % URI;  # IMPLIED
datetime % Datetime;  # IMPLIED>
```

Related command

DEL

ISINDEX

Defining searchable documents

Description

With this command you can define a file as searchable. In HTML 4.0 this command is not supported.

Application

The command ISINDEX is used to search HTML documents using keywords. You are provided with an entry field where you can enter your search string.

HTML 4.0 standard

CLASS, DIR, LANG, ID, TITLE, STYLE

The use of this command is no longer recommended in HTML; it has been replaced by other commands.

Start tag: required; end tag: not allowed.

Attributes

CLASS

Through the attribute CLASS the element can be assigned to a group (class). Enter one of the selectable class names. These groupings then provide easy access to all related elements so you can change the properties of the elements of a class with the help of cascading style sheets or other languages, or select a value.

DIR

This attribute is necessary to determine the text direction. This attribute can have the values:

LTR

This value determines the text direction from left to right (and is short for "left-to-right"). This is the default direction in the browser.

RTL

If the text should run contrary to the standard movement from the right to the left margin of the screen, choose the value RTL (short for "right-to-left").

ID

Through the ID attribute, the element will identify the document. Using ID a specific element can be accessed with the help of a script language to select or change values, for example.

LANG

This attribute indicates the language of the linked document. This is particularly important in search engines for identification purposes. Use the language codes according to ISO 639, for example "en" for English or "en-us" for American English.

PROMPT

With this attribute you can amend the predefined search text in a search for definite concepts.

STYLE

The attribute STYLE is used to determine specific properties in elements. Style settings are defined by cascading style sheets.

TITLE
> With this attribute additional information is assigned to selected elements. This information is displayed in the pop-up menu in many browsers, if the mouse pointer is on an element.

Example

```
<head>
<isindex prompt="Enter a search string">
</head>
```

ISMAP   <html attribute>
Defining server-side imagemaps

Description

With this attribute you show that you want to conduct a mapping, which contains a graphic to an imagemap program on the server. A browser can send the coordinates of the image to a server which then determines the necessary mapping with the help of this information.

Application

Today client-side imagemaps are started with the commands AREA and MAP. On the contrary, in a server-side solution, the possible coordinates are sent to the server. The browser simply submits the coordinates, which the visitor has selected on a graphic, to the server. Further processing is left to the server. The use of this attribute is optional.

Values

To activate this option, simply use the name of the attribute. You do not have to submit any value to this attribute. If the attribute is not used, then the option remains deactivated. This attribute is not case sensitive.

Example

```
<a href="inhalt.htm">
<img src="image.gif" ismap>
</a>
```

Accompanying element
IMG

KBD

Identifying texts which require keyboard input

Description

With this command sections of a document are identified which a user would enter text from a keyboard.

Application

The command KBD is used to identify sections where a user would enter text from a keyboard. This is mainly used in instructions for different computer programs, for example.

HTML 4.0 standard

CLASS, DIR, ID, LANG, STYLE, TITLE

Start tag: required; end tag: required.

Attributes

CLASS

Through the attribute CLASS the element can be assigned to a group (class). Enter one of the selectable class names. These groupings then provide easy access to all related elements so you can change the properties of the elements of a class with the help of cascading style sheets other languages, or select a value.

DIR

This attribute is necessary to determine the text direction. This attribute can have the values:

LTR

This value determines the text direction from left to right (and is short for"left-to-right"). This is the default direction in the browser.

RTL

If the text should run contrary to the standard movement from the right to the left margin of the screen, choose the value RTL (short for "right-to-left").

ID

Through the ID attribute, the element will identify the document. Using ID a specific element can be accessed with the help of a script language to select or change values, for example.

LANG

This attribute indicates the language of the linked document. This is particularly important in search engines for identification purposes. Use the language codes according to ISO 639, for example "en" for English or "en-us" for American English.

ONCLICK

This event takes place if you single-click on an element with the mouse. A given script is executed by this action.

ONDBLCLICK

This event takes place if you double-click on an element with the mouse. A given script is executed by this action.

ONKEYDOWN

This event takes place if you are in an element and a key is pressed and held down. This action executes a specific script.

ONKEYPRESS

This event takes place if you are in an element and a key is simultaneously pressed and released again. This action executes a determined script.

ONKEYUP

This event takes place if you are in an element and a key that was pressed is released. This action executes a specific script.

ONMOUSEDOWN

This event takes place if you are in an element and a mouse button is clicked and held down. A given script is executed by this action.

ONMOUSEMOVE

This event takes place if one moves the cursor over an object with the mouse. A given script is executed by this action.

ONMOUSEOUT

This event takes place if a mouse moves the cursor off an element. A given script is executed by this action.

ONMOUSEOVER

This event takes place if the mouse moves the cursor directly over the element (object). A given script is executed by this action.

ONMOUSEUP

This event takes place if you are in an element and a mouse button that was clicked and held down is released. A given script is executed by this action.

STYLE

The attribute STYLE can be used to change style settings, particularly the look of an element. As value of the attribute you give the corresponding options of a style sheet language (usually of CSS).

TITLE

Give the user further information about the element used by fixing a meaningful title with the help of the TITLE command. Navigation to your site is made easier for users who are dependent on speech synthesisers.

Example

```
<kbd>
DIR/p
</kbd>
```

Events

ONCLICK, ONDBLCLICK, ONKEYDOWN, ONKEYPRESS, ONKEYUP, ONMOUSEDOWN, ONMOUSEMOVE, ONMOUSEOUT, ONMOUSEOVER, ONMOUSEUP

Related commands

ACRONYM
CITE
CODE
DFN
EM
SAMP
STRONG
VAR

LABEL   \<html attribute\>

Indicating labels

Description

This attribute gives detailed information about an OPTION or an OPTIONGROUP.

Application

Most browsers cannot yet interpret this attribute. The use of this attribute is optional.

Values

For every command in which you use this attribute, there is a different validity range for the submitted value. Here is a list of the commands and possible values:

OPTION
  This attribute allows you to indicate a short name for an option. The browser can show this label as additional information.
OPTGROUP
  This attribute makes a label possible in the form of a character string for the selected entry groups.

Example

```
<option value="01" label="label">

<optgroup label="North Region">
<option label="North 1">Sheffield
```

```
<option label="North 2">Manchester
<option label="North 3">Liverpool
</optgroup>
```

Accompanying elements
OPTION
OPTGROUP

LABEL
Assigning additional information to form elements

Description
With this command, it is possible to assign information to control or form elements.

Application
The LABEL command is used to assign labels to control elements. These control elements can be check boxes, text fields, etc.

HTML 4.0 standard
ACCESSKEY, CLASS, DIR, FOR, ID, LANG, STYLE, TITLE

Start tag: required; end tag: required.

Attributes
ACCESSKEY

The ACCESSKEY attribute enables access to an element through a keyboard shortcut. So, the ACCESSKEY="A" instruction means that, when the user press the "A" key, the element is activated.

CLASS

Through the CLASS attribute the element can be assigned to a group (class). Enter one of the selectable class names. These groupings then provide easy access to all related elements so you can change the properties of the elements of a class with the help of cascading style sheets or other languages, or select a value.

DIR

This attribute is necessary to determine the text direction. This attribute can have the values:

LTR

> This value determines the text direction from left to right (and is short for "left-to-right"). This direction is predefined in the browser.

RTL

> If the text must run contrary to the standard direction from the right to the left margin of the screen, then choose the value RTL (short for "right-to-left").

DISABLED

With this attribute it is possible to deactivate buttons.

ID

Through the ID attribute, the element will provide a clear identification for the document. Using ID, a specific element can be accessed with the help of a script language to select or modify its value.

FOR

With this attribute a label is assigned to a form field with a corresponding ID.

LANG

This attribute indicates the language of the linked document. This is particularly important in search engines for identification purposes. Use the language codes according to ISO 639, for example "en" for English or "en-us" for American English.

ONBLUR

> This event is triggered when the element loses its focus because the mouse pointer is moved from a particular position on the element. By this action a given script is executed.

ONCLICK

> This event takes place if you single-click on an element with the mouse. A given script is executed by this action.

ONDBLCLICK

> This event takes place if you double-click on an element with the mouse. A given script is executed by this action.

ONKEYDOWN

> This event takes place if you are in an element and a key is pressed and held down. This action executes a specific script.

ONKEYPRESS

> This event takes place if you are in an element and a key is pressed and then released. This action executes a specific script.

ONKEYUP

> This event takes place if you are in an element and a key that was pressed is released. This action executes a specific script.

ONMOUSEDOWN

> This event takes place if you are in an element and a mouse button is clicked and held down. A given script is executed by this action.

ONMOUSEMOVE
> This event takes place if one moves the cursor over an object with the mouse. A given script is executed by this action.

ONMOUSEOUT
> This event takes place if a mouse moves the cursor off an element. By this action a given script is executed.

ONMOUSEOVER
> This event takes place if the mouse moves the cursor directly over the element (object). A given script is executed by this action.

ONMOUSEUP
> This event takes place if you are in an element and a mouse button that was clicked and held down is released. A given script is executed by this action.

ONFOCUS
> The ONFOCUS event is triggered when the current element is focused on. If the user goes on this field with a mouse click or the keyboard and the element is activated.

STYLE
> The STYLE attribute can be used to change style settings, in particular the appearence of the element. As the value of the attribute, you apply the corresponding options of a style sheet language (usually CSS).

TITLE
> Give the user further information about the element used by defining a meaningful title with the help of the TITLE command. Navigation on your Web site is made easier for users who are dependent on speech synthesizers.

Example

```
<label for="Residence">Residence </label>
<input type="text" id="Residence">
```

Events

ONBLUR, ONCLICK, ONDBLCLICK, ONFOCUS, ONKEYDOWN, ONKEYPRESS, ONKEYUP, ONMOUSEDOWN, ONMOUSEMOVE, ONMOUSEOVER, ONMOUSEOUT, ONMOUSEUPP

XML definition

```
<! ELEMENT LABEL - - (%inline;)* -(LABEL)>
<!ATTLIST LABEL
%attrs;
for          IDREF #     IMPLIED
accesskey %  Character;  IMPLIED
onfocus %    script;     IMPLIED
onblur %     script;     IMPLIED>
```

Related command
INPUT

LANG   <html attribute>

Indicating the language used

Description
With this attribute, it is possible to specify the language used in the document or in a particular section of a document.

Application
This attribute is helpful primarily in the search and identification of documents. It supports a search engine in the search for English pages or starts a corresponding translation program, for example. The use of this attribute is optional.

Values
Submit a language code to this attribute as a value. It gives information about the language used. The language code consists of two parts. As well as the language used (English, for example) the local identification is determined. This second detail is optional, though. Language codes are determined in the ISO 639. Valid values for the used language are for example:

FR French   DE German
IT Italian   ES Spanish
EN English   NL Dutch

In addition, besides the use of the language code (="EN" for English, for example) the detail of a country can optionally be inserted ("EN-US" for English with the local identification for the United States). You will find the complete list of country codes under the keyword ISO 3166.

DE Germany   US USA
UK Great Britain   NL Netherlands

Example
```
<div lang="en-uk"></div>
<html lang="de"></html>
<strong lang="de-ch"></strong>
```

Accompanying elements

A	FORM	OPTION
ABBR	H1	P
ACRONYM	H2	PRE
ADDRESS	H3	Q
AREA	H4	S
B	H5	SAMP
BDO	H6	SELECT
BIG	HEAD	SMALL
BLOCKQUOTE	HTML	SPAN
BODY	I	STRIKE
BUTTON	IMG	STRONG
CAPTION	INPUT	STYLE
CENTER	INS	SUB
CITE	ISINDEX	SUP
CODE	KBD	TABLE
COL	LABEL	TBODY
COLGROUP	LEGEND	TD
DD	LI	TEXTAREA
DEL	LINK	TFOOT
DFN	MAP	TH
DIR	MENU	THEAD
DIV	META	TITLE
DL	NOFRAMES	TR
DT	NOSCRIPT	TT
EM	OBJECT	U
FIELDSET	OL	UL
FONT	OPTGROUP	VAR

LANGUAGE   `<html attribute>`

Indicating script languages used

Description

Through this attribute, you can define the script language (computer language) used.

Application

Indicate the corresponding name for the script language used. Until now, these names have not been standardised. Therefore, the W3C recommends that you avoid this attribute for the time being. The use of this attribute is optional.

Values

You can submit an arbitrary string to this attribute as a value. This character string should not start or end with a space. The browser will filter this out if necessary.

Example

```
<script language="JavaScript">
<script language="VBScript">
<script language="Jscript">
```

Accompanying element

SCRIPT

LAYER

Placing areas

Description

With this command, it is possible to position different areas of a HTML file.

Application

The LAYER command occurs when an element of an HTML file should be defined as a unit. In this way, different components of a file, such as headings, graphics and text, can be combined in a layer.

HTML 4.0 standard

Layer is not an official language element of HTML. Layers are only interpreted by Netscape. Use style sheets conforming to HTML specifications.

Attributes

ABOVE

If you want to set different layers one on top of the other, you can determine through the ABOVE detail over which other layers the current layer should be. You must already have defined the layers whose names you indicate here.

ALIGN

This attribute determines where in a document a layer is embedded, how text is built up in or next to a graphic. The fixed values are oriented according to the normal position of the layers.

LEFT

With ALIGN=LEFT a layer is aligned to the left.

RIGHT

With ALIGN=RIGHT a layer is aligned to the right.

TOP

With ALIGN=TOP the layer is aligned to the top of the window.

BOTTOM

With ALIGN=BOTTOM the layer is aligned to the bottom of the window.

MIDDLE

With ALIGN=MIDDLE the layer is centre-aligned.

BACKGROUND

For every layer, a background image can be indicated. In the same way, with the BODY command, you can indicate a graphic for the background.

BELOW

If you set several layers one below the other, you can determine with the BELOW detail under which other layers the current layer should be. Submit the name of the above layer in the BELOW attribute as the value. You must indicate all layers you have previously defined whose names have been determined here BGCOLOR. As with BACKGROUND, with this attribute a background can be determined. Only a single colour can be indicated according to the HTML standard.

CLASS

Through the CLASS attribute the element can be assigned to a group (class). Enter one of the selectable class names. These groupings then provide you easy access to all related elements so you can change the properties of the elements of a class with the help of cascading style sheets or other languages, or select a value.

CLIP

You must submit two or four numbers separated by comma as a value to the CLIP attribute. With CLIP you can crop the range of layers. If you indicate four values, then these are interpreted as coordinates of an overflowed section. On the other hand, if you submit only two values, then these are treated as the height and width of a rectangle.

HEIGHT

This attribute defines the correct height of the selected area.

ID

Through the ID attribute, the element will provide identification for the document. Using ID, a specific element can be accessed with the help of a script language to select or modify values.

LEFT

Through LEFT you determine the correct position of the layer measured in pixels from the left margin.

NAME

> Through the NAME attribute a name can be assigned to the element. You should ensure that this name occurs only once in the document. This command is like to the ID attribute.

PAGEX

> Through PAGEX you determine the correct position of the layer measured in pixels from the left margin of the window (as in TOP).

PAGEY

> Through PAGEY you determine the correct position of the layer measured in pixels from the top margin of the window (as in TOP)

SRC

> Like in a frame, inside a layer you can display the contents of another HTML document. Give the URI of the other file through SRC.

TOP

> Through TOP you can determine the correct position of the layer measured in pixels from the upper margin of the document.

VISIBILITY

> Single layers can be displayed and deleted. This makes sense only if you want to change the visibility of the layers afterwards with the help of JavaScript. Three values can be submitted for this attribute:
>
> HIDE
>
>> Hides the specified layer.
>
> SHOW
>
>> Shows the layer. This is the default value.
>
> INHERIT
>
>> The layer is shown only if its sub-layer is also visible. This value makes sense only for interleaved layers.

WIDTH

> With this attribute you can determine the correct width of the layer.

Z-INDEX

> The position of the single interleaved layers can be determined with the help of the names through the ABOVE and BELOW attributes. Placing index numbers is simpler, using the Z-INDEX attribute. Layers with higher index numbers include layers with lower numbers.

Example

```
<layer top="10" left="50" width="200" height="150">
This is a layer
</layer>

<layer id="top" left="100" top="100">
Stack 1
</layer>
<layer id="bottom" below="top" left="200" top="200">
Layer 2
```

```
</layer>
<layer id="Center" above="bottom" left="300" top="300">
Layer 3
</layer>
```

Related command

ILAYER

LAYOUT ☺

Specifying the layout of a document

Description

The LAYOUT command is used to determine the look of the page.

Application

In principle, LAYOUT must be used in the head of the document.

Parameter

type
   Indicates the data type in which the layout is used.

Example

```
<layout>
< root-layout/>
<region id="video" top="10" left="10"
     width = "100" height = "100"/for >
</layout>

<layout type="string">
</layout>


<!-- Presetting: > --
<layout type="text/smil-basic-layout"/>
</layout>
```

LEGEND

Assigning a heading (caption) to a FIELDSET

Description

With this command, it is possible to assign headings to fieldsets. A fieldset is a group of form fields which has been arranged into a unit.

Application

The FIELDSET command is used when marked up elements are written with FIELDSET.

HTML 4.0 standard

ACCESSKEY, CLASS, DIR, ID, LANG, STYLE, TITLE

Start tag: required; end tag: required.

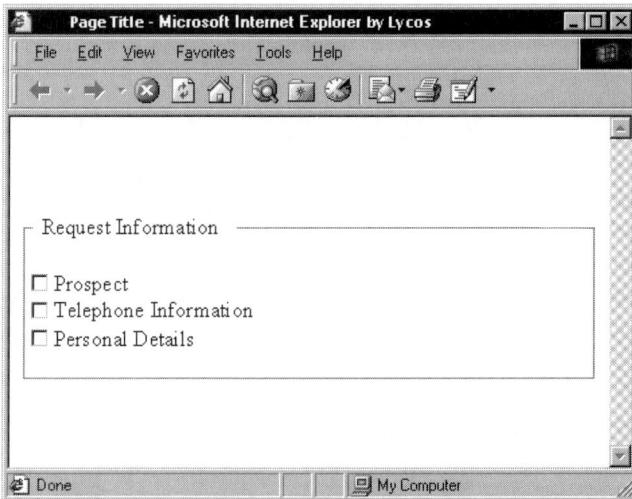

Form fields combined into a group and given a label

Attributes

ACCESSKEY

> The ACCESSKEY attribute enables access to an element through a keyboard shortcut. So, the instruction ACCESSKEY="A" means that, when the user presses the "A" key, the element is activated.

ALIGN

This attribute is responsible for determining the position of the legend. The legend can be aligned to all four edges of the rectangular group area.

TOP

The legend is placed at the top of the group. This is the default value.

BOTTOM

The legend is placed at the bottom of the group.

LEFT

Left alignment of the legend within the group.

RIGHT

Right alignment of the legend within the group.

CLASS

Through the CLASS attribute the element can be assigned to a group (class). Enter one of the selectable class names. These groupings then provide easy access to all related elements so you can change the properties of the elements of a class with the help of cascading style sheets or other languages, or select a value.

DIR

This attribute is necessary to determine the text direction. This attribute can have the values:

LTR

This value determines the text direction from left to right (and is short for "left-to-right"). This is the default direction in the browser.

RTL

If the text must run contrary to the standard direction from the right to the left margin of the screen, then you will choose the RTL value (short for "right-to-left").

ID

Through the ID attribute, the element will provide identification for the document. Using ID, a specific element can be accessed with the help of a script language to select or modify values.

LANG

This attribute indicates the language of the linked document. This is particularly important in search engines for identification purposes. Use the language codes according to ISO 639, for example "en" for English or "en-us" for American English.

ONCLICK

This event takes place if you single-click on an element with the mouse. A given script is executed by this action.

ONDBLCLICK

This event takes place if you double-click on an element with the mouse. A given script is executed by this action.

ONKEYDOWN

This event takes place if you are in an element and a key is pressed and held down. This action executes a specific script.

ONKEYPRESS

This event takes place if you are in an element and a key is pressed and released. This action executes a specific script.

ONKEYUP

This event takes place if you are in an element and a key that was pressed has been is released. This action executes a specific script.

ONMOUSEDOWN

This event takes place if you are in an element and a mouse button is clicked and held down. A given script is executed by this action.

ONMOUSEMOVE

This event takes place if one moves the cursor over an object with the mouse. A given script is executed by this action.

ONMOUSEOUT

This event takes place if a mouse moves the cursor off an element. This action executes a given script.

ONMOUSEOVER

This event takes place if the mouse moves the cursor directly over the element (object). A given script is executed by this action.

ONMOUSEUP

This event takes place if you are in an element and a mouse button that was clicked and held down is released. A given script is executed by this action.

STYLE

The STYLE attribute can be used to change style settings, in particular the way the element looks. As the value of the attribute, you apply the corresponding options of a style sheet language (usually CSS).

TITLE

Give the user further information about the element used by defining a meaningful title with the help of the TITLE command. Navigation in your Web site is made easier for users who are dependent on speech synthesizers.

Example

```
fieldset>
<legend>personal details</legend>
<input name="name" type="text">
<input name="surname" type="text">
<input name="residence" type="text">
</fieldset>

<fieldset>
<legend align="bottom">Information request </legend>
<input type="checkbox" name="prospect">
<input type="checkbox" name="telephone information">
<input type="checkbox" name="personal call">
</fieldset>
```

Events
ONCLICK, ONDBLCLICK, ONKEYDOWN, ONKEYPRESS, ONKEYUP, ONMOUSEDOWN, ONLOAD, ONUNLOAD, ONMOUSEMOVE, ONMOUSEOVER, ONMOUSEOUT, ONMOUSEUP

XML definition
```
<! ELEMENT LEGEND - - (%inline;)*>
<! ENTITY % LAlign "(top|bottom|left|right)">
<!ATTLIST LEGEND
% attrs;
accesskey % Character; # IMPLIED>
```

Related commands
FIELDSE
FORM
INPUT

CASCADING
STYLE SHEETS

letter-spacing
Space between letters

Description
Like the word-spacing function, letter-spacing does not handle spaces between whole words, but spaces between letters.

Parameter
The length of the separation between the single letters can be set as an absolute number or as a keyword for the default setting.

Example
```
<style type="text/css">
h1, h2 {letter-spacing:5}
h3, h4 {letter-spacing:normal}
</style>

<div style="letter-spacing:6">
</div>
```

LI
Selecting lists

W3C HTML 4.0 ✓

Description
With this command, it is possible to select a single item within a list.

Application
The Li command is used to select list entries. You must ensure that every list has at least one entry. The command for a single item must always be used in connection with an enclosing list container (such as UL or OL).

HTML 4.0 standard
CLASS, COMPACT, DIR, ID, LANG STYLE, TITLE, TYPE, START, VALUE

Start tag: required; end tag: optional.

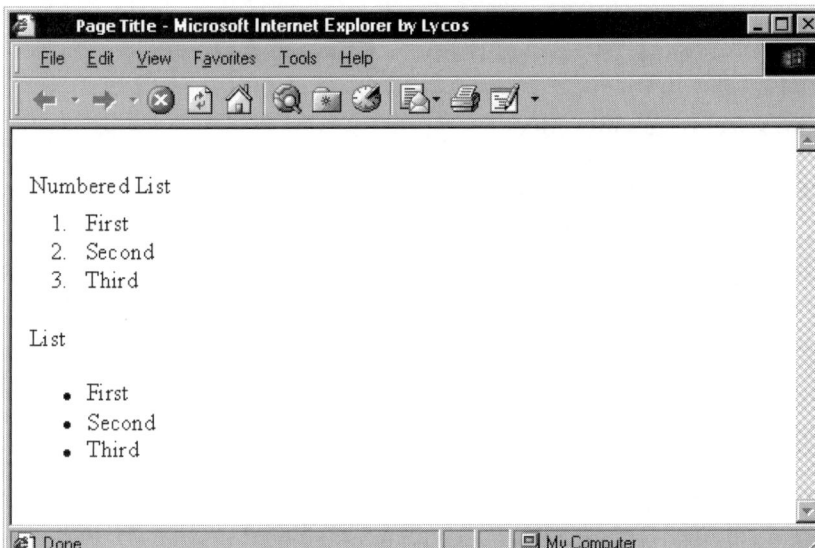

Comparison of numbered and bullet lists

Attributes

CLASS

Through the CLASS attribute, the element can be assigned to a group (class). Enter one of the selectable class names. These groupings provide easy access to all related elements so you can change the properties of the elements in a class with the help of cascading style sheets or other languages, or select a value.

COMPACT

Provided that this value is set, the browser tries to represent this in a compact form. The interpretation of this option is heavily dependent on the browser used.

DIR

This attribute is necessary to determine the text direction. This attribute can have the values:

LTR

This value determines the text direction from left to right (and is short for "left-to-right"). This is the default direction in the browser.

RTL

If the text must run contrary to the standard direction from the right to the left margin of the screen, then choose the value RTL (short for "right-to-left").

ID

Through the ID attribute, the element will provide a clear identification for the document. Using ID, a specific element can be accessed with the help of a script language, to select or modify values.

LANG

This attribute indicates the language of the linked document. This is particularly important in search engines for identification purposes. Use the language codes according to ISO 639, for example "en" for English or "en-us" for American English.

ONCLICK

This event takes place if you single-click on an element with the mouse. A given script is executed by this action.

ONDBLCLICK

This event takes place if you double-click on an element with the mouse. A given script is executed by this action.

ONKEYDOWN

This event takes place if you are in an element and a key is pressed and held down. This action executes a specific script.

ONKEYPRESS

This event takes place if you are in an element and a key is pressed and released. This action executes a specific script.

ONKEYUP

> This event takes place if you are in an element and a key that was pressed is released. This action executes a specific script.

ONMOUSEDOWN

> This event takes place if you are in an element and a mouse button is clicked and held down. A given script is executed by this action.

ONMOUSEMOVE

> This event takes place if one moves the cursor over an object with the mouse. A given script is executed by this action.

ONMOUSEOUT

> This event takes place if a mouse moves the cursor off an element. This action executes a given script.

ONMOUSEOVER

> This event takes place if the mouse moves the cursor directly over the element (object). A given script is executed by this action.

ONMOUSEUP

> This event takes place if you are in an element and a mouse button that was clicked and held down is released. A given script is executed by this action.

TYPE

> With this attribute you can determine the type of marker to be used before the corresponding list element within a list. To create an "unordered list" (non numeric list) with the UL command or an "ordered list" (numeric list) with OL, there are various possible values. The following settings apply to a UL:

> DISC

>> Diplays a diskette icon as the list symbol (not recognised by all browsers).

> SQUARE

>> With this value, you can select a small square as the list symbol.

> CIRCLE.

>> The CIRCLE value creates a small circle as a symbol.

> However, with this attribute, you can assign a list symbol to every element, even in OL. The following values are permitted:

> 1

>> Arabic numbers (1, 2, 3, ...); this is the default value.

> a

>> Lower case alpha-numeric characters (a, b, c, ...).

> A

>> Upper case alpha numeric characters (A, B, C, ...).

> i

>> Lower case Roman numerals (i, ii, iii, iv, ...).

> I

>> Upper case Roman numerals (I, II, III, IV, ...).

START

> This attribute is only used with a numbered list. You can indicate a start value and start the list with the value 100, for example.

STYLE
> The STYLE attribute can be used to change style settings, in particular the way the element looks. As a value of the attribute, you need to apply the corresponding options of a style sheet language (usually CSS).

TITLE
> Give the user further information about the element used by defining a meaningful title with the help of the TITLE command. Navigation in your Web site is made easier for users who are dependent on speech synthesizers.

VALUE
> With this attribute you can determine a numbering value freely within an OL.

Example

```
<ol>
     <li></li> first
     <li></li> second
     <li></li> third
</ol>
<ul>
     <li></li> first
     <li></li> second
     <li></li> third
</ul>
```

Events

ONCLICK, ONDBLCLICK, ONKEYDOWN, ONKEYPRESS, ONKEYUP, ONMOUSEDOWN, ONMOUSEMOVE, ONMOUSEOVER, ONMOUSEOUT, ONMOUSEUP

XML definition

```
<!ELEMENT LI-O(%flow;)*>
<!ATTLIST LI %attrs;>
```

Related commands

DIR
OL
UL

LINK   <html attribute>

Determining the colour of a hyperlink

Description

With this attribute, you can set the colour of the link in an HTML document. This command is not supported in HTML 4.0.

Application

Indicate the colour for hyperlinks not yet selected within the BODY tag. The use of this attribute is optional.

Values

Submit either a colour value in RGB syntax or a valid colour name to the attribute. For the RGB value, you indicate the colour code of the colours red, yellow and blue in hexadecimal notation: #RRGGBB (i. e. #008000 for green). Alternatively, you can use predefined colour names (i. e. YELLOW). Under the keyword **colorpalette** you will find a complete list of all standard colours. The 16 most frequently used primary colours are:

```
BLACK     = #000000    SILVER   = #C0C0C0
GRAY      = #808080    WHITE    = #FFFFFF
MAROON    = #800000    RED      = #FF0000
PURPLE    = #800080    FUCHSIA  = #FF00FF
GREEN     = #008000    LIME     = #00FF00
OLIVE     = #808000    YELLOW   = #FFFF00
NAVY      = #000080    BLUE     = #0000FF
TEAL      = #008080    AQUA     = #00FFFF
```

Example

```
<body alink="black">
<body vlink="red">
<body link="#00FFFF">
```

Accompanying element

BODY

LINK

Marking links

Description

With this command links between documents are defined. Unlike the A command, the LINK command is exclusively defined in the header of a document. It does not indicate any directly clickable link, but defines the relation between different pages of a project.

Application

The LINK command requires the detail of the HREF attribute. Through this attribute the browser is informed of the destination address to which it must go to produce a link. The LINK command does not produce a visible object in the browser, and the interpretation of the link depends on the program used.

HTML 4.0 standard

CHARSET, CLASS, DIR, HREF, HREFLANG, ID, LANG, MEDIA, REL, REV, STYLE, TITLE, TYPE

Start tag: required; end tag: not allowed.

Attributes

CHARSET

This attribute is used to determine the character encoding for data connected by the link. If the character set is not explicitly indicated, the browser determines the used character encoding.

CLASS

Through the CLASS attribute the element can be assigned to a group (class). Enter one of the selectable class names. These groupings then provide easy access to all related elements so you can change the properties of the elements of a class with the help of cascading style sheets or other languages, or select a value.

DIR

This attribute is necessary to determine the text direction. This attribute can have the values:

LTR

This value determines the text direction from left to right (and is short for "left-to-right"). This is the default direction in the browser.

RTL

If the text must run contrary to the standard direction from the right to the left margin of the screen, then choose the value RTL (short for "right-to-left").

ID

Through the ID attribute, the element will provide identification for the document. Using ID, a specific element can be accessed with the help of a script language to select or change values.

HREF

The HREF attribute indicates the linked element to which the link. You can use the standard notation for Internet addresses (URL). The link can refer to any Web site.

HREFLANG

This attribute indicates the language of the linked document. This is particularly important in search engines for identification purposes. Use the language codes according to ISO 639, for example "en" for English or "en-us" for American English.

MEDIA

This attribute can determine the output devices specified as suitable for the linked file. Possible values are:

ALL

This document is suitable for all devices.

AURAL

This document is intended for speech synthesisers.

BRAILLE

This document is optimised for the Braille keyboard.

HANDHELD

This document is optimised for handheld devices (small black and white screens, bitmapped graphics, limited bandwidth).

PRINT

This document is recommended for output to a printer.

PROJECTION

Recommended for a video player or projector.

SCREEN

This standard setting indicates that the document is optimised for computer screens.

TTY

Output optimised for terminal devices or computers with limited display capabilities.

TV

Especially suitable for output on a television-type devices (those with lower resolution and lower refresh rates than a computer screen).

ONCLICK

This event takes place if you single-click on an element with the mouse. A given script is executed by this action.

ONDBLCLICK

This event takes place if you double-click on an element with the mouse. A given script is executed by this action.

ONKEYDOWN

This event takes place if you are in an element and a key is pressed and held down. This action executes a specific script.

ONKEYPRESS

This event takes place if you are in an element and a key is pressed and released. This action executes a specific script.

ONKEYUP
> This event takes place if you are in an element and a key that was pressed is released. This action executes a specific script.

ONMOUSEDOWN
> This event takes place if you are in an element and a mouse button is clicked and held down. A given script is executed by this action.

ONMOUSEMOVE
> This event takes place if one moves the cursor over an object with the mouse. A given script is executed by this action.

ONMOUSEOUT
> This event takes place if a mouse moves the cursor off an element. This action executes a given script.

ONMOUSEOVER
> This event takes place if the mouse moves the cursor directly over the element (object). A given script is executed by this action.

ONMOUSEUP
> This event takes place if you are in an element and a mouse button that was clicked and held down is released. A given script is executed by this action.

REL
> With this attribute you can determine link types for the linked document, to define a reference to a glossary or the index, for example. These commands help the browser navigate through the site.

> ALTERNATE
>> Indicates an alternative version of the document: another language version or an abridged text version, for example.

> APPENDIX
>> Refers to a document serving as an appendix to the Web site.

> BOOKMARK
>> Indicates a special page which you can take as a bookmark into your browser.

> CHAPTER
>> Refers to the chapter of which the document is part.

> CONTENTS
>> Points to a table of contents in which all pages present are clearly listed.

> COPYRIGHT
>> In this page, you will find details about the originator of the document on this site.

> GLOSSARY
>> In this page, you will find a glossary which explains important concepts.

> HELP
>> Refers to a help page which helps with the navigation and usage of the site.

> INDEX
>> Refers to an index which contains all keywords of the Web site.

> NEXT
>> Indicates the next page on the current document.

PREV
 Indicates the previous document on this site.

SECTION
 Refers to the primary section which is part of the current document.

START
 Indicates the origin or start page of the Web site.

STYLESHEET
 Refers to an external style sheet in which details on the format of the current document can be found.

SUBSECTION
 Refers to a sub-section of this document.

REV
 Similar to REL, this attribute indicates the link back to the previous document. This attributes is rarely used. It does not indicate the jump destination, but the jump source, unlike a normal hyperlink.

ALTERNATE
 Indicates an alternative version of the document. Another language version or an abridged text version, for example.

APPENDIX
 Refers to an appendix of the Web site.

BOOKMARK
 Indicates a special page which you can take as a bookmark into your browser.

CHAPTER
 Refers to the chapter of which the document is part.

CONTENTS
 Points to a table of contents in which all pages present are clearly listed.

COPYRIGHT
 In this page, you will find details about the originator of the document on this site.

GLOSSARY
 In this page, you will find a glossary which explains important concepts.

HELP
 Refers to a help page which helps with the navigation and usage of the site.

INDEX
 Refers to an index which contains all keywords in the Web site.

NEXT
 Indicates the next page on the current document.

PREV
 Indicates the previous document on this site.

SECTION
 Refers to the primary section which is part of the current document.

START
 Indicates the origin or start page of the Web site.

STYLESHEET
> Refers to an external style sheet in which details on the format of the current document can be found.

SUBSECTION
> Refers to a sub-section of this document.

STYLE
> The STYLE attribute can be used to change style settings, in particular the appearance of the element. As the value of the attribute, you apply the corresponding options of a style sheet language (usually CSS).

TARGET
> The TARGET attribute is used to determine the name of a window in which the link is opened. This attribute is used if several windows are open or when a new window with a link needs to be open.

TITLE
> Gives the user further information about the element used by defining a meaningful title with the help of the TITLE command. Navigation in your Web site is made easier for users who are dependent on speech synthesisers.

TYPE
> Indicates the MIME type of the target document. Therefore, the browser is instructed to start a special display model for the content type and to display the document. For example, "text/plain" for normal text or "application/msword" for an MS Word document.

Example

```
<head>
<link rel="next" href="page3.htm">
<link rel="previous" href="page1.htm">
</head>

<head>
<link rev="Index" href="index.htm">
</head>
```

Events

ONCLICK, ONDBLCLICK, ONKEYDOWN, ONKEYPRESS, ONKEYUP, ONMOUSEDOWN, ONMOUSEMOVE, ONMOUSEOVER, ONMOUSEOUT, ONMOUSEUP

XML definition

```
<! ELEMENT LINK>
<!ATTLIST LINK
% attrs;

charset % Charset;#IMPLIED
href % URI;#IMPLIED
```

```
hreflang % LanguageCode;#IMPLIED
type  % ContentType;#IMPLIED
rel   % left type;#IMPLIED
rev   % left type;#IMPLIED
media % MediaDesc;#IMPLIED>
```

Related command
A

LISTING

Display formatted text

Description
With this command, it is possible to display all represented characters and letters in the same size.

Application
The LISTING command displays characters in exactly the same size. This type of representation is used to display the source text of programs.

HTML 4.0 standard
The PRE command is preferred to the LISTING command, because the latter is not an official HTML command.

Example
```
<listing>
Text section in non proportional letters
</listing>
```

Related commands
B
BIG
I
PLAINTEXT
PRE
S
SMALL

STRIKE
TT
U
XMP

Literal

Submitting values to an attribute

Description

As a rule, literals represent the value of an attribute. Through single or double quotation marks, restricted character strings are defined as literal data.

Application

A literal is a character string which is indicated in quotation marks. A literal must not be in the same quotation mark used to restrict (limit) the character string.

An external identifier can also be analysed without looking for a markup tag.

Example

```
<<address type="private">
<address id="123">
<address att="'literal'">
<address att="'literal"'>
```

LONGDESC   <html attribute>

Detailed description of an element

Description

This attribute defines a detailed description of the content of a frame or of an image. This completes the long description which can be indicated through the TITLE attribute.

Application

Indicate an additional detailed description of the element through LONGDESC. The use of this attribute is optional.

Values

A valid value for this attribute is the URI (Uniform Resource Identifier). The construction of a URI is as follows:

```
[protocol]: // [Domain]/[Directory]/[File]
```

Possible details for the used protocol are the following values:

ftp	File Transfer Protocol
http	Hypertext Transfer Protocol
gopher	Gopher Protocol
mailto	Electronic Mail Address
news	USENET News
nntp	USENET News (NNTP-access)
telnet	Reference to interactive sessions
wais	Wide Area Information Server
file	Host-specific file names
prospero	Prospero Directory Service

Example

```
<img
     src="auto.gif"
     title="Audi TT"
     "Audi TT year of construction 98 colours silver"=oldly
     "longdesc=Audi TT year of construction 98, 168 PS, 128.000 km,
silver metallic colour">
```

Accompanying elements

FRAME
IFRAME
IMG

MAP

Definition of an imagemap or a reference-sensitive graphic

Description

With the MAP command you can create a client-sided imagemap. Specific areas in a reference sensitive graphic can be assigned as links.

Application

Indicate the areas of the graphic to be assigned as links within the MAP through the AREA command. Give the imagemap a name through the NAME attribute.

HTML 4.0 standard

ACCESSKEY, ALT, CLASS, COORDS, DIR, HREF, ID, LANG, NOHREF, SHAPE, STYLE, TABINDEX, TITLE

Start tag: required; end tag: required.

Attributes

ONBLUR

The ONBLUR event is triggered when an input element loses its focus. The user must move to the next field with a mouse click or keyboard navigation. Through this event, which checks and reprocesses the entered values, a scriptcan be called up.

ONFOCUS

The ONFOCUS event is triggered when the current element is brought into focus. This happens when the user moves the mouse on to this field and clicks or uses the keyboard to activate the element.

NAME

You can assign a name to the imagemap through this attribute. Never use the same name for more than one imagemap within a document.

Example

```
<map name="location">
<area shape="circle" coords="242, 206, 8" href="place1.htm">
<area shape="circle" coords="198, 290, 8" href="place2.htm">
<area shape="circle" coords="182, 389, 8" href="place3.htm">
<area shape="circle" coords="100, 311, 8" href="place4.htm">
</map>
<img src="map.gif" usemap="#location">
```

Events

ONBLUR, ONFOCUS

Related commands

AREA

MARGINHEIGHT   \<html attribute\>

Distance from the top and bottom margin

Description

The MARGINHEIGHT attribute determines the distance from the top or bottom window margin.

Application

Indicate the distance as a single value. This distance is then automatically used both for the top and the bottom. The use of this attribute is optional.

Values

The value of this attribute indicates a size in pixels, therefore in microdots. Valid values are positive integer numbers. An input of ="100" corresponds to a size of 100 pixels, for example.

Example

```
<frame marginheight="10">
</frame>
```

Accompanying elements

FRAME
IFRAME

MARGINWIDTH   \<html attribute\>

Distance from the left and right margin

Description

The MARGINWIDTH attribute indicates the distance of the window content from the left and right picture margin. The value chosen must be larger than zero. The default distance depends on the browser's settings.

Application

Indicate the distance as a single value. This distance is then automatically adjusted to the same value on the left and right. The use of this attribute is optional.

Values

The value of this attribute indicates a size in pixels, therefore in microdots. Valid values are positive integer numbers. An input of ="100" corresponds to a size of 100 pixels, for example.

Example

```
<frame margin width="10">
</frame>
```

Accompanying elements

FRAME
IFRAME

MARQUEE

Defining text as a scrolling document

Description

The text defined with MARQUEE is shown as scrollable text in the document. Scroll direction, as well as scrolling speed and text behaviour, can be precisely defined.

Application

The text which should scroll through the screen is enclosed within the MARQUEE tags. With this attribute you set parameters for the scrolling text.

HTML 4.0 standard

The command introduced by Microsoft works with the new Netscape generation too, but it is not part of the official HTML standard.

Attributes

ALIGN

This attribute determines the appearance of the text when it is scrolling. The following values are possible:

TOP
> The scrolling text is above the marquee.

MIDDLE
> The scrolling text is in the top centre of the marquee.

BOTTOM
> The text is below the marquee.

ALTERNATE
> The ALTERNATE attribute, which does not contain a value, causes the text to scroll from one side to the other of the screen margin, with a sort of "ping pong" effect.

BEHAVIOR
> Two values are possible for BEHAVIOR:

SLIDE
> The text can be stopped and moved completely into the image.

SCROLL
> This gives a scrollable text. The text scrolls from one side into the image and on the other side it disappears off the screen completely.

BGCOLOR
> The colour of the background is determine with this attribute.

DIRECTION
> You can scroll the text to the left with the value LEFT and to the right with the value RIGHT.

HEIGHT
> With this attribute the height of the marquee is indicated in pixels.

HSPACE
> With this attribute the left and right margins are determined outside the marquee.

LOOP
> Indicates the number of repetitions as the value of LOOP. In LOOP="1" the text is scrolled once through the screen. LOOP="infinite" causes an infinite repetition of the operation.

SCROLLAMOUNT
> The value you submit to this attribute determines the number of pixels the text will move by when scrolling. The smaller the number, the "smoother" the movement of the text.

SCROLLDELAY
> With SCROLLDELAY you can indicate the delay in milliseconds between two scroll steps and the moving through the defined distance. The higher this value, the slower your text will move.

VSPACE
> With this attribute the upper and lower margin is determined outside the marquee.

WIDTH
> With this attribute the width of the marquee is assigned in pixels.

Example

```
<marquee behavior=scroll loop=infinite>

This text is scrolled on the screen...

</marquee>
```

MAXLENGTH   <html attribute>

Determining the maximum input length

Description

You can limit the number of characters the user can enter in text fields. For example, you can define a limit of 7 characters for a postcode field.

Application

With TYPE=TEXT you can create a text field where the user can enter the number of characters determined by the MAXLENGTH attribute. This attribute should not be mistaken for the length of the field, which is shown on the window. This is determined through SIZE. The PASSWORD input type also evaluates this detail, while other fields have the value left without meaning. The use of this attribute is optional.

Values

Valid values for this attribute are integer numbers. The number must contain at least one of the numbers from 0 to 9 (="9").

Example

```
<input
    name="PLZ"
    type="text"
    size="7"
    value="D-"
    maxlength="7">
```

Accompanying element
INPUT

MEDIA   <html attribute>
Assigning output devices

Description
This attribute determines which output devices are best suited for the linked file.

Application
Enter one of the keywords below as the value of this attribute. You can create and indicate special pages for speech synthesisers or printed output.

Values
ALL
> This document is suitable for output on all media.

AURAL
> This document was orginally meant for output from an electronic speech synthesiser.

BRAILLE
> This document is optimised for output from a Braille keyboard.

HANDHELD
> This document is optimised for output on handheld devices (small black and white screens, bitmapped graphics, limited bandwidth).

PRINT
> This document is recommended for output from a printer.

PROJECTION
> Recommended for output from a video player or projector.

SCREEN
> This standard setting states that the document is optimised for the most frequently used output, especially computer screens.

TTY
> Output optimised for terminals or devices with limited display capabilities.

TV
> Especially suitable for output on television-type devices (with lower resolution and lower refresh rate than a computer screen).

Example
```
<link rev="Index" href="index.htm" media="aural">
```

Accompanying elements
LINK
STYLE

MENU
Marking up menu lists

W3C HTML 4.0 ✔

Description
With this command, you can select menu lists.

Application
The MENU command is used to determine menu lists. Short entries, no longer than a line, are contained in these menu lists. This command is not supported in version 4.0 of HTML.

HTML 4.0 standard
ID, CLASS, LANG, DIR, TITLE, STYLE

The use of this command is no longer recommended in the current HTML version; it has been replaced by other commands.

Start tag: required; end tag: required.

Attributes
CLASS

Through the CLASS attribute the element can be assigned to a group (class). Enter one of the selectable class names. These groupings then provide easy access to all related elements so you can change the properties of the elements of a class with the help of cascading style sheets or other languages, or select a value.

DIR

This attribute is required to determine the text direction. This attribute can have the values:

LTR

This value determines the text direction from the left to the right (and is short for "left-to-right"). This is the default direction in the browser.

RTL

If the text must run contrary to the standard direction from the right to the left margin of the screen, choose the value RTL (short for "right-to-left").

ID

Through the ID attribute, the element will provide identification for the document. Using ID, a specific element can be accessed with the help of a script language to select or modify values.

LANG
> This attribute indicates the language of the linked document. This is particularly important in search engines for identification purposes. Use the language codes according to ISO 639, for example "en" for English or "en-us" for American English.

ONCLICK
> This event takes place if you single-click on an element with the mouse. A given script is executed by this action.

ONDBLCLICK
> This event takes place if you double-click on an element with the mouse. A given script is executed by this action.

ONKEYDOWN
> This event takes place if you are in an element and a key is pressed and held down. This action executes a specific script.

ONKEYPRESS
> This event takes place if you are in an element and a key is pressed and released. This action executes a specific script.

ONKEYUP
> This event takes place if you are in an element and a key that was pressed is released. This action executes a specific script.

ONMOUSEDOWN
> This event takes place if you are in an element and a mouse button is clicked and held down. A given script is executed by this action.

ONMOUSEMOVE
> This event takes place if one moves the cursor over an object with the mouse. A given script is executed by this action.

ONMOUSEOUT
> This event takes place if a mouse moves the cursor off an element. This action executes a given script.

ONMOUSEOVER
> This event takes place if the mouse moves the cursor directly over the element (object). A given script is executed by this action.

ONMOUSEUP
> This event takes place if you are in an element and a mouse button that was clicked and held down is released. A given script is executed by this action.

STYLE
> The STYLE attribute can be used to change style settings, in particular the way the element looks. As the value of the attribute, you apply the corresponding options of a style sheet language (usually CSS).

TITLE
> Give the user further information about the element used by defining a meaningful title with the help of the TITLE command. Navigation in your Web site is made easier for users who are dependent on voice response.

Example

```
<menu>
<li>Entry 1 </li>
<li>Entry 2 </li>
<li>Entry 3 </li>
</menu>
```

Events

ONCLICK, ONDBLCLICK, ONKEYDOWN, ONKEYPRESS, ONKEYUP, ONMOUSEDOWN, ONMOUSEMOVE, ONMOUSEOVER, ONMOUSEOUT, ONMOUSEUP

Related commands

D112
LI
OL
UL

META   ☺

Indicating additional information about the document

Description

Through the META tag you can indicate further META information about the content of the SMIL document. The name of the author or copyright specifications are part of this information, for example.

Application

The META command is used within the document head. Two attributes must be submitted to the command. The contents of the META tag must be indicated besides the attribute name which can accept one of the fixed values conerning CONTENT.

Parameter

CONTENT

This attribute can accept any value and contains the content of the META tag: the name of the author or a short description of the site, for example.

NAME

The NAME attribute determines the information provided with CONTENT. NAME can accept the following values:

ABSTRACT

A short description of the content of the site.

AUTHOR
>   The author of the document.

BASE
>   The URL base for all multimedia clips.

COPYRIGHT
>   Information about the originator and copyright.

TITLE
>   A clear and descriptive title for the presentation.

Example

```
<meta name="title" content="HTML/XML Reference"/>
<meta name="author" content="Gunter Wielage"/>
<meta name="copyright" content="(c) 2000 M&T Verlag"/>
<meta name="base" content="http://www.wielage.de"/>

<meta name="title"
      content="contents"
      skip-content="true"/>
```

META

W3C HTML 4.0 ✓

Information concerning an HTML document

Description

With this elementary command the properties of a document which cannot be described by other elements can be specified. The defined instructions are not displayed in the browser but can be interpreted only by search engines or servers.

Application

The META command is used to describe information about an HTML document. With this command, documents can be processed for search engines, for example, by indicating keywords in the content of the document.

HTML 4.0 standard

CONTENT, DIR, HTTP-EQUIV, LANG, NAME, SCHEME

Start tag: required; end tag: not allowed.

Attributes

CONTENT

The use of this attribute is mandatory. With this attribute, instructions concerning the content of a document can be executed. In addition, you must determine the information you wish to provide, using HTTP-EQUIV or NAME.

HTTP-EQUIV

With the HTTP-EQUIV attribute introduced by Netscape, a name can be assigned to the meta information. The NAME attribute also fulfils a similar purpose. Define the information you wish to provide in HTTP-EQUIV. Then indicate the information through the value of the CONTENT attribute.

An official definition of the possible value is not provided by the W3C. The following content types are far more common and can be used:

CONTENT-LANGUAGE

Indicates the language of the HTML document. Use the common definitions of a language of HTML as values for CONTENT ("en" for English, "en-uk" for English/Great Britain, for example).

CONTENT-SCRIPT-TYPE

If the document uses script languages, indicate with this value the predefined script language ("text/vbscript" or "text/javascript").

CONTENT-STYLE-TYPE

Indicates the standard style language. "Use "text/css" for style sheets, for example.

CONTENT-TYPE

Through CONTENT-TYPE you can indicate the type of predefined character set. For example: "text/html; charset=iso-8859-1" for the Western European character set.

EXPIRES

Through EXPIRES you can determine when your page should be updated. If it is stored (cached) in a proxy cache, then this reloads your page after the set period of time and requests the new version of your page.

PRAGMA

Submit the "no-cache" value to CONTENT to prevent your pages from being stored (cached) in the cache memory with CONTENT.

REFRESH

With REFRESH you instruct your browser to automatically load another HTML document after a certain number of seconds. The current document can naturally be transmitted again, for example in live pictures of a video camera. Indicate the number of seconds, followed by the URL of the document to be loaded:

```
CONTENT="10; URL=seite2.html"
```

LANG

Through meta tags you can indicate keywords or a description of your site for a search engine, and in addition through the LANG attribute you can indicate the language of the keywords. In this way you can indicate the same keywords in German and English, for example.

NAME

The NAME attribute is used almost in the same way as the HTTP-EQUIV attribute. They are however different in the way they are processed by the server.

AUTHOR

Through AUTHOR you describe the author of the HTML document.

DATE

With DATE you give the date your document was created.

DESCRIPTION

With DESCRIPTION you give a short description of the page contents.

GENERATOR

Most HTML editors insert this meta tag automatically to indicate the software with which the site has been created. This detail can be helpful particularly when the project has been created by a team, and a number of different individuals or groups may have created different sections.

KEYWORDS

This is one of the most important meta tags. With this tag you provide a keyword to a search engine which will locate your site. Each individual keyword is entered, separated by a comma or a blank space, through CONTENT.

REVISIT-AFTER

You inform a search robot (or "spider"), when it revisits your site, so that the updated information is available at all times.

ROBOTS

The ROBOTS option is especially designed for search engine robots. With this option you instruct the robot whether your site should be indexed in search engines. Through CONTENT two concepts separated by commas are indicated:

INDEX, NOINDEX

Indicate INDEX if the robot should include this page into the index. If you want to prevent a photo from being indexed, maybe because it is confidential company information or you think it is only of internal interest, you indicate NOINDEX. The page will then not be included in the index.

FOLLOW, NOFOLLOW

Through FOLLOW and NOFOLLOW you determine how a spider should handle the links on your page. Using FOLLOW the spider will examine and include all linked pages into the index. With NOFOLLOW the spider interrupts its journey through the links and only takes the current page.

SCHEME

The SCHEME attribute defines the format that should be used to transfer a document.

Example

```
<head>
<title>
 <meta scheme="ISBN" name="identifier"
content="3-8272-548 X" >

<meta http-equiv="content-language" content="de">
<meta http-equiv="content-script-type"
"content="text/vbscript">

<meta http-equiv="content-style-type" content="text/css">

<meta http-equiv="content-type"
content= "text/html; charse = iso-8859-1>

<meta http-equiv="expires"
content="Thu, 24 Jun 1999 12:00:00 GMT",>

<meta http-equiv="pragma" content="no-cache">

<meta http-equiv="refresh"
content="10;UR ="page2.htm >

<meta name="keywords"lang="en"
content="second-hand cars, cars">

<meta name="keywords"lang="en"content="used cars cars">
<meta name="author"content="Gunter Wielage">

<meta name="generator"content="Frontpage 2000">
<meta name="date"content="1999-06-25T12:00:00+00:00">
<meta name="description"lang="en"
content="second-hand car stock exchange">

<meta name="revisit-after"content="30 days">
<meta name="robots" content="index, follow">
</head>
```

XML definition

```
<!ELEMENT META>
<!ATTLIST META
% i18n;
```

```
http-equiv NAME#IMPLIED
name NAME#IMPLIED
content CDATA#REQUIRED
scheme CDATA#IMPLIED>
```

Related commands
HEAD
HTML

METHOD   <html attribute>

Determining an assignment method

Description
You have a choice of two transmission modes if data from a form has to be sent to the server. In these circumstances, you are dependent on the software used by the server when deciding on the settings.

Application
This attribute must be used when assigning the data of a form to the server.

Values
GET

The METHOD=GET setting saves all data from a form in the QUERY_STRING, the standard environmental variables of a WWW server. The contents of these environmental variables are then selected with the help of a CGI program or script.

POST

The METHOD=POST setting causes inputs to be treated as commands In this case, an evaluation program must automatically detect the length of the transmitted data. This usually happens to CONTENT_LENGTH with the help of the standard environmental variables.

Example
```
<form method="post">
<form method="get">
```

Accompanying element
FORM

MULTICOL

Defining multi-column tables

Description
With this command, it is possible to define tables with several columns.

Application
The MULTICOL command is used to define tables split into several columns. Currently, this command is only interpreted by Netscape version 3.0 and is not officially part of HTML.

Attributes
COLS

> The number of columns can be determined with the attribute. The MULTICOL command requires the detail of this attribute.

GUTTER

> This attribute is used to determine the distance between columns in pixels. The default value is 10. By assigning larger or smaller values, the distance between columns is correspondingly increased or reduced.

WIDTH

> This attribute is used to determine the column width in pixels. With the input WIDTH="0", a column is assigned an optimal width. Other permissible values can be integers for the number of pixels per column, or percentage of the screen width.

Example

```
<multicol cols=5 width=300 gutter=10>
There are many ways to present text with titles, tables and pictures
</multicol>
```

Related command
TABLE

Multiple <html attribute>

Allowing multiple selection

Description
The use of this attribute provides users with several choices. It activates multiple selection, which means that several entries can be selected by using the Ctrl key.

Application
This option only can be turned on or off. Further values are not permitted. The use of this attribute is optional. The standard setting permits only the choice of a single entry.

If you intend to create a single-line drop-down field, you must not use multiple selection, which can only be used to accommodate choices in lists of more than one line.

Values
To activate this option, simply use the name of the attribute. You do not need to submit any value to this attribute. If the attribute is not used, then the option remains deactivated. This attribute is not case-sensitive.

Example
```
<select name="Pasta" size=5 multiple>
<option value="P101">Spaghetti Napoli
<option value="P102">Spaghetti Bolognese
<option value="P103">Spaghetti al Pesto
<option value="P104">Spaghetti Mare e Monti
<option value="P105">Spaghetti Aglio e Olio
<option value="P106">Spaghetti Carbonara
</select>
```

Accompanying element
SELECT

Name <html attribute>

Assigning a clear name

Description

With the NAME attribute a name can be assigned to the element. You should ensure that names appear only once in the document. This command is comparable to the ID attribute.

Application

The use of this attribute is optional for some commands (A, APPLET, OBJECT, PARAM). A name is required (button, FRAME, IFRAME, input, MAP, META, SELECT, TEXTAREA) for most elements.

Values

You can submit any string to this attribute as a value. This character string should not start or end with a blank space, if possible. The browser will filter these out if necessary.

Example

```
<input name="name" type="text">
<meta name="keywords"content="Wort1, Wort2, Wort3">
```

Accompanying elements

AA
APPLET
BUTTON
FRAME
IFRAME
INPUT
MAP
META
OBJECT
PARAM
SELECT
TEATAREA

Name

Rules for the definition of separate XML commands

Description
A name or token is a valid name for a markup or an attribute name, for example.

Application
A valid name must begin with a letter. Additional punctuation marks, letters, numbers, underlines and hyphens are permitted.

Colons should be avoided if possible, as well as the letters XML at the beginning of a name (in both upper and lower case).

Example
```
<address>
<chapter_5>
<the_xml_reference_book>
</in-valid__name_123>
```

NOBR

Prevention of line breaks

Description
With this command you can prevent automatic line breaks.

Application
The NOBR command (abbreviation for "Nobreak") is used when you do not wish line breaks to be automatically created. The text is then displayed in a long line which can be viewed with the help of a horizontal scroll bar.

HTML 4.0 standard
This command is not part of the official HTML commands, but it is interpreted by Netscape and Internet Explorer.

Example
```
<nobr>
    This is a line without line breaks.
</nobr>
```

Related command
BR

NOEMBED

Alternative output for multimedia elements

Description
Using the NOEMBED command you can produce output which is displayed if the browser does not know the EMBED command. In this way, a single image or a .GIF animation can be displayed as an alternative to a video file.

Application
The EMBED command is always required in Netscape when there is a video sequence. Of course, any browser (such as Explorer) which does not know this command will not know the NOEMBED command either. But it will display the text or the graphic in the NOEMBED container. The command is then recognised by the Netscape browser and, instead of the NOEMBED area, the video is shown.

Example
```
<noembed>
<img src="animation.gif">
</noembed>
</embed src="video.avi">
```

Related commands
EMBED
NOFRAMES

NOFRAMES

Representation of alternative text for frames

Description
With this command, it is possible to indicate alternative text in case a browser is unable to show frames.

Application

This command is used to identify document sections which cannot contain or represent any frames. Insert the NOFRAMES container in the FRAMESET definition at the end of the document. Browsers which recognise frames will then simply ignore this part.

HTML 4.0 standard

CLASS, DIR, ID, LANG, STYLE, TITLE

Start tag: required; end tag: required.

```
Page Title - Microsoft Internet Explorer by Lycos          _ □ ✕
File   Edit   View   Favorites   Tools   Help

←  ·  →  ·  ⊗  ⟳  ⌂  ⌂  Q  ⊡  ⊘  ⧉·  ⊜  ⊒  ·

  Your browser cannot display frames. We recommend that you use a
  current browser.

  Microsoft Internet Explorer
  Netscape Communicator



Done                                   My Computer
```

A note appears on browsers which do not support frames

Attributes

CLASS

Through the CLASS attribute the element can be assigned to a group (class). Enter one of the selectable class names as a value. These groupings then provide easy access to all related elements so you can change the properties of the elements of a class with the help of cascading style sheets or other languages, or select a value.

DIR

This attribute is necessary to determine the text direction. This attribute can have the values:

LTR

This value determines the text direction from left to right (and is short for "left-to-right"). This is the default direction in the browser.

RTL

> If the text must run contrary to the standard direction from the right to the left margin of the screen, then choose the value RTL (short for "right-to-left").

ID

> Through the ID attribute, the element will provide identification for the document. Using ID, a specific element can be accessed with the help of a script language to select or modify values.

LANG

> This attribute indicates the language of the linked document. This is particularly important in search engines for identification purposes. Use the language codes according to ISO 639, for example "en" for English or "en-us" for American English.

STYLE

> The STYLE attribute is used to determine specific properties in the representation of elements. The style used is defined by the cascading style sheets.

TITLE

> Give the user further information about the element used by defining a meaningful title with the TITLE command. Navigation in your Web site is made easier for users who are dependent on voice response.

Example

```
<html>
<head>
<title>Page with and without frames </title>
</head>
<frameset cols="60%, 40%">
<frame src="left.htm">
<frame src="right.htm">
<noframes>
Unfortunately, your Browser cannot show frames.
We recommend that you use a current browser.
<a href="http://www.microsoft.co.uk">
Microsoft Internet Explorer</a>
<a href="http://www.netscape.co.uk">
Netscape Communicator</a>
</noframes>
</frameset>
```

Related commands

FRAMESET
FRAME
IFRAME

NOHREF   \<html attribute>
Deactivating hyperlink

Description
If this attribute is indicated for a hyperlink, it will be deactivated.

Application
You should already be familiar with this attribute because it has already been used for reference-sensitive graphics. If you want to break a hyperlink, without deleting it, simply deactivate it with this command. The use of this attribute is optional.

Values
To activate this option, use the name of the attribute. You do not need to submit any value to this attribute. If the attribute is not used, then the option remains deactivated. This attribute is not case-sensitive.

Example
```
<area shape=rect coords="1,1,249,49" href="seite3">
<area shape=rect coords="1,51,149,299" nohref>
<area shape=rect coords="251,1,399,399" href="seite2.htm">
>
```

Accompanying element
AREA

NORESIZE   \<html attribute>
Preventing resizing of a frame

Description
This attribute stops users from modifying the size of a frame window.

Application
Users can usually modify the size of frames by dragging them with the mouse. This should usually be left to the discretion of the user. But sometimes it may be useful to apply the NORESIZE attribute. If you use a frame as a menu bar, for example, you could define this as a fixed size. Other areas of the screen can be left as variable sizes. The use of this attribute is optional.

Values

To activate this option, simply use the name of the attribute. You do not need to submit any value to this attribute. If the attribute is not used, then the option remains deactivated. This attribute is not case-sensitive.

Example

```
<html>
<head>
<title>Frame-test</title>
</head>
<frameset cols="40%,150">
<frame src="menu.htm" name="Menu"noresize>
<frame src="title.htm" name="Data">
</frameset>
</html
```

Accompanying element

FRAME

NOSCRIPT

W3C HTML 4.0 ✔

Providing alternative contents

Description

With this command, it is possible to select alternative contents for browsers that are unable to support script.

Application

The NOSCRIPT command is used to select alternative text if the browser used is unable to support script.

HTML 4.0 standard

CLASS, DIR, ID, LANG, STYLE, TITLE

Start tag: required; end tag: required.

Attributes

CLASS

Through the CLASS attribute the element can be assigned to a group (class). Enter one of the free selectable class names as a value. These groupings then provide easy access to all related elements so you can change all properties of the elements in a class with the help of cascading style sheets or other languages, or select a value.

DIR

This attribute is necessary to determine the text direction. This attribute can have the values:

LTR

This value determines the text direction from left to right (and is short for "left-to-right"). This is the default direction in the browser.

RTL

If the text must run contrary to the standard direction from the right to the left margin of the screen, then choose the value RTL (short for "right-to-left").

ID

Through the ID attribute, the element will provide a clear identification for the document. Using ID, a specific element can be accessed with the help of a script language to select or modify values.

LANG

This attribute indicates the language of the linked document. This is particularly important in search engines for identification purposes. Use the language codes according to ISO 639, for example "en" for English or "en-us" for American English.

STYLE

The STYLE attribute is used to determine specific properties in the appearance of elements. Styles used are defined by cascading style sheets.

TITLE

Give the user further information about the element used by defining a meaningful title with the TITLE command. Navigation in your Web site is made easier for users who are dependent on voice response.

Example

```
<head>
<title>Title text</title>
<script language="JavaScript">
<!--
 UserName=window.prompt("your name:","surname");
//-->
</script>
</head>
<body>
```

```
<script language="JavaScript">
<!--
document.write(" <h1> hello "+UserName+" !</h1>");

//-->
</script>
<noscript>
<b>this text is shown, if JavaScript does not work</b>
</noscript>
</body>
</html>
<head>
<title>HTML reference: Reference of HTML commands </title>
further details in the file head
</head>
```

Events

ONCLICK, ONDBLCLICK, ONKEYDOWN, ONKEYPRESS, ONKEYUP, ONMOUSEDOWN, ONMOUSEMOVE, ONMOUSEOVER, ONMOUSEOUT, ONMOUSEUP

Related command

SCRIPT

NOSHADE <html attribute>

Preventing the 3D effect in dividing lines

Description

If you use this attribute, dividing lines between the single sections are represented without 3D effects.

Application

The use of this attribute is optional in connection with the HR command.

Values

To activate this option, simply use the name of the attribute. You do not need to submit any value to this attribute. If the attribute is not used, then the option remains deactivated. This attribute is not case-sensitive.

Example

```
<hr noshade>
<hr size="5" width="65%" align="right" noshade>
```

Accompanying element

HR

NOTATION

Defining data formats

Description

With Notation, data formats are defined which can be referred to when rendering or processing binary data. This command determines the application with which external data, which are not intended for processing by the parser, should be processed. Notation could also determine the application that should be opened when processing data in specific formats.

Application

As well as the SYSTEM option to access applications assigned through an URL, PUBLIC can also be chosen as a keyword for the definition of access.

Currently, the problem with using Notation is that the structure of the submitted value is not yet standardised. You can indicate all possible information about the program name up to the URL path. It is then up to the application to decide how to interpret and handle the values provided. As long as this important interface is not standardised, the use of Notation is always dependent on the application.

Example

```
<! NOTATION htm PUBLIC"-//W3C//DTD HTML 3.2//EN">
<! NOTATION gif87a SYSTEM "GIF">
<! NOTATION doc SYSTEM"winword.exe">
<! NOTATION xsl SYSTEM"Microsoft Excel 9.0">
```

NOWRAP   <html attribute>
Preventing automatic line breaks in tables

Description

This attribute ensures that text is not automatically inserted within cells because of automatic line breaks. If you still want line breaks, you must enter these manually with the BR command.

Application

Enter the NOSHADE attribute in the table cell or in the table head to turn off automatic line breaks. The use of this attribute is optional.

Values

To activate this option, simply use the name of the attribute. You do not need to submit any value to this attribute. If the attribute is not used, then the option remains deactivated. This attribute is not case-sensitive.

Example

```
<table>
<tr>
<td nowrap>Cell 1 </td>
<td nowrap>Cell 2 <br>here continue</td>
</tr>
```

Accompanying elements
TD
TH

OBJECT   <html attribute>
Determining a class for a Java applet

Description

This attribute is used to execute an APPLET class code, depending on the path of a CODEBASE attribute. When it starts an APPLET execution only the start() method and not the init () method will be used.

Application

This attribute can be used as an alternative to the CODE command. These attributes should not be used simultaneously, because this leads to an error. The attribute contains the class names of the applets but not their implementation.

Values

You can submit any string to this attribute as the value. If possible, this character string should not start or end with a blank space. The processin browser will filter these out if necessary.

Accompanying element

APPLET

OBJECT

W3C HTML 4.0 ✔

Inserting objects into an HTML document

Description

With this simple command it is possible to insert every kind of object in to an HTML document.

Application

The OBJECT command is used to insert any object into an HTML document, including graphics, images, controls etc.

HTML 4.0 standard

CLASS, DIR, ID, LANG STYLE, TITLE, DECLARE, CLASSID, CODEBASE, DATA, TYPE, CODE-TYPE, ARCHIVE, STANDBY, HEIGHT, WIDTH, USEMAP, NAME, TABINDEX

Start tag: required; end tag: required.

Attributes

ALIGN
This attribute is responsible for aligning of the object. The following values can be used:
BASELINE
With this value the bottom end of the corresponding object is at the bottom of the surrounding text.

CENTER
> With this value the corresponding object is centred between the right and left margin. The following text is displayed under this.

RIGHT
> The object is right-aligned. If there is text that goes with it, it is displayed at the right of the object.

LEFT
> The object is left-aligned. If there is text that goes with it, it is displayed at the left of the object.

MIDDLE
> If this value is indicated, the object is on the base line of the surrounding text.

TEXTBOTTOM
> If this value is indicated, the bottom of the object is at the bottom of the surrounding text.

TEXTMIDDLE
> If this value is indicated, the middle of the object is in the centre between the base line and the top of the surrounding text.

ARCHIVE
> With this attribute a list of archives is submitted which contains Java classes or other resources. The contents of these lists, which are represented separated by commas, should be loaded before the execution of a Java applet.

BORDER
> If you assign a value which is larger than 0 to this attribute, a browser sets a margin around the embedded object.

CLASS
> This attribute executes an assignment to a class or a group of classes. The use of classes is helpful if elements need to be modified. The change then does not affect a single element, but every element belonging to the class.

CLASSID
> This attribute is used to identify program files (classid = class identifier). Ensure that this detail is in quotation marks. The detail consists of the following solid string: `java:` -followed by the name `.class-file` (and the executable Java program file).

CODEBASE
> This attribute identifies the code base of an object. Sometimes, the instruction `codebase=` may be also required if parts of a Java applet need to be reloaded by a special Internet server.

CODETYPE
> With the help of this attribute, the media type of the corresponding object is determined.

DATA
> With this attribute, the location of the object's data is identified.

DECLARE
With this attribute, an object is changed into a definition. This attribute is submitted to the application if you wish to create cross-references to an object or if the object is a parameter of another object.

DIR
This attribute is necessary to determine the text direction. This attribute can have the values:

LTR
This value determines the text direction from left to right (and is short for "left-to-right"). This is the default direction in the browser.

RTL
If the text must run contrary to the standard direction from the right to the left margin of the screen, then choose the value RTL (short for "right-to-left").

HEIGHT
With this attribute the height of an object to be linked is indicated in pixels.

HSPACE
With this attribute, the amount of space to be inserted to the left and right of the element is determined, which is the space between the text and the object.

ID
This attribute can assign a unique identifier to a highlighted element.

LANG
This attribute indicates the language of the linked document. This is particularly important in search engines for identification purposes. Use the language codes according to ISO 639, for example "en" for English or "en-us" for American English..

ONCLICK
This event takes place if you single-click on an element with the mouse. A given script is executed by this action.

ONDBLCLICK
This event takes place if you double-click on an element with the mouse. A given script is executed by this action.

ONKEYDOWN
This event takes place if you are in an element and a key is pressed and held down. This action executes a specific script.

ONKEYPRESS
This event takes place if you are in an element and a key is pressed and released. This action executes a specific script.

ONKEYUP
This event takes place if you are in an element and a key that was pressed is released. This action executes a specific script.

ONMOUSEDOWN
This event takes place if you are in an element and a mouse button is clicked and held down. A given script is executed by this action.

ONMOUSEMOVE

This event takes place if one moves the cursor over an object with the mouse. A given script is executed by this action.

ONMOUSEOUT

This event takes place if a mouse moves the cursor off an element. This action executes a given script.

ONMOUSEOVER

This event takes place if the mouse moves the cursor directly over the element (object). A given script is executed by this action.

ONMOUSEUP

This event takes place if you are in an element and a mouse button that was clicked and held down is released. A given script is executed by this action.

STANDBY

This attribute provides the message to be displayed while the object is uploaded.

STYLE

The STYLE attribute is used to determine specific properties in the appearance of elements. Styles used are defined by cascading style sheets.

TABINDEX

This attribute assigns a command to the position of an element by using positive or negative integers. Elements which are provided with this attribute can be selected with the tab key one after the other.

TYPE

With this attribute, the internet media type is indicated for the relevant object.

USEMAP

This attribute determines the imagemap to be used in connection with an object.

VSPACE

This attribute determines the amount of space to be inserted at the top and bottom of the element between the text and the object.

WIDTH

This attribute determines the width of an object to be embedded in pixels.

TITLE

Give the user further information about the element usedby defining a meaningful title with the help of the TITLE command. Navigation in your Web site is made easier for users who are dependent on voice response.

Example

```
<object classid="java:animation" "codebase=../java/"
code type = "application/java vm">
<param name=animation_text
value="Here there is an animated text">
</object>
```

XML definition

```
<! ELEMENT OBJECT - - (PARAM | %flow;)*>
<!ATTLIST OBJECT
% attrs;

classid      %URI;           #IMPLIED
CODEBASE     %URI;           #IMPLIED
data         %URI;           #IMPLIED
type         %ContentType;   #IMPLIED
code type    %ContentType;   #IMPLIED
archives     %URI;           #IMPLIED
standby      %text;          #IMPLIED
height       %Length;        #IMPLIED
width        %Length;        #IMPLIED
usemap       %URI;           #IMPLIED
name         CDATA           #IMPLIED
tabindex     NUMBER          #IMPLIED
% reserved;>
```

Related commands

EMBED

IMG

OL

Indicating ordered or numbered lists

Description

With this command, you can indicate numbered lists.

Application

The OL command ("ordered list") is used if lists are to be numbered. An enumeration character is then placed at the beginning of each line in the list.

HTML 4.0 standard

CLASS, COMPACT, DIR, ID, LANG, START, STYLE, TITLE, TYPE, VALUE

Start tag: required; end tag: required.

Attributes

CLASS

Through the CLASS attribute the element can be assigned to a group (class). Enter one of the free selectable class names as a value. These groupings then provide easy access to all related elements so you can change the properties of the elements of a class with the help of cascading style sheets or other languages, or select a value.

COMPACT

If this value is set, the browser tries to represent this enumeration in a compact form. The interpretation of this option depends on the browser used.

DIR

This attribute is necessary to determine the text direction. This attribute can have the values:

LTR

This value determines the text direction from left to right (and is short for "left-to-right"). This is the default direction in the browser.

RTL

If the text must run contrary to the standard direction from the right to the left margin of the screen, then choose the value RTL (short for "right-to-left").

ID

Through the ID attribute, the element will provide identification for the document. Using ID, a specific element can be accessed with the help of a script language to select or modify values.

LANG

This attribute indicates the language of the linked document. This is particularly important in search engines for identification purposes. Use the language codes according to ISO 639, for example "en" for English or "en-us" for American English.

TYPE

You can set an enumeration character before every element with this attribute within an OL (Ordered List). The following results are valid:

1

Arabic numbers (1, 2, 3, ...); this value is the default.

a

Lower case alpha-numerical (a, b, c ...).

A

Upper case alpha-numerical (A, B, C, ...).

i

Lower case Roman numerals (I, ii, iii, iv, ...).

I

Upper case Roman numerals (I, II, III, IV, ...).

START
> This attribute can only be used in connection with a numbered list. You can indicate a start value and start the list with the value 100, for example.

STYLE
> The STYLE attribute can be used to change style settings, in particular the appearance of the element. As the value of the attribute, you apply the corresponding options of a style sheet language (usually CSS).

TITLE
> Give the user further information about the element used by defining a meaningful title with the help of the TITLE command. Navigation in your Web site is made easier for users who are dependent on speech synthesizers.

Example

```
<ol start="10" type="I">
<li>first</li>
<li value="3">second</li>
<li>third</li>
</ol>
```

Events

ONCLICK, ONDBLCLICK, ONKEYDOWN, ONKEYPRESS, ONKEYUP, ONMOUSEDOWN, ONMOUSEMOVE, ONMOUSEOVER, ONMOUSEOUT, ONMOUSEUP

XML definition

```
<! ELEMENT OL - - (LI)+>
<! ATTLIST OL %attrs;>
```

Related commands

LI
UL

OPTGROUP

Defining menu structures

Description

This command is used to create a structure for groups which have the same content.

Application

The OPTGROUP command creates a logical order for group elements. This command is useful when a user must select from a large number of options. The OPTGROUP element must be defined within the SELECT command.

HTML 4.0 standard

CLASS, DISABLED, DIR, ID, LABEL, LANG, NAME, STYLE, TITLE

Start tag: required; end tag: required.

Attributes

DISABLED

With this attribute, you can deactivate buttons which are part of the element.

LABEL

This attribute creates a label in the form of a character string for the selected entry groups.

Example

```
<select name="location" size=3>
     <optgroup label="North Region">
     <option label="North 1">Sheffield
     <option label="North 2">Liverpool
     <option label="North 3">Manchester
     </optgroup>
     <optgroup label="South Region">
     <option label="South 1">Brighton
     <option label="South 2">London
     <option label="South 3">Dover
     </optgroup>
     <optgroup label="West Region">
     <option label="West 1">Bristol
     <option label="West 2">Cardiff
     <option label="West 3">Preston
     </optgroup>
</select>
```

Events

ONBLUR, ONCHANGE, ONFOCUS

XML definition

```
<! ELEMENT OPTGROUP - - (OPTION)+>
<!ATTLIST OPTGROUP
% attrs;
```

```
disabled (disabled) # IMPLIED
label      % text;  # REQUIRED>
```

Related commands
FORM
INPUT
OPTION
SELECT

OPTION

Indicating choices

Description
This command is used to select choices within data, which have been selected with SELECT.

Application
With the OPTION markup users can check off and select one or more options from a choice list. The OPTION command is used to determine the individual entries in the choice list.

HTML 4.0 standard
CLASS, DIR, DISABLED, ID, LABEL, LANG, MULTIPLE, NAME, SIZE, STYLE, TABINDEX, TITLE

Start tag: required; end tag: optional.

Attributes
CLASS
> Through the CLASS attribute the element can be assigned to a group (class). Enter one of the free selectable class names as the value. These groupings provide easy access to all related elements so you can change the properties of the elements of a class with the help of cascading style sheets or other languages, or select a value.

DIR
> This attribute is necessary to determine the text direction. This attribute can have the values:
>
> LTR
>> This value determines the text direction from left to right (and is short for "left-to-right"). This is the default direction in the browser.

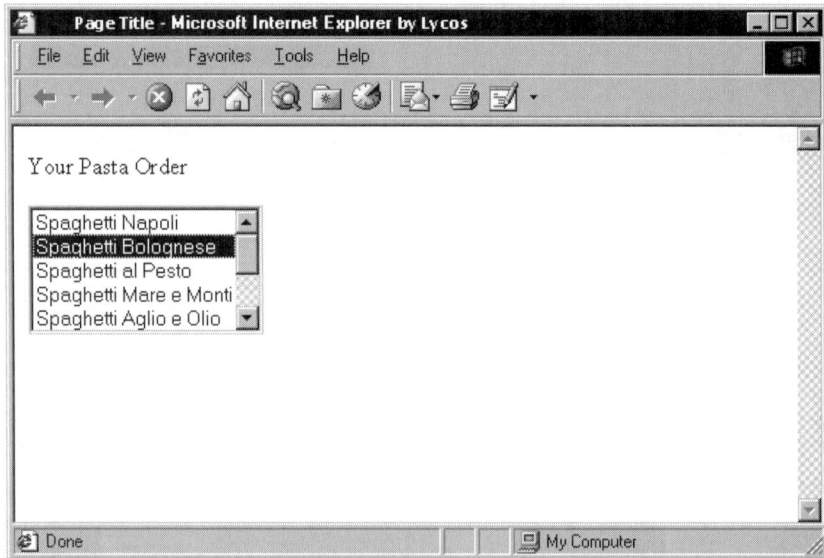

Choice list created with SELECT and OPTION

RTL

> If the text must run contrary to the standard direction from the right to the left margin of the screen, then choose the value RTL (short for "right-to-left").

DISABLED

> The use of this attribute deactivates the relating button and prevents an input.

ID

> ID identifies the document. Using ID, a specific element can be accessed with the help of a script language to select or modify values.

LABEL

> This attribute allows you to indicate a short label for an option. The browser can display this label as additional information.

LANG

> This attribute indicates the language of the linked document. This is particularly important in search engines for identification purposes. Use the language codes according to ISO 639, for exampl "en" for English or "en-us" for American English.

MULTIPLE

> The use of this attribute provides a user with several choices. It activates the multiple selection, which means several entries can be selected by pressing the Ctrl key. The standard setting permits only the choice of a single entry.

NAME

> This attribute assigns a name to an option display.

ONBLUR

The ONBLUR event is triggered when an input element loses focus. The user has moved to the next field with a mouse click or keyboard. This event can call a script which checks and reprocesses the entered values.

ONCHANGE

This event takes place if the contents of the entry field are changed. This action executes a given script.

ONCLICK

This event takes place if you single-click on an element with the mouse. A given script is executed by this action.

ONDBLCLICK

This event takes place if you double-click on an element with the mouse. A given script is executed by this action.

ONKEYDOWN

This event takes place if you are in an element and a key is pressed and held down. This action executes a specific script.

ONKEYPRESS

This event takes place if you are in an element and a key is pressed and released. This action executes a specific script.

ONKEYUP

This event takes place if you are in an element and a key that was pressed is released. This action executes a specific script.

ONMOUSEDOWN

This event takes place if you are in an element and a mouse button is clicked and held down. A given script is executed by this action.

ONMOUSEMOVE

This event takes place if one moves the cursor over an object with the mouse. A given script is executed by this action.

ONMOUSEOUT

This event takes place if a mouse moves the cursor off an element. This action executes a given script.

ONMOUSEOVER

This event takes place if the mouse moves the cursor directly over the element (object). A given script is executed by this action.

ONMOUSEUP

This event takes place if you are in an element and a mouse button that was clicked and held down is released. A given script is executed by this action.

ONFOCUS

The ONFOCUS event is triggered when the current element is focused on. If the user goes on this field with a mouse click or the keyboard, the element is activated.

SELECTED

This attribute sets the option as preselected.

SIZE
> With this attribute you determine the number of lines containing choices, to be provided for the user.

STYLE
> The STYLE attribute is used to determine specific properties in the appearance of labelled elements. Styles used are defined by cascading style sheets.

TABINDEX
> This attribute assigns an order position to an element by using positive or negative integers. Elements provided with this attribute can be selected one after the other with the Tab key.

TITLE
> With this attribute, the selected elements receives additional information. This information is displayed in a pop-up window in many browsers if the mouse pointer is on the element.

VALUE
> This attribute assigns a value to every choice. You should use a different value for each choice.

Example

```
<p>Your pasta order: </p>

<select name="Pasta" size=5>
<option value="P101">Spaghetti Napoli
<option value="P102">Spaghetti Bolognese
<option value="P103">Spaghetti al Pesto
<option value="P104">Spaghetti Mare e Monti
<option value="P105">Spaghetti Aglio e Olio
<option value="P106">Spaghetti Carbonara
<option value="P107">Spaghetti  Alfredo
<option value="P108">Spaghetti  Diavolo
<option value="P109">Spaghetti  Nettuno
</select>
```

Events

ONBLUR, ONCHANGE, ONCLICK, ONDBLCLICK, ONFOCUS, ONKEYDOWN, ONKEYPRESS, ONKEYUP, ONMOUSEDOWN, ONMOUSEMOVE, ONMOUSEOVER, ONMOUSEOUT, ONMOUSEUP

XML definition

```
<! ELEMENT OPTION - O (#PCDATA)>
<!ATTLIST OPTION
% attrs;

selected (selected) # IMPLIED
disabled (disabled) # IMPLIED
```

```
label      % text;  # IMPLIED
value CDATA # IMPLIED>
```

Related commands
FORM
INPUT
OPTION

P
Defining paragraphs

Description
This command defines paragraphs within an HTML document.

Application
The P command is used to select sections of an HTML text. This tag is usually applied to text. If you want to avoid inserting a blank line in a paragraph defined with the P command, simply insert the BR command.

HTML 4.0 standard
CLASS, DIR, ID, LANG, STYLE, TITLE

Start tag: required; end tag: optional.

Attributes
ALIGN

This attribute is responsible for determining the alignment of paragraphs.

LEFT

Paragraphs are aligned to the left.

RIGHT

Paragraphs are aligned to the right.

CENTER

Paragraphs are centre-aligned.

CLASS

Through the CLASS attribute the element can be assigned to a group (class). Enter one of the free selectable class names as a value. These groupings then provide easy access to all related elements so you can change all properties of the elements of a class with the help of cascading style sheets or other languages, or select a value.

DIR

This attribute is necessary to determine the text direction. This attribute can have the values:

LTR

This value determines the text direction from left to right (and is short for "left-to-right"). This is the default direction in the browser.

RTL

If the text must run contrary to the standard direction from the right to the left margin of the screen, then choose the value RTL (short for "right-to-left").

ID

Through the ID attribute, the element will provide identification for the document. Using ID, a specific element can be accessed with the help of a script language to select or modify values.

LANG

This attribute indicates the language of the linked document. This is particularly important in search engines for identification purposes. Use the language codes according to ISO 639, for example "en" for English or "en-us" for American English

ONCLICK

This event takes place if you single-click on an element with the mouse. A given script is executed by this action.

ONDBLCLICK

This event takes place if you double-click on an element with the mouse. A given script is executed by this action.

ONKEYDOWN

This event takes place if you are in an element and a key is pressed and held down. This action executes a specific script.

ONKEYPRESS

This event takes place if you are in an element and a key is pressed and released. This action executes a specific script.

ONKEYUP

This event takes place if you are in an element and a key that was pressed is released. This action executes a specific script.

ONMOUSEDOWN

This event takes place if you are in an element and a mouse button is clicked and held down. A given script is executed by this action.

ONMOUSEMOVE

This event takes place if one moves the cursor over an object with the mouse. A given script is executed by this action.

ONMOUSEOUT

This event takes place if a mouse moves the cursor off an element. This action executes a given script.

ONMOUSEOVER

This event takes place if the mouse moves the cursor directly over the element (object). A given script is executed by this action.

ONMOUSEUP

This event takes place if you are in an element and a mouse button that was clicked and held down is released. A given script is executed by this action.

STYLE

The STYLE attribute is used to determine specific properties in the appearance of labelled elements. Styles used are defined by cascading style sheets.

TITLE

Through this attribute, elements are defined with additional information. This information is displayed by many browsers in pop up windows, when the mouse pointer moves on the element.

Example

```
<p align="right"></p> The first paragraph ends here.
<p align="left">The next paragraph starts here. </p>
```

Events

ONCLICK, ONDBLCLICK, ONKEYDOWN, ONKEYPRESS, ONKEYUP, ONMOUSEDOWN, ONMOUSEMOVE, ONMOUSEOVER, ONMOUSEOUT, ONMOUSEUP

XML definition

```
<! ELEMENT P - O (%inline;)* -- paragraph -->
<! ATTLIST P %attrs;>
```

Related commands

BR
DIV

padding-bottom

CASCADING
STYLE SHEETS

Space between text and margin

Description

This command indicates the space between the margin of the element and the contents of the element in the bottom border. (Padding separates the text from the border.)

Parameter

Indicate the space required as a numerical value.

Example

```
<style type="text/css">
h1, h2 {padding-bottom:5}
h3, h4 {padding-bottom:9}
</style>

<div style="padding-bottom:8">
</div>
```

padding-left

Space between text and margin

Description

This command indicates the space between the margin of the element and the contents of the element on the left border.

Parameter

Indicate the space required as a numerical value.

Example

```
<style type="text/css">

h1, h2 {padding-left:5}
h3, h4 {padding-left:9}
</style>

<div style="padding-left:8">
</div>
```

padding-right

Space between text and margin

Description

This command indicates the space between the margin of the element and the contents of the element on the right border.

Parameter

Indicate the space required as a numerical value.

Example

```
<style type="text/css">
h1, h2 {padding-right:5}
h3, h4 {padding-right:9}
</style>

<div style="padding-right:8">
</div>
```

padding-top

Space between text and margin

Description

This command indicates the space between the margin of the element and the contents of the element on the top border,

Parameter

Indicate the space required as a numerical value.

Example

```
<style type="text/css">
h1, h2 {padding-top:5}
h3, h4 {padding-top:9}
</style>

<div style="padding-top:8">
</div>
```

PAR

Summarising sequences into a group

Description

By summarising several multimedia sequences into a group, you can ensure that they are played in parallel.

Application

No further attributes for the basic function of summarising to a group are necessary.

Parameter

abstract
> This attribute indicates a short description for the group.

author
> The author of the group is indicated by this attribute.

begin
> Indicates the reproduction time. You can use the definitions h, min, s or ms as units.

copyright
> Information about the originator and the copyright can be submitted as a value of this attribute.

dur
> Indicates the complete duration of a group. You can use the definitions h, min, s or ms as units.

end
> Indicates the end of the group. This value is the opposite of the attribute begin. You can use the definitions h, min, s or ms as units. Do not use end together with endsync.

endsync
> Indicates the end of the complete group with respect to the processing of the single clips. Three values are valid for this attribute:
>
> first
> > As soon as the first clip has ended, all other sequences will also end.
>
> last
> > The complete sequence is ended only when the last clip has been displayed in full.
>
> id
> > The complete group ends if the clip specified has been displayed in full.

id
> Through the ID attribute, the element will provide identification for the document. Using ID, other elements of this area can be accessed.

repeat
> The complete group is repeated as many times as specified.

title
> Gives the complete group a title with a short description of the content.

Example

```
<par repeat="2" begin="5s">
    <video src="video.avi">
```

```
          <textstream id="text"src="subtitle.rt">
</par>
```

PARAM

Submitting a set of values

Description
With this command, it is possible to submit a set of values to Java applets.

Application
The PARAM command (abbreviation for parameter) submits parameters to applets and objects. A PARAM element is required for any submitted parameter.

HTML 4.0 standard
ID, NAME, VALUE, VALUETYPE, TYPE

Start tag: required; end tag: not allowed.

Attributes
ID
   This attribute can assign a unique identifier to a defined element.
NAME
   This attribute determines the name of the parameter to be submitted.
TYPE
   This attribute specifies the content type of the data source. This option is valid only if the setting VALUETYP setting is chosen with the REF setting.
VALUE
   This attribute provides the value of a corresponding parameter to the content.
VALUETYPE
   The VALUETYPE attribute identifies the data submitted in the VALUE. Three valid values are available:
   DATA
      This data type causes the data submitted in VALUE to be submitted to the applet as pure text information. This is the default value.
   REF
      The value, submitted in the VALUE, is a reference to a URI. This indicates a storage location where the runtime variables are stored.
   OBJECT
      The value in VALUE refers to a connected OBJECT declaration in the same document. Indicate the corresponding ID of the object as the reference.

Example

```
<applet code="AnimText.class"
<width="150"height="100"hspace="500">
<param name="text"value="Animating text">
<param name="type"value="wave">
<param name="bgcolor"value="yellow">
<param name="fgcolor"value="red">
<param name="style"value="bold">
<param name="min"value="10">
<param name="max"value="40">
</applet>
```

XML definition

```
<!ELEMENT PARAM>
<!ATTLIST PARAM
id    ID                # IMPLIED
name CDATA # REQUIRED
value CDATA # IMPLIED
type % ContentType;  # IMPLIED>
```

Related commands

APPLET

OBJECT

Parameter entity

Entities in DTD use

Description

While general entities are defined in DTD and only enter into action in the XML document in connection with the parser, parameter entities only concern DTD. In the parsing process, these entities are replaced by the substitution text within DTD.

Application

The difference between general entities and parameter entities is in the per cent sign ("%") found in the syntax. While the per cent sign should be separated by blank spaces in the entity definition, the entity is called by the name or the abbreviation of the entities precceded by a per cent sign.

The same element lists regularly appear in DTD, therefore they can all be defined as entities, so they will always be called.

Example

```
<!ENTITY%structure"chapter|paragraph|sentence">
```

The call of the parameter entity is then carried out in the document with a preceding percentage sign and a final semi-colon. The percentage sign has no special meaning outside DTD, also used in XML documents.

```
%structure;
```

In practice, such parameter entities could always be used if the same character strings are frequently used. The following listing

```
<!ELEMENT DOCUMENT(chapter|paragraph|sentence)*>
```

can easily be replaced by an entity in the DTD:

```
<! ELEMENT DOCUMENT (%structure;)*>
```

Or also as an addition to other elements:

```
<! ELEMENT DOCUMENT (book|%structure;|word)*>
```

PLAINTEXT

Displaying preformatted text

Description

With this command, it is possible to display all characters and letters in the same size.

Application

The PLAINTEXT command enables characters to be displayed in exactly the same size. This way of representing characters is used to represent flow text. Instead of this command, use the PRE command, since LISTING is not defined in version 4.0 of HTML.

Example

```
<plaintext>
Text paragraph not in proportional font
</plaintext>
```

Related commands

B
BIG
I
LISTING
PRE
S
SMALL
STRIKE
TT
U
XMP

PRE

W3C HTML 4.0

Displaying preformatted text

Description

With this command, it is possible to display all represented characters and letters in the same size.

Application

The PRE command enables characters to be displayed in exactly the same size. This is useful for displaying tables, for example, where it is important to be able to retain a standard appearance. Blank spaces are not removed, which is also important in some cases.

HTML 4.0 standard

CLASS, DIR, ID, LANG, STYLE, TITLE, WIDTH

Start tag: required; end tag: required.

Attributes

CLASS

Through the CLASS attribute the element can be assigned to a group (class). Enter one of the free selectable class names as a value. These groupings then provide easy access to all related elements so you can change all the properties of the elements of a class with the help of cascading style sheets or other languages, or select a value.

DIR

This attribute is required to determine the text direction. This attribute can have the values:

LTR

This value determines the text direction from left to right (and is short for "keft-to-right"). This is the default direction in the browser:

RTL

If the text must run contrary to the standard direction from the right to the left margin of the screen, then choose the value RTL (short for "right-to-left").

ID

Through the ID attribute, the element will provide identification for the document. Using ID, a specific element can be accessed with the help of a script language to select or modify values.

LANG

This attribute indicates the language of the linked document. This is particularly important in search engines for identification purposes. Use the language codes according to ISO 639, for example "en" for English or "en-us" for American English.

ONCLICK

This event takes place if you single-click on an element with the mouse. A given script is executed by this action.

ONDBLCLICK

This event takes place if you double-click on an element with the mouse. A given script is executed by this action.

ONKEYDOWN

This event takes place if you are in an element and a key is pressed and held down. This action executes a specific script.

ONKEYPRESS

This event takes place if you are in an element and a key is pressed and released. This action executes a specific script.

ONKEYUP

This event takes place if you are in an element and a key that was pressed is released. This action executes a specific script.

ONMOUSEDOWN

This event takes place if you are in an element and a mouse button is clicked and held down. A given script is executed by this action.

ONMOUSEMOVE

This event takes place if one moves the cursor over an object with the mouse. A given script is executed by this action.

ONMOUSEOUT

This event takes place if a mouse moves the cursor off an element. This action executes a given script.

ONMOUSEOVER
> This event takes place if the mouse moves the cursor directly over the element (object). A given script is executed by this action.

ONMOUSEUP
> This event takes place if you are in the described element and a mouse button that was clicked and held down is released. A given script is executed by this action.

STYLE
> The STYLE attribute can be used to change style settings, in particular the appearance of an element. As the value of the attribute, you apply the options of a style sheet language (usually CSS).

TITLE
> Give the user further information about the element used by defining a meaningful title with the help of the command TITLE. Navigation in your Web site is made easier for users who are dependent on speech synthesizers.

WIDTH
> With this attribute you can determine the line width. The width is not currently interpreted by browsers, and the use of this attribute is no longer recommended in HTML 4.0.

Example

```
<pre>
FUNCTION Easter calculation (year: INTEGER): INTEGER;

VAR a,b, c, d, e, f, g, h, i, k, l, m: INTEGER;

BEGIN
a   :=  year MOD 19;
b   :=  year DIV 100;
c   :=  year MOD 100;
d   :=  b DIV 4;
e   :=  b MOD 4;
f   :=  ( b + 8 ) DIV 25;
g   :=  ( b  f + 1 ) DIV 3;
h   :=  ( 19 * a + b  d  g + 15 ) MOD 30;
i   :=  c DIV 4;
k   :=  c MOD 4;
l   :=  ( 32 + 2 * e + 2 * i  h  k ) MOD 7;
m   :=  ( a + 11 * h + 22 * l ) DIV 451;
Easter :=  h + l  7 * m + 22;
END{FUNC};
</pre>
```

Events

ONCLICK, ONDBLCLICK, ONKEYDOWN, ONKEYPRESS, ONKEYUP, ONMOUSEDOWN, ONMOUSEMOVE, ONMOUSEOVER, ONMOUSEOUT, ONMOUSEUP

XML definition

```
<!ENTITY % pre.exclusion "IMG|OBJECT|BIG|SMALL|SUB|SUP">

<!ELEMENT PRE - - (%inline;)* -(%pre.exclusion;)>
<!ATTLIST PRE
% attrs;>
```

Related commands

B
BIG
I
LISTING
PLAINTEXT
S
SMALL
STRIKE
TT
U
XMP

Processing Instruction (PI)

Commands executed by the parser

Description

Processing instructions are always passed directly on to the application.

Application

Names which start with xml are not allowed to process instructions. They are already preallocated for typical XML PIs.

When a tag in a typical XML document is opened and closed with a question mark ("<?... ?>", this is the structure of a processing instruction or short PI. Processing instructions which start with the XML keyword are reserved for the XML standard definition. This processing instruction informs the parser that it must be active and a DTD file must be loaded, for example.

Example

```
<?xml version="1.0"?>
<?xml version="1.0" standalone="yes"?>
<?xml encoding="UTF-8"?>
```

PROFILE   <html attribute>
Indicating the source of a META data profile

Description

With the PROFILE attribute, one or more external files can be described. In these files, which are separated by blank spaces, META information is given on the corresponding files. This attribute is not yet supported by most browsers. The implementation of the function is still at discussion stage.

Application

The use of this attribute is optional and is not yet supported. As an alternative, you can use the META tag, which is popular.

Values

A valid value for this attribute is a URI (Uniform Resource Identifier). The construction of a URI is as follows:

```
[protocol]://[domain]/[directory]/[file]
```

Valid details for the used protocol are the following values:

ftp	File Transfer Protocol
http	Hypertext Transfer Protocol
gopher	Gopher Protocol
mailto	Electronic Mail Address
news	USENET News
nntp	USENET News (NNTP-access)
telnet	Reference to interactive sessions
wais	Wide Area Information Server
file	Host-specific file names
prospero	Prospero Directory Service

Example
```
<head profile="http://www.pott-it.de/profiles/meta">
```

Accompanying element
HEAD

PROLOG

Construction of a XML document

Description

The document consists of three data divisions, in which the use of the first two parts is optional. The processing instruction and the document type definition are in the Prolog, which is the introduction of the XML document. The content of the file then follows.

Every valid XML document must contain a prolog at the beginning of the source file.

Application

In the following example, we are going to show you the overall basic framework, consisting of three parts, the processing instruction, document type definition and content of the document. The first two parts are in the prolog.

Processing Instruction
`<?xml version="1.0"standalone="no"encoding="ISO-8859-1"?>`

Document Type Definition
`<!DOCTYPE Address SYSTEM "Address.dtd">`

Content of the document

`<ADDRESS>`
`[...]`
`</ADDRESS>`

Example
```
<?xml version="1.0"?>
<?xml version="1.0" encoding="UTF-16"?>
```

PROMPT <html attribute>
Defining input fields for search forms

Description
With this attribute, predefined search text can be amended when searching for specific concepts. The user sees a prompt when the search function is started in the Browser.

Application
Submit the text to this attribute, with which the visitor is invited to input a search string. Most browsers do not support this feature. The use of this attribute is optional. It is recommended that the search input is executed through input forms.

Values
You can submit any string to this attribute as the value. If possible, this character string should not start or end with a blank space. The processing browser will filter these out if necessary.

Example
```
<isindex promt="Please insert a search string:">

<form>
Please enter a search string:

<input type="text">
</form>
```

Accompanying element
ISINDEX

Q
Indicating short quotations

Description
Quotations are marked with this command. If the original quotation needs to be accessed on the World Wide Web, you should provide the quotation with a hyperlink.

Application

The Q command is used to identify quotes from other media. Unlike the BLOCKQUOTA command, the Q command should be used to indicate short quotations such as single sentences or words.

HTML 4.0 standard

CLASS, CITE, DIR, ID, LANG, STYLE, TITLE

Start tag: required; end tag: required.

Attributes

CITE

    With this attribute you may indicate a source document for the used quotation.

CLASS

    Through the CLASS attribute the element can be assigned to a group (class). Enter one of the free selectable class names as a value. These groupings then provide easy access to all related elements so you can change the properties of the elements of a class with the help of cascading style sheets or other languages or select a value.

DIR

    This attribute is necessary to determine the text direction. This attribute can have the values:

    LTR

        This value determines the text direction from left to right (and is short for "left-to-right"). This is the default direction in the browser.

    RTL

        If the text must run contrary to the standard direction from the right to the left margin of the screen, choose the value RTL (short for "right-to-left").

ID

    Through the ID attribute, the element will provide identification for the document. Using ID, a specific element can be accessed with the help of a script language to select or modify values.

LANG

    This attribute indicates the language of the linked document. This is particularly important in search engines for identification purposes. Use the language codes according to ISO 639, for example "en" for English or "en-us" for American English.

ONCLICK

    This event takes place if you single-click on an element with the mouse. A given script is executed by this action.

ONDBLCLICK

    This event takes place if you double-click on an element with the mouse. A given script is executed by this action.

ONKEYDOWN

> This event takes place if you are in an element and a key is pressed and held down. This action executes a specific script.

ONKEYPRESS

> This event takes place if you are in an element and a key is pressed and released. This action executes a specific script.

ONKEYUP

> This event takes place if you are in an element and a key that was pressed is released. This action executes a specific script.

ONMOUSEDOWN

> This event takes place if you are in an element and a mouse button is clicked and held down. A given script is executed by this action.

ONMOUSEMOVE

> This event takes place if one moves the cursor over an object with the mouse. A given script is executed by this action.

ONMOUSEOUT

> This event takes place if a mouse moves the cursor off an element. This action executes a given script.

ONMOUSEOVER

> This event takes place if the mouse moves the cursor directly over the element (object). A given script is executed by this action.

ONMOUSEUP

> This event takes place if you are in an element and a mouse button that was clicked and held down is released. A given script is executed by this action.

STYLE

> The STYLE attribute can be used to change style settings, in particular the appearance of the element. As the value of the attribute, you apply the corresponding options of a style sheet language (usually CSS).

TITLE

> Give the user further information about the element used by defining a meaningful title with the help of the title command. Navigation in your Web site is made easier for users who are dependent on speech synthesisers.

Example

```
A <q>quotation</q> formatted with the Q command
```

Events

```
ONCLICK, ONDBLCLICK, ONKEYDOWN, ONKEYPRESS, ONKEYUP, ONMOUSEDOWN,
ONMOUSEMOVE, ONMOUSEOVER, ONMOUSEOUT, ONMOUSEUP
```

XML definition

```
<! ELEMENT Q - - (%inline;)*>
<!ATTLIST Q
% attrs;
```

```
cite % URI;   # IMPLIED>
```

Related commands

ACRONYM
CODE
DFN
EM
KBD
SAMP
STRONG
Q
VAR

READONLY   <html attribute>

Identifying entry fields as read-only

Description

This attribute marks an entry field as read-only. Other alterations, such as describing the entry
field, are not allowed, but the element can be selected with the Tab key.

Application

This attribute can occur, for example, if some fields of a form have been
deactivated. In addition, write-protected fields could be used for output from data
of a JavaScript program. The use of this attribute is optional.

Values

To activate this option, simply use the name of the attribute. You do not need to
submit any value to this attribute. If the attribute is not used, then the option
remains deactivated. This attribute is not case-sensitive.

Example

```
<textarea cols="60" rows="3" readonly">

<input type=checkbox name="Program" value="Word" readonly>
<input type=checkbox name="Program" value="Excel">
<input type=checkbox name="Program" value="Access">
```

Accompanying elements
INPUT
TEXTAREA

REGION ☺

Defining a rectangle within the window

Description
With REGION you can define a separate rectangular area within the main window.

Application
This command must always be used within a LAYOUT container.

Parameter
BACKGROUND-COLOR
> Determines the background colour of the defined area.

FIT
> Indicates how the size of the embedded rectangle will change, if shape and region do not have the same measures.
> Four values are valid for this attribute: FILL, HIDDEN, MEET, SLICE.

HEIGHT
> Through the HEIGHT attribute, you indicate the height of the restricted region.

ID
> Gives a name to the region.

LEFT
> Indicates the separation of the region to the left margin.

TOP
> Indicates the separation of the region to the top margin of the window.

WIDTH
> The WIDTH attribute sets the width of the restricted region.

Z-INDEX
> Defines the location of this region in the order of the overlaying regions.

Example
```
<layout>
     < root layout/>
     <region id="video" top="10" left="10"
width = "100" height = "100"/for>
</layout>

<region
id="identifier"
left="integer"
```

```
top="integer"
z-index="integer"
width="integer"
height="integer"
title="string"
fit="fill "
skip-content="true"/>
```

REL   <html attribute>
Determining link types (from the jump source)

Description
With this attribute, link types can be determined for linked documents. In this way, a reference to a glossary can be defined, or the table of contents of the presentation can be created. These details make it possible for the browser to create navigation help.

Application
A direct assignment of the accompanying file is usually executed with the help of the LINK command. A help file can be referred to in the document head. However, most browsers do not support this function, and it remains invisible to the user.

Values
The following values can be submitted to the attribute:

ALTERNATE
> Indicates an alternative version of the document; another language version or an abridged text version, for example.

APPENDIX
> Refers to a document serving as an appendix of the Web site.

BOOKMARK
> Indicates a special page which you can bookmark to your browser.

CHAPTER
> Refers to the chapter of which the document is part.

CONTENTS
> Points to a table of contents in which all pages present are clearly listed.

COPYRIGHT
> In this page you will find details about the originator of the document on this site.

GLOSSARY
> In this page you will find a glossary in which important concepts are explained.

HELP
> Refers to a help page which helps with the navigation and usage of the site.

INDEX
> Refers to an index which contains all keywords in the Web site.

NEXT
> Indicates the next page on the current document.

PREV
> Indicates the previous document of this site.

SECTION
> Refers to the primary section which is part of the current document.

START
> Indicates the origin or start page of the Web site.

STYLESHEET
> Refers to an external style sheet in which details on the format of the current document can be found.

SUBSECTION
> Refers to a sub-section of this document.

Example

```
<link href="index.htm" rel="Index">
<link href="page2.htm" rel="Next">
<link href="help.htm" rel="Help">

DOCUMENT  A:

<link href="document_b.htm" rev="Next">
DOCUMENT B:
<link href="document_a.htm" rel="Next">
```

Accompanying elements
A
LINK

REV <html attribute>
Determining the link type (from the jump destination)

Description

This attribute indicates a link back to the previous document, like REL. This is only rarely applied. It does not indicate the jump destination, but the jump source, unlike a normal hyperlink.

Application

A direct assignment of the accompanying file is usually executed with the help of the LINK command, so a help file can already be referred in the document head. Most browsers do not support this function, and it remains invisible to the user.

Values

The following values can be submitted to the attribute:

ALTERNATE
Indicates an alternative version of the document; another language version or one shortened text version, for example.

APPENDIX
Refers to an appendix of the Web site.

BOOKMARK
Indicates a special page which you can bookmark to your browser.

CHAPTER
Refers to the chapter of which the document is part.

CONTENTS
Points to a table of contents in which all pages present are clearly listed.

COPYRIGHT
In this page you will find details about the originator of the document.

GLOSSARY
In this page you will find a glossary in which important concepts are explained.

HELP
Refers to a help page which helps with the navigation and usage of the site.

INDEX
Refers to an index which contains all keywords of the Web site.

NEXT
This indicates the next page on the current document.

PREV
Indicates the previous document visited on this site.

SECTION
Refers to the primary section which is part of the current document.

START
Indicates the origin or start page of the Web site.

STYLESHEET
Refers to an external style sheet in which details on the format of the current document can be found.

SUBSECTION
Refers to a sub-section of this document.

Example

```
<link href="index.htm" rev="Index">

<link href="page2.htm" rev="Next">
```

```
<link href="help.htm" rev="Help">

Document A:
<link href="document_b.htm" rev="Next">

Document B:
<link href="document_a.htm" rel="Next">
```

Accompanying elements
A
LINK

root

Basic construction rule

Description
This indicates a basic construction rule. It provides the basic HTML structure for the document. All other elements are inserted in this structure.

Application
With the basic construction rule, the basic structure of the document is determined, for example an HTML document. Before the parser compiles the document, it finds this construction rule indicated by the keyword root rule and then inserts all other elements in this structure.

Example
```
<rule>

    < root/>
    <html>
         <head>
         <title>New page </title>
         </head>
    <body>
    < children/>
    </body>
</html>

</rule>
```

ROOT-LAYOUT ☺
Determining window size

Description
With the help of ROOT-LAYOUT the properties of the window can be set, such as width, height and title.

Application
This command must always be set within the LAYOUT container.

Parameter
BACKGROUND-COLOR
> Determines the background colour. The value can be submitted as a colour designation or a hexadecimal number.

HEIGHT
> Indicates the height of the area in pixels.

ID
> This identifies the document. Using ID, other elements of this area can be accessed.

WIDTH
> Indicates the width of the area in pixels.

Example
```
<root-layout
    id="identifier"
    width="integer"
    height="integer"
    title="string"
    skip-content="true"/>
```

ROWS <html attribute>
Defining rows

Description
This attribute helps to determine the height of rows within a frame. In connection with the entry field TEXTAREA, you indicate the number of rows to be displayed.

Application

The value for the width of the frame can be indicated in pixels or as a percentage of the total height of the screen. Height details of single lines are separated by commas.

For the text field you submit a single value to the attribute, which indicates the number of rows to be displayed.

Values

This attribute is used when there is scope for submitting the value. Below, we have listed the commands and their possible values:

FRAMESET

You can indicate the size of this in pixels, in percentage or in the relative length. Submit an integer value to the attribute for the detail of the size in pixels. Every pixel corresponds to a microdot in the chosen resolution. The detail in per cent is determined using a number from 1 to 100 followed by a per cent sign (="50%"). The detail of the relative length is determined as an integer followed by an asterisk (="1*").

The browser processes all data at the same time. First, it assigns the vertical or horizontal position to the pixel details, then it processes the percentage details and the remaining position is then assigned according to the appropriate numbers. If the remainder is a width of 100 pixels, for example, then an instruction ="2*, 3*" will correspond to a width of 40 and 60 pixels.

TEXTAREA

Valid values for this attribute are integers. The number must contain at least one number between 0 and 9 (="9").

Example

```
<textarea cols="60" rows="3">
Please enter text ...
</textarea>

<frameset rows="40%,60%">
<frame src="reference.htm" name="reference">
<frame src="title.htm" name="Data">
</frameset>
```

Accompanying elements

FRAMESET
TEXTAREA

ROWSPAN   **\<html attribute\>**

Combining cells within several rows

Description

With the help of this attribute, it is possible to select several cells of a table within rows. You can use this option if a cell should be higher than the other cells in the table.

Application

Instead of defining several cells, you indicate only a single cell, which you provide with the ROWSPAN attribute. Submit the number of rows you would like to connect to the attribute as the value. The use of this attribute is optional.

Values

Valid values for this attribute are integers. The number must contain at least one number between 0 and 9 (="9").

Example

```
<table border>

<tr>
<td rowspan=2>A </td>
<td>B </td>
</tr>

<tr>
<td>C </td>
</tr>

<tr>
<td>E </td>
<td>F </td>
</tr>

</table>
```

Accompanying elements

TD
TH

rule

Definition of a construction rule

Description

A single style instruction or construction rule consists of two connected parts:

The pattern determines to which XML command the following style instruction refers. The pattern is the criterion when the defined output form needs to be converted into mark-ups.

If the given pattern is recognised in the XML document, then the transformation of the element follows into the specified output form. As well as passive elements, an "action" instruction can contain dynamic instructions, such as calling JavaScript or another script language, for example.

Example

```
<rule>
        <target-element type="adrese">
    <DIV>
        < children/>
    </DIV>
</rule>
```

RULES   <html attribute>

Displaying borders

Description

The RULES attribute sets the border of the table which is to be displayed.

Application

In a table, you can usually decide whether the frame and rules should be shown or not. Through the RULES attribute the rules to be displayed can be set precisely.

Values

The following values are valid for this attribute:

ALL
    Shows all rules between cells (standard setting).

COLS
    Shows only the horizontal rules between columns.
GROUPS
    The single elements of the table are framed with rules (head, body and foot).
NONE
    No interior table rules are displayed.
ROWS
    Displays only horizontal rules between rows.

Example

```
<table rules="rows" border="5">
</table>

<table rules="none" border="3">
</table>
```

Accompanying element
TABLE

S

Displaying strikethrough text

Description
With this command, text can be displayed as strikethrough. This tag is not supported in HTML 4.0.

Application
The S command (which is an abbreviation of "strike") is converted with the help of style sheets in version 4.0 of HTML.

HTML 4.0 standard
CLASS, DIR, ID, LANG, STYLE, TITLE

The use of this command is no longer supported in the current HTML version; it has been replaced by other commands.

Start tag: required; end tag: required.

Attributes

CLASS

Through the CLASS attribute the element can be assigned to a group (class). Enter one of the free selectable class names as a value. These groupings then provide easy access to all related elements so you can change all the properties of the elements of a class with the help of cascading style sheets or other languages, or select a value.

DIR

This attribute is necessary to determine the text direction. This attribute can have the values:

LTR

This value determines the text direction from left to right (and is short for "left-to-right"). This is the default direction in the browser.

RTL

If the text must run contrary to the standard direction from the right to the left margin of the screen, choose the value RTL (short for "right-to-left").

ID

This identifies the document. Using ID, a specific element can be accessed with the help of a script language to select or modify values.

LANG

This attribute indicates the language of the linked document. This is particularly important in search engines for identification purposes. Use the language codes according to ISO 639, for example "en" for English or "en-us" for American English.

ONCLICK

This event takes place if you single-click on an element with the mouse. A given script is executed by this action.

ONDBLCLICK

This event takes place if you double-click on an element with the mouse. A given script is executed by this action.

ONKEYDOWN

This event takes place if you are in an element and a key is pressed and held down. This action executes a specific script.

ONKEYPRESS

This event takes place if you are in an element and a key is pressed and released. This action executes a specific script.

ONKEYUP

This event takes place if you are in an element and a key that was pressed is released. This action executes a specific script.

ONMOUSEDOWN

This event takes place if you are in an element and a mouse button is clicked and held down. A given script is executed by this action.

ONMOUSEMOVE

This event takes place if one moves the cursor over an object with the mouse. A given script is executed by this action.

ONMOUSEOUT

This event takes place if a mouse moves the cursor off an element. A given script is executed by this action.

ONMOUSEOVER

This event takes place if the mouse moves the cursor directly over the element (object). A given script is executed by this action.

ONMOUSEUP

This event takes place if you are in an element and a mouse button that was clicked and held down is released. A given script is executed by this action.

STYLE

The STYLE attribute can be used to change style settings, in particular the appearance of an element. As a value of the attribute you apply the corresponding options of a style sheet language (usually CSS).

TITLE

Give the user further information about the element used by defining a meaningful title with the help of the TITLE command. Navigation in your Web site is made easier for users who are dependent on speech synthesisers.

Example

```
This is <S> strikethrough </S>text!
```

Events

ONCLICK, ONDBLCLICK, ONKEYDOWN, ONKEYPRESS, ONKEYUP, ONMOUSEDOWN, ONMOUSEMOVE, ONMOUSEOVER, ONMOUSEOUT, ONMOUSEUP

Related commands

B
BIG
I
LISTING
PLAINTEXT
PRE
SMALL
STRIKE
TT
U
XMP

SAMP

W3C HTML 4.0

Indicating samples

Description

With this command, areas of text can be set as samples. These samples can be initiated by different programs.

Application

The SAMP command ("sample" = example) is used to identify specific text sections by samples. Unlike the KBD command, with the SMP command it is possible to indicate output on the screen.

HTML 4.0 standard

CLASS, DIR, ID, LANG, STYLE, TITLE

Start tag: required; end tag: required.

Attributes

CLASS

> Through the CLASS attribute the element can be assigned to a group (class). Enter one of the free selectable class names as a value. These groupings then provide easy access to all related elements so you can change all the properties of the elements of a class with the help of cascading style sheets or other languages, or select a value.

DIR

> This attribute is necessary to determine the text direction. This attribute can have the values:

> LTR

>> This value determines the text direction from left to right (and is short for "left-to-right"). This is the default direction in the browser.

> RTL

>> If the text must run contrary to the standard direction from the right to the left margin of the screen, choose the value RTL (short for "right-to-left").

ID

> This identifies the document. Using ID, a specific element can be accessed with the help of a script language to select or modify values.

LANG

> This attribute indicates the language of the linked document. This is particularly important in search engines for identification purposes. Use the language codes according to ISO 639, for example "en" for English or "en-us" for American English.

ONCLICK
> This event takes place if you single-click on an element with the mouse. A given script is executed by this action.

ONDBLCLICK
> This event takes place if you double-click on an element with the mouse. A given script is executed by this action.

ONKEYDOWN
> This event takes place if you are in an element and a key is pressed and held down. This action executes a specific script.

ONKEYPRESS
> This event takes place if you are in an element and a key is pressed and released. This action executes a specific script.

ONKEYUP
> This event takes place if you are in an element and a key that was pressed is released. This action executes a specific script.

ONMOUSEDOWN
> This event takes place if you are in an element and a mouse button is clicked and held down. A given script is executed by this action.

ONMOUSEMOVE
> This event takes place if one moves the cursor over an object with the mouse. A given script is executed by this action.

ONMOUSEOUT
> This event takes place if a mouse moves the cursor off an element. This executes a given script.

ONMOUSEOVER
> This event takes place if the mouse moves the cursor directly over the element (object). A given script is executed by this action.

ONMOUSEUP
> This event takes place if you are in the described element and a mouse button that was clicked and held down is released. A given script is executed by this action.

STYLE
> The STYLE attribute can be used to change style settings, in particular the appearance of the element looks. As the value of the attribute, you apply the corresponding options of a style sheet language (usually CSS).

TITLE
> Give the user further information about the element used by defining a meaningful title with the help of the title command. Navigation in your Web site is made easier for users who are dependent on a speech synthesiser.

Example

```
<samp>
general protection injury (violation)!
</samp>
```

Events

ONCLICK, ONDBLCLICK, ONKEYDOWN, ONKEYPRESS, ONKEYUP, ONMOUSEDOWN, ONMOUSEMOVE, ONMOUSEOVER, ONMOUSEOUT, ONMOUSEUP

Related commands

ACRONYM
CITE
CODE
DFN
EM
KBD
STRONG
VAR

<u>SCHEME</u>   <html attribute>

Determining the type of a META data profile

Description

The SCHEME attribute decides which format should be used to transfer a document.

Application

The SCHEME attribute is used with the META command. Through PROFILE, a meta data profile can be assigned to this command. This attribute decides the data format in which the meta information is written. Currently, this is still being developed, so there are no details on its use yet. The use of this attribute is optional.

Values

You can submit any string to this attribute as the value. If possible, this character string should not start or end with a blank space. The processing browser may filter these out.

Accompanying element

META

SCOPE   **\<html attribute>**

Indicating data relations in a table

Description
This attribute indicates the data cells which contain the accompanying header information for the current cell.

Application
The command can be used as an alternative to the HEADER attribute for simple tables. The use of this attribute is optional.

Values
ROW
> The current cell contains header information for the rest of the row.

COL
> The current cell contains header information for the rest of the column.

COLGROUP
> The current cell contains header information for other elements of a column group (COLGROUP).

ROWGROUP
> The current cell contains header information for other elements of a row group (ROWGROUP).

Example
```
<table>
<tr>
<td scope="col">Heading 1 </td>
<td scope="col">Heading 2 </td>
</tr>

<tr>
<td>Content 1 </td>
<td>Contentf 2 </td>
</tr>
</table>
>
```

Accompanying elements
TD
TH

SCRIPT

Inserting scripts

Description

With this command, it is possible to insert scripts into an HTML document.

Application

The SCRIPT commands determine the marking-up of inline scripts to be inserted into an HTML document. Text marked with this command is usually not displayed. However, it is recommended that scripts be marked with comments to ensure that the text is not displayed by older browsers either.

HTML 4.0 standard

CHARSET, DEFER, SRC, TYPE

Start tag: required; end tag: required.

Attributes

CHARSET

This attribute is used to determine the character set for linked data. If the character set is not indicated explicitly, the browser should determine the used character set.

DEFER

This attribute is used if no changes are made to a HTML document to be represented by a script.

LANGUAGE

With this attribute, it is possible to determine the script language of a document. In most cases it is JavaScript. Other possible details for the language are JScript and VBScript. This attribute is not supported in HTML 4.0.

SRC

This attribute defines the source of an external script. Submit a URI as the value for SRC.

TYPE

This element defines the script language used to program the code routines used for the script elements or the external script files. The script language is defined as content type (for example, "text/javascript"). There is no default value for this attribute.

Example

```
<head>
<title>Title text </title>
```

```
<script language="JavaScript">
<!--
UserName = window.prompt ("your name:", "surname" );
//-->
</script>
</head>
<body>
<script language="JavaScript">
<!--
document.write("<h1> hello "+UserName+" !</h1>");

//-->
</script>
</body>
</html>
```

XML definition

```
<! ELEMENT SCRIPT>
<!ATTLIST SCRIPT
charset     %Charset;       #IMPLIED
type        %ContentType;   #REQUIRED
src         %URI;           #IMPLIED
event       CDATA           #IMPLIED
for         %URI;           #IMPLIED>
```

SCROLLING   <html attribute>

Preventing frame contents from scrolling

Description
With this attribute you can influence the scroll properties of a frame.

Application

When the content of a frame is too large to be viewed on one screen, a scroll bar is usually displayed. Several frames are used on a page, so it is easy to display two scroll bars per frame but it is difficult to see the content. With the SCROLLING attribute, the properties of the scroll bars can be changed. The use of this attribute is optional.

Values

YES
   Scroll bars are always displayed.

NO
> Scroll bars are always hidden.

AUTO
> Scroll bars are displayed when required (standard setting).

Example

```
<frame scrolling="yes">
<frame scrolling="no">
```

Accompanying elements

FRAME

IFRAME

<u>SELECT</u>

Defining a menu

Description

This command is used to determine menus or drop-down menus within forms. Visitors to a Web site are not allowed any input in this field, but can only select entries from the list provided.

Application

With SELECT you can define menus and drop-down fields. The use of the command should take place within a form definition. Within the SELECT section you determine the individual entries of the list using the OPTION command. The markup OPTION is not usually closed.

HTML 4.0 standard

CLASS, DIR, DISABLED, ID, LANG, MULTIPLE, NAME, SIZE, STYLE, TABINDEX, TITLE

Start tag: required; end tag: required.

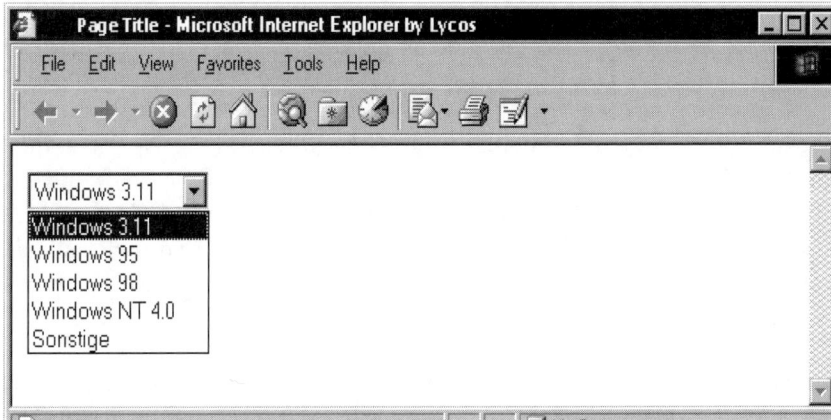

A simple list as a drop-down menu

Attributes

CLASS

Through the CLASS attribute the element can be assigned to a group (class). Enter one of the free selectable class names as a value. These groupings then provide easy access to all related elements so you can change all the properties of the elements of a class with the help of cascading style sheets or other languages or select a value.

DIR

This attribute is necessary to determine the text direction. This attribute can have the values:

LTR

This value determines the text direction from left to right (and is short for "left-to-right"). This is the default direction in the browser.

RTL

If the text must run contrary to the standard direction from the right to the left margin of the screen, then choose the value RTL (short for "right-to-left").

DISABLED

Deactivate buttons with this attribute.

ID

This identifies the document. Using ID, a specific element can be accessed with the help of a script language to select or modify values.

LANG

This attribute indicates the language of the linked document. This is particularly important in search engines for identification purposes. Use the language codes according to ISO 639, for example `"en"` for English or `"en-us"` for American English.

NAME

This applies to all form fields, to define a name. Usually, you receive the mailed forms from the Web server as an email message. The names of the fields and the selected entries of the menu are in this email, listed in the same order as they appear in the form. You therefore need to select a name which you will be able to remember, because you or somebody else will need to make sense of the received message.

MULTIPLE

The visitor has the option of selecting more menu entries by pressing the Ctrl key and clicking on them at the same time as using the MULTIPLE element. The MULTIPLE attribute does not require any value. When using MULTIPLE, you should set the size of the field with SIZE using a value larger than 1 to make things easier for the user.

ONBLUR

This event is triggered when the mouse pointer is moved from a specific position over the designated element. This action executes a given script.

ONCHANGE

This event is triggered when the contents of the entry field are changed. By this action a given script is executed.

ONCLICK

This event takes place if you single-click on an element with the mouse. A given script is executed by this action.

ONDBLCLICK

This event takes place if you double-click on an element with the mouse. A given script is executed by this action.

ONKEYDOWN

This event takes place if you are in an element and a key is pressed and held down. This action executes a specific script.

ONKEYPRESS

This event takes place if you are in an element and a key is pressed and released. This action executes a specific script.

ONKEYUP

This event takes place if you are in an element and a key that was pressed is released. This action executes a specific script.

ONMOUSEDOWN

This event takes place if you are in an element and a mouse button is clicked and held down. A given script is executed by this action.

ONMOUSEMOVE

This event takes place if one moves the cursor over an object with the mouse. A given script is executed by this action.

ONMOUSEOUT

This event takes place if a mouse moves the cursor off an element. This executes a given script.

ONMOUSEOVER

This event takes place if the mouse moves the cursor directly over the element (object). A given script is executed by this action.

ONMOUSEUP

This event takes place if you are in an element and a mouse button that was clicked and held down is released. A given script is executed by this action.

ONFOCUS

The ONFOCUS event is triggered when the current element is focused on. If the user goes on this field with a mouse click or the keyboard and the element is activated.

SIZE

The menu only shows a single field by default. If you click on it, you open a drop-down menu. However, you can change the number of fields to be displayed. In this case, indicate a higher value for SIZE. A drop-down menu will not be displayed, but a field which several lines will appear.

STYLE

The STYLE attribute can be used to change style settings, particularly the appearance of an element. As a value of the attribute you submit the corresponding options of a Cascading Style Sheet language (usually CSS).

TABINDEX

This attribute assigns an order to an element by the use of positive or negative integers. Elements provided with this attribute can be selected with the Tab key one after the other.

TITLE

Through this attribute, additional information can be assigned to selected elements. This information is displayed in a pop-up window in many browsers, if the mouse pointer is on the element.

Example

```
<select name="operating system" size="3" multiple>
<option>Windows   3.11
<option>Windows   95
<option>Windows  98
<option>Windows   NT   4.0
<option>Other
</select>
Events
```

Events

ONBLUR, ONCHANGE, ONCLICK, ONFOCUS, ONDBLCLICK, ONKEYDOWN, ONKEYPRESS, ONKEYUP, ONMOUSEDOWN, ONMOUSEMOVE, ONMOUSEOVER, ONMOUSEOUT, ONMOUSEUP

XML definition

```
<! ELEMENT SELECT - - (OPTGROUP|OPTION)+>
<!ATTLIST SELECT
% attrs;

name      CDATA      #IMPLIED
size      NUMBER     #IMPLIED
multiple  (multiple) #IMPLIED
disabled  (disabled) #IMPLIED
tabindex  NUMBER     #IMPLIED
onfocus   %script;   #IMPLIED
onblur    %script;   #IMPLIED
onchange  %script;   #IMPLIED
% reserved;>
```

Related commands

FORM
INPUT
OPTION

SELECTED   <html attribute>

Selecting single option fields as a preselection

Description

This attribute selects choices which are displayed to users as preselected.

Application

Activate the preselection of an option field by assigning the SELECTED attribute. The use of this attribute is optional.

Values

To activate this option, you simply use the name of the attribute. You do not need to submit any value to this attribute. If the attribute is not used, then the option remains deactivated. This attribute is not case-sensitive.

Example

```
<select name="Pasta" size=5>
<option value="P101">Spaghetti Napoli
<option value="P102">Spaghetti Bolognese
<option value="P103">Spaghetti al Pesto
<option value="P104">Spaghetti Mare e Monti
<option value="P105">Spaghetti Aglio e Olio
<option value="P106"selected>Spaghetti Carbonara
<option value="P107">Spaghetti Alfredo
<option value="P108">Spaghetti Diavolo
<option value="P109">Spaghetti Nettuno
</select>
```

Accompanying element

OPTION

select-elements

Filtering elements

Description

One of the new additions to XSL is the ability to restructure the content of an XML document and to filter out sub-sections. A mailing list could thus be distributed sorted by first names, and then according to surnames, for example. The `<select-elements>` tag, which replaces the `<children/>` element, provides XSL with the ability to filter elements.

Application

The `<select-elements>` tag within the action section replaces the `<children/>` element.

Parameter

`from`

> When elements must be filtered out from a document, and these elements are not immediate descendants of the pattern of the construction rule, the FROM attribute is used. The two values "descendants" and "children" can be submitted for this attribute. The second value corresponds to the presetting and refers to the immediate descendant ("children") of the source element, as described above.

Example

```
<select-elements from="descendants">
</select-elements>

    <select-elements from="children">
</select-elements>

<rule>
    <target-element type="list"/>
    <div>
    <select-elements from="descendants">
        <target-element type="surname"/>
    <select-element>
    </div>
</rule>
```

SEQ ☺

Playing clips sequentially

Description

All media clips within the seq container are played sequentially. Alternatively, you can use the PAR command to represent clips in parallel.

Parameter

`abstract`

A short description of the contents of the element.

`id`

This identifies the document. Using ID, other elements from this area can be accessed.

`author`

With this attribute the author of the media group can be indicated.

copyright
: Information about the originator and the copyright can be submitted as a value of this attribute.

dur
: Indicates the complete ending time of the group. You can use h, min, s or ms as units.

end
: Indicates the end of the group. This value refers to the BEGIN attribute. You can use h, min, s or ms as units.

repeat
: Repeats the complete group for the required number of times.

title
: Gives the complete group a title with a short description of the content.

Example

```
<seq id="identifier"
     title = "string"
     abstract = "string"
     author = "string"
     copyright = "string"
     begin = "clock-value"
     ends = "clock-value"
     major = "clock-value"
     repeat = "integer"
     system-bitrate = "integer"
     system-captions = "on |off"
     system-language = "coma-separated cunning"
     system-overdub-or captions = "captions | overdub"
     system-required = "string"
     system-screen-depth = "integer"
     system-screen-size = "integerXinteger"/
         system-bitrate = "integer"
     system-captions = "on |off"
     system-language = "coma-separated cunning"
     system-overdub-or captions = "captions | overdub"
     system-required = "string"
     system-screen-depth = "integer"
     system-screen-size = "integerXinteger"/>
```

SHAPE   \<html attribute\>

Determining the shape of a reference sensitive area

Description

With the SHAPE attribute, the area which represents the link can be determined. So in a reference-sensitive graphic, round, rectangular and polygonal areas can be selected.

Application

Through this attribute you indicate the shape of the area. The chosen form is then used for the interpretation of coordinate details executed under COORDS.

Values

The following details are valid:

DEFAULT
Complete area.
RECT
Rectangle; $x1$ = left top edge, left pixel, $y1$ = left top corner, top pixel, $x2$ = right lower corner, left pixel, $y2$ = right lower corner, top pixel.
CIRCLE
Circle; x = centre, left pixel, y = centre, top pixel, R = radius in pixels.
POLY
Polygon; $x1$-xn, x = pixel at a left corner, $y1$-yn, y = pixel at a top corner.

Example

```
<area shape=rect coords="1,1,249,49" href="seite3.htm">
<area shape=circle coords="1,51,299" nohref>
<area shape=poly coords="251,1,39,99,567" href="next.htm">
```

Accompanying elements

A
AREA

size

This determines page size

Description

This allows you to decide the size of the entire page.

Parameter

Indicates width and height as a numerical value. The following keywords are valid:

`auto`
> The standard setting of the output media.

`landscape`
> The standard format in landscape format.

`portrait`
> The standard format in portrait format.

Example

```
<style type="text/css">
h1, h2 {size:20 cm 10 cm}
h3, h4 {size:landscape}
</style>

<div style="size:portrait">
</div>
```

SIZE   <html attribute>

Setting size information

Description

This command has different effects for every element to which you assign a size. In the following, all possible combinations will be discussed.

Application

`INPUT`
> With this attribute, the size of an entry field is indicated. If the given value exceeds the area to be represented, the entered text will be scrollable.

`HR`
> With this attribute, you can indicate the height of the dividing lines in pixels.

`BASEFONT, FONT`
> The `SIZE` attribute is used to determine the font size. The values 1-7 are available for the size input. If this number is not determined explicitly, the default font size is 3.

`SELECT`
> With this attribute, you determine how many lines are displayed for the user to choose from.

Values

For every command with which you use this attribute, different validity ranges exist for the submitted value. The following is a list of commands and possible values:

HR

> The value of this attribute indicates a size in pixels, therefore in microdots. Valid values are positive integers (Integer Values). Inputting of ="100" corresponds to a size of 100 pixels, for example.

FONT, INPUT, BASEFONT, SELECT

> You can submit any string to this attribute as a value. If possible, this character string should not start or end with a blank space. The processing browser will filter these out if necessary.

Example

```
<basefont size="2">
<font-face="Arial" size="+2">
<font-face="Arial" size="3">

<hr size="5">

<select name="Pasta" size=2>
<option value="P101">Spaghetti Napoli
<option value="P102">Spaghetti Bolognese
<option value="P103">Spaghetti Pesto
</select>

<input type="text" size="20">
```

Accompanying elements

BASEFONT
FONT
HR
INPUT
SELECT

SMALL

Displaying text in a smaller font

Description

With this command, standard text can be made smaller. Follow three steps to reduce text size.

Application

The SMALL command sets text which should be displayed as smaller in a container between `<small>` and `</small>`. These containers can be nested into each other.

HTML 4.0 standard

CLASS, DIR, ID, LANG, STYLE, TITLE

Start tag: required; end tag: required.

Attribute

CLASS

Through the CLASS attribute the element can be assigned to a group (class). Enter one of the free selectable class names as a value. These groupings then provide easy access to all related elements so you can change all the properties of the elements of a class with the help of cascading style sheets or other languages, or select a value.

DIR

This attribute is necessary to determine the text direction. This attribute can have the values:

LTR

This value determines the text direction from left to right (and is short for "left-to-right"). This is the default direction in the browser.

RTL

If the text should must run contrary to the standard direction from the right to the left margin of the screen, then choose the value RTL (short for "right-to-left").

ID

This identifies the document. Using ID, a specific element can be accessed with the help of a script language to select or change values, for example.

LANG

This attribute indicates the language of the linked document. This is particularly important in search engines for identification purposes. Use the language codes according to ISO 639, for example "en" for English or "en-us" for American English.

ONCLICK
> This event takes place if you single-click on an element with the mouse. A given script is executed by this action.

ONDBLCLICK
> This event takes place if you double-click on an element with the mouse. A given script is executed by this action.

ONKEYDOWN
> This event takes place if you are in an element and a key is pressed and held down. This action executes a specific script.

ONKEYPRESS
> This event takes place if you are in an element and a key is pressed and released. This action executes a specific script.

ONKEYUP
> This event takes place if you are in an element and a key that was pressed is released. This action executes a specific script.

ONMOUSEDOWN
> This event takes place if you are in an element and a mouse button is clicked and held down. A given script is executed by this action.

ONMOUSEMOVE
> This event takes place if one moves the cursor over an object with the mouse. A given script is executed by this action.

ONMOUSEOUT
> This event takes place if a mouse moves the cursor off an element. This action executes a given script.

ONMOUSEOVER
> This event takes place if the mouse moves the cursor directly over the element (object). A given script is executed by this action.

ONMOUSEUP
> This event takes place if you are in an element and a mouse button that was clicked and held down is released. A given script is executed by this action.

STYLE
> The STYLE attribute is used to determine specific properties in relation to the representation of labelled elements. Styles used are defined by cascading style sheets.

TITLE
> Through this attribute, additional information can be assigned to selected elements. This information is displayed in a pop-up window in many browsers, if the mouse pointer is on the element.

Example

```
This was a <small>small</small> misunderstanding!
```

Events

ONCLICK, ONDBLCLICK, ONKEYDOWN, ONKEYPRESS, ONKEYUP, ONMOUSEDOWN, ONMOUSEMOVE, ONMOUSEOVER, ONMOUSEOUT, ONMOUSEUP

Related commands

B
BIG
I
LISTING
PLAINTEXT
PRE
S
STRIKE
TT
U
XMP

SMIL

Basic structure of a SMIL document

Description

As in HTML, SMIL encloses the complete document. Every SMIL document starts with the enclosing SMIL tag. Within the document, another two sub-divisions are possible: the head (HEAD) and the document body (BODY).

Application

A SMIL (Synchronized Multimedia Integration Language) document starts with this command and ends with the end tag.

Example

```
<smil>
<head>
<!-- head information -->
<layout>... </layout>
</head>
<body>
</body>
</smil>
```

SPACER

N

Inserting invisible objects

Description

With this command, invisible objects can be inserted into an HTML document.

Application

The SPACER command is used to represent objects which will be invisible in an HTML document. These are rectangles of different size. The effect of these invisible pictures on the surrounding text is the same as with referenced graphics.

HTML 4.0 standard

This SPACER command is not part of the official HTML standard, H was introduced by Netscape and is not interpreted by Explorer.

Attributes

ALIGN

This attribute is responsible for determining the alignment of the invisible rectangle. You can use the following values:

RIGHT

The invisible rectangle is right-aligned. The text to be displayed flows around the rectangle to the left.

LEFT

The invisible rectangle is left-aligned. The text to be displayed flows in around the rectangle to the right.

HEIGHT

With this attribute, the height of an invisible rectangle to be inserted is indicated in pixels.

TYPE

The value of this attribute determines the form of the invisible object. Three valid values can be chosen:

BLOCK

With this value you determine that the object to be inserted is a rectangle.

HORIZONTAL

With this value the following object is inserted horizontally.

VERTICAL

With this value the following object is inserted vertically.

WIDTH

With this attribute the width of the invisible rectangle to be inserted is set in pixels.

Example

```
<spacer type="block" width="100" height="50" align="left">
The is the text ...

<spacer type="horizontal" size="100">
The new paragraph starts here ...

<spacer type="vertical" size="100">
The last paragraph starts here
```

Related command

IMG

SPAN   <html attribute>

Setting columns in a table

Description

With this attribute, you can set the number of columns within a table. Valid values for this attribute are positive integers.

Application

The use of this attribute has the advantage that the browser knows immediately how large the corresponding table should be. Thus the screen does not need to be resized. The use of this attribute is optional.

Values

Valid values for this attribute are integers. The number must contain at least one number between 0 and 9 (="9").

Example

```
<colgroup span="10" width="20">
</colgroup>
```

Accompanying elements

COL
COLGROUP

SPAN

W3C HTML 4.0 ✔

Structuring a document

Description

With this command, HTML documents can be structured.

Application

The SPAN command is used to structure a document, just like the DIV command. This command replaces the not currently supported CENTRE tag. The command is used if sections of an HTML document must be centred. The SPAN command is mandatory, unlike the DIV tag, since with this command no lateral paragraph alignment is allowed.

Attributes

ALIGN

This attribute determines the alignment within a table column.

LEFT

Left alignment of data within a page. Default setting.

RIGHT

Right alignment of data within a page.

CENTER

Centred alignment of data within a page.

JUSTIFY

Justifies a page (text is full width of page).

CLASS

Through the CLASS attribute the element can be assigned to a group (class). Enter one of the free selectable class names as a value. These groupings then provide easy access to all related elements so you can change all the properties of the elements of a class with the help of cascading style sheets or other languages, or select a value.

DIR

This attribute is required to determine the text direction. This attribute can have the values:

LTR

This value determines the text direction from left to right (and is short for "left-to-right"). This is the default direction in the browser.

RTL

If the text should must run contrary to the standard direction from the right to the left margin of the screen, then choose the value RTL (short for "right-to-left").

ID

This identifies a document. Using ID, a specific element can be accessed with the help of a script language to select or change values.

LANG

This attribute indicates the language of the linked document. This is particularly important in search engines for identification purposes. Use the language codes according to ISO 639, for example "en" for English or "en-us" for American English.

ONCLICK

This event takes place if you single-click on an element with the mouse. A given script is executed by this action.

ONDBLCLICK

This event takes place if you double-click on an element with the mouse. A given script is executed by this action.

ONKEYDOWN

This event takes place if you are in an element and a key is pressed and held down. This action executes a specific script.

ONKEYPRESS

This event takes place if you are in an element and a key is simultaneously pressed and released again. This action executes a specific script.

ONKEYUP

This event takes place if you are in an element and a key that was pressed is released. This action executes a specific script.

ONMOUSEDOWN

This event takes place if you are in an element and a mouse button is clicked and held down. A given script is executed by this action.

ONMOUSEMOVE

This event takes place if one moves the cursor over an object with the mouse. A given script is executed by this action.

ONMOUSEOUT

This event takes place if a mouse moves the cursor off an element. This action executes a given script.

ONMOUSEOVER

This event takes place if the mouse moves the cursor directly over the element (object). A given script is executed by this action.

ONMOUSEUP

This event takes place if you are in an element and a mouse button that was clicked and held down is released. A given script is executed by this action.

STYLE

The STYLE attribute is used to determine specific properties in labelled elements. Style settings are defined by cascading style sheets.

TITLE

Through this attribute selected elements can be assigned with additional information. This information is displayed in a pop-up window in many browsers, if the mouse pointer is on the element.

Example

```
<span align="center">
Centred text
</span>
```

Events

ONCLICK, ONDBLCLICK, ONKEYDOWN, ONKEYPRESS, ONKEYUP, ONMOUSEDOWN, ONMOUSEMOVE, ONMOUSEOVER, ONMOUSEOUT, ONMOUSEUP

XML definition

```
<! ELEMENT SPAN>
<!ATTLIST SPAN
% attrs;

% reserved;>
```

Related commands

DIV

P

SRC   \<html attribute\>

Indicating data source

Description

With this attribute, the data source of an element is determined with its URI.

Application

The use of this attribute is required as well as the INPUT and SCRIPT commands.

Values

A valid value for this attribute is a URI (Uniform Resource Identifier). The construction of a URI is as follows:

```
[protocol]: // [Domain]/[Directory]/[File]
```

Possible details for the used protocol are the following values:

ftp   File Transfer Protocol
http   Hypertext Transfer Protocol
gopher   Gopher Protocol
mailto   Electronic Mail Address
news   USENET News
nntp   USENET News (NNTP access)
telnet   Reference to interactive sessions
wais   Wide Area Information Server
file   Host-specific file names
prospero   Prospero Directory Service

Example

```
<img src="bild.gif">

<img src="http://www.image.co.uk/image.gif">

<frameset cols="40%,60%">
<frame src="reference.htm" name="Reference">
<frame src="title.htm" name="Data">
</frameset>
```

Accompanying elements

FRAME
IFRAME
IMG
INPUT
SCRIPT

STANDBY   <html attribute>

Information during download

Description

This attribute indicates any messages to be displayed during the construction of an object.

Application

Downloading a multimedia object can take some time. Therefore, you need to provide the user with some information so that they are aware of what is happening. The browser will display this information in the status bar. The use of this attribute is optional.

Values

You can submit any string to this attribute as the value. If possible, this character string should not start or end with a blank space. The processing browser will filter these out if necessary.

Example

```
<object
    classid = "anim.py"
    standby = > "Please wait, object downloading"
</object>
```

Accompanying element

OBJECT

START <html attribute>

Indicating the start value for numbered lists

Description

START gives you the option of indicating a start value for list. You can let a numbered list start with the value 100, for example, rather than with the default value of 1.

Application

This attribute is only used in connection with a numbered list. The use of this attribute is optional.

Values

Valid values for this attribute are integers. The number must contain at least one number from 0 to 9 (="9").

Example

```
<ol start="3">
    <li>first</li>
    <li>second</li>
    <li>third</li>
</ol>
```

Accompanying element

OL

STRIKE

Displaying strikethrough text

Description

With this command text can be displayed as strikethrough. This command is not supported in HTML 4.0.

Application

The Strike command has been replaced by style sheets.

HTML 4.0 standard

CLASS, DIR, ID, LANG, STYLE, TITLE

The use of this command is no longer recommended in the current HTML version, as it has been replaced by other commands.

Start tag: required; end tag: required.

Attributes

CLASS

> Through the CLASS attribute the element can be assigned to a group (class). Enter one of the free selectable class names as a value. These groupings then provide easy access to all related elements so you can change all the properties of the elements of a class with the help of cascading style sheets or other languages, or select a value.

DIR

> This attribute is necessary to determine the text direction. This attribute can have the values:

> LTR

> > This value determines the text direction from left to right (and is short for "left-to-right"). This is the default direction in the browser.

> RTL

> > If the text should must run contrary to the standard direction from the right to the left margin of the screen, choose the value RTL (short for "right-to-left").

ID

> This identifies a document. Using ID, a specific element can be accessed with the help of a script language to select or change values, for example.

LANG

> This attribute indicates the language of the linked document. This is particularly important in search engines for identification purposes. Use the language codes according to ISO 639, for example "en" for English or "en-us" for American English.

ONCLICK

> This event takes place if you single-click on an element with the mouse. A given script is executed by this action.

ONDBLCLICK

> This event takes place if you double-click on an element with the mouse. A given script is executed by this action.

ONKEYDOWN

> This event takes place if you are in an element and a key is pressed and held down. This action executes a specific script.

ONKEYPRESS

> This event takes place if you are in an element and a key is simultaneously pressed and released again. This action executes a specific script.

ONKEYUP

> This event takes place if you are in an element and a key that was pressed is released. This action executes a specific script.

ONMOUSEDOWN

> This event takes place if you are in an element and a mouse button is clicked and held down. A given script is executed by this action.

ONMOUSEMOVE

> This event takes place if one moves the cursor over an object with the mouse. A given script is executed by this action.

ONMOUSEOUT

> This event takes place if a mouse moves the cursor off an element. This action executes a given script.

ONMOUSEOVER

> This event takes place if the mouse moves the cursor directly over the element (object). A given script is executed by this action.

ONMOUSEUP

> This event takes place if you are in an element and a mouse button that was clicked and held down is released. A given script is executed by this action.

STYLE

> The attribute STYLE can be used to change style settings, in particular the appearance of the element. As a value of the attribute you apply the corresponding options of a style sheet language (usually CSS).

TITLE

Give the user further information about the element used by determining a meaningful title with the help of the TITLE command. Navigation in your Web site is made particularly easy for users who are dependent on voice response.

Example

```
<strike>This is strikethrough text!</strike>
```

Events

ONCLICK, ONDBLCLICK, ONKEYDOWN, ONKEYPRESS, ONKEYUP, ONMOUSEDOWN, ONMOUSEMOVE, ONMOUSEOVER, ONMOUSEOUT, ONMOUSEUP

Related commands

B
BIG
I
LISTING
PLAINTEXT
PRE
S
SMALL
TT
U
XMP

STRONG

Highlighting text

Description

With this command, sections of text can be highlighted. Highlighting text in this way creates a stronger visual impact than with the EM command.

Application

The STRONG command is used when you wish to highlight parts of a text. This can also be achieved with the EM command. This command should not be used too often.

HTML 4.0 standard

CLASS, DIR, ID, LANG, STYLE, TITLE

Start tag: required; end tag: required.

Attributes

CLASS

Through the CLASS attribute the element can be assigned to a group (class). Enter one of the free selectable class names as a value. These groupings then provide easy access to all related elements so you can change all the properties of the elements of a class with the help of cascading style sheets or other languages or select a value.

DIR

This attribute is necessary to determine the text direction. This attribute can have the values:

LTR

This value determines the text direction from left to right (and is short for "left-to-right"). This is the default direction in the browser.

RTL

If the text should must run contrary to the standard direction from the right to the left margin of the screen, then choose the value RTL (short for "right-to-left").

ID

This identifies the document. Using ID, a specific element can be accessed with the help of a script language to select or change values, for example.

LANG

This attribute indicates the language of the linked document. This is particularly important in search engines for identification purposes. Use the language codes according to ISO 639, for example "en" for English or "en-us" for American English.

ONCLICK

This event takes place if you single-click on an element with the mouse. A given script is executed by this action.

ONDBLCLICK

This event takes place if you double-click on an element with the mouse. A given script is executed by this action.

ONKEYDOWN

This event takes place if you are in an element and a key is pressed and held down. This action executes a specific script.

ONKEYPRESS

This event takes place if you are in an element and a key is simultaneously pressed and released again. This action executes a specific script.

ONKEYUP

This event takes place if you are in an element and a key that was pressed is released. This action executes a specific script.

ONMOUSEDOWN

This event takes place if you are in an element and a mouse button is clicked and held down. A given script is executed by this action.

ONMOUSEMOVE

This event takes place if one moves the cursor over an object with the mouse. A given script is executed by this action.

ONMOUSEOUT

This event takes place if a mouse moves the cursor off an element. This action executes a given script.

ONMOUSEOVER

This event takes place if the mouse moves the cursor directly over the element (object). A given script is executed by this action.

ONMOUSEUP

This event takes place if you are in an element and a mouse button that was clicked and held down is released. A given script is executed by this action.

STYLE

The attribute STYLE can be used to change style settings, in particular the appearance of an element. As a value of the attribute you apply the corresponding options of a style sheet language (usually CSS).

TITLE

Give the user further information about the element used by determining a meaningful title with the help of the TITLE command. Navigation in your Web site is made particularly easy for users who are dependent on voice response.

Example

```
<strong>
Switch off the power before you open the equipment!
</strong>
```

Events

ONCLICK, ONDBLCLICK, ONKEYDOWN, ONKEYPRESS, ONKEYUP, ONMOUSEDOWN, ONMOUSEMOVE, ONMOUSEOVER, ONMOUSEOUT, ONMOUSEUP

Related commands

ACRONYM
CITE
CODE
DFN
EM
KBD
SAMP
VAR

STYLE   <html attribute>

Inserting direct style sheets

Description

The STYLE attribute can be used to change style settings, and the appearence of an element .

Application

As the value of the attribute, submit the corresponding options of a style sheet language (usually CSS). The use of this attribute is optional.

Values

Use the style sheet commands listed in this book. One or more properties can be changed at the same time. Then indicate the single values, separated by semi-colons.

Example

```
<div style="font-size: 12pt">
<div style="colour: blue">
<div style="font-size: 24pt; colour=yellow">>
```

Accompanying elements

A	DL	KBD
ABBR	FONT	LABEL
ACRONYM	FORM	LEGEND
ADDRESS	FRAME	LINK
APPLET	FRAMESET	MAP
AREA	H1	MENU
B	H2	NOFRAMES
BDO	H4	SMALL
BODY	H5	SPAN
BR	H6	STRIKE
BUTTON	HR	STRONG
CAPTION	I	STYLE
CITE	IFRAME	TABLE
CODE	IMG	TBODY
COL	INPUT	TEXTAREA
DIV	INS	VAR

STYLE

Style definition in the header

Description

With this command, definitions for style presentations are determined in document headers.

Application

The STYLE command is used if style information must be defined in the header of a document. This type can be assigned to all elements of an HTML document which belong to a group with the CLASS attribute. The same applies to single elemenents indicated by the ID attribute.

This command must not be confused with the frequently used STYLE attribute.

HTML 4.0 standard

DIR, LANG, MEDIA, TITLE, TYPE

Start tag: required; end tag: required.

Attributes

DIR

   This attribute is necessary to determine the text direction. This attribute can have the values:

   LTR

      This value determines the text direction from left to right (and is short for "left-to-right"). This is the default direction in the browser.

   RTL

      If the text should must run contrary to the standard direction from the right to the left margin of the screen, then choose the value RTL (short for "right-to-left").

LANG

   This attribute indicates the language of the linked document. This is particularly important in search engines for identification purposes. Use the language codes according to ISO 639, for example "en" for English or "en-us" for American English.

MEDIA

   This attribute determines the preferred output for an HTML document. The following outputs are possible:

   SCREEN

      The SCREEN extension is the default for this attribute. This detail refers to the output to computer screens, and indicates the document as printable and viewable at the same time.

PRINT

> The PRINT extension indicates documents intended for printing, often Adobe .pdf files.

PROJECTION

> The PROJECTION extension indicates documents which are intended to be used exclusively with projectors.

BRAILLE

> This extension indicates documents which are intended for output in Braille.

AURAL

> Documents intended for speech synthesisers are marked with this extension.

ALL

> This extension indicates documents which are suitable for all types of output.

TITLE

> Through this attribute, selected elements are provided with additional information. In this case, the STYLE command is used to describe the style used. This information is displayed in a pop-up window in many browsers if the mouse pointer is on the element.

TYPE

> Indicate the language in the style sheets. Usually, the setting TYPE="text/css" for the use of cascading style sheets should be listed here.

Example

```
<head>
<title>Title text </title>

<style type="text/css">
<!--
body { margin: 1 cm }
h1 { font-size: 22 pt }
//-->
</style>

<style type="text/javascript">
<!--
with (tags.H2)
 {
   colour = "blue";
  fontSize = "16pt";
  marginTop = "1cm";
 }
//-->
</style>

</head>
```

XML definition

```
<! ELEMENT STYLE>
<!ATTLIST STYLE
% i18n;

type %ContentType; #REQUIRED
media %MediaDesc; #IMPLIED
title
```

Related command

HEAD

style-rule

Assigning style sheets to elements

Description

Fix style rules with the `<style-rule>` markup. These rules assign cascading style sheets to single elements.

Example

```
<style-rule>
        < target element/>
    <apply font-style="bold"/>
</style-rule>
```

SUB

Displaying subscript text

Description

This command is used to represent standard flow text as subscript. Text formatted in this way appears vertically aligned slightly below the baseline of the surrounding text and, depending on the browser used, is shown either in normal or a slightly reduced character size.

Application

The SUB command places text to be highlighted in the subscript position. This is particularly useful for displaying mathematical formulae or footnotes.

HTML 4.0 standard

CLASS, DIR, ID, LANG, STYLE, TITLE

Start tag: required; end tag: required.

Attributes

CLASS

> Through the CLASS attribute the element can be assigned to a group (class). Enter one of the free selectable class names as a value. These groupings then provide easy access to all related elements so you can change all the properties of the elements of a class with the help of cascading style sheets or other languages, or select a value.

DIR

> This attribute is necessary to determine the text direction. This attribute can have the values:
>
> LTR
>
>> This value determines the text direction from left to right (and is short for "left-to-right"). This is the default direction in the browser.
>
> RTL
>
>> If the text should must run contrary to the standard direction from the right to the left margin of the screen, then choose the value RTL (short for "right-to-left").

ID

> This identifies the document. Using ID, a specific element can be accessed with the help of a script language to select or change values, for example.

LANG

> This attribute indicates the language of the linked document. This is particularly important in search engines for identification purposes. Use the language codes according to ISO 639, for example "en" for English or "en-us" for American English.

ONCLICK

> This event takes place if you single-click on an element with the mouse. A given script is executed by this action.

ONDBLCLICK

> This event takes place if you double-click on an element with the mouse. A given script is executed by this action.

ONKEYDOWN

> This event takes place if you are in an element and a key is pressed and held down. This action executes a specific script.

ONKEYPRESS

> This event takes place if you are in an element and a key is simultaneously pressed and released again. This action executes a specific script.

ONKEYUP

> This event takes place if you are in an element and a key that was pressed is released. This action executes a specific script.

ONMOUSEDOWN

> This event takes place if you are in an element and a mouse button is clicked and held down. A given script is executed by this action.

ONMOUSEMOVE

> This event takes place if one moves the cursor over an object with the mouse. A given script is executed by this action.

ONMOUSEOUT

> This event takes place if a mouse moves the cursor off an element. This action executes a given script.

ONMOUSEOVER

> This event takes place if a mouse moves the cursor over an element. This action executes a given script.

ONMOUSEUP

> This event takes place if you are in an element and a mouse button that was clicked and held down is released. A given script is executed by this action.

STYLE

> The STYLE attribute is used to determine specific properties in the representation of labelled elements. Used style settings are defined by cascading style sheets.

TITLE

> Through this attribute selected elements can be assigned with additional information. This information is displayed in a pop up window in many browsers, if the mouse pointer is on the element.

Example

```
<sub>Subscript text</sub> here is
```

Events

ONCLICK, ONDBLCLICK, ONKEYDOWN, ONKEYPRESS, ONKEYUP, ONMOUSEDOWN, ONMOUSEMOVE, ONMOUSEOVER, ONMOUSEOUT, ONMOUSEUP

Related commands

B
I
S
SMALL
STRIKE
SUP
TT
U

SUMMARY   **\<html attribute>**

Summarises table content

Description

This attribute produces a summarised statement of the contents of a table.

Application

Supply a short summary of table contents with this attribute. The use of this attribute is optional.

Values

You can submit any string to this attribute as a value. If possible, this character string should not start or end with a blank space. The processing browser will filter these out if necessary.

Example

```
<table summary="Turnover figure 1999">
<tr>
<td>Cell 1 </td>
<td>Cell 2 </td>
</tr>
</table>
```

Accompanying element

TABLE

SUP

Displaying text as superscript

Description

This command, which is the opposite of the SUB command, is used to represent standard flow text. Text formatted in this way appears vertically aligned slightly above the baseline of the surrounding text and, depending on the browser used, is shown either in normal or in slightly reduced character size.

Application

The SUP command places text to be highlighted in the superscript position. This is particularly useful for the representation of mathematical formulae or footnotes. This command is also occasionally used to mark source links (references).

HTML 4.0 standard

CLASS, DIR, ID, LANG, STYLE, TITLE

Start tag: required; end tag: required.

Attribute

CLASS

> Through the CLASS attribute the element can be assigned to a group (class). Enter one of the free selectable class names as a value. These groupings then provide easy access to all related elements so you can change all the properties of the elements of a class with the help of cascading style sheets or other languages, or select a value.

DIR

> This attribute is necessary to determine the text direction. This attribute can have the values:

> LTR

>> This value determines the text direction from left to right (and is short for "left-to-right"). This is the default direction in the browser.

> RTL

>> If the text must run contrary to the standard direction from the right to the left margin of the screen, then choose the value RTL (short for "right-to-left").

ID

> This identifies the document. Using ID a specific element can be accessed with the help of a script language to select or change values, for example.

LANG

> This attribute indicates the language of the linked document. This is particularly important in search engines for identification purposes. Use the language codes according to ISO 639, for example "en" for English or "en-us" for American English.

ONCLICK

> This event takes place if you single-click on an element with the mouse. A given script is executed by this action.

ONDBLCLICK

> This event takes place if you double-click on an element with the mouse. A given script is executed by this action.

ONKEYDOWN

This event takes place if you are in an element and a key is pressed and held down. This action executes a specific script.

ONKEYPRESS

This event takes place if you are in an element and a key is simultaneously pressed and released again. This action executes a specific script.

ONKEYUP

This event takes place if you are in an element and a key that was presse is released. This action executes a specific script.

ONMOUSEDOWN

This event takes place if you are in an element and a mouse button is clicked and held down. A given script is executed by this action.

ONMOUSEMOVE

This event takes place if one moves the cursor over an object with the mouse. A given script is executed by this action.

ONMOUSEOUT

This event takes place if a mouse moves the cursor off an element. This action executes a given script.

ONMOUSEOVER

This event takes place if the mouse moves the cursor directly over the element (object). A given script is executed by this action.

ONMOUSEUP

This event takes place if you are in an element and a mouse button that was clicked and held down is released. A given script is executed by this action.

STYLE

The STYLE attribute is used to determine specific properties in the representation of labelled elements. Used style settings are defined by cascading style sheets.

TITLE

Through this attribute selected elements can be assigned with additional information. This information is displayed in a pop up window in many browsers, if the mouse pointer is on the element.

Example

`<sup>Superscript text</sup> Here is`

Events

ONCLICK, ONDBLCLICK, ONKEYDOWN, ONKEYPRESS, ONKEYUP, ONMOUSEDOWN, ONMOUSEMOVE, ONMOUSEOVER, ONMOUSEOUT, ONMOUSETUP

Related commands

I
S
SMALL
STRIKE
SUB
TT
U

SWITCH ☺

Playing selected media clips

Description

This command is used to automatically select and play one of several media clips. The selection could be executed according to languages or available frequency ranges, for example.

Parameter

ID

This identifies the document. Using ID, areas of other elements can be accessed.

TITLE

Gives the complete group a title with a short description of the contents.

Example

```
<switch id="identifier"
        title = "string">



</switch>
```

TABINDEX   <html attribute>

Determining tab order

Description

This attribute assigns an order to an element using positive or negative integers. Elements provided with this attribute can be selected with the Tab key one after the other. This simplifies operation for users who cannot use a mouse.

Application

Usually, all active elements in a page are automatically provided with a number for the tab order with an index to be used. The user can reach the next field by pressing the Tab key. If you want to change this order or the browser has not determined the order correctly, then you can change the index manually. Whether the index is serial or not is not important. The use of this attribute is optional.

Values

Valid values for this attribute are integers. The number must contain at least one of the numbers from 0 to 9 (="9").

Example

```
<input name="Field1" type="text" tabindex="1">
<input name="Field3" type="text" tabindex="100">
<input name="Field2" type="text" tabindex="99">
<input name="Field4" type="text" tabindex="101">
```

Accompanying elements

A
AREA
BUTTON
INPUT
OBJECT
SELECT
TEXTAREA

TABLE

W3C HTML 4.0

Defining tables

Description

Use this command to define tables.

Application

The TABLE command is used to define tables. Elements which determine the appearance of a table are then determined within this definition.

HTML 4.0 standard

BORDER, CELLPADDING, CELLSPACING, CLASS, DIR, FRAME, ID, LANG, RULES, STYLE, SUM-MARY, TITLE, WIDTH

Start tag: required; end tag: required.

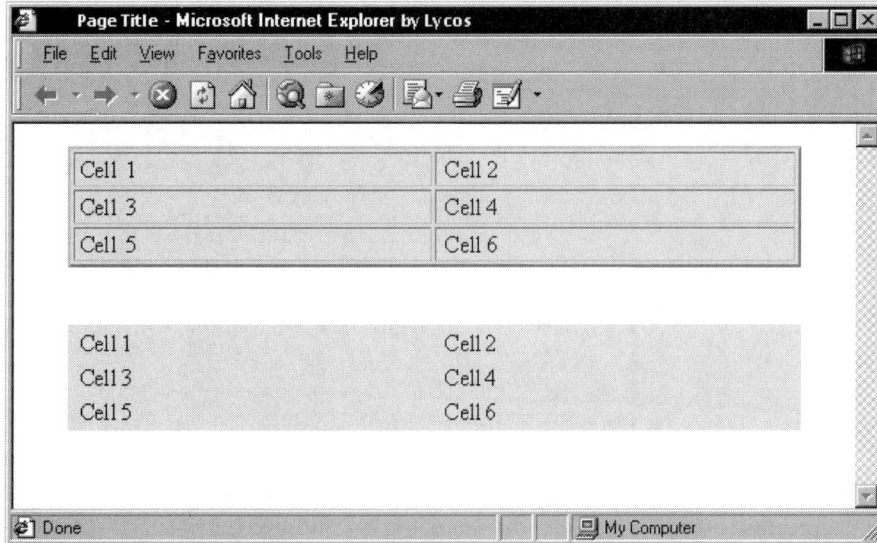

Tables with and without a frame

Attributes

ALIGN

This attribute is responsible for aligning tables.

LEFT

Left-alignment of a table.

RIGHT

Right-alignment of a table.

CENTER

Centre-alignment of a table.

BACKGROUND

This attribute refers to a background image to be inserted. This command is supported by current browsers but is not provided for in HTML.

BGcolour

Use this attribute to determine the background colour.

BORDER

This attribute creates borders around a table, of a specified thickness. With the value 0, you create an invisible table. The use of the BORDER attribute without another value causes a border of predefined width to be displayed.

BORDERCOLOR

Use this attribute to set the colour of the border. As well as the 16 defined colour keywords, up to 256 colours can be represented, indicated by hexadecimal numbers. In HTML 4.0 these settings are usually executed with style sheets. This attribute must be used together with the BORDER attribute. It is interpreted only by Explorer.

BORDERCOLORDARK

With this attribute, a dark colour is applied to a 3D border. This attribute is interpreted only by Explorer.

BORDERCOLORLIGHT

With this attribute, a bright colour is applied to a 3D border. This attribute is interpreted only by Explorer.

CELLPADDING

With this attribute, a rule between the cells is created measured in pixels.

CELLSPACING

With this attribute, a rule between cell margin and cell contents is created in pixels.

CLASS

Through the CLASS attribute the element can be assigned to a group (class). Enter one of the free selectable class names as a value. These groupings then provide easy access to all related elements so you can change all the properties of the elements of a class with the help of cascading style sheets or other languages, or select a value.

DIR

This attribute is necessary to determine the text direction. This attribute can have the values:

LTR

This value determines the text direction from left to right (and is short for "left-to-right"). This is the default direction in the browser.

RTL

If the text must run contrary to the standard direction from the right to the left margin of the screen, then choose the value RTL (short for "right-to-left").

FRAME

By default, using the BORDER attribute, a border is drawn around the table. With the FRAME attribute, this border can be adjusted. The following values are valid for FRAME:

ABOVE

Displays a border above the table only.

BELOW

Displays a border below the table only.

BORDER

Applies the default value. A frame is drawn around the complete table.

BOX

> This detail is identical to the value FRAME=BORDER or the BORDER command without the use of the FRAME attribute.

LHS

> Only produces a border on the left-hand side of the table (LHS = "left-hand side).

RHS

> Produces a border only on the right-hand side of the table (RHS = "right-hand side).

VOID

> With the VOID detail no border around the table will be displayed. Nevertheless, if you use the BORDER attribute, only the rules inside the table will be produced. The outer border is not displayed.

VSIDES

> Displays line borders to the left and right sides of the table only (VSIDES = "vertical sides").

HEIGHT

> Unlike the WIDTH attribute, the HEIGHT detail is not determined in the official HTML standard, but it interpreted by most browsers. With HEIGHT you indicate the height of the table on the page. If the contents of the table exceed the complete display, then this setting is ineffective.

HSPACE

> With the HSPACE attribute the space between the table and the text flowing around it can be determined exactly. With HSPACE you indicate the horizontal space and with VSPACE the vertical one. This attribute does not belong to the official HTML standard and is only interpreted by Netscape.

ID

> This identifies the document. Using ID, a specific element can be accessed with the help of a script language to select or change values, for example.

LANG

> This attribute indicates the language of the linked document. This is particularly important in search engines for identification purposes. Use the language codes according to ISO 639, for example "en" for English or "en-us" for American English.

ONCLICK

> This event takes place if you single-click on an element with the mouse. A given script is executed by this action.

ONDBLCLICK

> This event takes place if you double-click on an element with the mouse. A given script is executed by this action.

ONKEYDOWN

> This event takes place if you are in an element and a key is pressed and held down. This action executes a specific script.

ONKEYPRESS

This event takes place if you are in an element and a key is simultaneously pressed and released again. This action executes a specific script.

ONKEYUP

This event takes place if you are in an element and a key that was pressed is released. This action executes a specific script.

ONMOUSEDOWN

This event takes place if you are in an element and a mouse button is clicked and held down. A given script is executed by this action.

ONMOUSEMOVE

This event takes place if one moves the cursor over an object with the mouse. A given script is executed by this action.

ONMOUSEOUT

This event takes place if a mouse moves the cursor off an element. This action executes a given script.

ONMOUSEOVER

This event takes place if the mouse moves the cursor directly over the element (object). A given script is executed by this action.

ONMOUSEUP

This event takes place if you are in an element and a mouse button that was clicked and held down is released. A given script is executed by this action.

RULES

With the help of the RULES attribute you can decide exactly which table borders are to be displayed. The following are possible values for this attribute:

ALL

All lines between the table cells are displayed (standard setting).

COLS

Only the lines between the table columns are displayed.

GROUPS

The single elements of the table are framed with borders (head, body and table foot).

NONE

Interior table borders are not displayed.

ROWS

Only the borders between the single rows of a table are displayed.

STYLE

The STYLE attribute can be used to change style settings, particularly the appeaance of an element. As a value of the attribute you submit the corresponding options of a style sheet language (usually of CSS).

SUMMARY

The contents of a table can be summarised with the help of this attribute.

TITLE
> Give the user further information about the element used by determining a meaningful title with the help of the `title` command. Navigation in your Web site is made particularly easy for users who are dependent on a speech synthesiser.

VSPACE
> With `VSPACE`, the exact space between a table and text flowing around it is determined. With `HSPACE` you determine the horizontal space and with `VSPACE` the vertical space. This attribute does not belong to the official HTML standard and is only interpreted by Netscape.

WIDTH
> This attribute is used to determine the column width in pixels. With an input of `WIDTH="0"` you set the optimal width for this column. Other valid values can be supplied as integer or a percentage of the current available space on the screen.

Example

```
<table border="2" bgcolour="green" width="90%">

<tr>
<td>Cell 1 </td>
<td>Cell 2 </td>
</tr>

<tr>
<td>Cell 3 </td>
<td>Cell 4 </td>
</tr>

<tr>
<td>Cell 5 </td>
<td>Cell 6 </td>
</tr>
</table>
```

Events

```
ONCLICK, ONDBLCLICK, ONKEYDOWN, ONKEYPRESS, ONKEYUP, ONMOUSEDOWN,
ONMOUSEMOVE, ONMOUSEOVER, ONMOUSEOUT, ONMOUSEUP
```

XML definition

```
<!ELEMENT TABLE
(CAPTION ?, (COL* | COLGROUP*), THEAD ?, TFOOT ?, TBODY+) >
<!ATTLIST TABLE
%attrs;
```

361

```
summary           %text;      #IMPLIED
width             %Length;    #IMPLIED
bcommand          %pixel;     #IMPLIED
frame             %TFrame;    #IMPLIED
rules             %TRules;    #IMPLIED
cellspacing       %Length;    #IMPLIED
cellpadding       %Length;    #IMPLIED
% reserved;
datapagesize      CDATA       #IMPLIED>
```

Related commands

TD

TR

TARGET   <html attribute>

Indicating target windows of a link

Description

The TARGET attribute is used to determine the name of a window in which a link is opened. This attribute is used if several windows are open at the same time or if a new window with a link is to be opened.

Application

With the help of the TARGET attribute you can decide exactly in which frame or window to load a document. Indicate the name of the desired frame.

Values

TARGET allows also some additional predefined targets as well as the input of a name. The following concepts should be entered instead of frame names.

_blank

   Opens a new empty window.

_self

   Opens the document in the same window or frame in which this link was called.

_parent

   The document is opened in the parent frameset. If the document does not have any predecessors, then this value corresponds to the detail of _self.

_top

   If the document loads in the same window, it removes all frames and deletes the contents of the window.

Example
```
<a href="menu2.htm" target="Menu">
<a href="http://www.microsoft.co.uk" target="_top">
<a href="http://www.amazon.co.uk" target="_blank">
```

Accompanying elements
A
AREA
BASE
FORM
LINK

target-element

Defining patterns within a construction rule

Description
This defines a pattern within a construction rule, for the action. The target element is an integral constituent of a construction rule, but it does not need to contain any further attribute.

Application
Every construction rule must contain at least one pattern or target element. One exception are wildcards.

Parameter
type
> Contains the search pattern.

position
> Sometimes it is better to assign a specific format to select elements of a group. For example, a horizontal line could be inserted in a mailing list before the first element of the list and after the last element of the list.
> In XSL, there is a "position" attribute which is caused by the target element. Through position, you can determine that the first element of a group should be affected by the formatting, for example.

Keywords meaning

first-of-type	First descendant of an element of this type.
last-of-type	Last descendant of an element of this type.
first-of-any	First descendant of an element of any type.
last-of-any	Last descendant of an element of any type.

363

Example

```
<target-element type="list"/>
    < target-element/>
<target-element type="list" position="first-of-type"/>

<rule>
<target-element type="address" position="first-of-type"/>
<P>
    <children/>
</P>
</rule>
```

TBODY

Assignment of table rows

Description

With this command, rows are assigned to the body of a table.

Application

The TBODY command is used to assign rows to a table. This command is used to structure data contained in a table. When creating a table, make sure that this element is contained. The details on the table head are not evaluated by all browsers.

HTML 4.0 standard

ALIGN, CHAR, CHAROFF, CLASS, DIR, ID, LANG, STYLE, TITLE, VALIGN

Start tag: optional; end tag: optional.

Attributes

ALIGN

This attribute is responsible for determining the alignment of data within a table column.

LEFT

Left-alignment of data within a table. Default setting.

RIGHT

Right-alignment of data within a table.

CENTER

Centre-alignment of data within a table. Default presetting of table heads.

JUSTIFY

Justified a table.

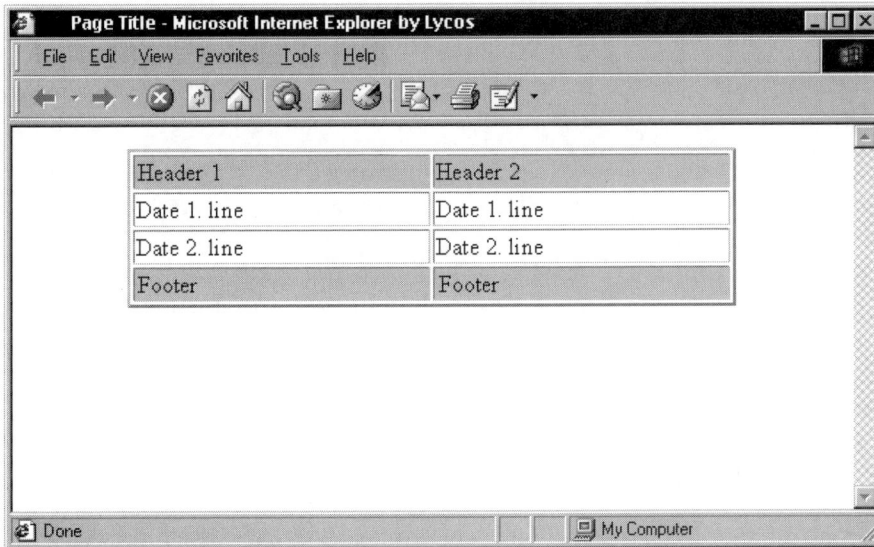

The three parts of a table: THEAD, TBODY and TFOOT

CHAR
> Alignment of data within a table for characters determined with the CHAR attribute.

CHAR
> With this attribute, characters from a valid character set can be determined, according to the way in which the data within the table are aligned. Be careful to distinguish between the use of upper and lower case characters in this attribute. The default character for alignment is the decimal point. Depending on the language used (LANG), this can be a comma or a full stop.

CHAROFF
> This attribute defines the offset to the first character which was formatted with the CHAR attribute.

CLASS
> Through the CLASS attribute the element can be assigned to a group (class). Enter one of the free selectable class names as a value. These groupings then provide easy access to all related elements so you can change all the properties of the elements of a class with the help of cascading style sheets or other languages, or select a value.

DIR
> This attribute is necessary to determine the text direction. This attribute can have the values:

> LTR
> > This value determines the text direction from left to right (and is short for "left-to-right"). This is the default direction in the browser.

RTL

If the text must run contrary to the standard direction from the right to the left margin of the screen, then choose the value RTL (short for "right-to-left").

ID

This identifies the document. Using ID, a specific element can be accessed with the help of a script language to select or change values, for example.

LANG

This attribute indicates the language of the linked document. This is particularly important in search engines for identification purposes. Use the language codes according to ISO 639, for example "en" for English or "en-us" for American English.

ONCLICK

This event takes place if you single-click on an element with the mouse. A given script is executed by this action.

ONDBLCLICK

This event takes place if you double-click on an element with the mouse. A given script is executed by this action.

ONKEYDOWN

This event takes place if you are in an element and a key is pressed and held down. This action executes a specific script.

ONKEYPRESS

This event takes place if you are in an element and a key is simultaneously pressed and released again. This action executes a specific script.

ONKEYUP

This event takes place if you are in an element and a key that was pressed is released. This action executes a specific script.

ONMOUSEDOWN

This event takes place if you are in an element and a mouse button is clicked and held down. A given script is executed by this action.

ONMOUSEMOVE

This event takes place if one moves the cursor over an object with the mouse. A given script is executed by this action.

ONMOUSEOUT

This event takes place if a mouse moves the cursor off an element. This action executes a given script.

ONMOUSEOVER

This event takes place if the mouse moves the cursor directly over the element (object). A given script is executed by this action.

ONMOUSEUP

This event takes place if you are in an element and a mouse button that was clicked and held down is released. A given script is executed by this action.

STYLE

The STYLE attribute can be used to change style settings, particularly the appearance of the element. As a value of the attribute you submit the corresponding option of a style sheet language (usually of CSS).

TITLE

Give the user additional information about the element used by determining a meaningful title with the TITLE command. Navigation in your site is made particularly easier for users who are dependent on speech synthesisers.

VALIGN

With this attribute the vertical alignment of text within a table can be determined. If this element is not used, all text is automatically centered aligned.

TOP

Highlighted text is aligned at the top.

BOTTOM

Highlighted text is aligned at the bottom.

MIDDLE

Highlighted text is centred.

BASELINE

Text in lines next to the highlighted text is aligned to the base line used.

Example

```
<table border>
<thead>
<tr>
<td>Heading 1 </td>
<td>Heading 2 </td>
</tr>
</thead>
<tbody>
<tr>
<td>Data 1st line </td>
<td>Data 1st line </td>
</tr>
<tr>
<td>Data 2nd line </td>
<td>Data 2nd line </td>
</tr>
</tbody>
<tfoot>
<tr>
<td>Foot </td>
<td>Foot </td>
</tr>
</tfoot>
</table>>
```

Events

ONCLICK, ONDBLCLICK, ONKEYDOWN, ONKEYPRESS, ONKEYUP, ONMOUSEDOWN, ONMOUSEMOVE, ONMOUSEOVER, ONMOUSEOUT, ONMOUSEUP

XML definition

```
<! ELEMENT TBODY O O (TR)+>
>>> <!ATTLIST (THEAD|TBODY|TFOOT)
% of attrs;
% cellhalign;
% cellvalign; >
```

Related commands

TABLE
TFOOT
THEAD

TD

Specifying data cell within a table

Description

With this command, you can mark individual data cells within tables.

Application

The TD command is used to mark data cells. This command determines that the following text is formatted to represent the first column in a table.

HTML 4.0 Standard

ABBR, ALIGN, AXIS, CHAR, CHAROFF, CLASS, COLSPAN, DIR, HEADERS, ID, LANG, ROWSPAN, SCOPE, STYLE, TITLE, VALIGN

Start tag: required; end tag: optional.

Attribute

ABBR

With this attribute, you can define a short description for a table cell. The first characters of the content are predefined.

ALIGN

This attribute is responsible for the alignment of the content within a cell.

LEFT

Left-alignment of the cell content.

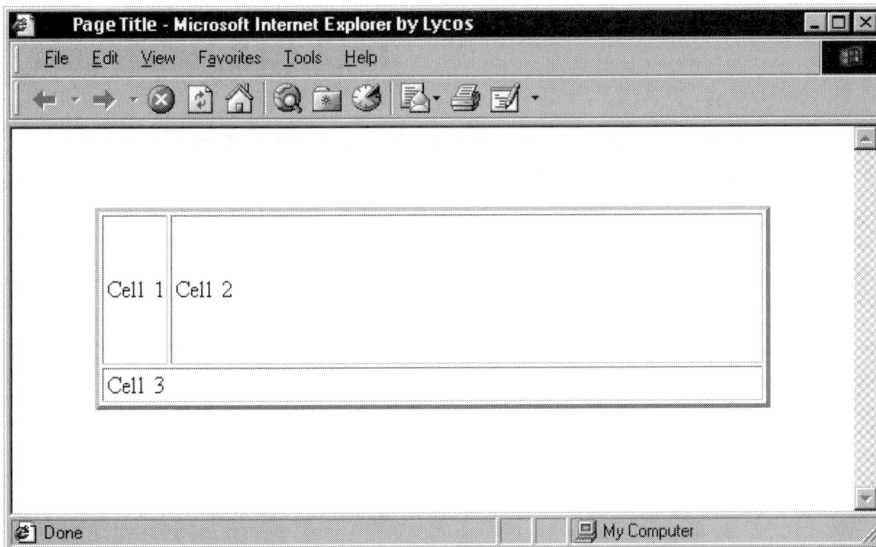

With COLSPAN attribute you can summarise cells

RIGHT
>Right-alignment of the cell content.

CENTER
>Centre-alignment of the cell content.

AXIS
>You can assign an element to a group of table elements which have similar contents with this attribute. The organisation of these table elements is carried out according to their hierarchy.

BGcolour
>With this attribute, the background colour is determined. Besides the 16 defined colour keywords, up to 256 colours can be represented, indicated by hexadecimal numbers. These settings are usually executed with style sheets in HTML 4.0.

CLASS
>Through the CLASS attribute the element can be assigned to a group (class). Enter one of the free selectable class names as a value. These groupings then provide easy access to all related elements so you can change all the properties of the elements of a class with the help of cascading style sheets or other languages, or select a value.

COLSPAN
>This attribute indicates the number of columns necessary for a cell. As a rule, if you want to expand (to span) a cell to three columns, indicate COLSPAN="3".

DIR
>This attribute is necessary to determine the text direction. This attribute can have the values:

LTR

This value determines the text direction from left to right (and is short for "left-to-right"). This is the default direction in the browser.

RTL

If the text must run contrary to the standard direction from the right to the left margin of the screen, then choose the value RTL (short for "right-to-left").

HEADERS

Through the HEADERS attribute a reference between cell contents and column header is produced. Here ID is assigned as a value for the column header. So, it is possible for language output systems, for example, to distribute cell contents together with a suitable column header.

HEIGHT

With HEIGHT you can set a precise height for a cell. At the same time, the width of the complete row is determined. Different cell heights within a row are not possible. The detail can be assigned in pixels or as a percentage.

ID

This identifies the document. Using ID, a specific element can be accessed with the help of a script language to select or change values, for example.

LANG

This attribute indicates the language of the linked document. This is particularly important in search engines for identification purposes. Use the language codes according to ISO 639, for example "en" for English or "en-us" for American English.

NOWRAP

This attribute determines that text is not automatically made into pages within a cell. If you want to insert line breaks, you must enter these manually with the BR command.

ONCLICK

This event takes place if you single-click on an element with the mouse. A given script is executed by this action.

ONDBLCLICK

This event takes place if you double-click on an element with the mouse. A given script is executed by this action.

ONKEYDOWN

This event takes place if you are in an element and a key is pressed and held down. This action executes a specific script.

ONKEYPRESS

This event takes place if you are in an element and a key is simultaneously pressed and released again. This action executes a specific script.

ONKEYUP

This event takes place if you are in an element and a key that was pressed is released. This action executes a specific script.

ONMOUSEDOWN

This event takes place if you are in an element and a mouse button is clicked and held down. A given script is executed by this action.

ONMOUSEMOVE

This event takes place if one moves the cursor over an object with the mouse. A given script is executed by this action.

ONMOUSEOUT

This event takes place if a mouse moves the cursor off an element. This action executes a given script.

ONMOUSEOVER

This event takes place if the mouse moves the cursor directly over the element (object). A given script is executed by this action.

ONMOUSEUP

This event takes place if you are in an element and a mouse button that was clicked and held down is released. A given script is executed by this action.

ROWSPAN

With this attribute you can set the number of rows necessary for a cell. As a rule only one row is needed.

SCOPE

This attribute indicates the set of data cells which contains the accompanying head information for the current cell. The command can be used as an alternative to HEADER for simple tables.

ROW

The current cell contains header information for the rest of the row.

COL

The current cell contains header information for the rest of the column.

COLGROUP

The current cell contains header information for the other elements of a column (COLGROUP).

ROWGROUP

The current cell contains header information for the other elements of a row (ROWGROUP).

STYLE

The STYLE attribute can be used to change style settings, particularly the look of the element. As a value of the attribute you submit the corresponding option of a style sheet language (usually of CSS).

TITLE

Give the user additional information about the element used by determining a meaningful title with the TITLE command. Navigation in your site is made easier for users who are dependent on speech synthesisers.

VALIGN

With this attribute the vertical alignment of content in a row can be determined. If this element is not used, all text is automatically centred.

TOP

Marked text is aligned at the top.

BOTTOM
>   Marked text is aligned at the bottom.

MIDDLE
>   Marked text is centred.

BASELINE
>   Both texts are aligned to a common baseline.

WIDTH
>   You can provide the cell with a definite width using WIDTH. The width of the entire column is determined simultaneously. Therefore, different details for cells in the same column are not possible. Width can be given in pixels or as a percentage.

Example

```
<table>
<tr>
<td width="10%" height="100">
          Cell 1
</td>
<td width="90%">
          Cell 2
</td>
<tr>
<td colspan="2">
          Cell 3
          </td>
     </tr>
</table>
```

Events

ONCLICK, ONDBLCLICK, ONKEYDOWN, ONKEYPRESS, ONKEYUP, ONMOUSEDOWN, ONMOUSEMOVE, ONMOUSEOVER, ONMOUSEOUT, ONMOUSEUPP

XML definition

```
<! ELEMENT (TH|TD) - O (%flow;)*>
<! ENTITY % Scope "(row|col|rowgroup|colgroup)">
<!ATTLIST (TH|TD)
%attrs;
abbr      % text;  # IMPLIED
axis       CDATA # IMPLIED
headers IDREFS # IMPLIED
scope % Scope;  # IMPLIED
rowspan NUMBER 1
colspan NUMBER 1
% cellhalign;
```

Related commands
TABLE
TH
TR

TEXT

☺

Diplaying a document

Description
This command allows you to display a document in a specific area of the window.

Parameter
abstract
> This attribute indicates a short description (abbreviation) for the group.

author
> This attribute is used to indicate the author of this media grouping.

begin
> Indicates the reproduction time. You can use h, min, s or ms as units.

copyright
> Information about the originator and the copyright can be submitted as values of this attribute.

dur
> Indicates the complete playing time of the group. You can use h, min, s or ms as units.

end
> Indicates the end time of the group. This value is the opposite of the attribute BEGIN. You can use h, min, s or ms as units.

id
> This identifies the document. Using ID, this area can be accessed by other elements.

repeat
> The complete group repeats for the specified number of times.

src
> Indicates the source of the media clip or the graphic. Here a valid URL is expected as a value.

title
> Gives the group a title with a short description of the contents.

Example
```
<text id="identifier"
     src="URL"
```

```
alt="string"
region="identifier"
title="string"
abstract="string"
author="string"
copyright="string"
longdesc="string"
type="string"
begin="clock-value"
end="clock-value"
dur="clock-value"
repeat="integer"
fill="remove|freeze"
system-bitrate="integer"
system-captions="on|off"
system-language="coma-separated-list"
system-overdub-or-caption="caption|overdub"
system-required="string"
system-screen-depth="integer"
system-screen-size="integerXinteger"/>
```

TEXT   **<html attribute>**

Determining text colour in a document

Description

This attribute is used to determine the text colour in an HTML document.

Application

The text colour for the complete document is indicated in the BODY tag. Naturally, you can change the colour of individual sections any time. The use of this attribute is optional. This command is not supported by HTML 4.0.

Values

Submit either a colour value in RGB syntax or a valid colour name to the attribute. For the RGB value, you indicate the values for the colours red, green and blue in hexadecimal notation: #RRGGBB (#008000 for green, for example). Alternatively, the predefined colour names (YELLOW, for example) can be used. Under the keyword colour table (colorpalette) you will find all standard colours. The following is a list of the16 most frequently used primary colours:

```
BLACK     = #000000  SILVER   = #COCOCO
GRAY      = #808080  WHITE    = #FFFFFF
MAROON    = #800000  RED      = #FF0000
```

```
PURPLE    = #800080  FUCHSIA   = #FF00FF
GREEN     = #008000  LIME      = #00FF00
OLIVE     = #808000  YELLOW    = #FFFF00
NAVY      = #000080  BLUE      = #0000FF
TEAL      = #008080  AQUA      = #00FFFF
```

Example

```
<body text="white" bgcolour="black">
<body text="#800000">
```

Accompanying element

BODY

text-align

Aligning text

Description

Text can be aligned vertically with this parameter.

Parameter

align
>   The alignment is executed by the keywords in HTML.

left
>   Left-alignment.

right
>   Right-alignment.

center
>   Centre-alignment.

justify
>   Text is justified.

Example

```
<style type="text/css">
h1, h2 { text-align: right }
h3, h4 { text-align: center }
</style>

<div style="text-align: justify">
</div>
</div>
```

TEXTAREA

Input of text within forms

Description

This command creates an area for users to input text.

Application

The TEXTAREA command is used to create an area for user input which is longer than one line (multiple line entries). Line breaks must be entered by the user. The text within the TEXTAREA container is provided as an initial value on accessing the page.

HTML 4.0 standard

ACCESSKEY, CLASS, COLS, DIR, DISABLED, ID, LANG, NAME, READONLY, ROWS, STYLE, TABINDEX, TITLE

Start tag: required; end tag: required.

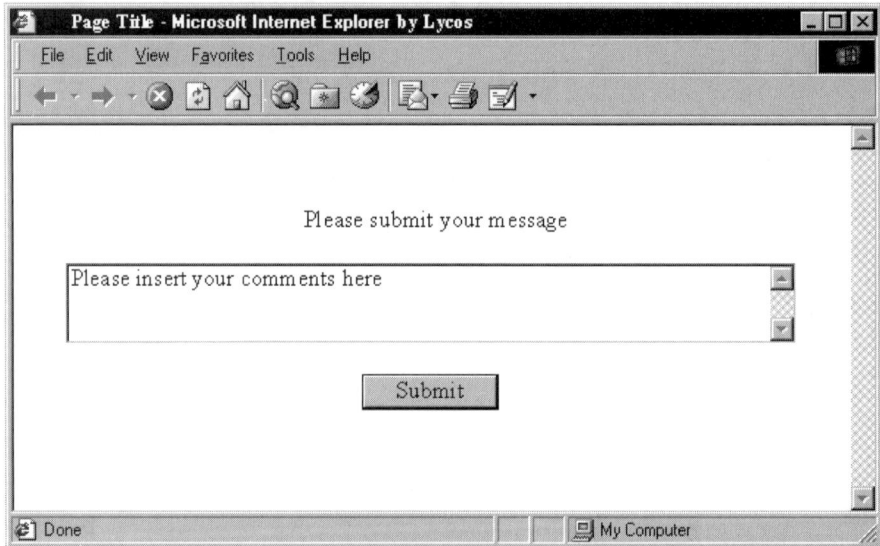

The TEXTAREA field for inputting text on multiple lines

Attributes

CLASS

Through the CLASS attribute the element can be assigned to a group (class). Enter one of the free selectable class names as a value. These groupings then provide easy access to all related elements so you can change all the properties of the elements of a class with the help of cascading style sheets or other languages, or select a value.

COLS

This attribute determines the width of the input window into characters.

DIR

This attribute is necessary to determine the text direction. This attribute can have the values:

LTR

This value determines the text direction from left to right (and is short for "left-to-right"). This is the default direction in the browser.

RTL

If the text must run contrary to the standard direction from the right to the left margin of the screen, then choose the value RTL (short for "right-to-left").

ID

This identifies for the document. Using ID, single elements can be accessed, for example with the help of a script language, to select and change values, for example.

DISABLED

With this attribute, it is possible to deactivate the entry field.

LANG

This attribute indicates the language of the linked document. This is particularly important in search engines for identification purposes. Use the language codes according to ISO 639, for example "en" for English or "en-us" for American English.

NAME

This attribute assigns a name to a text entry field.

ONBLUR

This event occurs when the mouse pointer is moved on the element. This action executes a given script.

ONCHANGE

This event occurs when the contents of the entry field are changed. This action executes a given script.

ONFOCUS

The ONFOCUS event occurs when the current element is focused on. If the user moves onto this field with the mouse or with the keyboard.

ONCLICK

This event takes place if you single-click on an element with the mouse. A given script is executed by this action.

ONDBLCLICK
> This event takes place if you double-click on an element with the mouse. A given script is executed by this action.

ONKEYDOWN
> This event takes place if you are in an element and a key is pressed and held down. This action executes a specific script.

ONKEYPRESS
> This event takes place if you are in an element and a key is pressed and released. This action executes a specific script.

ONKEYUP
> This event takes place if you are in an element and a key that was pressed is released. This action executes a specific script.

ONMOUSEDOWN
> This event takes place if you are in an element and a mouse button is clicked and held down. A given script is executed by this action.

ONMOUSEMOVE
> This event takes place if one moves the cursor over an object with the mouse. A given script is executed by this action.

ONMOUSEOUT
> This event takes place if a mouse moves the cursor off an element. This action executes a given script.

ONMOUSEOVER
> This event takes place if the mouse moves the cursor directly over the element (object). A given script is executed by this action.

ONMOUSEUP
> This event takes place if you are in an element and a mouse button that was clicked and held down is released. A given script is executed by this action.

ONSELECT
> This event becomes active if the user selects a text in the entry field.

READONLY
> This attribute marks an entry field as read-only. Other alterations, like writing in the entry field, are not allowed.

ROWS
> This attribute determines the number of lines in an input window.

STYLE
> The STYLE attribute can be used to change style settings, particularly the appearance of the element. As a value of the attribute you submit the corresponding options of a style sheet language (usually CSS).

TABINDEX
> This attribute assigns an ordered position to an element by using positive or negative integers. Elements which are provided with this attribute can be selected with the Tab key one after the other.

TITLE

Give the user additional information about the element used by determining a meaningful title with the help of the TITLE command. Navigation in your site is made particularly easier for users who are dependent on speech synthesisers.

WRAP

Although not provided in the official HTML, line breaks can automatically be created with the WRAP attribute. Netscape and Internet Explorer interpret this attribute. Two values are possible:

VIRTUAL

The text is visibly made into pages while the user inputs text. When transmitting the data to the server, the line breaks are removed again.

PHYSICAL

During the input of data, the text entered is automatically broken down into line breaks and is transmitted to the server in this way.

Example

```
<div align="center">
Please send us your message
</div>

<form>
>>> <textarea name="Comment" rows="3" cols="60"
    wrap = "virtual" >
Enter your comment here!
</textarea>
<br><br>
<input type=subMit value="Absenden">
</form>
```

Events

ONBLUR, ONCHANGE, ONCLICK, ONDBLCLICK, ONFOCUS, ONKEYDOWN, ONKEY-PRESS, ONKEYUP, ONMOUSEDOWN, ONMOUSEMOVE, ONMOUSEOVER, ONMOUSEOUT, ONMOUSEUP, ONSELECT

XML definition

```
<! ELEMENT TEXTAREA - - (#PCDATA)>
<!ATTLIST TEXTAREA
% attrs;
name        CDATA           #IMPLIED
rows        NUMBER          #REQUIRED
cols        NUMBER          #REQUIRED
disabled    (disabled)      #IMPLIED
readonly    (readonly)      #IMPLIED
tabindex    NUMBER          #IMPLIED
accesskey   %Character;     #IMPLIED
onfocus     %script;        #IMPLIED
```

```
onblur      % script;      #IMPLIED
onselect    % script;      #IMPLIED
onchange    % script;      #IMPLIED
% reserved;>
```

Related command
INPUT

text-decoration

CASCADING STYLE SHEETS

Adding features to text

Description
Through the text-decoration parameter, optional attributes to "decorate" the text can be determined, such as underlining or blinking.

Parameter
none
> No particular text decoration (standard setting).

underline
> Text underlined.

overline
> Line over text.

line-through
> Text crossed out.

blink
> Text blinking.

Example
```
<style type="text/css">
h1, h2 { text-decoration: blink }
h3, h4 { text-decoration: underline }
</style>

<div style="text-decoration: underline">
</div>
```

text-indent

Indenting text

Description

With this command, the first line of each paragraph can be indented.

Parameter

Positive and negative numerical details are allowed. A negative number causes a left indent.

Example

```
<style type="text/css">
h1, h2 { text-indent: 10mm }
h3, h4 { text-indent: -1cm }
</style>

<div style="text-indent: 12mm">
</div>
```

text-shadow

Adding a shadow to text

Description

Text can be shadowed with this attribute.

Parameter

Indicate either the colour of the shadow, or the keyword NONE to prevent a shadow from being displayed.

Example

```
<style type="text/css">
h1, h2 { text-shadow: black }
h3, h4 { text-shadow: gray }
</style>

<div style="text-shadow: none">
</div>
```

text-transform

Changing text

Description

Text-transform changes character size, for example from upper to lower case.

Parameter

transform

> The following keywords can be used to transform the letter size:

> No alterations (standard setting).

capitalize

> The first letter of every word is changed to a capital letter.

uppercase

> All letters are changed into upper case.

lowercase

> All letters are changed into lower case.

Example

```
<style type="text/css">
h1, h2 { text-transform: capitalize }
h3, h4 { text-transform: none }
</style>

<div style="text-transform: capitalize">
</div>
```

TFOOT

Assignment of table rows

Description

With this command, table rows are assigned to the foot of the table.

Application

The TFOOT command is used to assign rows to the foot of a table. By this assignment the table footer appears on every page in a printout.

HTML 4.0 standard

ALIGN, CHAR, CHAROFF, CLASS, DIR, ID, LANG, STYLE, TITLE, VALIGN

Start tag: required; end tag: optional.

Attributes

ALIGN

This attribute is responsible for determining the alignment of data within a table column.

LEFT

Left-alignment of data within a table. Default setting.

RIGHT

Right-alignment of data within a table.

CENTER

Alignment of data centred within a table. Default presetting for the table foot.

JUSTIFY

Table text justified.

CHAR

Alignment of characters determined within a table with the CHAR attribute.

CHAR

With this attribute, a character can be determined from a valid character set, on which data in the table are aligned. Be careful to distinguish the use of upper and lower characters using this attribute. The default character for the alignment is the decimal point. Depending on the language used (LANG), this can be a comma or a full stop, for example.

CHAROFF

This attribute defines the offset to the first character which was formatted with the CHAR attribute.

CLASS

Through the CLASS attribute the element can be assigned to a group (class). Enter one of the free selectable class names as a value. These groupings then provide easy access to all related elements so you can change all the properties of the elements of a class with the help of cascading style sheets or other languages, or select a value.

DIR

This attribute is necessary to determine the text direction. This attribute can have the values:

LTR

This value determines the text direction from the left to the right (and is short for "left-to-right"). This is the default direction in the browser.

RTL

If the text must run contrary to the standard direction from the right to the left margin of the screen, then choose the value RTL (short for "right-to-left").

ID

This attribute can assign a document unique identifier to a marked element.

LANG

This attribute indicates the language of the linked document. This is particularly important in search engines for identification purposes. Use the language codes according to ISO 639, for example "en" for English or "en-us" for American English.

ONCLICK

This event takes place if you single-click on an element with the mouse. A given script is executed by this action.

ONDBLCLICK

This event takes place if you double-click on an element with the mouse. A given script is executed by this action.

ONKEYDOWN

This event takes place if you are in an element and a key is pressed and held down. This action executes a specific script.

ONKEYPRESS

This event takes place if you are in an element and a key is simultaneously pressed and released again. This action executes a specific script.

ONKEYUP

This event takes place if you are in an element and a key that was pressed is released. This action executes a specific script.

ONMOUSEDOWN

This event takes place if you are in an element and a mouse button is clicked and held down. A given script is executed by this action.

ONMOUSEMOVE

This event takes place if one moves the cursor over an object with the mouse. A given script is executed by this action.

ONMOUSEOUT

This event takes place if a mouse moves the cursor off an element. This action executes a given script.

ONMOUSEOVER

This event takes place if the mouse moves the cursor directly over the element (object). A given script is executed by this action.

ONMOUSEUP

This event takes place if you are in an element and a mouse button that was clicked and held down is released. A given script is executed by this action.

STYLE

The attribute STYLE can be used to change style settings, in particular the appearance of the element. As a value of the attribute you apply the corresponding options of a style sheet language (usually CSS).

TITLE

Give the user further information about the element used by determining a meaningful title with the help of the TITLE command. Navigation in your Web site is made easier for users who are dependent on voice response.

VALIGN

This attribute determines the horizontal alignment of text within a table. If this element is not used, all text is automatically centred.

TOP

Marked text aligned at the top.

BOTTOM

Marked text aligned at the bottom.

MIDDLE

Marked text centred.

BASELINE

All text aligned on a common baseline.

Example

```
<table border>
<thead>
<tr>
<td>Heading 1 </td>
<td>Heading 2 </td>
</tr>
</thead>

<tbody>
<tr>
<td>Data 1st line </td>
<td>Data 1st line </td>
</tr>

<tr>
<td>Data 2nd line </td>
<td>Data 2nd line </td>
</tr>

</tbody>
<tfoot>
<tr>
<td>Foot </td>
<td>Foot </td>
</tr>
</tfoot>
```

```
</table>
```

Events

```
ONCLICK, ONDBLCLICK, ONKEYDOWN, ONKEYPRESS, ONKEYUP, ONMOUSEDOWN,
ONMOUSEMOVE, ONMOUSEOVER, ONMOUSEOUT, ONMOUSEUP
```

XML-Definition

```
<! ELEMENT TFOOT - O (TR)+>
<!ATTLIST (THEAD|TBODY|TFOOT
% attrs;
% cellhalign;
% cellvalign;>
```

Related commands

TABLE
TBODY
THEAD

TH

Naming table columns

Description

With this command, it is possible to provide single table columns with a name.

Application

The TH command is used to distribute a list of cell headers. The cell header contains additional information about the contents of a cell or column besides the name. As a rule, such headers are centred and displayed in bold.

HTML 4.0 standard

```
ABBR, ALIGN, AXIS, CHAR, CHAROFF, CLASS, COLSPAN, DIR, HEADERS, ID,
LANG, ROWSPAN, SCOPE, STYLE, TITLE, VALIGN
```

Start tag: required; end tag: optional.

Attributes

ABBR
> With this attribute, it is possible to define a short description for a table cell. The first characters of the contents are predefined.

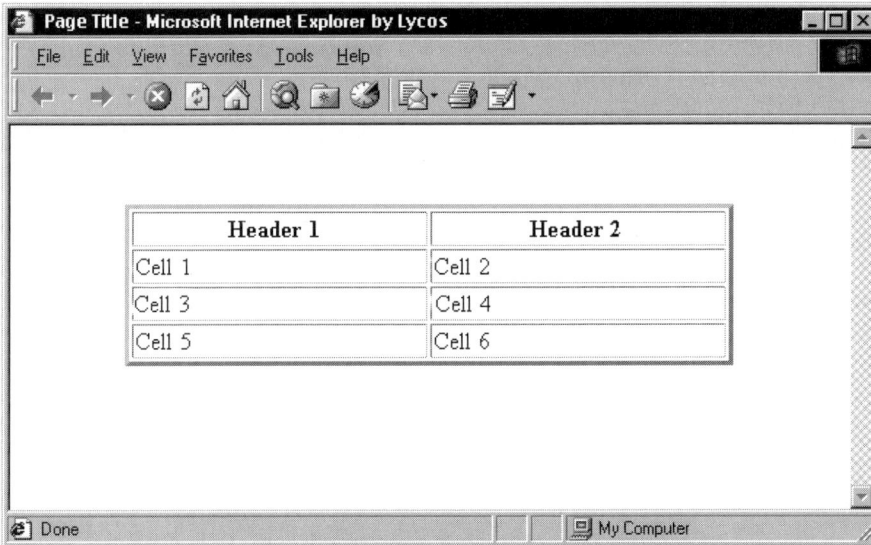

Table headers with TH

ALIGN

This attribute is responsible for the alignment of the cell contents within a cell.

LEFT

Left-alignment of the cell contents.

RIGHT

Right-alignment of the cell contents.

CENTER

Centre-alignment of the cell contents.

AXIS

You can assign an element to a group of table elements which have similar contents with this attribute. The organisation of these table elements is executed according to a hierarchy.

BGcolour

With this attribute, the colour of the background is determined. Up to 256 colours can be displayed, indicated by hexadecimal nembers, besides the 16 defined colour keywords. In HTML 4.0, these settings are usually executed with style sheets.

CLASS

Through the CLASS attribute the element can be assigned to a group (class). Enter one of the free selectable class names as a value. These groupings then provide easy access to all related elements so you can change all the properties of the elements of a class with the help of cascading style sheets or other languages or select a value.

BGcolour

With this attribute, the colour of the background is determined. Besides the 16 defined colour keywords, up to 256 colours can be represented, which are indiciated by hexadecimal numbers. These settings are usually executed by style sheets in HTML 4.0.

DIR

This attribute is necessary to determine the text direction. This attribute can have the values:

LTR

This value determines the text direction from left to right (and is short for "left-to-right"). This is the default direction in the browser.

RTL

If the text must run contrary to the standard direction from the right to the left margin of the screen, then choose the value RTL (short for "right-to-left").

HEADERS

Through the HEADERS attribute a reference between cell contents and column header is produced. Here ID is assigned as a value for the column header. This make it possible for language output systems, for example, to distribute cell contents together with a suitable column header.

HEIGHT

With HEIGHT you can provide a cell with a precise height. At the same time, the width of the complete row is determined. Different cell heights within a row are not possible. Height can be given in pixels or as a percentage.

ID

This identifies the document. Using ID, a specific element can be accessed with the help of a script language to select or change values, for example.

LANG

This attribute indicates the language of the linked document. This is particularly important in search engines for identification purposes. Use the language codes according to ISO 639, for example "en" for English or "en-us" for American English.

NOWRAP

With this attribute text is not automatically made into pages within a cell. If you want to insert line breaks, you must enter these manually with the BR command.

ONCLICK

This event takes place if you single-click on an element with the mouse. A given script is executed by this action.

ONDBLCLICK

This event takes place if you double-click on an element with the mouse. A given script is executed by this action.

ONKEYDOWN

This event takes place if you are in an element and a key is pressed and held down. This action executes a specific script.

ONKEYPRESS

This event takes place if you are in an element and a key is simultaneously pressed and released again. This action executes a specific script.

ONKEYUP

This event takes place if you are in an element and a key that was pressed is released. This action executes a specific script.

ONMOUSEDOWN

This event takes place if you are in an element and a mouse button is clicked and held down. A given script is executed by this action.

ONMOUSEMOVE

This event takes place if one moves the cursor over an object with the mouse. A given script is executed by this action.

ONMOUSEOUT

This event takes place if a mouse moves the cursor off an element. This action executes a given script.

ONMOUSEOVER

This event takes place if the mouse moves the cursor directly over the element (object). A given script is executed by this action.

ONMOUSEUP

This event takes place if you are in the described element and a mouse button that was clicked and held down is released. A given script is executed by this action.

ROWSPAN

With this attribute the number of rows necessary for a cell is set. As a rule only one row is needed.

SCOPE

This attribute indicates the set of data cells which contains the accompanying head information for the current cell. The command can be used as an alternative to HEADER for simple tables.

ROW

The current cell contains header information for the rest of the row.

COL

The current cell contains header information for the rest of the column.

COLGROUP

The current cell contains header information for the other elements of a column (COLGROUP).

ROWGROUP

The current cell contains header information for the other elements of a row (ROWGROUP).

STYLE
> The STYLE attribute can be used to change style settings, particularly the appearance of the element. As a value of the attribute you submit the corresponding option of a style sheet language (usually of CSS).

TITLE
> Give the user additional information about the element used by determining a meaningful title with the TITLE command. Navigation in your site is made easier for users who are dependent on speech synthesisers.

VALIGN
> With this attribute the vertical alignment of content in a row can be determined. If this element is not used, all texts are automatically centred.
>
> TOP
> > Marked text is aligned at the top.
>
> BOTTOM
> > Marked text is aligned at the bottom.
>
> MIDDLE
> > Marked text is centred.
>
> BASELINE
> > All text is aligned to a common baseline.

WIDTH
> You can set the cell width using WIDTH. At the same time, the width of the entire column is determined. Therefore, different settings for cells in the same column are not possible. This can be given in pixels or as a percentage.

Example

```
<table>
<tr>
<th>Header 1 </th>
<th>Header 2 </th>
<tr>
<td>Cell 1 </td>
<td>Cell 2 </td>
</tr>
</table>
```

Events

ONCLICK, ONDBLCLICK, ONKEYDOWN, ONKEYPRESS, ONKEYUP, ONMOUSEDOWN, ONMOUSEMOVE, ONMOUSEOVER, ONMOUSEOUT, ONMOUSEUP

XML definition

```
<! ELEMENT (TH|TD) - 0 (%flow;)*>
<! ENTITY % Scope "(row|col|rowgroup|colgroup)">
<!ATTLIST (TH|TD)
%attrs;
abbr % text;  # IMPLIED
```

```
axis CDATA # IMPLIED
headers IDREFS # IMPLIED
scope % Scope; # IMPLIED
rowspan NUMBER 1
colspan NUMBER 1
% cellhalign;
% cellvalign;>
```

Related commands

TABLE
TD
TH
TR

THEAD

Assignment of table rows

Description

With this command, table rows are assigned to the table header.

Application

The THEAD command (abbreviation for "Table Head") is used to assign rows to a table head. With this assignment, the table header appears on every printed page when printing.

HTML 4.0 standard

ALIGN, CHAR, CHAROFF, CLASS, DIR, ID, LANG, STYLE, TITLE, VALIGN

Start tag: required; end tag: optional.

Attributes

ALIGN

This attribute is responsible for determining the alignment of data within a table column.

LEFT

Left-alignment of data within a table. Default setting.

RIGHT

Right-alignment of data within a table.

CENTER

Centre-alignment of data within a table. Default setting for the table footer.

JUSTIFY
Table justification.

CHAR
Alignment of characters determined within a table with the CHAR attribute.

CHAR
With this attribute, a character can be determined from a valid character set, on which data in the table are aligned. Be careful to distinguish the use of upper and lower case characters when using this attribute. The default character for the alignment is the decimal point. Depending on the language used (LANG), this can be a comma or a full stop.

CHAROFF
This attribute defines the offset to the first character which was formatted with the CHAR attribute.

CLASS
Through the CLASS attribute the element can be assigned to a group (class). Enter one of the free selectable class names as a value. These groupings then provide easy access to all related elements so you can change all the properties of the elements of a class with the help of cascading style sheets or other languages, or select a value.

DIR
This attribute is necessary to determine the text direction. This attribute can have the values:

LTR
This value determines the text direction from left to right (and is short for "left-to-right"). This is the default direction in the browser.

RTL
If the text must run contrary to the standard direction from the right to the left margin of the screen, then choose the value RTL (short for "right-to-left").

ID
This attribute can assign a document unique identifier to a marked element.

LANG
This attribute indicates the language of the linked document. This is particularly important in search engines for identification purposes. Use the language codes according to ISO 639, for example "en" for English or "en-us" for American English.

ONCLICK
This event takes place if you single-click on an element with the mouse. A given script is executed by this action.

ONDBLCLICK
This event takes place if you double-click on an element with the mouse. A given script is executed by this action.

ONKEYDOWN

This event takes place if you are in an element and a key is pressed and held down. This action executes a specific script.

ONKEYPRESS

This event takes place if you are in an element and a key is simultaneously pressed and released again. This action executes a specific script.

ONKEYUP

This event takes place if you are in an element and a key that was pressed is released. This action executes a specific script.

ONMOUSEDOWN

This event takes place if you are in an element and a mouse button is clicked and held down. A given script is executed by this action.

ONMOUSEMOVE

This event takes place if one moves the cursor over an object with the mouse. A given script is executed by this action.

ONMOUSEOUT

This event takes place if a mouse moves the cursor off an element. This action executes a given script.

ONMOUSEOVER

This event takes place if the mouse moves the cursor directly over the element (object). A given script is executed by this action.

ONMOUSEUP

This event takes place if you are in an element and a mouse button that was clicked and held down is released. A given script is executed by this action.

STYLE

The STYLEattribute can be used to change style settings, in particular the appearance of an element. As a value of the attribute you apply the corresponding options of a style sheet language (usually CSS).

TITLE

Give the user further information about the element used by determining a meaningful title with the help of the TITLE command. Navigation in your Web site is made easier for users who are dependent on voice response.

VALIGN

With this attribute the horizontal alignment of text within a table can be determined. If this element is not used, all text is automatically centred.

TOP

Marked text aligned at the top.

BOTTOM

Marked text aligned at the bottom.

MIDDLE

Marked text centred.

BASELINE

Text aligned on a common baseline.

Example

```
<table border>
<thead>
<tr>
<td>Header 1</td>
<td>Header 2</td>
</tr>
</thead>

<tbody>
<tr>
<td>Data 1st cell</td>
<td>Data 1st cell</td>
</tr>
<tr>
<td>Data 2nd cell</td>
<td>Data 2nd cell</td>
</tr>
</tbody>
<tfoot>
<tr>
<td>Foot</td>
<td>Foot</td>
</tr>
</tfoot>
</table>
```

Events

ONCLICK, ONDBLCLICK, ONKEYDOWN, ONKEYPRESS, ONKEYUP, ONMOUSEDOWN, ONMOUSEMOVE, ONMOUSEOVER, ONMOUSEOUT, ONMOUSEUP

XML definition

```
<! ELEMENT THEAD - O (TR)+>
<!ATTLIST (THEAD|TBODY|TFOOT)
%attrs;
%cellhalign;
%cellvalign;>
```

Related commands

TABLE
TFOOT
THEAD

TITLE   **\<html attribute>**

Indicating titles of an element

Description

Give the user additional information about the element used by giving it a title using the TITLE command. Navigation in your site is made easier for users who are dependent on a speech synthesiser.

Application

Through the TITLE attribute you can add a short description or a title with almost every command.

Values

You can submit any string to this attribute as a value. If possible, this character string should not start or end with a blank space. The processing browser will filter these out if necessary.

Example

```
<p title="summary"></p>
<h1 title="content overview"></h1>
<a title="Link to a search engine"></a>
```

Accompanying elements

A	COL	H3
ABBR	COLGROUP	H4
ACRONYM	DD	H5
ADDRESS	DEL	H6
APPLET	DFN	HR
AREA	DIR	I
B	DIV	IFRAME
BDO	DL	IMG
BIG	DT	INPUT
BLOCKQUOTE	EM	INS
BODY	FIELDSET	ISINDEX
BR	FONT	KBD
BUTTON	FORM	LABEL
CAPTION	FRAME	LEGEND
CENTER	FRAMESET	LI
CITE	H1	LINK
CODE	H2	MAP

MENU	SUB
NOFRAMES	SUP
NOSCRIPT	TABLE
OBJECT	TBODY
OL	TD
OPTGROUP	TEXTAREA
OPTION	TFOOT
P	TH
PRE	THEAD
Q	TR
S	TT
SAMP	U
SELECT	UL
SMALL	VAR
SPAN	
STRIKE	
STRONG	

TITLE

Information about the title of an HTML document

Description

The title of an HTML document is determined with this command.

Application

TITLE is the only command which is mandatory for an HTML document. Therefore, every HTML document must have a unique name. Every browser can recognise and represent titles. Titles are also frequently used to describe bookmark entries. You can use a special character encoding within this command in the form of entities.

HTML 4.0 standard

DIR, LANG

Start tag: required; end tag: required.

The entered title is shown on the title bar of the browser

Attributes

DIR

This attribute is necessary to determine the text direction. This attribute can have the values:

LTR

This value determines the text direction from left to right (and is short for "left-to-right"). This is the default direction in the browser.

RTL

If the text must run contrary to the standard direction from the right to the left margin of the screen, then choose the value RTL (short for "right-to-left").

LANG

This attribute indicates the language of the linked document. This is particularly important in search engines for identification purposes. Use the language codes according to ISO 639, for example "en" for English or "en-us" for American English.

Example

```
<head>
<title>Reference of HTML commands </title>
...
</head>
```

XML definition

```
<! ELEMENT TITLE - - (#PCDATA) -(%head.misc;)>
<! ATTLIST TITLE %i18n>
```

Related commands

BODY
HEAD

Token

Rules to define specific XML commands

Description

A name or token is a valid description for a mark-up or an attribute name, for example.

Application

A valid name must begin with a letter. Hyphens, punctuation marks, underscores, numbers and letters are also allowed.

Using the XML letters at the beginning of a name (both in upper and lower case), and colons should be avoided.

Example

```
<address>
<chapter1_5>
<das_xml_reference_book>
</a-valid__name_123>
```

top

Top position

Description

The space detail always corresponds to the distance of the window margin when positioning elements on the page. If you want to move this top position, you can do so using the top element.

Parameter

Indicate a numerical value for the top positioning.

Example

```
<style type="text/css">
h1, h2 {top:100 px}
h3, h4 {top:100}
</style>

<div style="top:100">
</div>
```

TR

Defining rows of a table

W3C HTML 4.0 ✓

Description

With this command it is possible to define single rows of a table.

Application

With the TR command, rows of a table are defined, sub-divided and structured within a table. A table row consists of a number of nested table cells.

HTML 4.0 standard

ALIGN, CHAR, CHAROFF, CLASS, DIR, ID, LANG, STYLE, TITLE, VALIGN

Start tag: required; end tag: optional.

Attributes

ALIGN

This attribute is responsible for determining the alignment of cell content within a cell.

LEFT

Left-alignment of cell contents.

RIGHT

Right-alignment of cell contents.

CENTER

Centre-alignment of cell content.

CHAR

Alignment of characters fixed within a table with the CHAR attribute.

CHAR

With this attribute, a character can be determined from a valid character set, on which data in the table is aligned. Be careful to distinguish between the use of upper and lower case characters when using this attribute. The default character for the alignment is the decimal point. Depending on the language used (LANG), this can be a comma or a full stop.

CHAROFF

This attribute shows the offset to the first character formatted with the CHAR attribute.

CLASS

Through the CLASS attribute, the element can be assigned to a group (class). Enter one of the free selectable class names as a value. These groupings then provide easy access to all related elements so you can change all the properties of the elements of a class with the help of cascading style sheets or other languages or select a value.

DIR

This attribute is necessary to determine the text direction. This attribute can have the values:

LTR

This value determines the text direction from left to right (and is short for "left-to-right"). This is the default direction in the browser.

RTL

If the text must run contrary to the standard direction from the right to the left margin of the screen, choose the value RTL (short for "right-to-left").

ID

This attribute identifies a document.

LANG

This attribute indicates the language of the linked document. This is particularly important in search engines for identification purposes. Use the language codes according to ISO 639, for example "en" for English or "en-us" for American English.

ONCLICK

This event takes place if you single-click on an element with the mouse. A given script is executed by this action.

ONDBLCLICK

This event takes place if you double-click on an element with the mouse. A given script is executed by this action.

ONKEYDOWN

This event takes place if you are in an element and a key is pressed and held down. This action executes a specific script.

ONKEYPRESS

This event takes place if you are in an element and a key is simultaneously pressed and released again. This action executes a specific script.

ONKEYUP

This event takes place if you are in an element and a key that was pressed is released. This action executes a specific script.

ONMOUSEDOWN

This event takes place if you are in an element and a mouse button is clicked and held down. A given script is executed by this action.

ONMOUSEMOVE

This event takes place if one moves the cursor over an object with the mouse. A given script is executed by this action.

ONMOUSEOUT

This event takes place if a mouse moves the cursor off an element. This action executes a given script.

ONMOUSEOVER

This event takes place if the mouse moves the cursor directly over the element (object). A given script is executed by this action.

ONMOUSEUP

This event takes place if you are in an element and a mouse button that was clicked and held down is released. A given script is executed by this action.

STYLE

The STYLE attribute can be used to change style settings, in particular the appearance of an element. As a value of the attribute you apply the corresponding options of a style sheet language (usually CSS).

TITLE

Give the user further information about the element used by determining a meaningful title with the help of the TITLE command. Navigation in your Web site is made easier for users who are dependent on voice response.

VALIGN

With this attribute the horizontal alignment of text within a table can be determined. If this element is not used, all text is automatically centred.

TOP

Marked text aligned at the top.

BOTTOM

Marked text aligned at the bottom.

MIDDLE

Marked text centred.

BASELINE

Text aligned to a common baseline.

Example

```
<table>
<tr>
     <td>first row</td>
</tr>
<tr>
     <td>second row</td>
</tr>
</table>
```

Events

ONCLICK, ONDBLCLICK, ONKEYDOWN, ONKEYPRESS, ONKEYUP, ONMOUSEDOWN, ONMOUSEMOVE, ONMOUSEOVER, ONMOUSEOUT, ONMOUSEUP

XML definition

```
<! ELEMENT TR - 0 (TH|TD)+>
<!ATTLIST TR
% attrs;
% cellhalign;
% cellvalign;>
```

Related commands

TD
TH

TT

Display of non-proportional fonts

Description

With this command, it is possible to display all displayed characters and letters in the same size.

Application

The TT command enables characters to be displayed in exactly the same size. With this non-proportional repesentation, it is possible to set monospaced letters. This kind of text is also described as teletext. Courier is an example of a monospace font.

HTML 4.0 standard

CLASS, DIR, ID, LANG, STYLE, TITLE

Start tag: required; end tag: required.

Attributes

CLASS

Through the CLASS attribute the element can be assigned to a group (class). Enter one of the free selectable class names as a value. These groupings then provide easy access to all related elements so you can change all the properties of the elements of a class with the help of cascading style sheets or other languages, or select a value.

DIR

This attribute is necessary to determine the text direction. This attribute can have the values:

LTR

This value determines the text direction from left to right (and is short for "left-to-right"). This is the default direction in the browser.

RTL

If the text must run contrary to the standard direction from the right to the left margin of the screen, choose the value RTL (short for "right-to-left").

ID

The ID attribute, identifies the document. Using ID, a specific element can be accessed with the help of a script language to select or change values, for example.

LANG

This attribute indicates the language of the linked document. This is particularly important in search engines for identification purposes. Use the language codes according to ISO 639, for example "en" for English or "en-us" for American English.

ONCLICK

This event takes place if you single-click on an element with the mouse. A given script is executed by this action.

ONDBLCLICK

This event takes place if you double-click on an element with the mouse. A given script is executed by this action.

ONKEYDOWN

This event takes place if you are in an element and a key is pressed and held down. This action executes a specific script.

ONKEYPRESS

This event takes place if you are in an element and a key is simultaneously pressed and released again. This action executes a specific script.

ONKEYUP

This event takes place if you are in an element and a key that was pressed is released. This action executes a specific script.

ONMOUSEDOWN

This event takes place if you are in an element and a mouse button is clicked and held down. A given script is executed by this action.

ONMOUSEMOVE

This event takes place if one moves the cursor over an object with the mouse. A given script is executed by this action.

ONMOUSEOUT

This event takes place if a mouse moves the cursor off an element. This action executes a given script.

ONMOUSEOVER

This event takes place if the mouse moves the cursor directly over the element (object). A given script is executed by this action.

ONMOUSEUP

This event takes place if you are in an element and a mouse button that was clicked and held down is released. A given script is executed by this action.

STYLE

The attribute STYLE is used to determine specific properties of elements. Used style settings are defined by cascading style sheets.

TITLE
Through this attribute selected elements can be assigned with additional information. This information is displayed in a pop-up window in many browsers, if the mouse pointer is on the element.

Example

```
<TT>
Here is a non-proportional font!
</tt>
```

Events

ONCLICK, ONDBLCLICK, ONKEYDOWN, ONKEYPRESS, ONKEYUP, ONMOUSEDOWN, ONMOUSEMOVE, ONMOUSEOVER, ONMOUSEOUT, ONMOUSEUP

Related commands

B
BIG
I
LISTING
PLAINTEXT
PRE
S
SMALL
STRIKE
U
XMP

TYPE <html attribute>

Indicating data type

Description

The meaning of the values of the TYPE attribute depend strongly on the command which has been set. The following is a list of all possible values assigned to the commands.

Values

For every command with which you use this attribute, there are various possible values. In the following list we have listed the individual commands and possible values:

A, LINK, OBJECT, PARAM, SCRIPT, STYLE

Valid values for the attribute are the "content types". Special data formats are marked with these; a Microsoft Word document or an Adobe PDF document, for example. Use the definitions which you can find under the **MIME-types** keyword, to describe the data format. Several values can be indicated, separated by commas.

INPUT

With this attribute, you determine the type of control element you want to use. You can choose from the following input types:

BUTTON

Creates a simple button, Windows style. Through this button various actions can be started, such as a script, for example. You can produce graphic buttons with the IMAGE option.

CHECKBOX

Creates check boxes. A check box allows the user to choose an option by "checking" the field. For every check box, two states are possible, selected and deselected.

FILE

This control type permits the user to select a file so that its contents can be transmitted with a form.

HIDDEN

This value produces a hidden dialog field. The entry field does not appear on the screen. It is used to transmit additional information to the server, which the user does not have to enter. The value of the field can be indicated with VALUE.

IMAGE

With IMAGE you can create a graphic button. The image displayed as a graphic button must be indicated through SRC. The coordinates, with which the user has selected the graphic (X and Y values), are transmitted to the server as a result.

PASSWORD

Creates a simple single-line entry field. However, the letters entered are not displayed, but are replaced by asterisks. In this way, passwords or other confidential information cannot be read from the screen. Data in this field are transferred unencrypted to the server.

RADIO

A radio button or an option button permits the user to select one of many options. The radio buttons, which belong to decision commands, are summarised in a group by receiving the same name. In a group a radio button may be selected on its own.

RESET

If the Reset button is activated by a visitor, then all data in the form are deleted and returned to their original status.

SUBMIT
> If the Submit button is activated by the visitor, then all data in the form are transmitted to the server by the browser.

TEXT
> Produces a simple single-line entry field.

LI, UL
> This attribute determines the type of character used in front of a list element. Different values are available if you do not create a numbered list with UL, or if you create an ordered list with OL. The following settings apply to a UL:

DISC
> Displays a diskette icon as a list symbol (this does not work in all browsers).

SQUARE
> With this value you can select a small square as a list symbol.

CIRCLE
> You get a small circle as a list symbol with the CIRCLE value.

LI, OL
> With this attribute, you can set a character in front of every element, also within an OL (ordered list). The following values are available:

1
> Arabic numbers (1, 2, 3, ...); this value is the default.

a
> Lower case letter (a, b, c ...).

A
> Upper case letter (A, B, C, ...).

i
> Lower case Roman numerals (i, ii, iii, iv, ...).

I
> Upper case Roman numerals (I, II, III, IV, ...).

TYPE
> With this attribute it is possible to fix the kind of button or its purpose.

SUBMIT
> With TYPE=SUBMIT you can produce an entry field. Using this entry field, a user can mail a form. Within a form there can be several mail buttons. However, you have to assign a name to every button using the NAME attribute.

RESET
> With TYPE=RESET it is possible to create an entry field where input can be deleted. The default values for the presets are moved back to the exit values.

BUTTON
> TYPE=BUTTON creates a button which starts a script when clicked on, for example. This option makes it possible to interact with visitors without interpreting data over the server.

Example

```
<input type="text">
<input type="radio">
<button type="submit">
```

Accompanying elements

A
BUTTON
INPUT
LI
LINK
OBJECT
OL
PARAM
SCRIPT
STYLE
UL

U

Underlining text

Description

With this command, standard flow text can be displayed as underlined. This tag is not supported in HTML 4.0.

Application

The U command ("underline") represents underlined text. Ensure that you do not create text that could be confused with hyperlink text.

HTML 4.0 standard

CLASS, DIR, ID, LANG, STYLE, TITLE

The use of this command is no longer recommended in HTML 4.0, and has been replaced by other commands.

Start tag: required; end tag: required.

Attributes

CLASS

Through the CLASS attribute the element can be assigned to a group (class). Enter one of the free selectable class names as a value. These groupings then provide easy access to all related elements so you can change all the properties of the elements of a class with the help of cascading style sheets or other languages, or select a value.

DIR

This attribute is necessary to determine the text direction. This attribute can have the values:

LTR

This value determines the text direction from left to right (and is short for "left-to-right"). This is the default direction in the browser.

RTL

If the text should must run contrary to the standard direction from the right to the left margin of the screen, choose the value RTL (short for "right-to-left").

ID

The ID attribute identifies the document. Using ID, a specific element can be accessed with the help of a script language to select or modify values.

LANG

This attribute indicates the language of the linked document. This is particularly important in search engines for identification purposes. Use the language codes according to ISO 639, for example "en" for English or "en-us" for American English.

ONCLICK

This event takes place if you single-click on an element with the mouse. A given script is executed by this action.

ONDBLCLICK

This event takes place if you double-click on an element with the mouse. A given script is executed by this action.

ONKEYDOWN

This event takes place if you are in an element and a key is pressed and held down. This action executes a specific script.

ONKEYPRESS

This event takes place if you are in an element and a key pressed and released. This action executes a specific script.

ONKEYUP

This event takes place if you are in an element and a key that was pressed is released. This action executes a specific script.

ONMOUSEDOWN

This event takes place if you are in an element and a mouse button is clicked and held down. A given script is executed by this action.

ONMOUSEMOVE
This event takes place if one moves the cursor over an object with the mouse. A given script is executed by this action.
ONMOUSEOUT
This event takes place if a mouse moves the cursor off an element. This action executes a given script.
ONMOUSEOVER
This event takes place if the mouse moves the cursor directly over the element (object). A given script is executed by this action.
ONMOUSEUP
This event takes place if you are in an element and a mouse button that was clicked and held down is released. A given script is executed by this action.
STYLE
The STYLE attribute can be used to change style settings, in particular the way the element looks. As a value of the attribute you apply the corresponding options of a style sheet language (usually CSS).
TITLE
Give the user further information about the element used by determining a meaningful title with the help of the TITLE command. Navigation in your Web site is made easier for users who are dependent on voice response.

Example

```
<u>an underlined textlooks like this!</u>
```

Events

ONCLICK, ONDBLCLICK, ONKEYDOWN, ONKEYPRESS, ONKEYUP, ONMOUSEDOWN, ONMOUSEMOVE, ONMOUSEOVER, ONMOUSEOUT, ONMOUSEUP

Related commands

B
BIG
I
LISTING
PLAINTEXT
PRE
S
SMALL
STRIKE
STRONG
TT

UL

W3C HTML 4.0 ✔

Indicating unnumbered (or unordered) lists

Description

With this command, it is possible to indicate lists which are not numbered.

Application

The UL command is used to set lists which are not numbered. This type of list can be also described as a bullet list.

HTML 4.0 standard

CLASS, DIR, ID, LANG, STYLE, TITLE

Start tag: required; end tag: required..

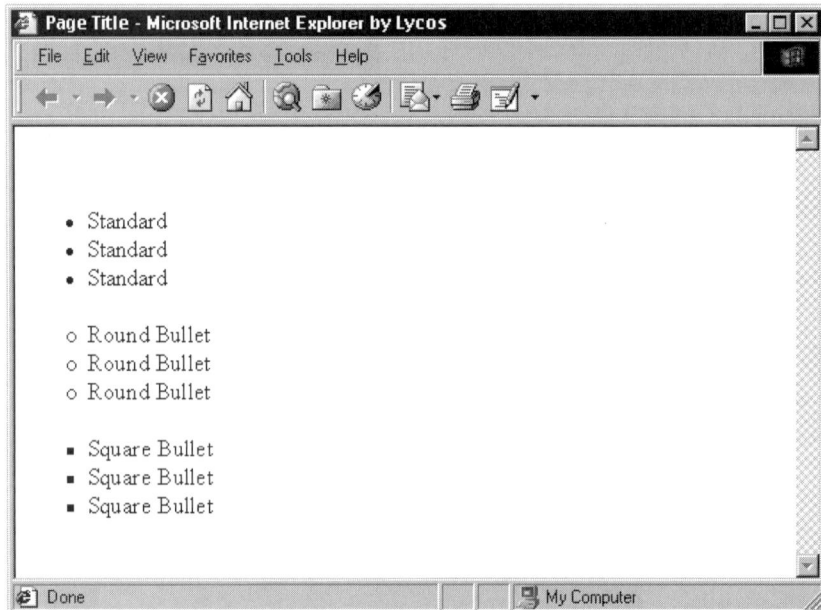

Different types of bullet for a bullet list

Attributes

CLASS

> Through the CLASS attribute the element can be assigned to a group (class). Enter one of the free selectable class names as a value. These groupings then provide easy access to all related elements so you can change all the properties of the elements of a class with the help of cascading style sheets or other languages, or select a value.

COMPACT

> This attribute means that the list entries are very short and can be represented in a compact form. It is interpreted by most browsers.

DIR

> This attribute is necessary to determine the text direction. This attribute can have the values:
>
> > LTR
> >
> > > This value determines the text direction from left to right (and is short for "left-to-right"). This is the default direction in the browser.
> >
> > RTL
> >
> > > If the text must run contrary to the standard direction from the right to the left margin of the screen, choose the value RTL (short for "right-to-left").

ID

> This identifies the document. Using ID, single elements can be accessed with the help of a script language to choose or change values, for example.

LANG

> This attribute indicates the language of the linked document. This is particularly important in search engines for identification purposes. Use the language codes according to ISO 639, for example "en" for English or "en-us" for American English.

ONCLICK

> This event takes place if you single-click on an element with the mouse. A given script is executed by this action.

ONDBLCLICK

> This event takes place if you double-click on an element with the mouse. A given script is executed by this action.

ONKEYDOWN

> This event takes place if you are in an element and a key is pressed and held down. This action executes a specific script.

ONKEYPRESS

> This event takes place if you are in an element and a key is simultaneously pressed and released again. This action executes a specific script.

ONKEYUP

> This event takes place if you are in an element and a key that was pressed is released. This action executes a specific script.

ONMOUSEDOWN

This event takes place if you are in an element and a mouse button is clicked and held down. A given script is executed by this action.

ONMOUSEMOVE

This event takes place if one moves the cursor over an object with the mouse. A given script is executed by this action.

ONMOUSEOUT

This event takes place if a mouse moves the cursor off an element. This action executes a given script.

ONMOUSEOVER

This event takes place if the mouse moves the cursor directly over the element (object). A given script is executed by this action.

ONMOUSEUP

This event takes place if you are in an element and a mouse button that was clicked and held down is released. A given script is executed by this action.

TYPE

With this attribute you can determine the character type within a list in front of a corresponding list element. You can use different values if you create an unordered list (not numbered) with the UL command or an ordered list (numbered list) with the OL command. The following settings apply to a UL:

DISC

Displays a diskette icon as a list symbol (this does not work in all browsers).

SQUARE

With this value you can select a small square as a list symbol.

CIRCLE

You get a small circle as a list symbol with this value.

START

This attribute is used exclusively with a numbered list. It gives you the option to indicate a start value and to start the list with another value than the default 1.

STYLE

The STYLE attribute can be used to change style settings, in particular the look of the element. As a value of the attribute you apply the corresponding options of a style sheet language (usually CSS).

TITLE

Give the user further information about the element used by determining a meaningful title with the help of the TITLE command. Navigation in your Web site is made easier for users who are dependent on voice response.

Example

```
<ul type="circle">
<li>first</li>
<li >second</li>
<li>third</li>
</ul>
```

Events

ONCLICK, ONDBLCLICK, ONKEYDOWN, ONKEYPRESS, ONKEYUP, ONMOUSEDOWN, ONMOUSEMOVE, ONMOUSEOVER, ONMOUSEOUT, ONMOUSEUP

XML definition

```
<! ELEMENT UL - - (LI)+>
<! ATTLIST UL %attrs;>
```

Related commands

LI
OL

Unicode-standard

In the following overview, you will be able to find the Unicode standard, taken from the official W3C specifications for XML 1.0. With this standard characters are divided into three groups: letters, numbers and extenders. Letters can be further divided into base, idiographic and combining characters.

Letter	BaseChar | Ideographic
BaseChar	[#x0041-#x005A] | [#x0061-#x007A] | [#x00C0-#x00D6] | [#x00D8-#x00F6] | [#x00F8-#x00FF] | [#x0100-#x0131] | [#x0134-#x013E] | [#x0141-#x0148] | [#x014A-#x017E] | [#x0180-#x01C3] | [#x01CD-#x01F0] | [#x01F4-#x01F5] | [#x01FA-#x0217] | [#x0250-#x02A8] | [#x02BB-#x02C1] | #x0386 | [#x0388-#x038A] | #x038C | [#x038E-#x03A1] | [#x03A3-#x03CE] | [#x03D0-#x03D6] | #x03DA | #x03DC | #x03DE | #x03E0 | [#x03E2-#x03F3] | [#x0401-#x040C] | [#x040E-#x044F] | [#x0451-#x045C] | [#x045E-#x0481] | [#x0490-#x04C4] | [#x04C7-#x04C8] | [#x04CB-#x04CC] | [#x04D0-#x04EB] | [#x04EE-#x04F5] | [#x04F8-#x04F9] | [#x0531-#x0556] | #x0559 | [#x0561-#x0586] | [#x05D0-#x05EA] | [#x05F0-#x05F2] | [#x0621-#x063A] | [#x0641-#x064A] | [#x0671-#x06B7] | [#x06BA-#x06BE] | [#x06C0-#x06CE] | [#x06D0-#x06D3] | #x06D5 | [#x06E5-#x06E6] | [#x0905-#x0939] | #x093D | [#x0958-#x0961] | [#x0985-#x098C] | [#x098F-#x0990] | [#x0993-#x09A8] | [#x09AA-#x09B0] | #x09B2 | [#x09B6-#x09B9] | [#x09DC-#x09DD] | [#x09DF-#x09E1] | [#x09F0-#x09F1] | [#x0A05-#x0A0A] | [#x0A0F-#x0A10] | [#x0A13-#x0A28] | [#x0A2A-#x0A30] | [#x0A32-#x0A33] | [#x0A35-#x0A36] | [#x0A38-#x0A39] |

Letter	BaseChar	Ideographic
	[#x0A59-#x0A5C] | #x0A5E | [#x0A72-#x0A74] | [#x0A85-#x0A8B] | #x0A8D | [#x0A8F-#x0A91] | [#x0A93-#x0AA8] | [#x0AAA-#x0AB0] | [#x0AB2-#x0AB3] | [#x0AB5-#x0AB9] | #x0ABD | #x0AE0 | [#x0B05-#x0B0C] | [#x0B0F-#x0B10] | [#x0B13-#x0B28] | [#x0B2A-#x0B30] | [#x0B32-#x0B33] | [#x0B36-#x0B39] | #x0B3D | [#x0B5C-#x0B5D] | [#x0B5F-#x0B61] | [#x0B85-#x0B8A] | [#x0B8E-#x0B90] | [#x0B92-#x0B95] | [#x0B99-#x0B9A] | #x0B9C | [#x0B9E-#x0B9F] | [#x0BA3-#x0BA4] | [#x0BA8-#x0BAA] | [#x0BAE-#x0BB5] | [#x0BB7-#x0BB9] | [#x0C05-#x0C0C] | [#x0C0E-#x0C10] | [#x0C12-#x0C28] | [#x0C2A-#x0C33] | [#x0C35-#x0C39] | [#x0C60-#x0C61] | [#x0C85-#x0C8C] | [#x0C8E-#x0C90] | [#x0C92-#x0CA8] | [#x0CAA-#x0CB3] | [#x0CB5-#x0CB9] | #x0CDE | [#x0CE0-#x0CE1] | [#x0D05-#x0D0C] | [#x0D0E-#x0D10] | [#x0D12-#x0D28] | [#x0D2A-#x0D39] | [#x0D60-#x0D61] | [#x0E01-#x0E2E] | #x0E30 | [#x0E32-#x0E33] | [#x0E40-#x0E45] | [#x0E81-#x0E82] | #x0E84 | [#x0E87-#x0E88] | #x0E8A | #x0E8D | [#x0E94-#x0E97] | [#x0E99-#x0E9F] | [#x0EA1-#x0EA3] | #x0EA5 | #x0EA7 | [#x0EAA-#x0EAB] | [#x0EAD-#x0EAE] | #x0EB0 | [#x0EB2-#x0EB3] | #x0EBD | [#x0EC0-#x0EC4] | [#x0F40-#x0F47] | [#x0F49-#x0F69] | [#x10A0-#x10C5] | [#x10D0-#x10F6] | #x1100 | [#x1102-#x1103] | [#x1105-#x1107] | #x1109 | [#x110B-#x110C] | [#x110E-#x1112] | #x113C | #x113E | #x1140 | #x114C | #x114E | #x1150 | [#x1154-#x1155] | #x1159 | [#x115F-#x1161] | #x1163 | #x1165 | #x1167 | #x1169 | [#x116D-#x116E] | [#x1172-#x1173] | #x1175 | #x119E | #x11A8 | #x11AB | [#x11AE-#x11AF] | [#x11B7-#x11B8] | #x11BA | [#x11BC-#x11C2] | #x11EB | #x11F0 | #x11F9 | [#x1E00-#x1E9B] | [#x1EA0-#x1EF9] | [#x1F00-#x1F15] | [#x1F18-#x1F1D] | [#x1F20-#x1F45] | [#x1F48-#x1F4D] | [#x1F50-#x1F57] | #x1F59 | #x1F5B | #x1F5D | [#x1F5F-#x1F7D] | [#x1F80-#x1FB4] | [#x1FB6-#x1FBC] | #x1FBE | [#x1FC2-#x1FC4] | [#x1FC6-#x1FCC] | [#x1FD0-#x1FD3] | [#x1FD6-#x1FDB] | [#x1FE0-#x1FEC] | [#x1FF2-#x1FF4] | [#x1FF6-#x1FFC] | #x2126 | [#x212A-#x212B] | #x212E | [#x2180-#x2182] | [#x3041-#x3094] | [#x30A1-#x30FA] | [#x3105-#x312C] | [#xAC00-#xD7A3]	
Ideographic	[#x4E00-#x9FA5] | #x3007 | [#x3021-#x3029]	

Letter	BaseChar	Ideographic
Combining Character	[#x0300-#x0345] | [#x0360-#x0361] | [#x0483-#x0486] | [#x0591-#x05A1] | [#x05A3-#x05B9] | [#x05BB-#x05BD] | #x05BF | [#x05C1-#x05C2] | #x05C4 | [#x064B-#x0652] | #x0670 | [#x06D6-#x06DC] | [#x06DD-#x06DF] | [#x06E0-#x06E4] | [#x06E7-#x06E8] | [#x06EA-#x06ED] | [#x0901-#x0903] | #x093C | [#x093E-#x094C] | #x094D | [#x0951-#x0954] | [#x0962-#x0963] | [#x0981-#x0983] | #x09BC | #x09BE | #x09BF | [#x09C0-#x09C4] | [#x09C7-#x09C8] | [#x09CB-#x09CD] | #x09D7 | [#x09E2-#x09E3] | #x0A02 | #x0A3C | #x0A3E | #x0A3F | [#x0A40-#x0A42] | [#x0A47-#x0A48] | [#x0A4B-#x0A4D] | [#x0A70-#x0A71] | [#x0A81-#x0A83] | #x0ABC | [#x0ABE-#x0AC5] | [#x0AC7-#x0AC9] | [#x0ACB-#x0ACD] | [#x0B01-#x0B03] | #x0B3C | [#x0B3E-#x0B43] | [#x0B47-#x0B48] | [#x0B4B-#x0B4D] | [#x0B56-#x0B57] | [#x0B82-#x0B83] | [#x0BBE-#x0BC2] | [#x0BC6-#x0BC8] | [#x0BCA-#x0BCD] | #x0BD7 | [#x0C01-#x0C03] | [#x0C3E-#x0C44] | [#x0C46-#x0C48] | [#x0C4A-#x0C4D] | [#x0C55-#x0C56] | [#x0C82-#x0C83] | [#x0CBE-#x0CC4] | [#x0CC6-#x0CC8] | [#x0CCA-#x0CCD] | [#x0CD5-#x0CD6] | [#x0D02-#x0D03] | [#x0D3E-#x0D43] | [#x0D46-#x0D48] | [#x0D4A-#x0D4D] | #x0D57 | #x0E31 | [#x0E34-#x0E3A] | [#x0E47-#x0E4E] | #x0EB1 | [#x0EB4-#x0EB9] | [#x0EBB-#x0EBC] | [#x0EC8-#x0ECD] | [#x0F18-#x0F19] | #x0F35 | #x0F37 | #x0F39 | #x0F3E | #x0F3F | [#x0F71-#x0F84] | [#x0F86-#x0F8B] | [#x0F90-#x0F95] | #x0F97 | [#x0F99-#x0FAD] | [#x0FB1-#x0FB7] | #x0FB9 | [#x20D0-#x20DC] | #x20E1 | [#x302A-#x302F] | #x3099 | #x309A
Number	[#x0030-#x0039] | [#x0660-#x0669] | [#x06F0-#x06F9] | [#x0966-#x096F] | [#x09E6-#x09EF] | [#x0A66-#x0A6F] | [#x0AE6-#x0AEF] | [#x0B66-#x0B6F] | [#x0BE7-#x0BEF] | [#x0C66-#x0C6F] | [#x0CE6-#x0CEF] | [#x0D66-#x0D6F] | [#x0E50-#x0E59] | [#x0ED0-#x0ED9] | [#x0F20-#x0F29]
Extender	#x00B7 | #x02D0 | #x02D1 | #x0387 | #x0640 | #x0E46 | #x0EC6 | #x3005 | [#x3031-#x3035] | [#x309D-#x309E] | [#x30FC-#x30FE]

(Source: www.w3c.org/xml)

USEMAP <html attribute>
Client-sided imagemaps

Description
This attribute is used for client-sided imagemaps.

Application
With this command, you assign an image or an object to a predefined imagemap.

Values
A valid value for this attribute is the URI (Uniform Resource Identifier). The construction of a URI is as follows:

```
[protocol]://[domain]/[directory]/[file]
```

Possible protocols used are the following:

ftp	File Transfer Protocol
http	Hypertext Transfer Protocol
gopher	Gopher Protocol
mailto	Electronic Mail Address
news	USENET News
nntp	USENET News (NNTP access)
telnet	Reference to interactive sessions
wais	Wide Area Information Server
file	Host-specific file names
prospero	Prospero Directory Service

Example
```
<map name="Test image">
<area shape=rect coords="1,1,249,49" href="#anchor">
<area shape=rect coords="1,51,149,299" href="file.htm">
<area shape=rect coords="251,1,399,399" href="file.htm">
<area shape=rect coords="151,51,249,299"
href =" http://www.cybertechnics.co.uk /">
<area shape=rect coords="1,301,249,399" nohref>
</map>
<img src="hypgraph.gif" usemap="#Test image" border=0>>
```

Accompanying elements
IMG
INPUT
OBJECT

Validity

Prerequisite for valid XML documents

Description

XML documents must be valid. Three points decide whether a XML document has validity or not:

- It is a well-formed document .

- An accompanying internal or external DTD exists and is available.

- The document is valid in relation to the rules of the DTD.

Application

This means that if a DTD is missing it already affects the validity of the document. XML documents without DTD cannot be valid documents according to the specification. Since the processing of the DTD is not easy to check, many parsers fail to check the validity of documents.

As can be seen from the conditions for validity, the conclusion is that every valid document must also be a well-formed document. The check on validity includes the check on now well it is formed.

In many cases, the far-reaching check on validity is unnecessary. When the document structure is simple, for example, no DTD is required.

The simplest valid XML document with integrated DTD definition of an element should at least consist of the following lines:

Example

```
<?xml version = "1.0" ?>
<!DOCTYPE document [
<! ELEMENT data (#PCDATA)>
]>
<data>Here are data ...</data>

<?xml version="1.0"?>
<!DOCTYPE document [
<! ELEMENT data (#PCDATA)>
]>
<data>
This document is
<technically>well-formed </technically>
but not
<technically>valid </technically>.
</data>
```

VALIGN   \<html attribute\>
Vertical alignment

Description
With this attribute, the vertical alignment of text within a table can be determined. If this element is not used, all text will automatically be centred.

Application
Usually, cell contents are displayed with the same distance from the cell margin at the top and the bottom, but with this attribute you can change the alignment. The use of this attribute is optional.

Values
TOP
   Selected text is aligned at the top.
BOTTOM
   Selected text is aligned at the bottom.
MIDDLE
   Selected text is centre-aligned.
BASELINE
   Text is aligned to a common baseline.

Example
```
<table border>
<tr>
<td valign="top">Data</td>
<td valign="bottom">Data</td>
</tr>
</table>
```

Accompanying elements
COL
COLGROUP
TBODY
TD
TFOOT
TH
THEAD
TR

VALUE   \<html attribute\>

Assigning value

Description

This attribute assigns a value to an element. In active form elements, this value will be submitted to the server when you click the Submit button.

Values

Different validity ranges exist for each command with which you use this attribute. The following is a list of individual commands and possible values:

BUTTON, INPUT, OPTION, PARAM

You can submit any string to this attribute as a value. If possible, this character string should not start or end with a blank space. The processing browser will filter these out if necessary.

LI

Valid values for this attribute are integers. The number must contain at least one number ranging from 0 to 9 (="9").

Example

```
<button name="I'm a button. Select me".
"type="button"  value="go back"onClick="history.back()">
<input name="name"type="text" value="name">

<ol start="10" type="I">
<li>first</li>
<li value="3">second</li>
<li>third</li>
</ol>
```

Accompanying elements

BUTTON
INPUT
LI
OPTION
PARAM

VALUETYPE <html attribute>

Indicating data type for VALUE

Description

The VALUETYPE attribute indicates the data type to be submitted in VALUE. This determines how the transferred values are to be interpreted.

Application

Specify the given values through VALUETYPE in connection with the PARAM command. There are three valid values:

Values

DATA

    This value submits data submitted in VALUE as pure text to the applet. This is the default value.

REF

    This value contains a URI. This indicates where runtime variables are saved.

OBJECT

    This value refers to a connected OBJECT declaration in the same document. Indicate the corresponding ID of the object as a reference.

Example

```
<object classid="anim.py">
<param name="height" value="10" valuetype="data">
<param name="width" value="10" valuetype="data">
</object>
```

Accompanying element

PARAM

VAR

W3C HTML 4.0 ✔

Indicating variables and parameters (program argument)

Description

Variables and parameters are determined with this command. However, the use of this command should be limited to variables and parameters which occur within a running text.

Application

The `VAR` command is used to identify variables. This occurs in the first line of explanatory texts executed relating to computer proceedings. Variables with the `CODE` command should be formatted within program listings which are inline for publication.

HTML 4.0 standard

`CLASS, DIR, ID, LANG, STYLE, TITLE`

Start tag: required; end tag: required.

Attributes

`CLASS`

Through the `CLASS` attribute the element can be assigned to a group (class). Enter one of the free selectable class names as a value. These groupings then provide easy access to all related elements so you can change all the properties of the elements of a class with the help of cascading style sheets or other languages, or select a value.

`DIR`

This attribute is necessary to determine the text direction. This attribute can have the values:

`LTR`

This value determines the text direction from left to right (and is short for "left-to-right"). This is the default direction in the browser.

`RTL`

If the text must run contrary to the standard direction from the right to the left margin of the screen, choose the value RTL (short for "right-to-left").

`LANG`

This attribute indicates the language of the linked document. This is particularly important in search engines for identification purposes. Use the language codes according to ISO 639, for example "en" for English or "en-us" for American English.

`ONCLICK`

This event takes place if you single-click on an element with the mouse. A given script is executed by this action.

`ONDBLCLICK`

This event takes place if you double-click on an element with the mouse. A given script is executed by this action.

`ONKEYDOWN`

This event takes place if you are in an element and a key is pressed and held down. This action executes a specific script.

ONKEYPRESS

This event takes place if you are in an element and a key is simultaneously pressed and released again. This action executes a specific script.

ONKEYUP

This event takes place if you are in an element and a key that was pressed is released. This action executes a specific script.

ONMOUSEDOWN

This event takes place if you are in an element and a mouse button is clicked and held down. A given script is executed by this action.

ONMOUSEMOVE

This event takes place if one moves the cursor over an object with the mouse. A given script is executed by this action.

ONMOUSEOUT

This event takes place if a mouse moves the cursor off an element. This action iexecutes a given script.

ONMOUSEOVER

This event takes place if the mouse moves the cursor directly over the element (object). A given script is executed by this action.

ONMOUSEUP

This event takes place if you are in an element and a mouse button that was clicked and held down is released. A given script is executed by this action.

STYLE

The STYLE attribute is used to determine specific properties in the appearance of elements. Used style settings are defined by cascading style sheets.

TITLE

Through this attribute, selected elements can be assigned with additional information. This information is displayed in a pop-up window in many browsers, if the mouse pointer is on the element.

Example

```
<var>
file name
</var>
```

Events

ONCLICK, ONDBLCLICK, ONKEYDOWN, ONKEYPRESS, ONKEYUP, ONMOUSEDOWN, ONMOUSEMOVE, ONMOUSEOVER, ONMOUSEOUT, ONMOUSEUP

Related commands

ACRONYM
CITE
CODE
DFN
EM

KBD
SAMP
STRONG

VERSION <html attribute>
Indicating the HTML version used

Description
You can indicate the HTML used with this command.

Application
The use of this attribute is no longer supported. Use the DOCTYPE command to give the version number at the beginning of your HTML document instead.

Values
You can submit any string to this attribute as a value. If possible, this character string should not start or end at this with a blank space. The processing browser will filter these out if necessary

A clear standard for the detail of the version number is not defined.

Example
```
<html version="2.0">
<html version="4.0">
<html version="4">
```

Accompanying element
HTML

VIDEO ☺
Reproduction of a video sequence

Description
This command allows the representation of a graphic in a specific region of the window.

Parameter

abstract
> Indicates a short description for the group with the help of this attribute.

author
> Through this attribute, an author for this media grouping is indicated.

begin
> Indicates the reproduction time. You can use h, min, s or ms as units.

copyright
> Information about the originator and the copyright can be submitted as values of this attribute.

dur
> Indicates the complete duration of the group. You can use the h, min, s or ms as units.

end
> Indicates the end of the group. This value is the opposite of the attribute begin. You can use the h, min, s or ms descriptions as units.

id
> This identifies the document. Through ID, this area can be accessed by other elements.

repeat
> The complete group repeats in the said number.

src
> Indicates the source of the media clip or the graphic. Here a valid URL is required as a value for this attribute.

title
> Gives the complete group a title with a short description of the content.

Example

```
<video id="identifier"
       src="URL"
       alt="string"
       region="identifier"
       title="string"
       abstract="string"
       author="string"
       copyright="string"
       longdesc="string"
       type="string"
       begin="clock-value"
       end="clock-value"
       dur="clock-value"
       clip-begin="clock-value"
       clip-end="clock-value"
       repeat="integer"
       fill="remove|freeze"
       system-bitrate="integer"
```

```
system-captions="on|off"
system-language="coma-separated-list"
system-overdub-or-caption="caption|overdub"
system-required="string"
system-screen-depth="integer"
system-screen-size="integerXinteger" />>
```

VLINK   <html attribute>
Colour of a visited link

Description

This attribute determines the colour of the link activated by a user.

Application

In this case, besides the 16 defined colour keywords, up to 256 colours can be represented with hexadecimal numbers. This command is not supported in HTML 4.0.

The use of this attribute is optional.

Values

Submit either a colour value in RGB syntax or a valid colour name to the attribute. For the RGB value you indicate the value of the colours red, green and blue in hexadecimal numbers: #RRGGBB (#008000 for green, for example). Alternatively, you can use predefined colour names (i. e. YELLOW). Under the keyword colour table (**colour palette**) you will find all standard colours. The following is a list of the 16 most frequently used primary colours:

```
BLACK     = #000000      SILVER    = #C0C0C0
GRAY      = #808080      WHITE     = #FFFFFF
MAROON    = #800000      RED       = #FF0000
PURPLE    = #800080      FUCHSIA   = #FF00FF
GREEN     = #008000      LIME      = #00FF00
OLIVE     = #808000      YELLOW    = #FFFF00
NAVY      = #000080      BLUE      = #0000FF
TEAL      = #008080      AQUA      = #00FFFF
```

Example

```
<body alink="black">
<body vlink="red">
<body link="#00FFFF">
```

Accompanying element
BODY

VSPACE <html attribute>

Determining vertical space in an element

Description
With this attribute, the vertical separation of an embedded object is determined in proportion to its environment within a window.

Application
The use of this attribute is optional.

Values
The value of this attribute indicates a size in pixels, therefore in microdots. Valid values are positive integers. The input of ="100" corresponds to 100 pixels, for example.

Example
```
<img src="image.gif" vspace="100" hspace="20">
```

Accompanying elements
APPLET
IMG
OBJECT

WBR

Allowing word breaks

Description
With this command you can create word.

Application
The WBR command is used to create word breaks in pages. This also works with text marked with the NOBR command. As a rule, the browser software looks after

the rows and creates a word break, if a blank space occurs in a suitable place. In very long words, or words divided by hyphens, it may be sensible to create a line break. This command is not part of the official HTML standard, but is supported by all common browsers.

Example

```
The word <wbr>(antidisestablish) <wbr>
ment <wbr> arianism
is a long word.
```

Related commands

BR
NOBR

Well-formed code

Converting XML specifications

Description

When working with XML, you will meet the same concept over and over again, in relation to correct specification conversion: well-formed code. A well-formed document means that the construct in question observes the official rules of the W3C for constructing XML documents. A well-formed document consists of a prolog and at least one element.

Application

The complete document must be included in a single root element. Transferred to the language HTML, this means that a document without the enclosing `<html>`-tag is not well-formed.

All absolute attributes required are indicated.

The values of the attributes are to the right of values and correspond to the given type.

In this way, the inserted elements are correctly nested. If a start-tag of an element is found in the content of an other element, then its end-tag must also be found in the content of the other element. With the conversion of XML into SGML, it is important to know that SGML documents should also be well-formed.

Example

```
<?XML version="1.0"?>
<document>
```

```
        <data>Text</data>
</document>
```

WIDTH   **\<html attribute>**
Determining the width of an element

Description
This attribute is used to determine the width of an element.

Application
For each command with which you use this attribute, various validity ranges exist for the submitted value. The following is a list of individual commands and possible values:

Values
COL, COLGROUP

Some elements allow three different sets of information for this attribute: you can indicate the size in pixels, as a percentage or a length. Submit an integer value to the attribute for the size in pixels. Every pixel corresponds to a microdot in the chosen resolution. The detail in percentage is executed via a number ranging from 1 to 100 and a percent sign (="50%"). The detail executes the length as an integer with an asterisk (="1*").

The browser proceeds with the simultaneous use of the three data items in this command. First, it allocates the vertical or horizontal position according to pixel details, then it processes the percentage details and the remaining place is then distributed according to the related numbers. If a width has been left in 100 pixels, then a detail of ="2*, 3*" corresponds to a width of 40 and 60 pixels.

APPLET, HR, IFRAME, IMG, OBJECT, TABLE

The value of these attributes indicate a size in pixels or a percentage. Valid values for pixels are positive integers. The input ="100" corresponds to 100 pixels. A percentage detail corresponds to the percentage of the available horizontal or vertical window width in the browser. An input ="30%" corresponds to a width of 30 per cent.

TD, TH

The value of these attributes indicate a size in pixels, therefore in microdots. Valid values are positive integers. The input ="100" corresponds to 100 pixels, for example.

PRE
>
> Valid values for this attribute are integers. The number must contain a number ranging from 0 to 9 (="9").

Example

```
<table>
<td width="40%"></td>
<td width="20%"></td>
<td width="40%"></td>
</table>

<table>
<td width="40%"></td>
<td width="100"></td>
<td width="*"></td>
</table>
```

Accompanying elements

APPLET
COL
COLGROUP
HR
IFRAME
IMG
OBJECT
PRE
TABLE
TD
TH

word-spacing

Space between words

Description
Determines the space between individual words .

Parameter
The length of the space between words can normally be set as an absolute number or as a keyword for the default setting.

Example

```
<style type="text/css">
h1, h2 { word-spacing: 10 mm}
h3, h4 { word-spacing: normal}
</style>

<div style="word-spacing: 10%">
</div>
```

XML

Defines the beginning of an XML document

Description

A data object is a document if it consists of a presentation and at least a number of elements. At a minumum it needs an XML command and an element which encloses the rest of the content.

Application

A root element, which encloses all other elements, must be present in the document. In addition, you define the type and the version of the XML document in the presentation.

Parameter

VERSION

Currently, version 1.0 is the only possible version detail. But with a view to further developments of the language, this could be updated.

STANDALONE

The STANDALONE option in the processing of messages indicates whether or not the parser must enter an external DTD. The value "YES" shows that no external files must be consulted. The value "NO" shows that an external file exists. The file name must be indicated in the DOCTYPE definition.

ENCODING

The character set used within a document can be set in the ENCODING keyword in the processing message.

The standard ISO/IEC 10646 is also available, besides the standard ISO 8859 with its sub-structures. Every XML processor must be able to read at least format UTF 8 and UTF 16.

Example

```
<?xml version="1.0">
<document>
```

```
        <content>
        Here is the text ...
        </content>
</document>
```

xml : lang

Identifying the language

Description

The xml:lang attribute is used to define the language used in a document.

Example

```
<?xml version="1.0"?>
<prosa xml:lang="de">
<p xml:lang="en">English</p>
<p xml:lang="en-US">English (USA)</p>
<p xml:lang="en_UK">English (United Kingdom)</p>
<p xml:lang="de">german</p>
<p xml:lang="de-DE">German (Germany)</p>
<p xml:lang="de-CH">German (Switzerland)</p>
</prosa>
```

xml : stylesheet

Combining documents with style sheets

Description

This links a XML or HTML document with a style sheet.

Parameter

href

This command refers either to a cascading style sheet or an XSL style sheet.

type

Indicates the type of style sheet information.

Example

```
<?xml:Stylesheet href="customers.css" type="text/css"?>
<?xml:Stylesheet href="customers.xsl" type="text/xsl"?>
```

XMP

N

Displaying preformatted text

Description

With this command, it is possible to display all represented characters and letters in the same size.

Application

The XMP command allows characters to be displayed in exactly the same font size. This kind of representation is used to represent source codes. However, instead of this command, the PRE command is preferred since LISTING is not supported in HTML 4.0.

Example

```
<xmp>Text paragraph in non-proportional document</xmp>
```

Related commands

B
BIG
I
LISTING
PLAINTEXT
PRE
S
SMALL
STRIKE
TT
U

XSL

Base structure of an XSL document

Description

Determines the start and end of an XSL document and is used with style sheets.

Application

The content of an XSL file is enclosed with the markup `<xsl>`. The content consists of the following rules which are marked with `<rule>`. The base framework of a XSL file looks like this:

Example

```
<xsl>
<rule>
     <!--construction rule 1 -->
</rule>
<rule>
     <!-- construction rule 2 -->
</rule>
</xsl>
```

z-index

Positioning layers

Description

If several elements overlap, you can determine the layer position of the elements with this command.

Parameter

Choose a numeric value for the layer. Lower numbers are covered by elements with higher numbers, so that layer 1 will be under layer 2, which will be under layer 3.

Example

```
<style type="text/css">
h1, h2 {z-index:5}
h3, h4 {z-index:99}
</style>

<div style="z-index:3">
</div>
```

Practice

new reference

This part explains all the tools required for successful programming and demonstrates various operations with the use of practical examples.

Category: Basics

Indicating document types

Application

The SGML standard must be determined in the first line of every document, concerning the language used. You assign the HTML version used with the DOCTYPE command and the corresponding parameters.

Implementation

Insert the DOCTYPE command in the first line of the document. Within the command, provide a reference to the accompanying DTD (Document Type Definition). Which version should be used in this definition and which commands and attributes are permitted? There are some permitted attributes which access DTDs in the W3C. It is likely that other DTDs will be available in XML in future.

```
"-//W3C//DTD HTML 2.0//EN"
```

This string states that you use a W3C DTD in HTML 2.0. The suffix //EN indicates the language of the DTD (not the language which you use in your document).

If you use commands that are based on HTML 3.2, then insert the string shown below into your DOCTYPE definition.

```
"-//W3C//DTD HTML 3.2//EN"
```

If you already use HTML 4.0, then insert the string into shown below your document.

```
"-//W3C//DTD HTML 4.0//EN"
```

The string above shows that you also use cascading style sheets or script in your document as well as HTML 4.0 elements.

```
"-//W3C//DTD HTML 4.0 Transitional//EN"
```

If the definition of a frameset is contained in your document, then you indicate this with the string shown below. Only use this definition for the part that contains the frame definition.

```
"-//W3C//DTD HTML 4.0 Frameset//EN"
```

Example

```
<!DOCTYPE HTML PUBLIC "-//W3C//DTD HTML 3.2//EN">
<head>
```

```
<title>HTML 3.2 Document</title>
</head>
<body>
...

<!DOCTYPE HTML PUBLIC"-//W3C//DTD HTML 4.0//EN">
<head>
<title>HTML 4.0 Document</title>
</head>
<body>
```

Using framesets

Application

The correct use of frames is not alway simple, so you must carefully plan and keep an overview of individual documents. To give you a basis for the correct layout with frames, we will show you some completed example framesets. You can adapt these to your own needs quickly and easily.

Implementation

With the help of the FRAMESET command, the monitor is split into three sections, for example. The three accompanying documents are then indicated by FRAME within this container.

Example

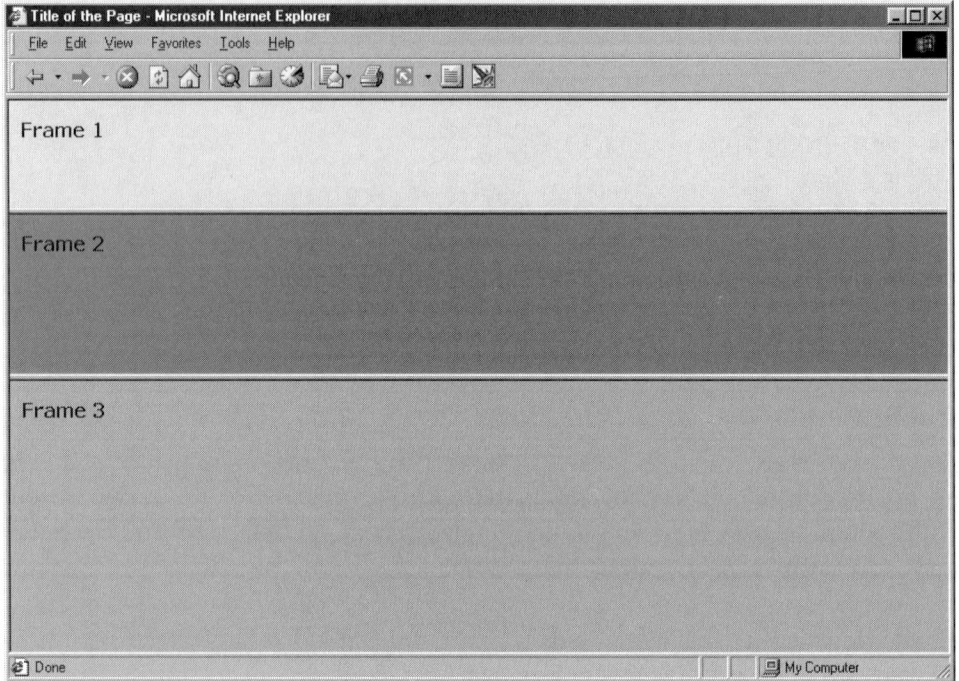

The following example is displayed in the browser shown above

```
frameset rows="20%, 30%, 50%">
      <frame src="frame1.htm" name="Links">
      <frame src="frame2.htm" name="Middle">
      <frame src="frame3.htm" name="Right">
</frameset>
<noframe>
</noframes>
```

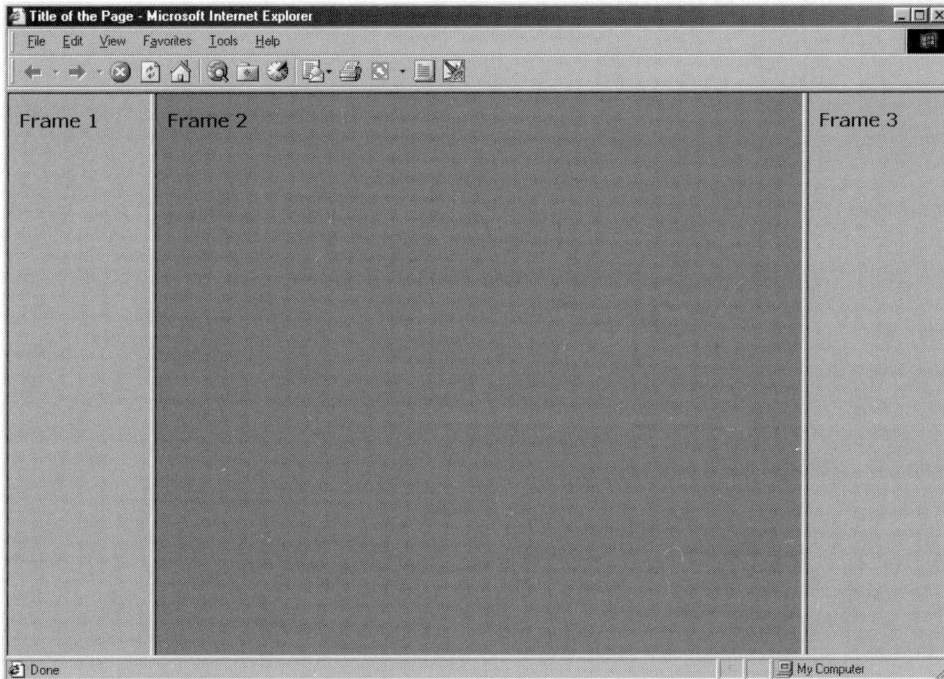

Instead of rows we have used columns in this example

```
<frameset cols="130, *, 130">
    <frame src="frame1.htm" name="Above">
    <frame src="frame2.htm" name="Middle">
    <frame src="frame3.htm" name="Below">
</frameset>
<noframes>
</noframes>
```

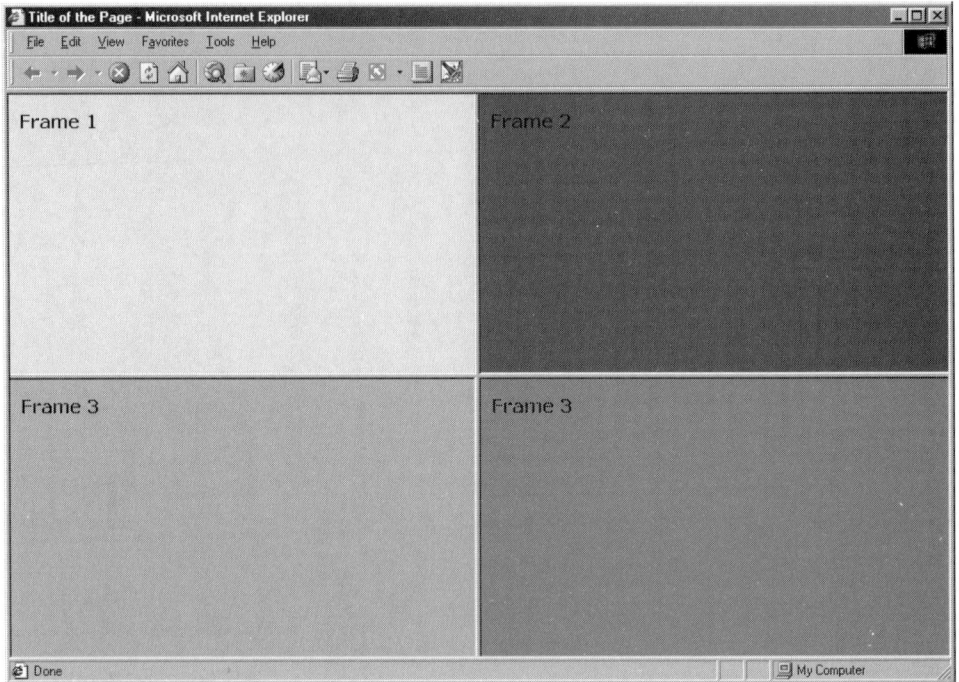

In this example, the monitor has been split into four equal areas

```
<frameset rows="50%,*">
<frameset cols="50%,*">
     <frame src="frame1.htm">
     <frame src="frame2.htm">
</frameset>
<frameset cols="50%,*">
     <frame src="frame3.htm">
     <frame src="frame4.htm">
</frameset>
</frameset>
```

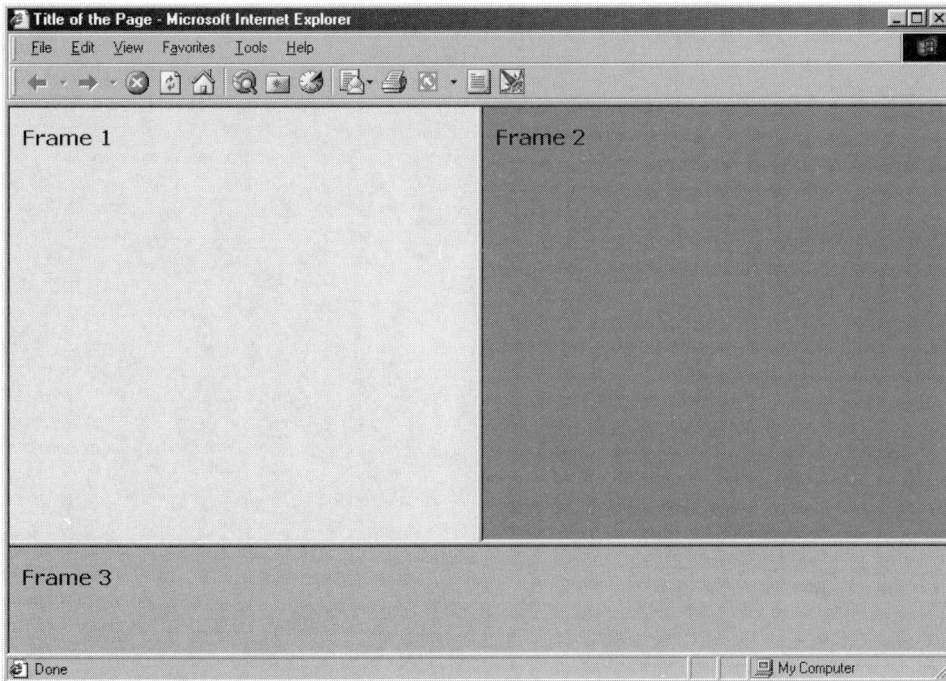

The DA range of applications frequently use this example for menu bars

```
<frameset rows="*,20%">
<frameset cols="50%,*">
      <frame src="frame1.htm">
      <frame src="frame2.htm">
</frameset>
      <frame src="frame3.htm">
</frameset>
```

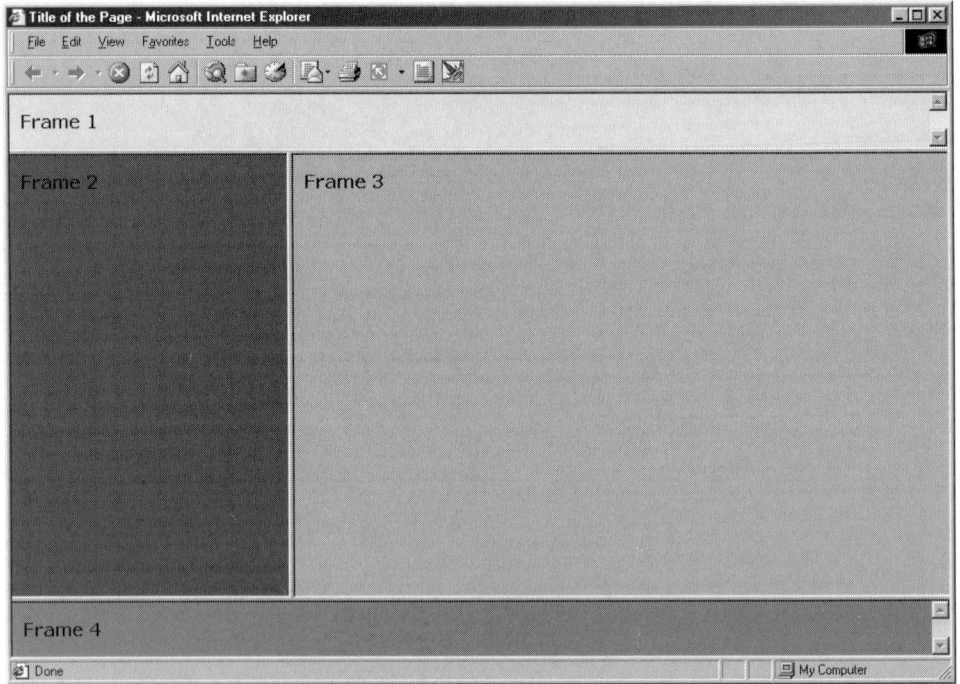

The following example could be used for different menu bars

```
<frameset rows="10%,*,10%">
     <frame src="frame1.htm">
<frameset cols="30%,*">
     <frame src="frame2.htm">
     <frame src="frame3.htm">
</frameset>
     <frame src="frame4.htm">
</frameset>
```

Tips

You may need two or more FRAMESETS to split your monitor into columns and rows.

Changing the content of several frames simultaneously

Application

You may wish to change not only the content of frame links, but also the content of two or more frames at the same time. While it is easy to modify a single frame in HTML, modifying several frames can be a little more complicated.

Implementation

It is not possible to change the contents of several frames simultaneously without using JavaScript. The following example will provide you with a simple solution for this case. The onClick event will regard the content of the first frame as the changes to be made to the second frame. The traditional solution is still chosen for the first frame, with TARGET.

A JavaScript function, which replaces the contents of three frames, is defined in the second example. The URL of the site to be displayed will submit the index of the frames whose contents are referred to in this function. This function can easily be extended to additional frames.

Example

```
<a language="JavaScript" herf="page1.htm" target="Frame1"
onClick="parent.frame2.location.href='page2.htm'">
```

Our next example contains three areas in total (frames) to be replaced

```
<html>
<head>
<script language="JavaScript">
<!--
function ThreeFrames (URL1, F1, URL2, F2, URL3, F3)
{
parent.frames[F1].location.href=URL1;
parent.frames[F2].location.href=URL2;
parent.frames[F3].location.href=URL3;
}
//-->
</script>
</head>
<body bgcolor="white">

<br><br>
<br><br>

<center>
<a href="javascript:ThreeFrames
('title02.htm', 1,
```

```
'links02.htm', 2,
'right02.htm', 3)">

<img src=english.gif" border="0"></a>

<br><br>

<a href="javascript:ThreeFrames
('title02e.htm', 1,
'links02e.htm', 2,
'right02e.htm', 3)">
<img src="english.gif" border="0"><br>
</center>
</body>
</html>
```

The three documents have been replaced

Special characters

Application

Displaying special characters can cause problems if the font which has been used does not support these characters.

HTML provides two solutions for this problem. Special characters can be changed into entities. These are abbreviations for special characters, according to the standard ASCII font, which can be represented by any browser.

The second solution is that the font used can be indicated for the complete document. If another system wishes to display these sites, it can switch automatically to this font. This is therefore the best solution.

Implementation

Provided that you have not indicated a specific font in your HTML document, special strings, called entities, must replace special characters.

The following table represents all the ISO 8859-1 characters. All special characters can be inserted as abbreviations or as universal code.

Unicode in HTML	Code	Description	Name in HTML
		Non-breaking space	
&#161;	¡	Inverted exclamation mark	&iexcl;
&#162;	¢	Cent sign	&cent;
&#163;	£	Pound sign	&pound;
&#164;	¤	Currency sign	&curren;
&#165;	¥	Yen sign	&yen;
&#166;	≠	Open line (*)	&brvbar;
&#167;	§	Section	&sect;
&#168;	¨	Umlaut	&uml;
&#169;	©	Copyright	&copy;
&#170;	ª	Ordinal	&ordf;
&#171;	«	Left-angle quote	&laquo;
&#172;	¬	Not sign	&not;
&#173;	-	Soft hyphen	&shy;
&#174;	®	Registered trademark	&reg;
&#175;	¯	Macron accent	&macr;

Unicode in HTML	Code	Description	Name in HTML
&#176;	°	Degree sign	&deg;
&#177;	±	Plus or minus	&plusmn;
&#178;	^{2}	Superscript two	&sup2;
&#179;	^{3}	Superscript three	&sup3;
&#180;	'	Acute accent	&acute;
&#181;	µ	Micro sign	&micro;
&#182;	¶	Paragraph sign	&para;
&#183;	·	Middle dot	&middot;
&#184;	¸	Cedilla (*)	&cedil;
&#185;	^{1}	Superscript 1 (*)	&sup1;
&#186;	º	Ordinal	&ordm;
&#187;	»	Right-angle quote,	&raquo;
&#188;	$\frac{1}{4}$	One quarter (*)	&frac14;
&#189;	$\frac{1}{2}$	Half (*)	&frac12;
&#190;	$\frac{3}{4}$	Three quarters (*)	&frac34;
&#191;	¿	Inverted question mark	&iquest;
&#192;	À	Capital A, grave accent	&Agrave;
&#193;	Á	Capital A, acute accent	&Aacute;
&#194;	Â	Capital A, circumflex accent	&Acirc;
&#195;	Ã	Capital A, tilde	&Atilde;
&#196;	Ä	Capital A, umlaut	&Auml;
&#197;	Å	Capital A, ring	&Aring;
&#198;	Æ	Capital A diphhtong	&AElig;
&#199;	Ç	Capital C, cedilla	&Ccedil;
&#200;	È	Capital E, grave accent	&Egrave;
&#201;	É	Capital E, acute accent	&Eacute;
&#202;	Ê	Capital E, circumflex accent	&Ecirc;
&#203;	Ë	Capital E, umlaut	&Euml;
&#204;	Ì	Capital I, grave accent	&Igrave;
&#205;	Í	Capital I, acute accent	&Iacute;
&#206;	Î	Capital I, circumflex accent	&Icirc;
&#207;	Ï	Capital I, umlaut	&Iuml;
&#208;	Ð	Capital Eth (Icelandic) (*)	&ETH;
&#209;	Ñ	Capital N, tilde	&Ntilde;
&#210;	Ò	Capital O, grave accent	&Ograve;

Unicode in HTML	Code	Description	Name in HTML
&#211;	Ó	Capital O, acute accent	&Oacute;
&#212;	Ô	Capital O, circumflex accent	&Ocirc;
&#213;	Õ	Capital O, tilde	&Otilde;
&#214;	Ö	Capital O, umlaut	&Ouml;
&#215;	×	Multiply sign (*)	&times;
&#216;	Ø	Capital O, slash	&Oslash;
&#217;	Ù	Capital U, grave accent	&Ugrave;
&#218;	Ú	Capital U, acute accent	&Uacute;
&#219;	Û	Capital U, circumflex accent	&Ucirc;
&#220;	Ü	Capital U, umlaut	&Uuml;
&#221;	Ý	Capital Y, acute accent (*)	&Yacute;
&#222;	Þ	Capital (Icelandic) (*)	&THORN;
&#223;	ß	Small sharp s, German (ligature)	&szlig;
&#224;	à	Small a, grave accent	&agrave;
&#225;	á	Small a, acute accent	&aacute;
&#226;	â	Small a, circumflex accent	&acirc;
&#227;	ã	Small a, tilde	&atilde;
&#228;	ä	Small a, umlaut	&auml;
&#229;	å	Small a, ring	&aring;
&#230;	æ	Small a diphthong	&aelig;
&#231;	ç	Small c, cedilla	&ccedil;
&#232;	è	Small e, grave accent	&egrave;
&#233;	é	Small e, acute accent	&eacute;
&#234;	ê	Small e, circumflex accent	&ecirc;
&#235;	ë	Small e, umlaut	&euml;
&#236;	ì	Small i, grave accent	&igrave;
&#237;	í	Small i, acute accent	&iacute;
&#238;	î	Small i, circumflex accent	&icirc;
&#239;	ï	Small i, umlaut	&iuml;
&#240;	ð	small eth (Icelandic) (*)	&eth;
&#241;	ñ	Small n, tilde	&ntilde;
&#242;	ò	Small o, grave accent	&ograve;
&#243;	ó	Small o, acute accent	&oacute;
&#244;	ô	Small o, circumflex accent	&ocirc;
&#245;	õ	Small o, tilde	&otilde;

Unicode in HTML	Code	Description	Name in HTML
&#246;	ö	Small o, umlaut	&ouml;
&#247;	÷	Division sign	&divide;
&#248;	ø	Small o, slash	&oslash;
&#249;	ù	Small u, grave accent	&ugrave;
&#250;	ú	Small u, acute accent	&uacute;
&#251;	û	Small u, circumflex accent	&ucirc;
&#252;	ü	Small u, umlaut	&uuml;
&#253;	ý	Small y, acute accent	&yacute;
&#254;	þ	Small thorn (Icelandic) (*)	&thorn;
&#255;	ÿ	Small y, umlaut	&yuml;

Some characters are not displayed on MacIntosh computers correctly, despite general support for the font. An asterisk indicates these characters.

Example

Characters in ISO 8859-1 as displayed by the browser

```
<html>
<head>
```

```
<meta
     http-equiv="content-type"
     content="text/html; CHARSET=iso8859-1">
</head>
<body>
</body>
</html>
```

Indicating the language used

Application

ISO 639 defines the uniform language codes world wide. This means that every language in the world has been assigned an abbreviation consisting of two letters.

Implementation

These abbreviations are used when you wish to indicate the language used in your HTML document. Do not confuse these abbreviations with the country codes. For example, there is a distinction between English as a language, and the country England.

A	
aa	Afar
ab	Abkhazian
af	Afrikaans
am	Amharic
ar	Arabic
as	Assamese
ay	Aymara
az	Azerbaijani
B	
ba	Bashkir
be	Byelorussian
bg	Bulgarian
bh	Bihari
bi	Bislama
bn	Bengali; Bangla
bo	Tibetan
br	Breton

C	
ca	Catalan
co	Corsican
cs	Czech
cy	Welsh
D	
da	Danish
de	German
dz	Bhutani
E	
el	Greek
en	English
eo	Esperanto
es	Spanish
et	Estonian
eu	Basque
F	
fa	Persian
fi	Finnish
fj	Fijian
fo	Faeroese
fr	French
fy	Frisian
G	
ga	Irish
gd	Scots, Gaelic
gl	Galician
gn	Guarani
gu	Gujarati
H	
ha	Hausa
hi	Hindi
hr	Croatian
hu	Hungarian
hy	Armenian
I	

ia	Interlingua
ie	Interlingue
ik	Inupiak
in	Indonesian
is	Icelandic
it	Italian
iw	Hebrew
J	
ja	Japanese
ji	Yiddish
jw	Javanese
K	
ka	Georgian
kk	Kazakh
kl	Greenlandic
km	Cambodian
kn	Kannada
ko	Korean
ks	Kashmiri
ku	Kurdish
ky	Kirghiz
L	
la	Latin
ln	Lingala
lo	Laothian
lt	Lithuanian
lv	Latvian, Lettish
M	
mg	Malagasy
mi	Maori
mk	Macedonian
ml	Malayalam
mn	Mongolian
mo	Moldavian
mr	Marathi
ms	Malay

mt	Maltese
my	Burmese
N	
na	Nauru
ne	Nepali
nl	Dutch
no	Norwegian
O	
oc	Occitan
om	(Afan), Oromo
or	Oriya
P	
pa	Punjabi
pl	Polish
ps	Pashto, Pushto
pt	Portuguese
Q	
qu	Quechua
R	
rm	Rhaeto-Romance
rn	Kirundi
ro	Romanian
ru	Russian
rw	Kinyarwanda
S	
sa	Sanskrit
sd	Sindhi
sg	Sangro
sh	Serbo-Croatian
si	Singhalese
sk	Slovak
sl	Slovenian
sm	Samoan
sn	Shona
so	Somali
sq	Albanian

sr	Serbian
ss	Siswati
st	Sesotho
su	Sundanese
sv	Swedish
sw	Swahili
T	
ta	Tamil
te	Tegulu
tg	Tajik
th	Thai
ti	Tigrinya
tk	Turkmen
tl	Tagalog
tn	Setswana
to	Tonga
tr	Turkish
ts	Tsonga
tt	Tatar
tw	Twi
U	
uk	Ukrainian
ur	Urdu
uz	Uzbek
V	
vi	Vietnamese
vo	Volapuk
W	
wo	Wolof
X	
xh	Xhosa
Y	
yo	Yoruba
Z	
zh	Chinese
zu	Zulu

Example

```
<a href="english.htm" hreflang="en">
<a href="german1.htm hreflang="de-ch">
<a href="german2.htm hreflang="de-de">
<div lang="en-uk"></div>
<html lang="de"></html>
```

Links within a document

Application

This allows you not only to create links to other documents, which are called hyperlinks within the WWW, but also internal links to areas within the same document. You can therefore move quickly to individual text sections within a longer document without having to read through the whole text. In this way, outside visitors are also provided with jump destinations within a document.

Implementation

You will first need to define the jump destinations in the target document; this is slightly different from creating hyperlinks, where the file name or the name of the document is sufficient as a jump destination. This happens when the command is used without the HREF attribute, but with the markup tag. You simply define an area with its name.

If you wish to create links, then provide the name of the link with a left-angle single quote as the jump destination. If the link is with another document, you must also indicate the name of the document, in front of the quote.

Example

```
Example
<html>
<body>

<a name="Top">

<a href="#Section1">Section 1</a>
<a href="#Section2">Section 2</a>
<a href="#Section3">Section 3</a>
<a href="#Section4">Section 4</a>
<a href="#Section5">Section 5</a>

</a>
```

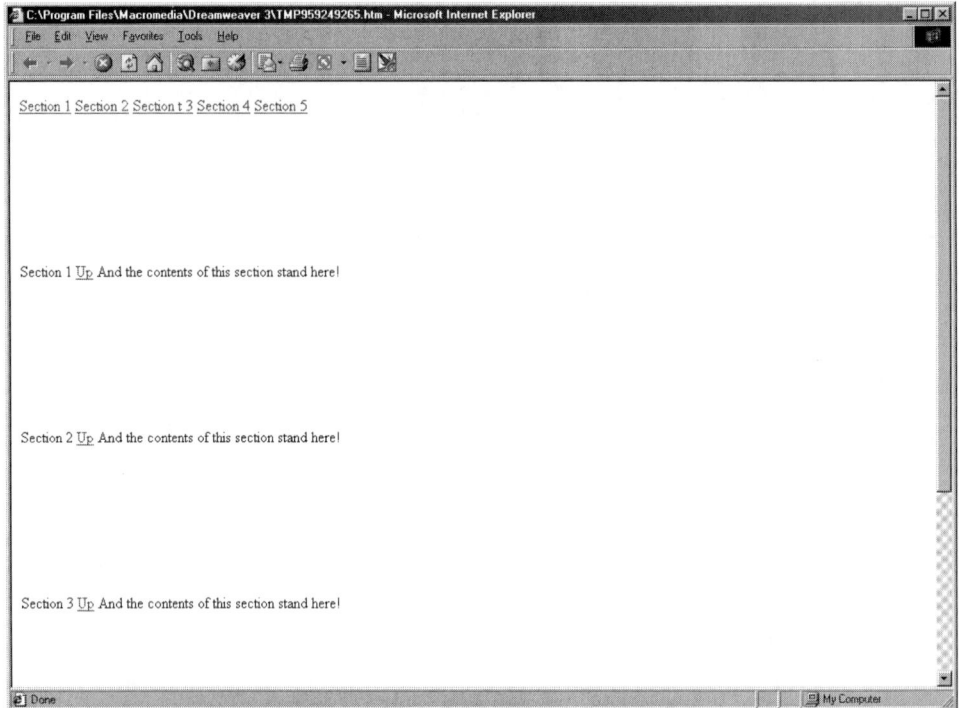

Creating links within a document

```
<br><br><br><br>
<br><br><br><br><br>
<a name="Section1">Section 1</a>
<a href="#Top">Up</a>
And the contents of this section stand here!

<br><br><br><br>
<br><br><br><br><br>
<a name="Section2">Section 2</a>
<a href="#Top">Up</a>
And the contents of this section stand here!

<br><br><br><br>
<br><br><br><br><br>
<a name="Section3">Section 3</a>
<a href="#Top">Up</a>
And the contents of this section stand here!

<br><br><br><br>
<br><br><br><br><br>
<a name="Section4">Section 4</a>
<a href="#Top">Up</a>
And the contents of this section stand here!
```

```
<br><br><br><br>
<br><br><br><br><br>
<a name="Section5">Section 5</a>
<a href="#Top">Up</a>
And the contents of this section stand here!

</body>
</html>
```

Tips

Make sure that when specifying the name of a section, you differentiate between lower and upper case characters.

The following example works:

```
The following example works:
<a name="Section2">
<a href="#Section2">
<a href="page2.htm#Section2">
```

The following example does not work:

```
<a name="Section2">
<a href="#section2">
<a href="page2.htm#section2">
```

Documents in HTML 4.0

Application

To provide you with a short summary of the changes to HTML 4.0 from the previous version HTML 3.2, we have briefly listed the main differences.

Implementation

As well as adding new commands which have been made available to the programmer, a whole batch of commands have been removed in HTML 4.0. These should be replaced with the new recommended commands. Do not continue to use old commands.

The following new commands were introduced:

```
ACRONYM    new command
BUTTON     new command
COLGROUP   new command
```

```
DEL         new command
FIELDSET    new command
INS         new command
PUTTING     new command
Q           new command
```

The use of the following commands is no longer recommended in HTML 4.0. The following list shows the old commands (left) and what they have been replaced by right.

```
APPLET      replaced by: OBJECT
BASEFONT    replaced by: STYLE
CENTER      replaced by: DIV ALIGN="CENTER"
DIR         replaced by: UL
FONT        replaced by: STYLE
ISINDEX     replaced by: INPUT
MENU        replaced by: UL
S           replaced by: STYLE
STRIKE      replaced by: STYLE
U           replaced by: STYLE
```

The following are still used in HTML 4.0 but should be replaced with the ones indicated here:

```
LISTING     replaced by:    PRE
PLAINTEXT   replaced by:    PRE
XMP         replaced by:    PRE
```

Using country codes

Application

You can submit the language code to various commands through an attribute. It provides precise information about the language used. The language code consists of two parts; besides a language used (i. e. English) it also determines the local variation. This second detail is optional, though. Language codes are listed according to the ISO 639, and can be found under the ISO 639 keyword. The country code defines the country the document originates from or the language variation used. The detail of the language used is executed with the language code.

Implementation

ISO 3166 provides a standard for country codes. The current version of this standard allows three abbreviations for each country: A three-digit number, a two-letter version, and a three-letter version. Currently, the variant A2 is used in HTML documents.

Country	A2	A3	Number
AFGHANISTAN	AF	AFG	004
ALBANIA	AL	ALB	008
ALGERIA	DZ	DZA	012
AMERICAN SAMOA	AS	ASM	016
ANDORRA	AD	AND	020
ANGOLA	AO	AGO	024
ANGUILLA	AI	AIA	660
ANTARCTICA	AQ	ATA	010
ANTIGUA AND BARBUDA	AG	ATG	028
ARGENTINA	AR	ARG	032
ARMENIA	AM	ARM	051
ARUBA	AW	ABW	533
AUSTRALIA	AU	AUS	036
AUSTRIA	AT	AUT	040
AZERBAIJAN	AZ	AZE	031
BAHAMAS	BS	BHS	044
BAHRAIN	BH	BHR	048
BANGLADESH	BD	BGD	050
BARBADOS	BB	BRB	052
BELARUS	BY	BLR	112
BELGIUM	BE	BEL	056
BELIZE	BZ	BLZ	084
BENIN	BJ	BEN	204
BERMUDA	BM	BMU	060
BHUTAN	BT	BTN	064
BOLIVIA	BO	BOL	068
BOSNIA AND HERZEGOVINA	BA	BIH	070
BOTSWANA	BW	BWA	072
BOUVET ISLAND	BV	BVT	074
BRAZIL	BR	BRA	076

Country	A2	A3	Number
BRITISH INDIAN OCEAN TERRITORY	IO	IOT	086
BRUNEI DARUSSALAM	BN	BRN	096
BULGARIA	BG	BGR	100
BURKINA FASO	BF	BFA	854
BURUNDI	BI	BDI	108
CAMBODIA	KH	KHM	116
CAMEROON	CM	CMR	120
CANADA	CA	CAN	124
CAPE VERDE	CV	CPV	132
CAYMAN ISLANDS	KY	CYM	136
CENTRAL AFRICAN REPUBLIC	CF	CAF	140
CHAD	TD	TCD	148
CHILE	CL	CHL	152
CHINA	CN	CHN	156
CHRISTMAS ISLAND	CX	CXR	162
COCOS (KEELING) ISLANDS	CC	CCK	166
COLOMBIA	CO	COL	170
COMOROS	KM	COM	174
CONGO	CG	COG	178
COOK ISLANDS	CK	COK	184
COSTA RICA	CR	CRI	188
COTE D'IVOIRE	CI	CIV	384
CROATIA (HRYATSKA)	HR	HRV	191
CUBA	CU	CUB	192
CYPRUS	CY	CYP	196
CZECH REPUBLIC	CZ	CZE	203
DENMARK	DK	DNK	208
DJIBOUTI	DJ	DJI	262
DOMINICA	DM	DMA	212
DOMINICAN REPUBLIC	DO	DOM	214
EAST TIMOR	TP	TMP	626
ECUADOR	EC	ECU	218
EGYPT	EG	EGY	818
EL SALVADOR	SV	SLV	222
EQUATORIAL GUINEA	GQ	GNQ	226

Country	A2	A3	Number
ERITREA	ER	ERI	232
ESTONIA	EE	EST	233
ETHIOPIA	ET	ETH	231
FALKLAND ISLANDS (MALVINAS)	FK	FLK	238
FAROE ISLANDS	FO	FRO	234
FIJI	FJ	FJI	242
FINLAND	FI	FIN	246
FRANCE	FR	FRA	250
FRANCE, METROPOLITAN	FX	FXX	249
FRENCH GUIANA	GF	GUF	254
FRENCH POLYNESIA	PF	PYF	258
FRENCH SOUTHERN TERRITORIES	TF	ATF	260
GABON	GA	GAB	266
GAMBIA	GM	GMB	270
GEORGIA	GE	GEO	268
GERMANY	DE	DEU	276
GHANA	GH	GHA	288
GIBRALTAR	GI	GIB	292
GREECE	GR	GRC	300
GREENLAND	GL	GRL	304
GRENADA	GD	GRD	308
GUADELOUPE	GP	GLP	312
GUAM	GU	GUM	316
GUATEMALA	GT	GTM	320
GUINEA	GN	GIN	324
GUINEA-BISSAU	GW	GNB	624
GUYANA	GY	GUY	328
HAITI	HT	HTI	332
HEARD AND MCDONALD ISLANDS	HM	HMD	334
HONDURAS	HN	HND	340
HONG KONG	HK	HKG	344
HUNGARY	HU	HUN	348
ICELAND	IS	ISL	352
INDIA	IN	IND	356
INDONESIA	ID	IDN	360

Country	A2	A3	Number
IRAN (ISLAMIC REPUBLIC OF)	IR	IRN	364
IRAQ	IQ	IRQ	368
IRELAND	IE	IRL	372
ISRAEL	IL	ISR	376
ITALY	IT	ITA	380
JAMAICA	JM	JAM	388
JAPAN	JP	JPN	392
JORDAN	JO	JOR	400
KAZAKHSTAN	KZ	KAZ	398
KENYA	KE	KEN	404
KIRIBATIKI		KIR	296
KOREA, DEMOCRATIC REPUBLIC OF	KP	PRK	408
KOREA, REPUBLIC OF	KR	KOR	410
KUWAIT	KW	KWT	414
KYRGYZSTAN	KG	KGZ	417
LAO DEMOCRATIC REPUBLIC	LA	LAO	418
LATVIA	LV	LVA	428
LEBANON	LB	LBN	422
LESOTHO	LS	LSO	426
LIBERIA	LR	LBR	430
LIBYAN ARAB JAMAHIRIYA	LY	LBY	434
LIECHTENSTEIN	LI	LIE	438
LITHUANIA	LT	LTU	440
LUXEMBOURG	LU	LUX	442
MACAU	MO	MAC	446
MACEDONIA	MK	MKD	807
MADAGASCAR	MG	MDG	450
MALAWI	MW	MWI	454
MALAYSIA	MY	MYS	458
MALDIVES	MV	MDV	462
MALI	ML	MLI	466
MALTA	MT	MLT	470
MARSHALL ISLANDS	MH	MHL	584
MARTINIQUE	MQ	MTQ	474
MAURITANIA	MR	MRT	478

Country	A2	A3	Number
MAURITIUS	MU	MUS	480
MAYOTTE	YT	MYT	175
MEXICO	MX	MEX	484
MICRONESIA, FEDERATED STATES OF	FM	FSM	583
MOLDOVA, REPUBLIC OF	MD	MDA	498
MONACO	MC	MCO	492
MONGOLIA MN	MNG	496	
MONTSERRAT	MS	MSR	500
MOROCCO	MA	MAR	504
MOZAMBIQUE	MZ	MOZ	508
MYANMAR	MM	MMR	104
NAMIBIA	NA	NAM	516
NAURU	NR	NRU	520
NEPAL	NP	NPL	524
NETHERLANDS	NL	NLD	528
NETHERLANDS ANTILLES	AN	ANT	530
NEW CALEDONIA	NC	NCL	540
NEW ZEALAND	NZ	NZL	554
NICARAGUA	NI	NIC	558
NIGER	NE	NER	562
NIGERIA	NG	NGA	566
NIUE	NU	NIU	570
NORFOLK ISLAND	NF	NFK	574
NORTHERN MARIANA ISLANDS	MP	MNP	580
NORWAY	NO	NOR	578
OMAN	OM	OMN	512
PAKISTAN	PK	PAK	586
PALAU	PW	PLW	585
PANAMA	PA	PAN	591
PAPUA NEW GUINEA	PG	PNG	598
PARAGUAY	PY	PRY	600
PERU	PE	PER	604
PHILIPPINES	PH	PHL	608
PITCAIRN	PN	PCN	612
POLAND	PL	POL	616

Country	A2	A3	Number
PORTUGAL	PT	PRT	620
PUERTO RICO	PR	PRI	630
QATAR	QA	QAT	634
REUNION	RE	REU	638
ROMANIA	RO	ROM	642
RUSSIAN FEDERATION	RU	RUS	643
RWANDA	RW	RWA	646
SAINT KITTS AND NEVIS	KN	KNA	659
SAINT LUCIA	LC	LCA	662
SAINT VINCENT AND THE GRENADINES	VC	VCT	670
SAMOA	WS	WSM	882
SAN MARINO	SM	SMR	674
SAO TOME AND PRINCIPE	ST	STP	678
SAUDI ARABIA	SA	SAU	682
SENEGAL	SN	SEN	686
SEYCHELLES	SC	SYC	690
SIERRA LEONE	SL	SLE	694
SINGAPORE	SG	SGP	702
SLOVAKIA	SK	SVK	703
SLOVENIA	SI	SVN	705
SOLOMON ISLANDS	SB	SLB	090
SOMALIA	SO	SOM	706
SOUTH AFRICA	ZA	ZAF	710
SOUTH GEORGIA AND THE SOUTH SANDWICH ISLANDS	GS	SGS	239
SPAIN	ES	ESP	724
SRI LANKA	LK	LKA	144
ST. HELENA	SH	SHN	654
ST. PIERRE AND MIQUELON	PM	SPM	666
SUDAN	SD	SDN	736
SURINAME	SR	SUR	740
SVALBARD AND JAN MAYEN ISLANDS	SJ	SJM	744
SWAZILAND	SZ	SWZ	748
SWEDEN	SE	SWE	752
SWITZERLAND	CH	CHE	756

Country	A2	A3	Number
SYRIAN ARAB REPUBLIC	SY	SYR	760
TAIWAN, PROVINCE OF CHINA	TW	TWN	158
TAJIKISTAN	TJ	TJK	762
TANZANIA, UNITED REPUBLIC	TZ	TZA	834
THAILAND	TH	THA	764
TOGO	TG	TGO	768
TOKELAU	TK	TKL	772
TONGA	TO	TON	776
TRINIDAD AND TOBAGO	TT	TTO	780
TUNISIA	TN	TUN	788
TURKEY	TR	TUR	792
TURKMENISTAN	TM	TKM	795
TURKS AND CAICOS ISLANDS	TC	TCA	796
TUVALU	TV	TUV	798
UGANDA	UG	UGA	800
UKRAINE	UA	UKR	804
UNITED ARAB EMIRATES	AE	ARE	784
UNITED KINGDOM	GB	GBR	826
UNITED STATES	US	USA	840
UNITED STATES MINOR OUTLYING ISLANDS	UM	UMI	581
URUGUAY	UY	URY	858
UZBEKISTAN	UZ	UZB	860
VANUATU	VU	VUT	548
VATICAN CITY STATE	VA	VAT	336
VENEZUELA	VE	VEN	862
VIETNAM	VN	VNM	704
VIRGIN ISLANDS (BRITISH)	VG	VGB	092
VIRGIN ISLANDS (U.S.)	VI	VIR	850
WALLIS AND FUTUNA ISLANDS	WF	WLF	876
WESTERN SAHARA	EH	ESH	732
YEMEN	YE	YEM	887
YUGOSLAVIA	YU	YUG	891
ZAIRE	ZR	ZAR	180
ZAMBIA	ZM	ZMB	894

Country	A2	A3	Number
ZIMBABWE	ZW	ZWE	716

Example

```
<a href="english.htm" hreflang="en">
<a href="english1.htm" hreflang="en-uk">
<a href="german1.htm" hreflang="de-de">

<div lang="en-uk"></div>
<html lang="en"></html>
<strong lang="en-uk"></strong>
```

Background sound for Microsoft Internet Explorer and Netscape Navigator

Application

If you wish to insert background music, such as a MIDI file or a WAVE sound file, you will encounter the problem that until now, Microsoft Internet Explorer and Netscape Navigator do not handle sound in the same way.

Implementation

The solution requires additional effort but the outcome is then compatible with both systems. You must integrate two variants of the sound file. Netscape will ignore the commands which apply to Explorer and vice versa, so the background sound will be heard on each browser.

For Microsoft Internet Explorer, the sound file should be inserted at the head of the document and for Netscape it should be inserted in the body of the HTML document.

Example

```
<html>
<head>
<title>Page with background sound<title>
<!-- Microsoft: -->
<bgsound src="file.mid" loop=-1>
</head>
<body>
```

```
<!-- Netscape: -->
<embed src="file.mid" autostart=true loop=true
hidden=true height=0 width=0>
</body>
</html>
```

You can also use the following JavaScript alternative:

```
<script language="javascript">
<!--
var ver=navigator.appVersion;
if (ver.indexOf ("MSIE") !=-1)
{
document.write('<bgsound src="sound.wav" loop=infinite>')
}
else
document.write
('<embed
     src="sound.wav"
     height=2 width=2
     autostart=true
     hidden=true
     loop=true>')
// -->
</script>
```

Tables containing empty cells

Application

Table cells which are empty are not usually displayed. This can lead to problems in displaying a table.

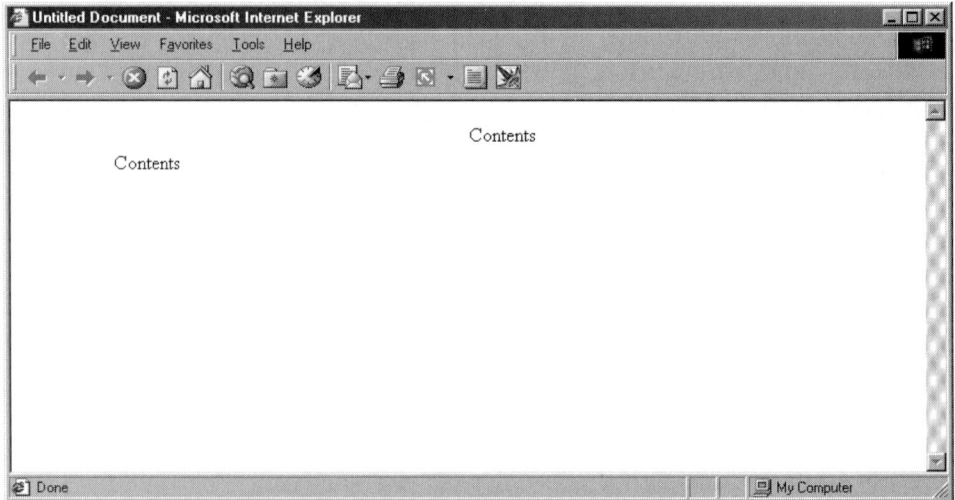

Table with empty cells

Implementation

The solution is relatively simple: insert invisible content in the empty cell, for example a blank space. However, if you only insert a blank space, this is ignored and the cell is still considered to be empty. But there is a trick to bypass this problem. You insert the entity of a blank in the table ( ) or).

Example

```
<table width="80%" border="1">
<tr>
    <td width="50%">  </td>
    <td>Contents</td>
</tr>
<tr>
    <td>  </td>
    <td>  </td>
</tr>
<tr>
    <td>Contents</td>
```

```
        <td>  </td>
</tr>
</table>
```

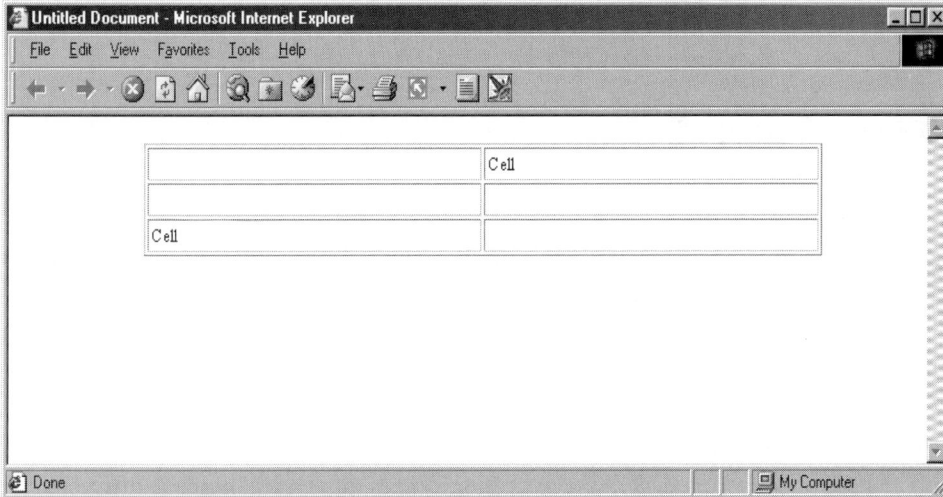

Using the above solution the table can be displayed.

Using external style sheets

Application

Style sheets can be defined and specified within the HTML document to which they apply. However, for large projects, it may be better to store style definitions in an external file. This has the advantage that a common design need only be set up in one file and the data does not have to appear again in each document. In this way, on the one hand, you save work and keep control of the situation, while on the other you also save time.

Implementation

Create an external style sheet file in which the style settings for the document are specified. You then link this file to each document with the LINK command.

Example

```
<html>
<head>
<link
    rel=stylesheet
```

```
        type="text/css"
        src="http://www.pott-it.de/mystyle.css">
</head>
<body>
</body>
</html>
```

Determining MIME types

Application

MIME types ("Multipurpose Internet Mail Extension" file) describe the content of a file. So you specify, for example, that the transmitted data is a MIDI Sound file or an AVI video sequence. Every data type can be described in a standard format and can be assigned to an application.

Implementation

With MIME types you describe the content types of data. These identify special data formats, for example, a Microsoft Word document or an Adobe PDF document. Use the definitions which you will find in the following table to specify the data format.

Every MIME type consists of a main type and a sub-type (such as text/html for an HTML file).

Type	Sub-type	Description
application	msexcel	Microsoft Excel table
application	mshelp	Microsoft Windows Help file
application	mspowerpoint	Microsoft PowerPoint presentation
application	msword	Microsoft Word document
application	pdf	Adobe Acrobat document
application	postscript	Adobe Postscript document
application	rtf	Microsoft RTF document
application	zip	ZIP file archive
audio	basic	AU and SND file
audio	mid	MIDI sound file
audio	wav	WAVE file
audio	x-pn-realaudio	RealAudio file

Type	Sub-type	Description
image	gif	GIF graphic file
image	jpeg	JPEG graphic file
image	tiff	TIFF graphic file
text	css	Cascading style sheet
text	html	HTML document
text	javascript	JavaScript file
text	plain	8-Bit text
video	avi	AVI-Video
video	mpeg	MPEG-Video
video	quicktime	Quicktime-Video

Example

```
<input accept="image/gif">
<input accept="text/html">
<input accept="text/css">

<object codetype="video/mpeg">
<object codetype="image/gif">

<form
     action="http://www.domain.de/action.cgi"
     enctype="text/html"
     method="post">
</form>
```

Defining a Font

The standard font is usually provided by the browser. This font is always used if no other font is explicitly indicated.

Implementation

This changes the standard font determined with the style sheets. You need to indicate another font for the Body command.

Example

```
<html>
<head>
<style>
<!--
     body {font-family: COMIC SANS MS}
```

471

```
-->
</style>
</head>
<body>
<h1>Example</h1>
</body>
</html>
```

Protecting source text

Application

As soon as your HTML document is published on the Internet, your source code becomes open to everybody who wishes to view it. Of course this also means that your pages and your design can be copied by anybody who should be so inclined, without paying you any royalties, and there is nothing you can do to protect your copyright. This is one of the accepted conditions for operating on the Internet, at least in principle. And a large number of people have in fact benefited from this freedom, by lifting code and learning tricks from work carried out and published. However, there are a few tips to follow so that people cannot enter your source code.

Implementation

Of course, no solution can offer absolute protection. So how do you create a shield for your documents? One simple option to protect oneself from inexperienced Web users is to fill the source code with blank lines, which should be placed at the beginning of the document. Insert a few hundred blank lines. Of course, these lines will not show up on your site in the browser. If somebody tries to look at the source code, they will think that the file is empty. Your source code becomes visible only if the user makes the effort to scroll to the end of the document.

Another option, which is demonstrated in the following example, is to remove the overview facility from your document by removing all unnecessary line breaks and blank spaces. This will make it difficult to follow the code. But remember to save a copy of the document for yourself so that you can work on it at a later stage. Currently, there are a number of programs that make your source code automatically illegible.

Example

```
<HTML><BODY bgcolor="white" link="gray"><br><div style="font-family:
Arial; font-size: 90%; color: gray; font-weight: bold" align="cen-
```

At first the file seems to be empty

ter">Standard and custom-built models measure for the-and control engineering
 <table width=90% border=0 cellspacing=1 cellpadding=1><tr> <td rowspan="3" valign="top"><IMG SRC="pro-dukt.jpg"></td><td width="20">   </td><td style="font-family: Arial; font-size: 100%; color: gray; font-weight: bold">L i n e a r - P o t e n t i o m e t e r</td></tr><tr><td width="20"> </td><td style="font-family: Arial; font-size: 90%; color: black;">Linear Potentiometer are used for measuring lengths. The push bar can be fetched back by means of the built-in tool or driven out in the key-board execution. With built-in electronics the linear Potentiometer works as a measure and a transducer.</td></tr><tr><td width="20"> </td><td align="right" style="font-family: Arial; font-size: 60%; color: gray; font-weight: bold"> <a href="">Overview<IMG align=absmiddle SRC="arrow.gif" border="0"></a></td></tr> </table><table width=90% border=0 cellspacing=1 cellpad-ding=1><tr><td rowspan="3" valign="top"><IMG SRC="produkt.jpg"></td><td width="20"> </td><td style="font-family: Arial; font-size: 100%; color: gray; font-weight: bold">L i n e a r - P o t e n t i o m e t e r</td></tr><tr><tr>

473

Using character sets

Application
This allows you to define the appropriate font for a document or input. The following list provides an overview of all available characters sets worldwide. If more than one name appears in a line, it means that there are alternative names for the same font.

Implementation
The list also shows the example for the corresponding name of the font. The fonts are usually taken from the ISO 8859 or the later ISO 10646.

ISO	Name	Font
ISO-8859-1	»Latin-1«	Western Europe
ISO-8559-2	»Latin-2«	Central Europe
ISO-8559-3	»Latin-3«	Esperanto, Galician, Maltese
ISO-8559-4	»Latin-4«	Estonian, Latvian, Lithuanian
ISO-8559-5		Cyrillic
ISO-8559-6		Arabic
ISO-8559-7		Modern Greek
ISO-8559-8		Hebrew
ISO-8559-9	»Latin-5«	Turkish
ISO-8559-10	»Latin-6«	Icelandic, Lappon

A
```
Adobe-Standard-Encoding, csAdobeStandardEncoding
Adobe-Symbol-Encoding, csHPPSMath
ANSI_X3.110-1983, iso-ir-99, CSA_T500-1983, NAPLPS, csISO99NAPLPS
ANSI_X3.4-1968, iso-ir-6, ANSI_X3.4-1986, ISO_646.irv:1991, ASCII,
ISO646-US, US-ASCII, us, IBM367, cp367, csASCII
ASMO_449, ISO_9036, arabic7, iso-ir-89, csISO89ASMO449
```

B
```
Big5, csBig5
BS_4730, iso-ir-4, ISO646-GB, gb, uk, csISO4UnitedKingdom
BS_viewdata, iso-ir-47, csISO047BSViewdata,
```

C
```
CSA_Z243.4-1985-1,iso-ir-121,ISO646-
```

CA,csa7-1, ca, csISO121Canadian1
CSA_Z243.4-1985-2, iso-ir-122, ISO646-CA2, csa7-2, csISO122Canadian2
CSA_Z243.4-1985-gr, iso-ir-123, csISO123CSAZ24341985gr
CSN_369103, iso-ir-139, csISO139CSN369103

D

DEC-MCS, dec, csDECMCS
DIN_66003, iso-ir-21, de, ISO646-DE, csISO21German
DS_2089, DS2089, ISO646-DK, dk, csISO646Danish

E

EBCDIC-AT-DE, csIBMEBCDICATDE
EBCDIC-AT-DE-A, csEBCDICATDEA
EBCDIC-CA-FR, csEBCDICCAFR
EBCDIC-DK-NO, csEBCDICDKNO
EBCDIC-DK-NO-A, csEBCDICDKNOA
EBCDIC-ES, csEBCDICES
EBCDIC-ES-A, csEBCDICESA
EBCDIC-ES-S, csEBCDICESS
EBCDIC-FI-SE, csEBCDICFISE
EBCDIC-FI-SE-A, csEBCDICFISEA
EBCDIC-FR, csEBCDICFR
EBCDIC-IT, csEBCDICIT
EBCDIC-PT, csEBCDICPT
EBCDIC-UK, csEBCDICUK
EBCDIC-US, csEBCDICUS
ECMA-cyrillic, iso-ir-111, csISO111ECMACyrillic
ES, iso-ir-17, ISO646-ES, csISO017Spanish
ES2, iso-ir-85, ISO646-ES2, csISO085Spanish2
EUC-KR, csEUCKR
Extended_UNIX_Code_Fixed_Width_for_Japanese, csEUCFixWidJapanese
Extended_UNIX_Code_Packed_Format_for_Japanese, csEUCPkdFmtJapanese,
EUC-JP

G

GB_1988-80, iso-ir-57, cn, ISO646-CN, csISO57GB1988
GB_2312-80, iso-ir-58, chinese, csISO58GB231280
GB2312, csGB2312
GOST_19768-74, ST_SEV_358-88, iso-ir-153, csISO153GOST1976874
greek7, iso-ir-88, csISO088Greek7
greek7-old, iso-ir-18, csISO018Greek7Old
greek-ccitt, iso-ir-150, csISO150, csISO150GreekCCITT

H

HP-DeskTop, csHPDesktop
HP-Legal, csHPLegal
HP-Math8, csHPMath8
HP-Pi-font, csHPPiFont
hp-roman8, roman8, r8, csHPRoman8
HZ-GB-2312

I

IBM037,cp037,ebcdic-cp-us,ebcdic-cp-ca,ebcdic-cp-wt,ebcdic-cp-nl,
csIBM037
IBM038, EBCDIC-INT, cp038, csIBM038
IBM1026, CP1026, csIBM1026
IBM273, CP273, csIBM273
IBM274, EBCDIC-BE, CP274, csIBM274
IBM275, EBCDIC-BR, cp275, csIBM275
IBM277, EBCDIC-CP-DK, EBCDIC-CP-NO, csIBM277
IBM278, CP278, ebcdic-cp-fi, ebcdic-cp-se, csIBM278
IBM280, CP280, ebcdic-cp-it, csIBM280
IBM281, EBCDIC-JP-E, cp281, csIBM281
IBM284, CP284, ebcdic-cp-es, csIBM284
IBM285, CP285, ebcdic-cp-gb, csIBM285
IBM290, cp290, EBCDIC-JP-kana, csIBM290
IBM297, cp297, ebcdic-cp-fr, csIBM297
IBM420, cp420, ebcdic-cp-ar1, csIBM420
IBM423, cp423, ebcdic-cp-gr, csIBM423
IBM424, cp424, ebcdic-cp-he, csIBM424
IBM437, cp437, 437, csPC8CodePage437
IBM500, CP500, ebcdic-cp-be, ebcdic-cp-ch, csIBM500
IBM775, cp775, csPC775Baltic
IBM850, cp850, 850, csPC850Multilingual
IBM851, cp851, 851, csIBM851
IBM852, cp852, 852, csPCp852
IBM855, cp855, 855, csIBM855
IBM857, cp857, 857, csIBM857
IBM860, cp860, 860, csIBM860
IBM861, cp861, 861, cp-is, csIBM861
IBM862, cp862, 862, csPC862LatinHebrew
IBM863, cp863, 863, csIBM863
IBM864, cp864, csIBM864
IBM865, cp865, 865, csIBM865
IBM866, cp866, 866, csIBM866
IBM868, CP868, cp-ar, csIBM868
IBM869, cp869, 869, cp-gr, csIBM869
IBM870, CP870, ebcdic-cp-roece, ebcdic-cp-yu, csIBM870
IBM871, CP871, ebcdic-cp-is, csIBM871
IBM880, cp880, EBCDIC-Cyrillic, csIBM880

```
IBM891, cp891, csIBM891
IBM903, cp903, csIBM903
IBM904, cp904, 904, csIBBM904
IBM905, CP905, ebcdic-cp-tr, csIBM905
IBM918, CP918, ebcdic-cp-ar2, csIBM918
IBM-Symbols, csIBMSymbols
IBM-Thai, csIBMThai
IEC_P27-1, iso-ir-143, csISO143IECP271
INIS, iso-ir-49, csISO49INIS,
INIS-8, iso-ir-50, csISO50INIS8
INIS-cyrillic, iso-ir-51, csISO51INISCyrillic
INVARIANT, csINVARIANT
ISO_10367-box, iso-ir-155, csISO10367Box
ISO_2033-1983, iso-ir-98, e13b, csISO2033
ISO_5427, iso-ir-37, csISO5427Cyrillic
ISO_5427:1981, iso-ir-54, ISO5427Cyrillic1981
ISO_5428:1980, iso-ir-55, csISO5428Greek
ISO_646.basic:1983, ref, csISO646basic1983
ISO_646.irv:1983, iso-ir-2, irv, csISO2IntlRefVersion
ISO_6937-2-25, iso-ir-152, csISO6937Add
ISO_6937-2-add, iso-ir-142, csISOTextComm
ISO_8859-1:1987,    iso-ir-100,    ISO_8859-1,ISO-8859-1,latin1,l1,
IBM819, CP819, csISOLatin1
ISO_8859-15
ISO_8859-2:1987,iso-ir-101,ISO_8859-2,ISO-8859-2,latin2,l2,
csISOLatin2
ISO_8859-3:1988,iso-ir-109,ISO_8859-3,ISO-8859-3,latin3,l3,
csISOLatin3
ISO_8859-4:1988,iso-ir-110,ISO_8859-4,ISO-8859-4,latin4,l4,
csISOLatin4
ISO_8859-5:1988,iso-ir-144,ISO_8859-5,ISO-8859-5,cyrillic,csISOLa-
tinCyrillic
ISO_8859-6:1987, iso-ir-127, ISO_8859-6, ISO-8859-6, ECMA-114, ASMO-
708, arabic, csISOLatinArabic
ISO_8859-6-E, csISO88596E
ISO_8859-6-I, csISO88596I
ISO_8859-7:1987, iso-ir-126, ISO_8859-7, ISO-8859-7, ELOT_928, ECMA-
118, greek, greek8, csISOLatinGreek
ISO_8859-8:1988, iso-ir-138, ISO_8859-8, ISO-8859-8, hebrew, csISO-
LatinHebrew
ISO_8859-8-E, csISO88598E
ISO_8859-8-I, csISO88598I
ISO_8859-9:1989, iso-ir-148, ISO_8859-9, ISO-8859-9, latin5, l5,
csISOLatin5
ISO_8859-supp, iso-ir-154, latin1-2-5, csISO8859Supp
ISO-10646-J-1
ISO-10646-UCS-2, csUnicode
ISO-10646-UCS-4, csUCS4
ISO-10646-UCS-Basic, csUnicodeASCII
ISO-10646-Unicode-Latin1, csUnicodeLatin1, ISO-10646
```

```
ISO-10646-UTF-1, csISO10646UTF1
ISO-2022-CN
ISO-2022-CN-EXT
ISO-2022-JP, csISO2022JP
ISO-2022-JP-2, csISO2022JP2
ISO-2022-KR, csISO2022KR
ISO-8859-1, csUnicodeIBM2039
ISO-8859-1-Windows-3.0-Latin-1, csWindows30Latin1
ISO-8859-1-Windows-3.1-Latin-1, csWindows31Latin1
ISO-8859-2-Windows-Latin-2, csWindows31Latin2
ISO-8859-9-Windows-Latin-5, csWindows31Latin5
iso-ir-103, csISO103T618bit
iso-ir-27, csISO27LatinGreek1
iso-ir-90, csISO90
ISO-Unicode-IBM-1261, csUnicodeIBM1261
ISO-Unicode-IBM-1264, csUnicodeIBM1264
ISO-Unicode-IBM-1265, csUnicodeIBM1265
ISO-Unicode-IBM-1268, csUnidoceIBM1268
ISO-Unicode-IBM-1276, csUnicodeIBM1276
IT, iso-ir-15, ISO646-IT, csISO15Italian
```

J

```
JIS_C6220-1969-jp,  JIS_C6220-1969,  iso-ir-13,  katakana,  x0201-7,
csISO13JISC6220jp
JIS_C6220-1969-ro, iso-ir-14, jp, ISO646-JP, csISO14JISC6220ro
JIS_C6226-1978, iso-ir-42, csISO42JISC62261978
JIS_C6226-1983, iso-ir-87, x0208, JIS_X0208-1983, csISO87JISX0208
JIS_C6229-1984-a, iso-ir-91, jp-ocr-a, csISO91JISC62291984a
JIS_C6229-1984-b,      iso-ir-92,      ISO646-JP-OCR-B,      jp-ocr-b,
csISO92JISC62991984b
JIS_C6229-1984-b-add,iso-ir-93, jp-ocr-b-add, csISO93JIS62291984badd
JIS_C6229-1984-hand, iso-ir-94, jp-ocr-hand, csISO94JIS62291984hand
JIS_C6229-1984-hand-add,iso-ir-95,jp-ocr-hand-add,
csISO95JIS62291984handadd
JIS_C6229-1984-kana, iso-ir-96, csISO96JISC62291984kana
JIS_Encoding, csJISEncoding
JIS_X0201, X0201, csHalfWidthKatakana
JIS_X0212-1990, x0212, iso-ir-159, csISO159JISX02121990
JUS_I.B1.002, iso-ir-141, ISO646-YU, js, yu, csISO141JUSIB1002
JUS_I.B1.003-mac, macedonian, iso-ir-147, csISO147Macedonian
JUS_I.B1.003-serb, iso-ir-146, serbian, csISO146Serbian
```

K

```
KOI8-R, csKOI8R
KOI8-U
KS_C_5601-1987,iso-ir-149,KS_C_5601-1989,KSC_5601,korean,
csKSC56011987
```

KSC5636, ISO646-KR, csKSC5636

L

latin6, iso-ir-157, l6, ISO_8859-10:1992, csISOLatin6
latin-greek, iso-ir-19, csISO019LatinGreek
Latin-greek-1
latin-lap, lap, iso-ir-158, csISO158Lap

M

macintosh, mac, csMacintosh
Microsoft-Publishing, csMicrosoftPublishing
MNEM, csMnem
MNEMONIC, csMnemonic
MSZ_7795.3, iso-ir-86, ISO646-HU, hu, csISO86Hungarian

N

NATS-DANO, iso-ir-9-1, csNATSDANO
NATS-DANO-ADD, iso-ir-9-2, csNATSDANOADD
NATS-SEFI, iso-ir-8-1, csNATSSEFI
NATS-SEFI-ADD, iso-ir-8-2, csNATSSEFIADD
NC_NC00-10:81, cuba, iso-ir-151, ISO646-CU, csISO151Cuba
NF_Z_62-010, iso-ir-69, ISO646-FR, fr, csISO069French
NF_Z_62-010_(1973), iso-ir-25, ISO646-FR1, csISO025French
NS_4551-1, iso-ir-60, ISO646-NO, no, csISO060DanishNorwegian, csISO060Norwegian1
NS_4551-2, ISO646-NO2, iso-ir-61, no2, csISO061Norwegian2

P

PC8-Danish-Norwegian, csPC8DanishNorwegian
PC8-Turkish, csPC8Turkish
PT, iso-ir-16, ISO646-PT, csISO016Portuguese
PT2, iso-ir-84, ISO646-PT2, csISO084Portuguese2

S

SEN_850200_B,iso-ir-10,FI,ISO646-FI,ISO646-SE, se, csISO010Swedish
SEN_850200_C, iso-ir-11, ISO646-SE2, se2, csISO011SwedishForNames
Shift_JIS, MS_Kanji, csShiftJIS

T

T.101-G2, iso-ir-128, csISO128T101G2
T.61-7bit, iso-ir-102, csISO102T617bit

```
T.61-8bit, T.61
TIS-620
```

U

```
UNICODE-1-1, csUnicode11
UNICODE-1-1-UTF-7, csUnicode11UTF7
UNKNOWN-8BIT, csUnknown8BiT
us-dk, csUSDK, dk-us, csDKUS
UTF-7
UTF-8
```

V

```
Ventura-International, csVenturaInternational
Ventura-Math, csVenturaMath
Ventura-US, csVenturaUS
videotex-suppl, iso-ir-70, csISO70VideotexSupp1
VIQR, csVIQR
VISCII, csVISCII
```

W

```
windows-1250
windows-1251
windows-1253
windows-1254
windows-1255
windows-1256
windows-1257
windows-1258
Windows-31J, csWindows31J
```

Example

```
<form accept-charset="ISO-8859-1">
<form accept-charset="ISO-8859-1, ISO-8859-2">
<a charset="iso-8859-1"></a>
<link charset="iso-8859-1">
<script charset="iso-8859-1">

<meta http-equiv="content-type"
content="text/html; charset=iso-8859-1">
```

Information on HTML

Application

All new Internet standards are provided as open access RFCs (request for comment). This is to ensure that everybody can actively participate in the creation and update of standards. You must therefore also make sure that these open standards are available freely to everybody.

Implementation

Numerous RFC documents also list the commands in the HTML language. We have listed below the most important ones, with their source.

Find out the content of all RFCs on the Internet at:
http://www.ietf.org/rfc.

[RFC850]
"Standard for Interchange of USENET Messages",
M. Horton, June 1983.
(Source: http://www.ietf.org/rfc/rfc00850.txt)

[RFC1468]
"Japanese Character Encoding for Internet Messages",
J. Murai, M. Crispin, and E. van der Poel, June 1993.
(Source: http://www.ietf.org/rfc/rfc01468.txt)

[RFC1555]
"Hebrew Character Encoding for Internet Messages",
H. Nussbacher and Y. Bourvine, December 1993.
(Source: http://www.ietf.org/rfc/rfc01555.txt)

[RFC1556]
"Handling of Bi-directional Texts in MIME",
H. Nussbacher, December 1993.
(Source: http://www.ietf.org/rfc/rfc01556.txt)

[RFC1630]
"Universal Resource Identifiers in WWW: A Unifying Syntax for the Expression of Names and Addresses of Objects on the Network as used in the World Wide Web",
T. Berners-Lee, June 1994.
(Source: http://www.ietf.org/rfc/rfc01630.txt)

[RFC1738]
"Uniform Resource Locators",
T. Berners-Lee, L. Masinter, and M. McCahill, December 1994.
(Source: http://www.ietf.org/rfc/rfc01738.txt)

[RFC1766]
"Tags for the Identification of Languages",
H. Alvestrand, March 1995.
(Source: http://www.ietf.org/rfc/rfc01766.txt)

[RFC1808]
"Relative Uniform Resource Locators",
R. Fielding, June 1995.
(Source: http://www.ietf.org/rfc/rfc01808.txt)

[RFC1866]
"HyperText Markup Language 2.0",
T. Berners-Lee and D. Connolly, November 1995.
(Source: http://www.ietf.org/rfc/rfc01866.txt)

[RFC1867]
"Form-based File Upload in HTML",
E. Nebel and L. Masinter, November 1995.
(Source: http://www.ietf.org/rfc/rfc01867.txt)

[RFC1942]
"HTML Tables", Dave Raggett, May 1996.
(Source: http://www.ietf.org/rfc/rfc01942.txt)

[RFC2044]
"UTF-8, a transformation format of Unicode and ISO 10646",
F. Yergeau, October 1996.
(Source: http://www.ietf.org/rfc/rfc02044.txt)

[RFC2045]
"Multipurpose Internet Mail Extensions (MIME)
Part One: Format of Internet Message Bodies",
N. Freed and N. Borenstein, November 1996.
(Source: http://www.ietf.org/rfc/rfc02045.txt)

[RFC2046]
"Multipurpose Internet Mail Extensions (MIME)
Part Two: Media Types",
N. Freed and N. Borenstein, November 1996.
(Source: http://www.ietf.org/rfc/rfc02046.txt)

[RFC2048]
"Multipurpose Internet Mail Extensions (MIME)
Part Four: Registration Procedure",
N. Freed, J. Klensin, and J. Postel, November 1996.
(Source: http://www.ietf.org/rfc/rfc02048.txt)

[RFC2068]
"HTTP Version 1.1 ",
R. Fielding, J. Gettys, J. Mogul, H. Frystyk Nielsen, and T. Berners-Lee,
January 1997.
(Source: http://www.ietf.org/rfc/rfc02068.txt)

[RFC2070]
"Internationalization of the HyperText Markup Language",
F. Yergeau, G. Nicol, G. Adams, and M. Dürst, January 1997.
(Source: http://www.ietf.org/rfc/rfc02070.txt)

[RFC2119]
"Key words for use in RFCs to Indicate Requirement Levels",
S. Bradner, March 1997.
(Source: http://www.ietf.org/rfc/rfc02119.txt)

[RFC2141]
"URN Syntax",
R. Moats, May 1997.
(Source: http://www.ietf.org/rfc/rfc02141.txt)

Extended Backus-Naur form (EBNF)

Application

The definitions of the official XML reference are defined in the EBN form. A special language was therefore created to be able to create uniform definitions: the Extended Backus-Naur form. This is also used for other standards.

Implementation

The XML has been defined by the W3C, just as the HTML standard. A single EBNF definition always consists of the following elements:

```
[Number] Name:=Definition
```

Printout	The following characters are valid
`[a-z]`	... all signs within the said interval
`[^a-z]`	... all signs outside the said interval
`[*abc]`	... all signs unless defined
`"character"`	... the given character string
`'character'`	... the given character string

Sample	Short	Meaning
`A?`	Optional	The use of the defined icon is optional.
`A B`	AND	The icons must occur in the stated command.
`A	B`	OR	Either the symbol A or B must be used.
`A - B`	OHNE	The symbol A must be used but B must not be used.
`A+`	Simple or multiple	The icon must appear at least once.
`A*`	Not at all, simple or multiple	The icon does not have to occur, but it may occur.

Example

(Definition of a comment in an EBN form)

```
[15]
Comment::=
'<!--' ((Char - '-') | ('-' Char - '-')))* '-->'
```

Grouping radio buttons

Application

Radio buttons are frequently used in forms. They are used to provide the user with a choice of options from which to select (radio buttons are also called option buttons). Make sure when programming that several radio buttons are always summarised to a group.

Implementation

The grouping of radio buttons is simple: give all fields which belong together in a selection the same name.

Example

```
<input name="Group1" type=radio checked value="1"> 1
<input name="Group1" type=radio value="2"> 2
```

```
<input name="Group1" type=radio value="3"> 3
Group 1<br>
```

```
<input name="Group2" type=radio checked value="1"> 1
<input name="Group2" type=radio value="2"> 2
<input name="Group2" type=radio value="3"> 3
Group 2<br>
```

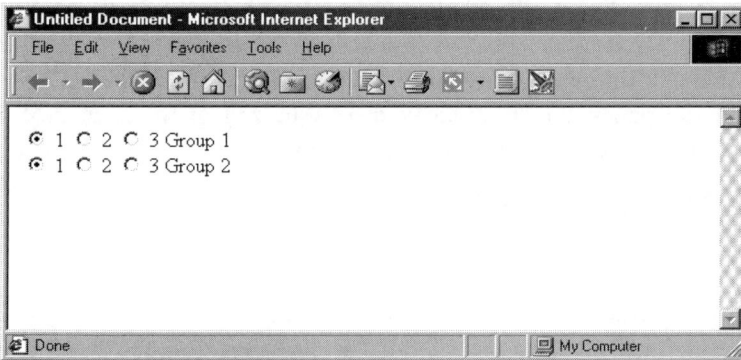

Grouping radio buttons for display in the browser

Category: Design Tricks

Frames and margins

Application

The fact that users work with different screen resolutions and with a variety of computer specifications is still a problem when creating Web pages. For example, even well designed pages may look poor on low resolution screens. Only part of the page may be displayed. If, on the other hand, you decide to opt for designing at low resolution, then the pages may be displayed as squeezed in the corner of a large screen, because they have been created for a small screen.

The solution to this problem is learning how to work with frames.

Implementation

We can create a frame by using several frames. The middle of the monitor is filled by a rectangle with a defined size. This size should be chosen so that it is visible at full resolution, but will also be visible at low resolution.

Using frames, we can centre-align the contents, both vertically and horizontally. The size of our page is defined by the size of our middle frame, therefore the display on screen will be fine, even if the browser window is reduced or the screen resolution changes.

Of course, it is not so easy to draw frames with frames, so we divide our screen into three columns. In this way we select the outer columns with about a 25% margin. The monitor is also divided into three parts. Here we leave an upper and a lower margin of about 15%. The field into which finally fill the contents remains in the middle.

Example

```
<frameset rows="25%,*,25%">
    <frame src="above.htm">
<frameset cols="15%,*,15%">
    <frame src="left.htm">
    <frame name="middle" SRC="middle.htm">
    <frame SRC="right.htm">
</frameset>
    <frame src="below.htm">
</frameset>
```

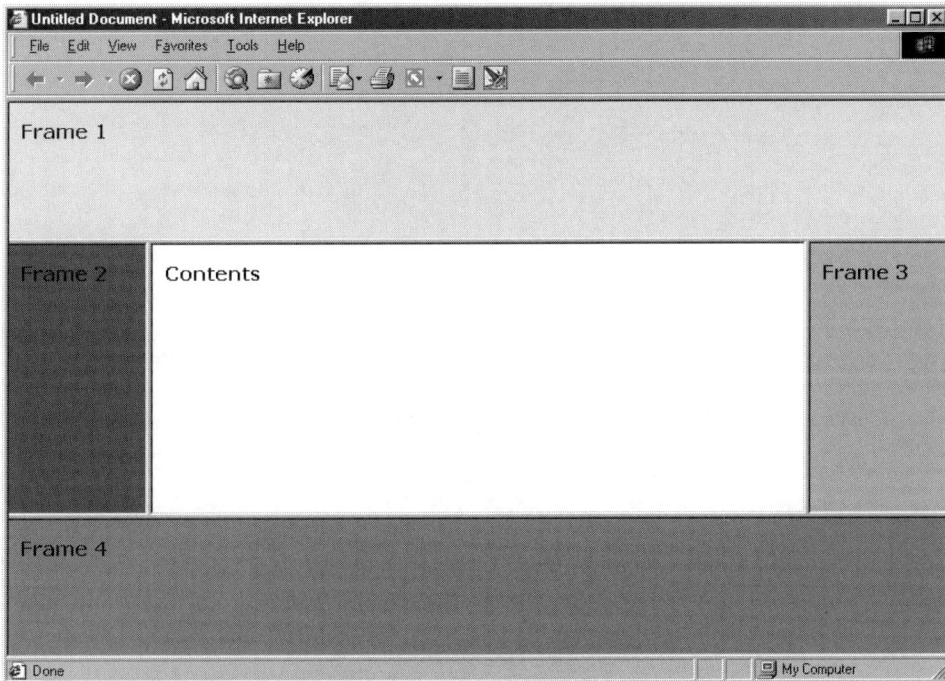

Frames are displayed with margins

Tip

When you have finished designing your page, remember to hide the frame edges and to adjust the scroll bar.

Invisible frames

Application

The use of Frames is now widespread after the command was finally given official status in HTML 4.0 as the appropriate tool for splitting browser windows. Frames can currently be found in many professional Web sites, as invisible frames solve all problems previously encountered with smaller screens, usually with a scroll bar.

Implementation

You will need a number of attributes to remove the display of unsightly frames, since Internet Explorer and Netscape Communicator support various commands. Use the three attributes FRAMESIZE, FRAMEBORDER and BORDER, and for all of them assign the value "0" to make frames totally invisible.

Example

```
<html>
<frameset>
<frame
     cols="60%, 40%"
     frameborder="0"
     border="0"
     framespacing="0">
...
</html>
```

The frame will disappear, because FRAMEBORDER has been assigned the value 0.

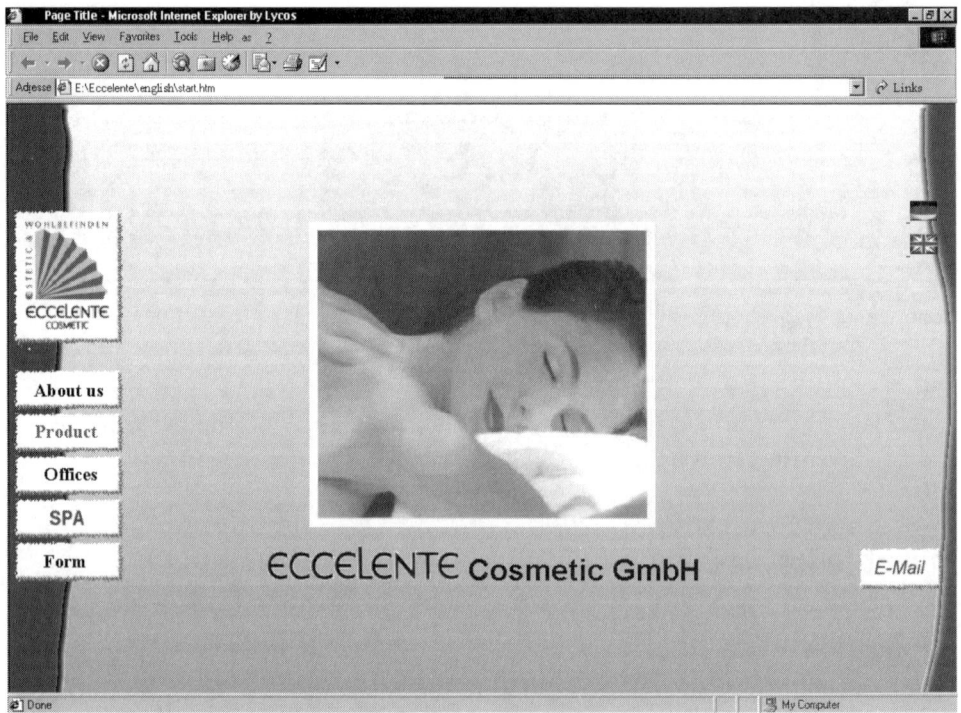

Three frames are hidden on this page

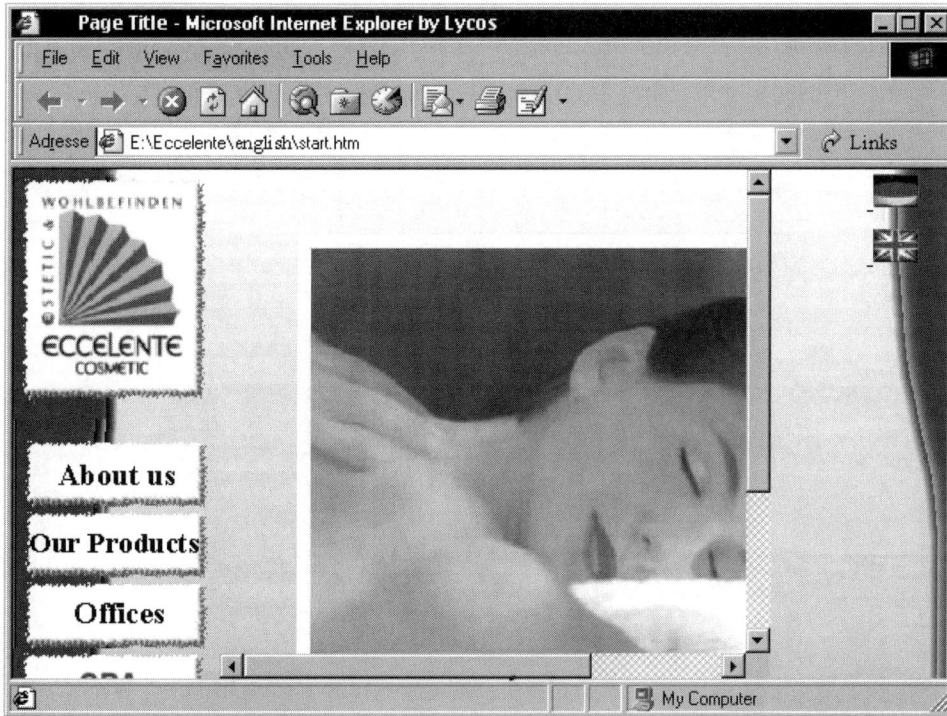

As soon as one reduces the window manually in the browser, frames are visible again

Tips

You need to adjust the SCROLLING attribute to remove scroll bars. The value NO prevents these bars from being displayed. By using YES, the scroll bars will be permanently displayed and adjusted automatically to the page contents.

Using blind GIF images

Application

HTML has some difficulties in allowing you to place elements precisely on a page. A popular trick for achieving a more exact layout is to use a "blind" GIF picture. These are invisible pictures used as dummies, to force the browser to move elements to where you want them to appear.

Implementation

First create a small picture with any graphics program, with the size 1 x 1 pixel. You can create a larger picture, if your graphics software is unable to create such a small picture. Save the picture in the .GIF format and assign the Transparency attribute to it.

Then link the picture into your HTML code, as with other graphic files, and change the size with the Width and Height attributes to the size you require.

The picture is used as a dummy, but it is not displayed because it is transparent.

Example

```
<img scr="empty.gif" width="100" height="200">
```

The picture `empty.gif` has a width of 100 microdots and a height of 200 microdots.

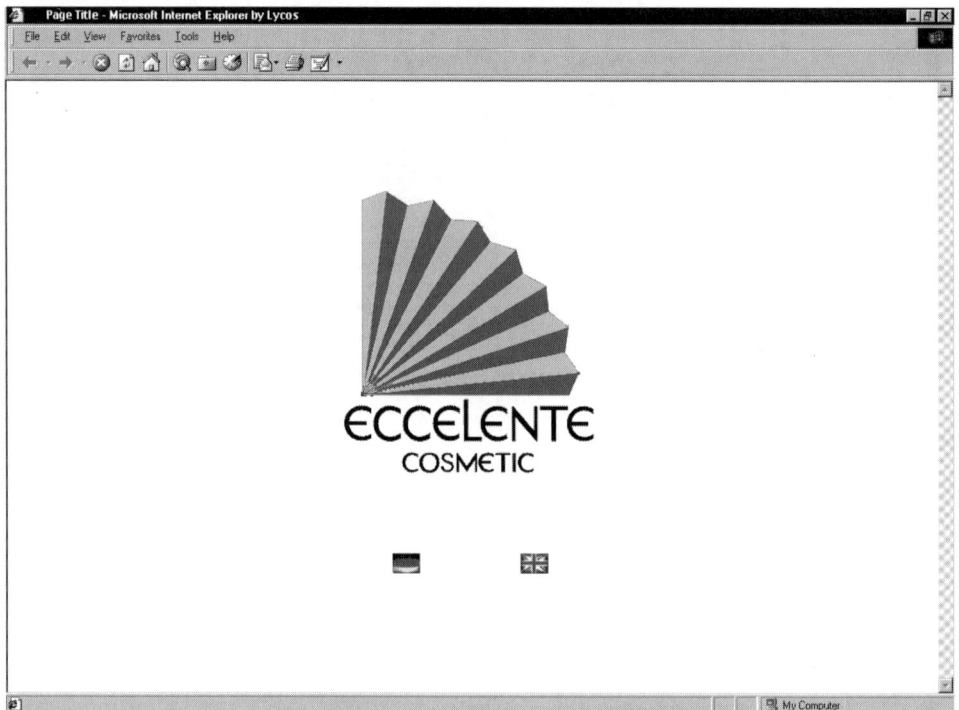

In the above example, the exact distance between the two country flags was determined with the help of an invisible picture

```
<a href="german/start.htm">
<img src="images/flag_g.gif" border="0"
alt="German" width="30" height="21"></a>

<img src="images/empty.gif" border="0"
width=100 height=10 alt="---">
```

```
<a href="english/start.htm">
<img src="images/flag_e.gif" border="0"
alt="English" width="30" height="21"></a>
```

Tip

Always use the same transparent picture for the whole of your Web site, so the browser can retrieve the graphic from the cache memory and does not have to upload again each time you want to use it.

Using alternative graphics

Application

With the command to insert an image, an alternative image source can be indicated with the real image source. The alternative image source is always displayed before the real graphic and sends a lower resolution picture first to a Web site.

The aim of this attribute is to provide the visitor to the Web site with a fast summary of its content.

Implementation

You should create a copy of the original image with your graphic processing program, and save it in the way that takes up least memory. You can do this by modifying resolution and colour density. Try not to modify the image size.

Example

```
<img scr="original.gif" lowscr="copy.gif">
```

Tip

You should only use an alternative graphic, if the original and the copy have a different size. Otherwise the additional effort of data download for the additional image is no longer worthwhile.

Retreiving pages from external frames

Application

A recurring problem in the use of frames is if your pages are loaded into external frames. In this case the frame contents are not completely displayed. In addition, the contents and external information fade fast.

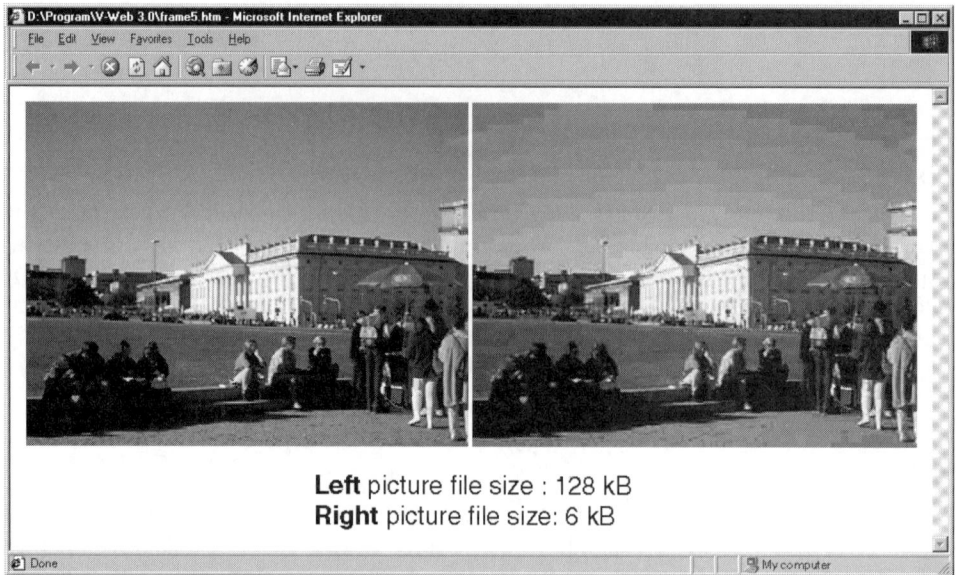

The same picture with different resolutions and colour density

Implementation

If you only call other frames, you can easily prevent these from being displayed within your framesets in which you start a new browser instance and display the document. It is more difficult if somebody else has integrated your contents into his site. In this case, you must use JavaScript. Insert the lines listed below at the head of your document. This then ensures that this page is always displayed in a separate window.

Example

```
JavaScript.
<html>
<head>
<title>Page title</title>

<script language="javascript">
<!--
     if (top.frames.length!=0)
     {
     top.location=location;
     }
-->
</script>

</head>
<body>
```

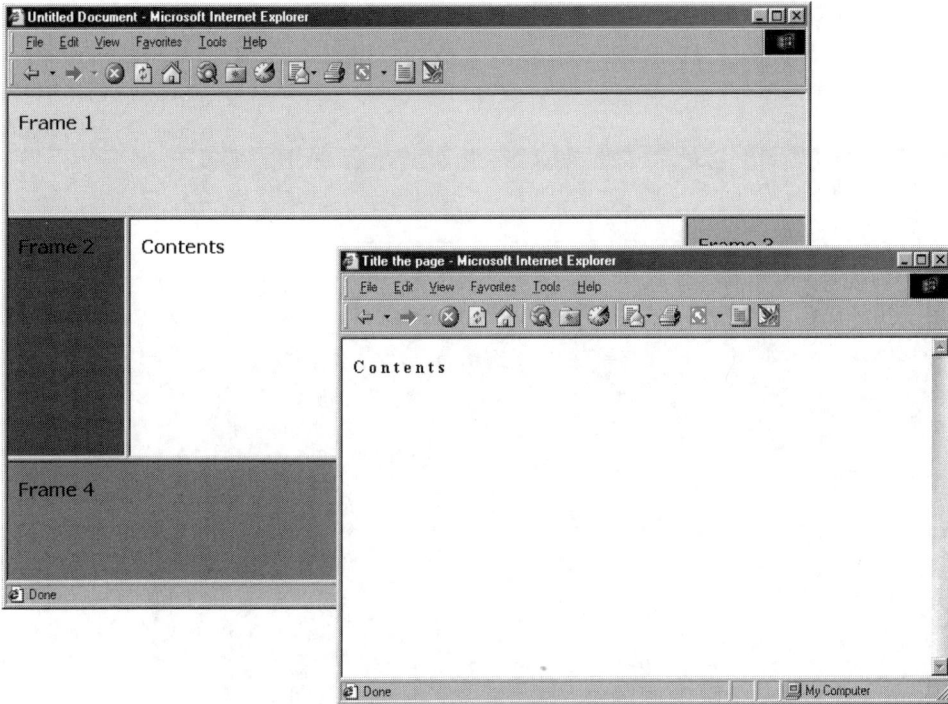

The document previously displayed within a frameset is automatically released from the external frame through the inserted frame

```
<b>content</b>
</body>
</html>
```

Adding an extra background colour

Application

If you choose a graphic background for an Internet page, you can add an extra background colour to it. The background graphic is always transferred a little later than text, but colour always appears immediately in an HTML document.

This can cause problems if one works with a dark background and white or bright letters. In this case the visitor will be able to view nothing more than a blank page of the document during the first few seconds of downloading. If a black background colour is indicated then white text can immediately be viewed.

Implementation

As well as adding a graphic background, you should also indicate the approximate colour of the graphic.

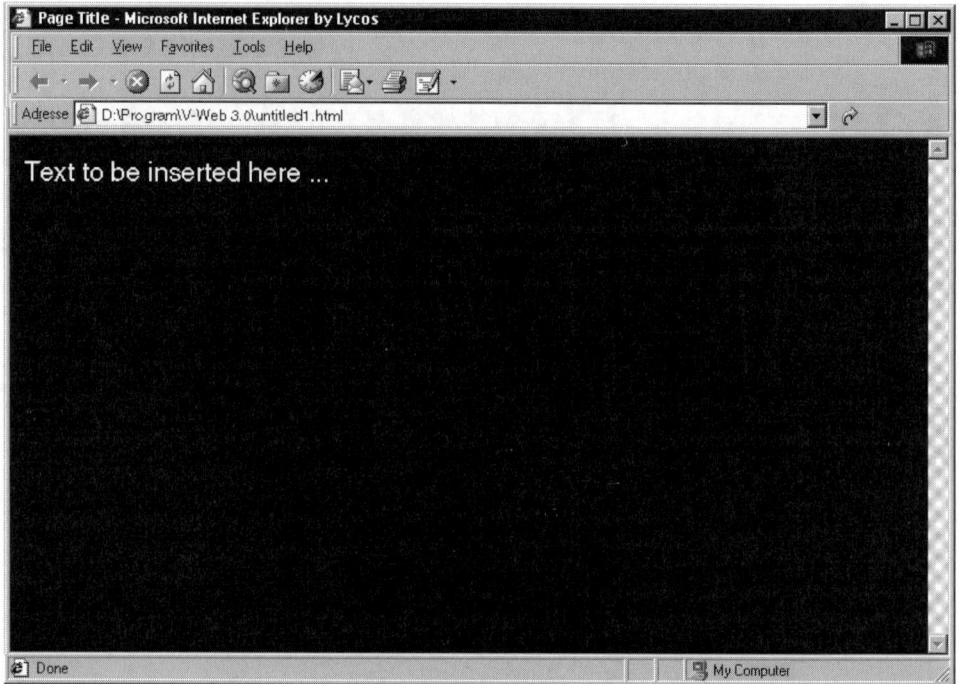

White letters on bright background can not be displayed well

Example

```
<body background="dark_background.gif" bgcolor="black">
```

Tip

You should always use this option if you use a background graphic. The additional download time will be small, and the desired effect will make your page to appear much more quickly.

Determining margins

Application

By inserting an invisible table you can easily and simply enforce margins for a HTML document. Insert a single table cell in the document.

Implementation

You must only insert a table with a single cell in the page. To assign a minimum size to the table, you fill the complete page despite the lack of concrete dimensional information. Centre the table to get even left and right margins.

Example

```
<div align=center>
<table width=90%>
     <tr>
          <td>
          Page content
          </td>
     </tr>
</table>

<html>
<body>
<div align=center>
<table width=80% height="95%">
<tr>
<td bgcolor=#FFFF00 align="center">
<b>Page content</b>
</td>
</tr>
</table>
</body>
</html>
```

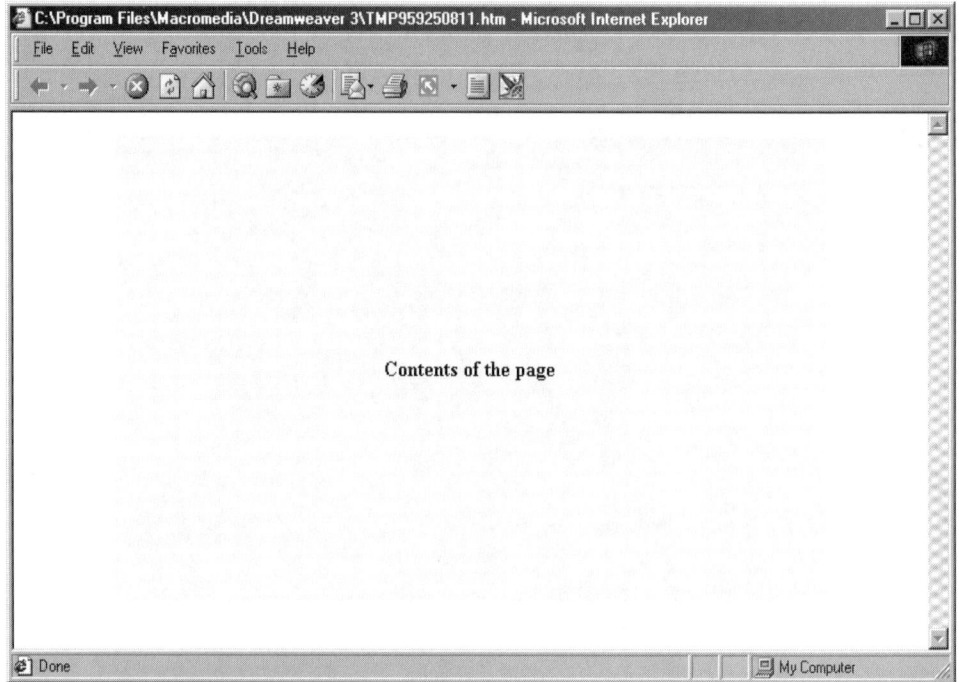

The above example displayed in the browser

Tip
Try inputting different percentage data for the width of a table to get optimal results.

Invisible tables

Application
Today tables are rarely used in their original form to represent information into tabular form, but they are almost always used in page layout. Since HTML does not recognise any options for placing elements on the page, tables help in doing this.

Since table frames can disappear with border=0, they make themselves invisible. For this reason these tables are also called "blind" tables.

Implementation

Insert a table containing the whole screen with a minimal width and height of 95 per cent. Centre this table. The partitioning of the table into single cells is up to you, depending on the content you want to insert here.

Example

```
<div align="center">
<table width="95%" height="95%" border="0">
     <tr>
          <td>
          </td>
     </tr>
</table>
</div>
```

Tips

This effect for Web page style can only be used if the content of your document is smaller than the display.

In designing a page, in order not to make the table "disappear", you should insert the attribute "Border=0" before ending the project. In this way you can keep a good overview of the used frames in the browser.

Opening a new browser window

Application

If there are external links on your site, you may find that the visitor you took so long to attract to your site soon leaves. This because when the visitor clicks on an external link on your site, then the new page is completely loaded into the browser and they forget about your site.

A better solution is to open a new browser window for each external link. Though the visitor may leave your site, it will always remain in the background, where he/she can return any time, and when he/she closes the browser window which is currently hiding it.

Implementation

Open a link in a new window with the TARGET attribute.

Do not have too many new windows open at once

Example

```
<a href="http://www.wielage.de" target="_blank">
```

Tip

You should test other jump destinations with TARGET indicated in the reference section.

Clickable images

Application

Imagemaps or clickable images are commonly used. These are used to provide graphics with the image area for the link. In this way you can provide a map with marked locations linked to other locations.

Imagemaps replace single buttons. Instead of many small buttons, these are grouped into a picture and the corresponding image area is selected.

Implementation

Very large imagemaps should be avoided because the user will wait for a long time for them to download. Nevertheless, menus with a size of up to 25 Kbyte are still safe. In this way you offer a good substitute to several small buttons and they are even faster in downloading.

Example

A menu with a Windows style icon bar created with a single imagemap

```
<MAP NAME="Main menu">
    <AREA
    SHAPE="RECT"
    COORDS="476, 1, 520, 45"
    HREF="help.htm">
    <AREA
    SHAPE="RECT"
    COORDS="431, 1, 473, 45"
    HREF="books.htm">
    <AREA
    SHAPE="RECT"
    COORDS="369, 1, 413, 45"
    HREF="register.htm">
    <AREA
    SHAPE="RECT"
    COORDS="307, 1, 345, 45"
    HREF="service.htm">
    <AREA
    SHAPE="RECT"
    COORDS="243, 1, 283, 45"
    HREF="search.htm">
    <AREA
```

499

```
        SHAPE="RECT"
        COORDS="189, 1, 228, 45"
        HREF="contact.htm">
        <AREA
        SHAPE="RECT"
        COORDS="128, 1, 165, 45"
        HREF="customers.htm">
        <AREA
        SHAPE="RECT"
        COORDS="67, 1, 107, 45"
        HREF="aboutus.htm">
        <AREA
        SHAPE="RECT"
        COORDS="3, 1, 56, 45"
        HREF="weblinks.htm">
</MAP>

<IMG border=0 width=607 height=50
      SRC="images/part2.gif"
      alt="main menu"
      usemap="#main menu">
```

Tip

Remember that there are still users with browsers which cannot display any imagemaps. It is better to offer an alternative menu in text form.

Autoloading a slide show

Application

Usually the user must be active to load the next page or site from the menu. In HTML it is possible to load the following Web site automatically.

This function is usually used to load a number of images or HTML pages automatically. It can be used in a picture gallery or a guide to your Internet site.

Implementation

With the REFRESH META tag another document can automatically be loaded into the browser after a predefined number of seconds. You can turn this function into an autoloading slideshow.

Example

Page 1.htm in document:

```
<meta http-equiv="refresh" content="10; URL=page2.htm">
<img src="dia1.jpg">
```

Page 2.htm in document:

```
<meta http-equiv="refresh" content="10; URL=page3.htm">
<img src="dia2.jpg">
Page 3.htm in document:
<meta http-equiv="refresh" content="10; URL=page4.htm">
<img src="dia3.jpg">
```

Tips

Do not exaggerate this effect; remember to leave visitors a way to navigate "normally" through the program. In addition, you must adjust the waiting time precisely for each image. If images close too fast, then the Web site is not completely loaded, the slower the whole show is, and the more boring it is for the visitor.

Recognising browser types

Application

Sometimes it can be useful or interesting to know which browser a visitor uses. Although the protocol of this kind of information is complex, an informative display can be rapidly created for the visitor.

Implementation

Nobody browses anonymously on the Net. A name or place of residence can be found out and through JavaScript it can be seen which browser, which browser version and which operating system are being used.

After you have integrated the following code into your Web site, any visitor can display the available information about his browser.

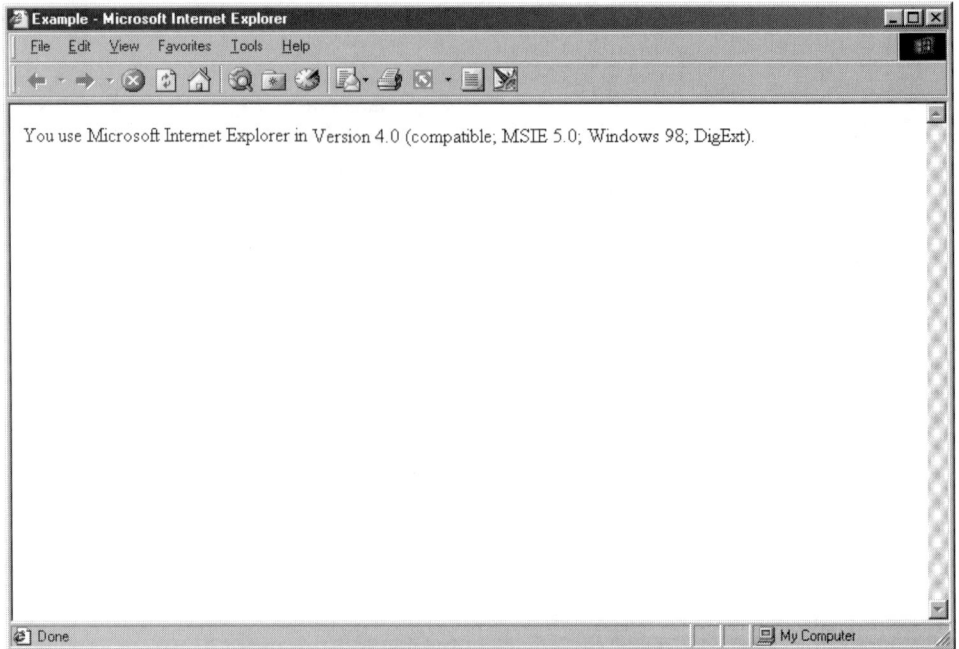

You can view this information about your browser

Example

```
<html>
<head>
<title>Example </title>
<script language="JavaScript">
<!--
document.write ("You use"
          + navigator.appName
          + " version "
          + navigator.appVersion+".")
// -->
</script>
</head>
<body>
</body>
</html>
```

Tip

This script works only with browsers which support JavaScript, and only if the JavaScript is activated.

Different versions

Application

Various differences between the available browsers is how they handle functions means that caution is required when using new commands.

One solution is to provide more versions of a document: a specially adapted version for every browser.

Implementation

Using a small JavaScript program, an automatic distinction between several browser versions can be set up. Therefore, for every recognised browser, a page specifically set up should be called. Import the script into your site and adapt the file names correspondingly.

Example

```
<html>
<head>
<title>Viewing the browser</title>

<script language="JavaScript">
<!--
    if ((navigator.appName=="Netscape") &&
    (parseInt(navigator.appVersion.substring(0,1)) >= 4))
    {
    location="netscape4.htm"
    }

else

    {if ((navigator.appName=="Netscape") &&
    (parseInt(navigator.appVersion.substring(0,1))==3))
    {
    location="netscape3.htm"
    }

else

    {if
    ((navigator.appName=="Microsoft Internet Explorer") &&
    (parseInt(navigator.appVersion.substring(0,1))>=4))
    {
    document.location="msie4.htm"
    }
```

```
else

    {if
    ((navigator.appName=="Microsoft Internet Explorer") &&
    (parseInt
    (navigator.appVersion.substring(0,1))==2))
    {
    location="msie3.htm"
    }

else
    {document.location="noscript.htm"
}
}
}
}
// -->
</script>
</head>
<body>
</body>
</html>
```

Tip

Be sure to create a page even for users (`noscript.htm`) whose browsers do not understand JavaScript or which have deactivated this function.

Using titles

Application

Almost every element offers the option of defining a separate title. It is not always necessary to do this, but you should always use a title: the title of the page.

The page title plays a special role in several ways. On one hand it is the effective criterion in searching with search engines. Only Web sites which have inserted the most important keywords, even in the title of the site, will be found. On the other hand many users pay attention to the content of the title which appears in the browser list.

You should therefore use a meaningful title. Page names like `"Page 1"` or `"welcome to my home page"` are not explicit or detailed enough.

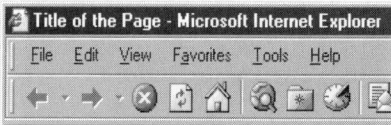

You can see the title of the page in the browser

Implementation

You should use a meaningful title for every page of your Web site. The title is used at the head of the document.

If you use frames, only the title bar of the first document is displayed in the browser. Nevertheless, you should always assign meaningful titles to all additional embedded documents.

Example

```
<html>
<head>
<title>collection of information HTML/XML </title>
</head>
<body>
</body>
</html>
```

Tip

Bookmarks are all also written containing a page title.

Inserting text correctly

Application

It is usually relatively time-consuming to place text exactly on the page. If you have grown accustomed to editing a text by inserting blank spaces, and aligning and indenting words, you will soon be disappointed with the HTML browser. Every position with more than one blank space is deleted.

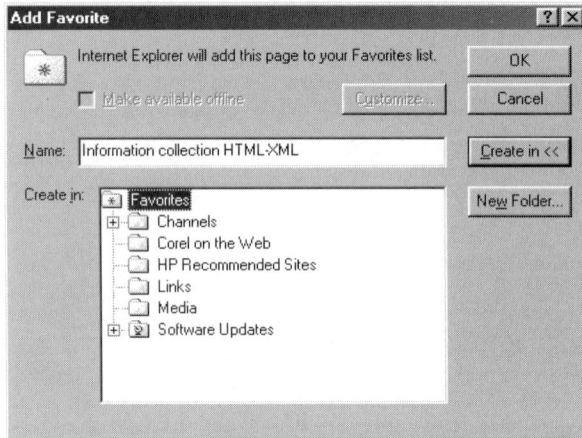

A Favorite (Bookmark) is defined in Internet Explorer

Implementation

One solution is using the PRE command. This command is created to use pre-formatted text without further processing. This is primarily useful for program listings but works even for small text effects.

Example

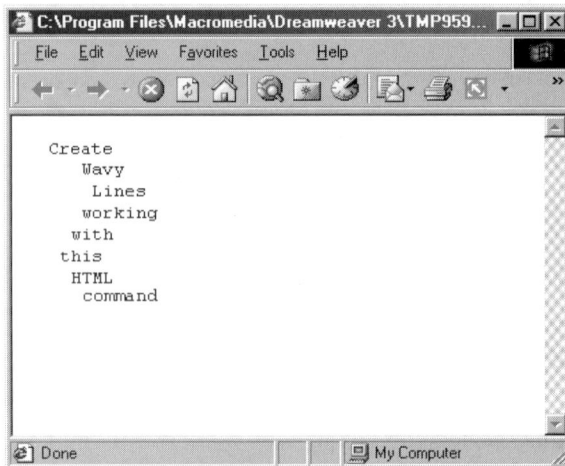

This effect can easily be created

```
<pre>
   Create
      Wavey
         Lines
      working
```

```
    with
     this
      HTML
       Command
</pre>
```

Start page

Application

Nowadays it is fashionable in Web design to open a start page with a site's navigation structure before the real site. Usually, this page contains some important current news or relevant information.

This page looks particularly professional if after several seconds the next page is loaded without a further mouse click.

Implementation

Create a demanding but technically simple page as your start page. In this way, visitors will not be overwhelmed by technical information like JavaScript or frames on the first page. After some seconds you will have the next page automatically loaded.

Example

```
<meta http-equiv="refresh"
content="10;URL="menu.htm >


<html>
<head>
<title>Error:The page doesn't exist any more! </title>
<meta http-equiv="refresh"content="5;URL="site2new.htm >
</head>
<body>
<center>
<font color="red"> <h1> Error ! </h1> </font>
<br>
<font size="+1">
The requested page does not exist on
this server. <br>
Click here to reach
the new page.
<br><br><br>
The new page will load automatically after 5 seconds
```

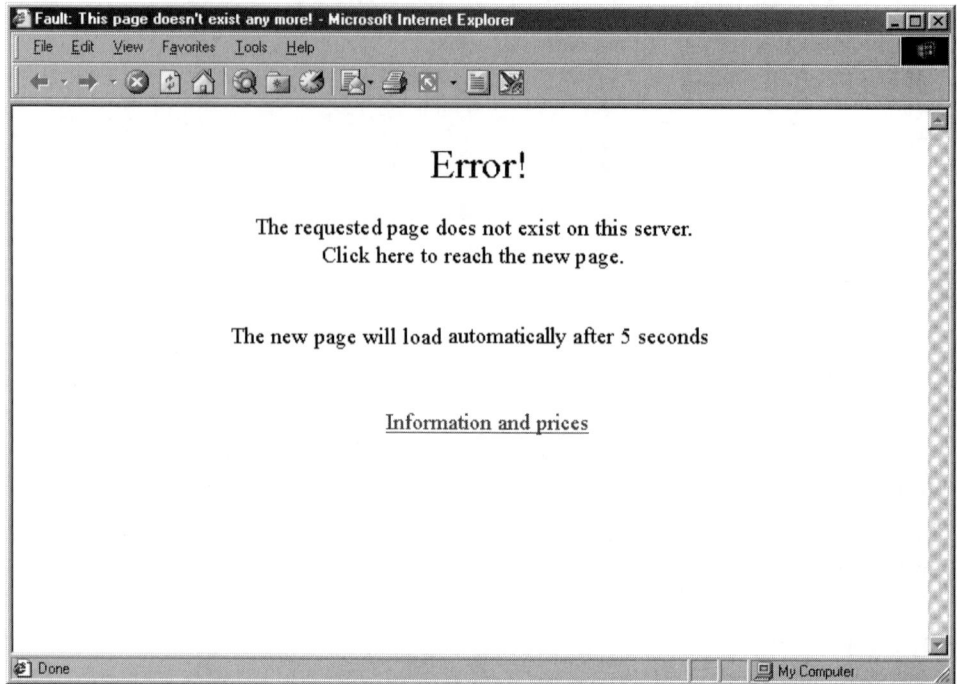

One use of the "refresh" function

```
<br><br><br>
<a href="site2new.htm">
Information and prices</a>
</font>
</center>
</body>
</html>
```

Tips

You should also install a page which moves automatically on to the next page if you remove the domain of your site. You should start the page with a message and an automatic refresh to another page. In this way visitors who found your site through old links can go back directly to your new home page.

Inserting an image in the top left corner of a window

Application

A picture can be inserted without any problem in the top left corner of the screen. A little separation is always kept to the top and left margin. However, if you want to use the entire page, leave some settings unstored.

Implementation

The objective is to set the space between the element and the margin to zero. You can do this using Style Sheets.

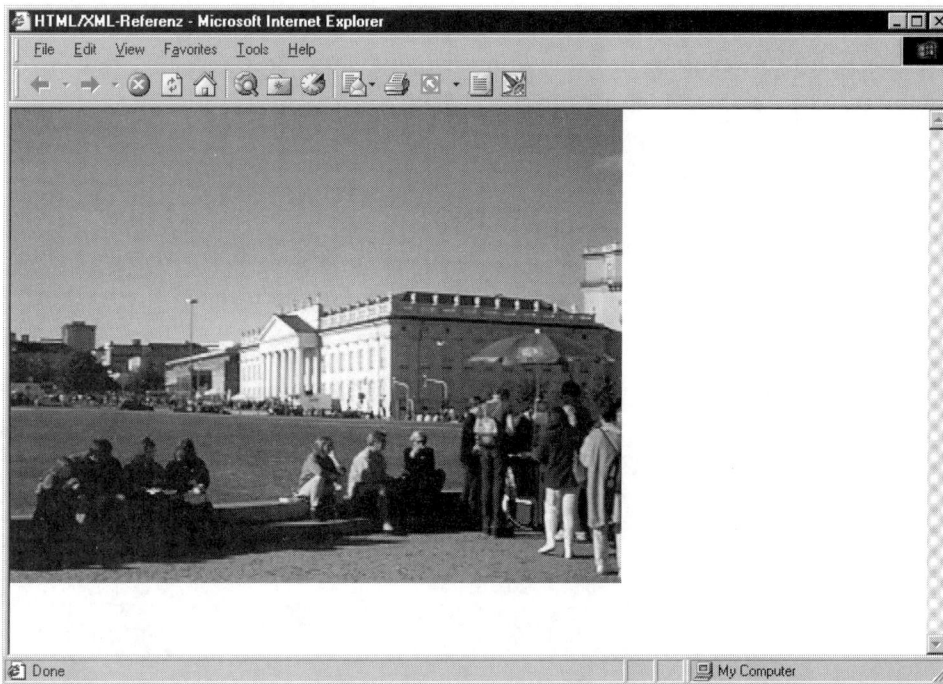

You can set images exactly in the top left corner of the browser window

Example

```
<html>
<head>
<style>
.null {position:absolute; top: 0pt; left: 0pt}
</style>
</head>
<body>
<div class="zero" id="zero">
```

```
...
</div>
</body>
</html>

<div style="position: absolute; top: 0 pt; left: 0pt">
</div>
```

Bookmarking your Web site

Application

Microsoft Internet Explorer organises frequently visited sites that you want to revisit as a list of Favorites. In a Favorites list you can collect as many sites as you want, especially ones you use the most frequently.

It is not so easy for a regular visitor to your Web site to save your site as a bookmark. You have to help out by incorporating an automated link.

Implementation

A small, embedded JavaScript enables visitors to your site to open the bookmark easily on your site by clicking on the corresponding button.

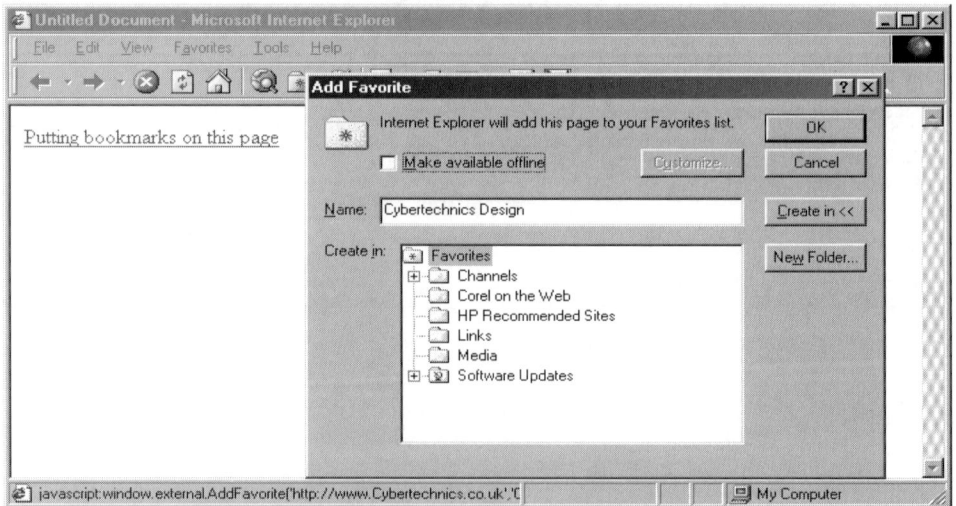

In Explorer a click on the link automatically opens the corresponding function

Example

```
<a
    href="javascript:window.external.AddFavorite
    ('http://www.pott-it.de',
    'Pott IT-Experts')">
    Putting bookmarks on this page
</a>
```

Tip

Unfortunately, this function works only with Microsoft Internet Explorer.

Style sheets supported by browsers

Application

Style sheets are not interpreted by all Browsers in the same way, like so many other commands. So you don't have to create an HTML page for every browser, there is a way of selecting the right commands using JavaScript.

Implementation

At first you need two external style sheet files for your document. This means that the style sheets are not directly defined in the document but in a separate file. You should create a style sheet file for Internet Explorer and one for Netscape Communicator.

An external style sheet file can easily be inserted into every HTML document. You need only decide with JavaScript which file this should be.

Example

```
html>
<head>

<script language="JavaScript">

    if
    ((navigator.appName.indexOf("Explorer"))>=0)
    &&
    (navigator.appVersion.indexOf('4.0')>=0))
    document.writeln
    ('<link
        rel=stylesheet
        href="netscape.css"
```

```
        type="text/css">');
if
((navigator.appName.indexOf("Netscape")>= 0)
&&
(navigator.appVersion.indexOf('4.0')>=0))
document.writeln
('<link
    rel=stylesheet
    href="explorer.css"
    type ="text/css">');
</script>

</head>
<body>
</body>
</html>
```

Using a watermark as a background

Application

Microsoft Internet Explorer offers a small and safe additional option to be used for the detail of the background graphic: the watermark effect. This means that the background graphic is not scrolled with the text bus remains fixed in the background.

Implementation

You should indicate the BGPROPERTIES="fixed" attribute in addition to the background image to create a solid immovable background.

Example

```
<background="back.gif"bgproperties="fixed">
```

Tip

This effect can be created in all browsers compatible with CSS using style sheets. You will find specific information about this in the reference section.

Changing the size of the browser window

Application

Help your visitors again and give them the opportunity to change the size of the browser window by a mouse click. In this way they can test different resolutions and screen measurements at the same time.

Implementation

What seems so spectacular can easily be created with a source code line and a little JavaScript. The effect is created over a form, which imports the mouse clicks and executes a corresponding JavaScript command.

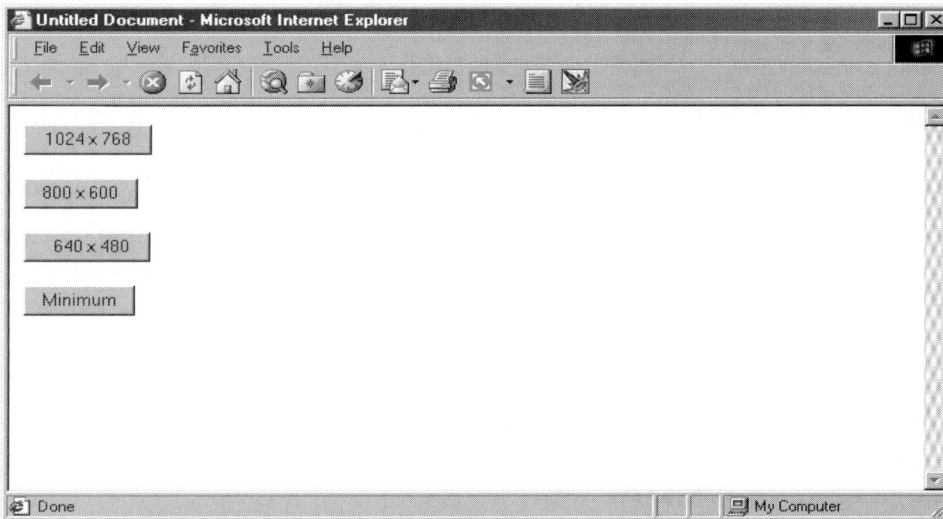

A small command with amazing results

Example

```
<form>
<input
type=button
onclick="window.resizeTo (1024.768)"
"value=1024 for x for 768" for>
</form>

<form>
<input
type=button
onclick="window.resizeTo (800.600)"
"value=800 for x for 600" for>
</form>

<form>
<input
type=button
onclick="window.resizeTo(640.480)"
"value=640 for x for 480"for>
</form>
```

```
<form>
 <input
type=button
onclick="window.resizeTo(0.0)"
value="minimise">
</form>
```

Tables with a background

Application

Tables with coloured backgrounds are usually pleasing to the eye but now they can not only be filled with solid colour backgrounds, but also with a background graphic.

Implementation

Indicate a suitable graphic as a background using the TABLE command. Choose the size of the graphic so that it fits into the table. Unfortunately, this command does not yet work with all browsers yet.

Example

```
<table
      border="3"
      background="back.gif"
      align="CENTER"
      width="100">

<tr>
      <td> </td>
</tr>
<tr>
      <td> </td>
</tr>
</table>
```

Fading effects

Application

Microsoft Explorer 4.0 provides an interesting effect where one page fades to the next. These effects may become active when you enter the page or exit it again. On other browsers these effects are simply ignored and do not lead to error messages. These effects are therefore much more interesting than any Java-Script displaying.

Implementation

These effects are created through the META command, which you submit as a HTTP-EQUIV or PAGE-EXIT value. As the CONTENT of the attribute you submit the settings of the desired effect. Set PAGE-ENTER if you want to insert an effect which becomes active on entering the site. Use PAGE-EXIT for the same effect when exiting the active page.

```
<meta http-equiv="page-enter"
content="revealtrans (duration=3, transition=23)">
```

Besides the type of the effect (under TRANSITION) you can still indicate the duration of the display or hide the fading effect with DURATION. You should not choose too long a duration (an approximate duration of 2 to 5 seconds is optimal). You should use this effect carefully, otherwise it will become unpopular very quickly with visitors to your site. One or a maximum of two pages should be equipped with this effect.

Effect	Value
Box in	0
Box out	1
Circle in	2
Circle out	3
Wipe up	4
Wipe down	5
Wipe right	6
Wipe left	7
Vertical blinds	8
Horizontal blinds	9
Checkerboard across	10
Checkerboard down	11
Random dissolve	12

Effect	Value
Split vertical in	13
Split vertical out	14
Split horizontal in	15
Split horizontal out	16
Strips left down	17
Strips left up	18
Strips right down	19
Strips right up	20
Random bars horizontal	21
Random bars vertical	22
Random	23

Example

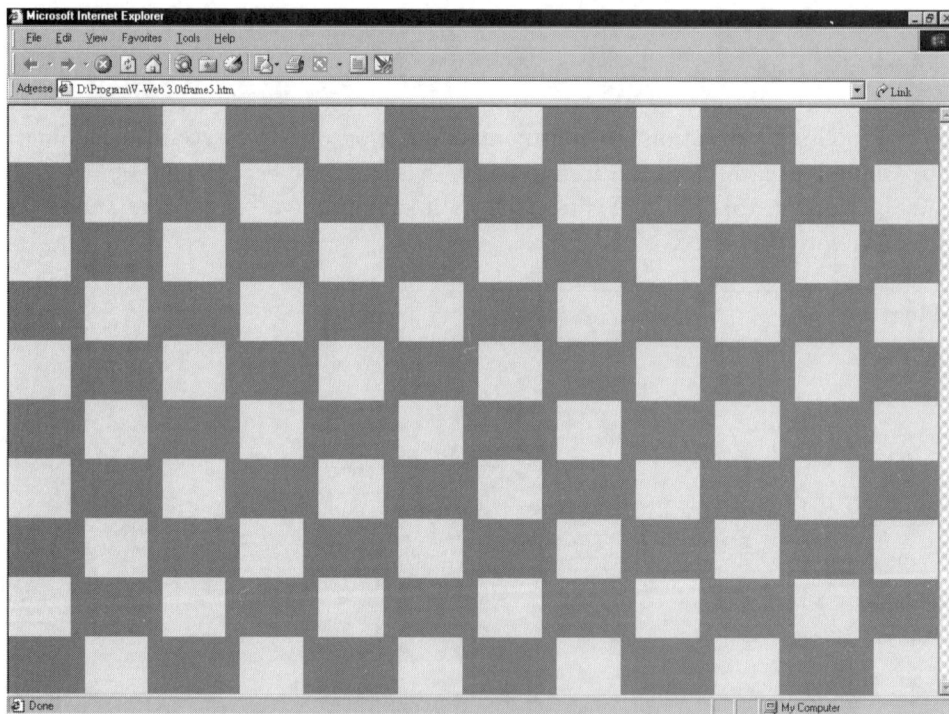

When entering the new page this is displayed slowly. Here the " Checkerboard across" effect (10) is displayed

```
<html>
<head>
<meta http-equiv="page-enter"
```

```
          "content=(for revealtrans duration=4.transition=10)"for>
</head>
<body bgcolor="yellow">
<b>content</b>
</body>
</html>

<meta http-equiv="page-exit"
"content="(for revealtrans duration=3.transition=23)">
```

Tips

If this function is not allowed by the browser, make sure that it only works if you actually move from a different page to a target page and that reloading of the page does not activate the effect. This makes the test of these effects a little more difficult.

Removing underlined hyperlinks

Application

A normal hyperlink is shown underlined in blue characters. You may like to differ from this traditional form and to remove this underlining. This can easily be adapted to a predefined layout.

Implementation

The solution is to be found in the style sheets. With the help of the `text-decoration` attribute it is possible to remove the underline. Using style sheets, other design options are also open to you. Colour and character type can also be modified, for example.

Example

```
<a href="http://www.cybertechnics.co.uk">
Normal Hyperlink
</a>

<br>
<a    href="http://www.cybertechnics.co.uk"    style="text-decoration:
none">
Hyperlink without underline
</a>
>
```

Hyperlinks with and without an underline

Buttons with rollover effects

Application

It is rare nowadays for an Internet page not to be provided with buttons with rollover effects. This means that if the visitor moves the mouse pointer over a graphic button, then this graphic is replaced and another graphic appears. The buttons react to mouse movements.

Implementation

These interactive buttons are created by JavaScript. At first you should create two graphics for every button, one for the normal condition and one for the active condition. The functions for the activated button and the deactivation of a button are entered in the document header. We have in addition a check of the built-in browser version. This ensures that in case that the browser cannot cope with this JavaScript version, it will not crash either.

The picture is then loaded in the body of the document through the `onMouseOver` event, which represents the activated condition. If the mouse moves away from the button again, then the old condition is produced through `onMouseOut`.

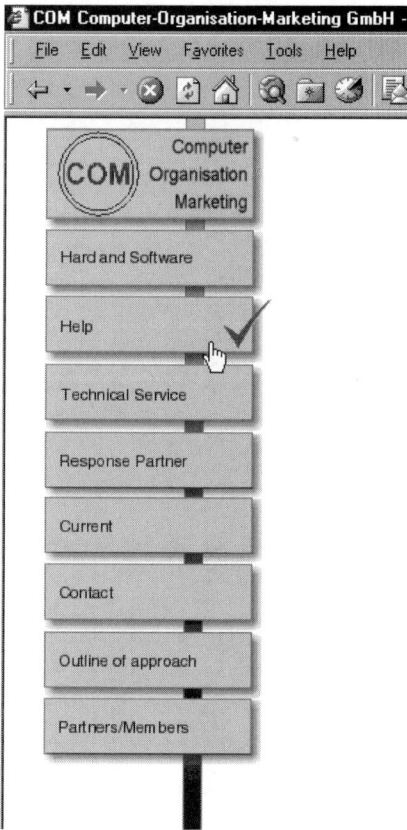

As soon as the visitor reaches one of the buttons with the mouse, this tick appears

Example

```
<html>
<head>
<title>Homepage</title>
<script language="JavaScript">
<!--
browser=0
if (navigator.userAgent.substring(0,9)
    =="Mozilla/3") {browser=1}
if (navigator.userAgent.substring(0,9)
    =="Mozilla/4") {browser=1}

if (browser==1)
{
var image1=new Array();
var image2=new Array();

image1[0]=new Image();
```

```
image1[0].src="images/button11.gif";
image2[0]=new Image()
image2[0].src="images/button12.gif"

image1[1]=new Image();
image1[1].src="images/button21.gif";
image2[1]=new Image()
image2[1].src="images/button22.gif"

image1[2]=new Image();
image1[2].src="images/button31.gif";
image2[2]=new Image()
image2[2].src="images/button32.gif"

image1[3]=new Image();
image1[3].src="images/button41.gif";
image2[3]=new Image()
image2[3].src="images/button42.gif"

image1[4]=new Image();
image1[4].src="images/button51.gif";
image2[4]=new Image()
image2[4].src="images/button52.gif"

image1[5]=new Image();
image1[5].src="images/button61.gif";
image2[5]=new Image()
image2[5].src="images/button62.gif"

image1[6]=new Image();
image1[6].src="images/button71.gif";
image2[6]=new Image()
image2[6].src="images/button72.gif"
}
var click=null

function 1(i)
{
    if (browser==1)
    {
    if (i==0) {document.images[0].src=image1[0].src}
    if (i==1) {document.images[1].src=image1[1].src}
    if (i ==
 2) {document.images[2].src=image1[2].src}
    if (i==3) {document.images[3].src=image1[3].src}
    if (i==4) {document.images[4].src=image1[4].src}
    if (i==5) {document.images[5].src=image1[5].src}
    if (i==6) {document.images[6].src=image1[6].src}
    }
}
```

```
function 2(i)
{
      if (browser==1)
      {
      if (i==0) {document.images[0].src=image2[0].src}
      if (i==1) {document.images[1].src=image2[1].src}
      if (i==2) {document.images[2].src=image2[2].src}
      if (i==3) {document.images[3].src=image2[3].src}
      if (i==4) {document.images[4].src=image2[4].src}
      if (i==5) {document.images[5].src=image2[5].src}
      if (i==6) {document.images[6].src=image2[6].src}
      }
}
// -->
</script>
</head>
<body>

<a
      target="Headframe"
      href="start.htm"
      onMouseOver="1(0); return true"
      onMouseOut="2(0)">
<img
      border="0"
      src="images/button11.gif"
      height="35"
      width="100"
      alt=" Introduction ">
</a>

<a
      target="Headframe"
      href="presence.htm"
      onMouseOver="1(1); return true"
      onMouseOut="2(1)">
<img
      border="0"
      src="images/button22.gif"
      height="35"
      width="100"
      alt=" cheap web presence ">
</a>

... further buttons...

</body>
```

```
</html>
```

In the next example we move to another step and determine three conditions for each button. These buttons represent the menu bar, which always remains displayed. If the user moves the mouse over one of these buttons, then this is activated. If the user selects the button, then this is marked as a selection. The document suitable for the menu item is then loaded. The visitor immediately sees which menu he is in. In this case, you must create three graphics (normal, activated and selected) for every button.

```
<html>
<head>
<title>Homepage</title>
<script language="JavaScript">
<!--
punkt=0;
browser=0;
if (navigator.userAgent.substring(0,9)
     =="Mozilla/3") {browser=1}
if (navigator.userAgent.substring(0,9)
     =="Mozilla/4") {browser=1}
if (browser==1)
{
var image1=new Array();
var image2=new Array();
var image=new Array();

image1[0]=new Image();
image1[0].src="menu1on.gif";
image2[0]=new Image()
image2[0].src="menu1.gif"
image[0]=new Image()
image[0].src="menu1g.gif"

image1[1]=new Image();
image1[1].src="menu2on.gif";
image2[1]=new Image()
image2[1].src="menu2.gif"
image[1]=new Image()
image[1].src="menu2g.gif"

image1[2]=new Image();
image1[2].src="menu3on.gif";
image2[2]=new Image()
image2[2].src="menu3.gif"
image[2]=new Image()
image[2].src="menu3g.gif"
}
```

```
var click=null


function 1(i)
{
     if (browser==1)
     {
     if (i==0) {document.images[0].src=image1[0].src}
     if (i > 0)
          {document.images[i].src=image1[i].src
          if (punkt==i)
          {document.images[i].src=image[i].src}}
          }
}
function 2(i)
{
     if (browser==1)
     {
     if (i==0) {document.images[0].src=image2[0].src}
     if (i> 0)
          {document.images[i].src=image2[i].src
          if (punkt==i)
          {document.images[i].src=image[i].src}}
     }
}
function gewaehlt(i)
{
     if (browser==1)
     {
     document.images[dot].src=image2[item].src;
     document.images[i].src=image[i].src;
     item=i;
     }
}

// -->
</script>
</head>
<body>
<a
     href="page1.htm" target="Headwindow"
     onMouseOver="1(0); return true"
     onMouseOut="2(0)">
     onClick="selected(0)">
<img src="menu1.gif" border="0"></a><br>

<a
     href="page2.htm" target="Headwindow"
     onMouseOver="1(1); return true"
     onMouseOut="2(1)"
```

```
        onClick="gewaehlt(1)">
<img src="menu2.gif" border="0"></a><br>


<a
     href="page3.htm" target="Headwindow"
     onMouseOver="1(2); return true"
     onMouseOut="2(2)"
     onClick="gewaehlt(2)">
<img src="menu3.gif" border="0"></a><br>
</body>
</html>
```

Creating forms optimally

Application

When using forms there is a recurring problem with inserting names of single entry fields. If names are simply inserted as text before the entry fields, then some inaccuracies will arise which are not, visually pleasing.

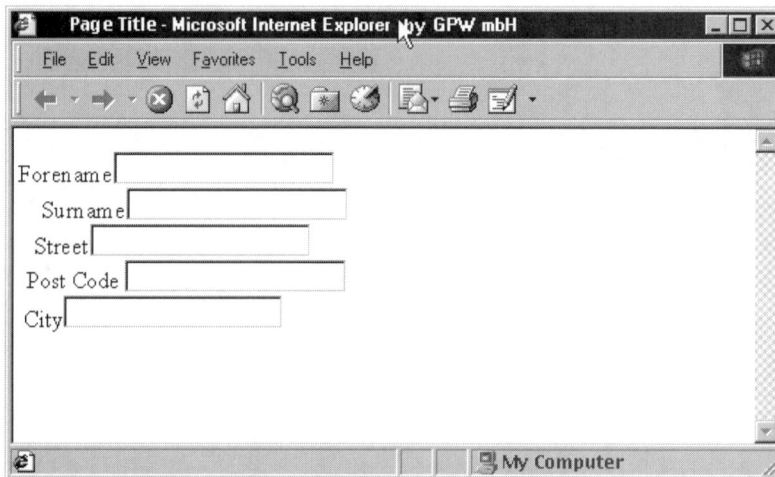

Problems with the names of entry fields

Implementation

The solution is a double-columned table. The first column contains the field names and the second column the entry field. The complete table is enclosed by the form. Make sure that the FORM container is not within a table cell. You can use the SUBMIT button behind the table.

Field names are inserted in a table

Example

```
<form
     name="command"
     action="feedback.cgi"
     method="POST">

<table border=0 cellpadding=0>
<tr>
     <td bgcolor="#C0C0C0" width="30%">
     <b>Company</b></td>
     <td bgcolor="#C0C0C0" width="70%">
     <input type=text name="Company" size="40"></td>
</tr>

<tr>
     <td bgcolor="#C0C0C0" width="30%">
     Contact person </td>
     <td bgcolor="#C0C0C0" width="70%">
     Sir
     <INPUT NAME=" Salutation " TYPE="RADIO" VALUE="Sir">
     Madam
     <INPUT NAME=" Salutation " TYPE="RADIO" VALUE="Madam"></td>
</tr>

<tr>
     <td bgcolor="#C0C0C0" width="30%">
     <b>Name</b></td>
     <td bgcolor="#C0C0C0" width="70%">
```

```
        <input type=text name="Name" size="40"></td>
</tr>

<tr>
        <td bgcolor="#C0C0C0" width="30%">
        Street</td>
        <td bgcolor="#C0C0C0" width="70%">
        <input type=text name="Street" size="40"></td>
</tr>

<tr>
        <td bgcolor="#C0C0C0" width="30%">
        City</td>
        <td bgcolor="#C0C0C0" width="70%">
        <input type=text name="City" size="40"></td>
</tr>

<tr>
        <td bgcolor="#C0C0C0" width="30%">Information</td>
        <td bgcolor="#C0C0C0" width="70%">
        <select name="Product">
        <option> Final consumer
        <option>Studio
        <option>Trade
        </select>
        </td>
</tr>

</table>

<br>
<input type="submit" value="Requesting Information">
</form>
```

Sound effects

Application

Provided that the sound system supports stereo or surround output, the direction from which the sound output is to be heard can be set.

Implementation

The style sheet command is used to implement this. This determines the surround effect of the sound output. The following parameters are used to decide the direction of the sound output.

```
center
```
in the centre
```
center behind
```
in the centre, behind
```
center-left
```
left of centre
```
center-left behind
```
left of centre, behind
```
center-right
```
right of centre
```
center-right behind
```
right of centre, behind
```
far-left
```
far left
```
far-left behind
```
far left, behind
```
left
```
from the left only
```
left behind
```
left, behind
```
left-side
```
left side
```
left-side behind
```
left side, behind
```
right
```
from the right only
```
right behind
```
right, behind
```
right-side
```
right side
```
right-side behind
```
right side, behind

Example

```
<style type="text/css">
h1, h2 {azimuth:right}
h3, h4 {azimuth:right behind}
</style>

<div style="azimuth: left">
</div>
```

Marking up images

Application

Labelling embedded images and positioning circulating text cause difficulties time and again. In this example, we show the most useful alignment commands.

Implementation

The ALIGN attribute of the IMG command is of great help in determining how text should be ordered around an image. With this attribute you decide exactly how the browser should operate.

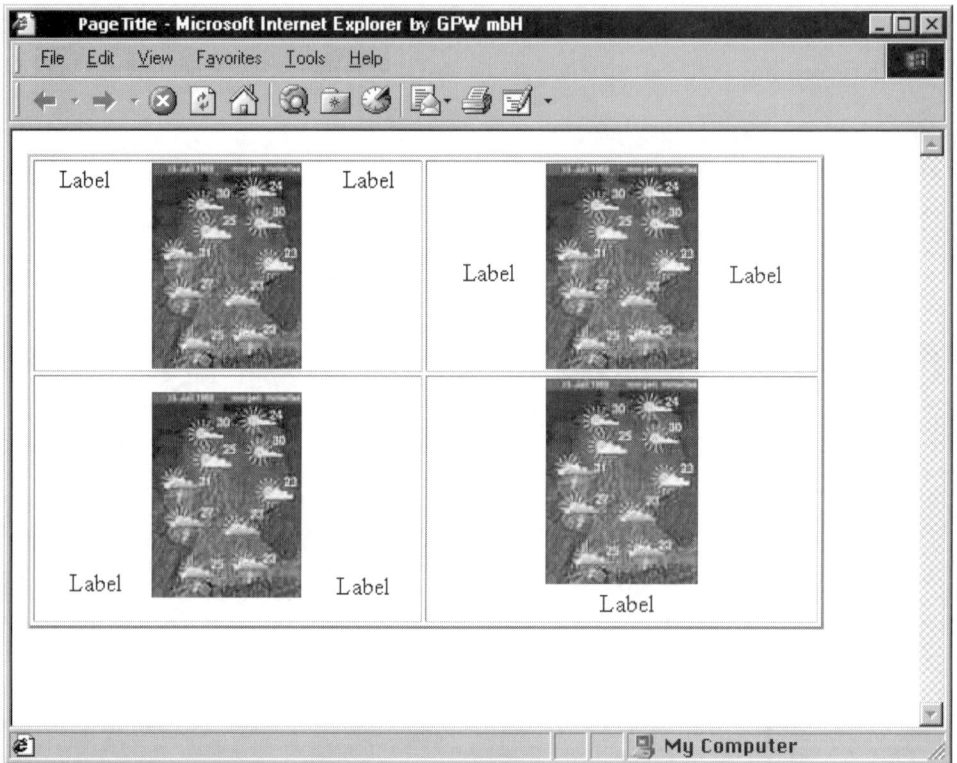

Different ways of labelling an image

Example

```
<html>
<body>

<table border="2">
<tr>
```

```
<td>
Label
<img src="clouds.jpg" align="top">
Label
</td>
</tr>

<tr>
<td>
Label
<img src="clouds.jpg" align="middle">
Label
</td>
</tr>

<tr>
<td>
Label
<img src="clouds.jpg" align="bottom">
Label
</td>
</tr>

<tr>
<td align="center">
<img src="clouds.jpg">
<br>
Label
</td>
</tr>

</body>
</html>
```

Category: User-friendliness

Optimising keyboard use

Application

HTML 4.0 provides several new ways of making Web sites navigable not only with the mouse but also with the keyboard. These extensions were designed especially for physically handicapped people who are instructed to use the keyboard. Optimise your pages bearing these handicapped people in mind!

Implementation

With the ACCESSKEY attribute you can set up a keyboard control for the element. Submit any character as the value. If the user presses the character on the keyboard, then the accompanying object is dialled.

Under most Windows programs one can move to the next or previous entry field using the Tab key. This function is also enabled in the Web browser. Through the TABINDEX attribute an element's task in the jump command is assigned. If the attribute is not used, then the browser accesses the HTML document according to the sequence of commands.

Both attributes can be used for almost all HTML commands which necessitate access or a selection (e.g. form fields or links).

Example

```
<a href="http://www.microsoft.com" accesskey="m">
<a href="http://www.microsoft.com" tabindex="2">
<a href="http://www.netscape.com" tabindex="1">
```

Tips

Use of the old attribute is very important for blind visitors to your Web site who are unable to view images or read their contents. Be sure to recognise this and add some descriptive text to every graphic.

User-friendly forms

Application

Forms should be used to encourage visitor to your site to contact you. Protect these when working with personal data. If you also want to know the email addresses of visitors, assure them that these addresses will not be distributed and they will not be bombarded with junk email.

Structure the input form explicitly and avoid asking for data which could be considered too personal. If you create a form with predefined entry fields you will receive some additional information.

Implementation

You can easily encourage visitors to fill out a form. You should provide as many options as you can, and radio buttons, tick boxes or drop-down menus where possible. Avoid fields in which the visitor has to enter too much text.

Through the VALUE attribute text fields can be given an initial value. Radio buttons and tick boxes can be activated with CHECKED.

Predefined entry fields are helpful for visitors

Example

```
<form
      action="feedback.cgi"
      method="POST"
      name="Info">
Name:
<input name="Name" size=40 maxlength=60 value="@"><br>
E-Mail-Address:
<input name="E-Mail" size=40 maxlength=40><br>
Post Code:
<input name="PLZ" size=7 maxlength=7 value=" "><br>

<input type=radio name="Use" value="Private">
Private<br>
<input type=radio name="Use" value="No">
Business<br>

Which operating system do you use?<br>
<select name="operating system">
<option>No idea
<option>Windows 95
<option>Windows 98
<option>Windows NT 4.0
<option>Windows 2000
<option>Linux
</select>

How do you assess your knowledge?<br>
<input type=radio name="Knowledge" value="Beginner">
Beginner
<input type=radio name="Knowledge" value="Advanced">
Advanced
<input type=radio name="Knowledge" value="Professional">
Professional

<input value="Mail now!" type=submit>
</form>
```

Tip

Avoid using the RESET button. The user may select it by mistake. There is a danger of all data being inadvertently deleted by the user and then he or she will not want to re-enter them. If the visitor does not wish to submit the form, he or she can leave the page without doing so.

Setting your page as a home page

Application

Every browser has a predefined start page. The users start surfing from this point when they start the browser. They can also go back to the home page at any time by clicking on the home page button.

Every user can choose a home page. It would be ideal if visitors indicated your site as their own home pages. You can ask them if they want to do this. The user merely has to select a button on your site and the rest then happens automatically.

Implementation

A small JavaScript can be created with this feature program. Unfortunately, it only works with Microsoft Internet Explorer. As soon the button is pressed, an option asking whether the user would like to select this address as a home page appears.

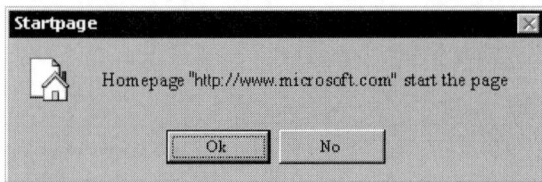

Confirmation in progress

Example

```
<a href="test.htm" class="chlnk"
onmouseover="this.style.behavior='url(#default#homepage)';
this.setHomePage('http://www.cybertechnics.co.uk);">
Determine Homepage
</a>
```

Windows tool tips

Application

No doubt you are already familiar with Windows the tool tips. This information is also available in HTML documents, but only with the Microsoft browser until recently.

Implementation

Almost all elements can be given a title. This title is used in Microsoft Explorer to display a small tool tip by moving over it with the mouse.

Tool tips provide additional operational information

Example

```
<div title="Tooltips">
</div>

<td title="Table cell">
</td>
```

Tips

This attribute exists for almost all HTML elements.

Menu selection by drop-down field

Application

If you wish to make as many menu items available as possible, there is an alternative. The visitor can access all menu entries via a drop-down list. This selection method requires only a single line on the page. There is room in every HTML document for access to the complete page structure.

Implementation

Implementation is executed using a small JavaScript program. A form element can also be used as a control element. The button confirming selection also originates from the form functions.

Example

```
<html>
<head>
<script language="JavaScript">
<!--
```

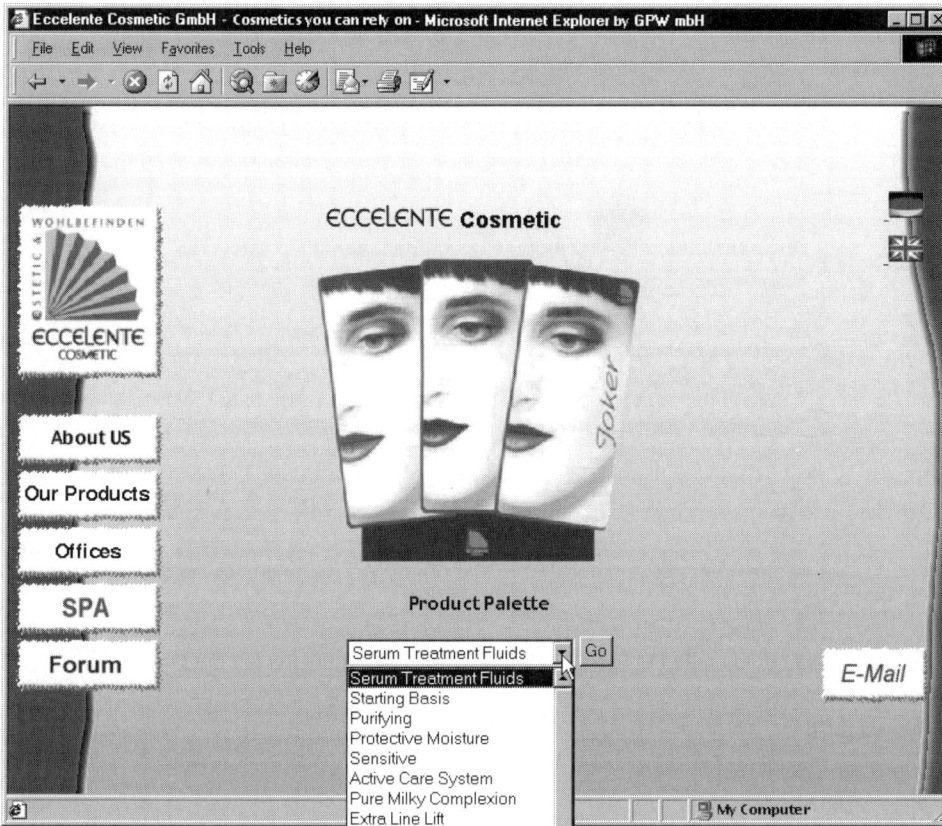

An alternative menu selection: by drop-down menu

```
function goto_export()
{
     var selectedIndex=document.form1.to.selectedIndex;
     {
     var selection
     =document.form1.to.options[selectedIndex].value;
     self.location=selection;
     }
}
// -->
</script>
</head>

<body>

<form name="form1">
<font face="Arial,Helvetica"><b>Product Palette</b><br><br>

<select name="to" size="1">
```

```
<option value="page1.htm">Serum Treatment Fluids</option>
<option value="page2.htm">Starting Basis</option>
<option value="page3.htm">Purifying</option>
<option value="page4.htm">Protective Moisture</option>
<option value="page5.htm">Sensitive</option>
<option value="page6.htm">Active Care System</option>
<option value="page7.htm">Pure Milky Complexion</option>
<option value="page8.htm">Extra Line Lift</option>
<option value="page9.htm">Eye zone Contours</option>
<option value="page10.htm">Body styling</option>
<option value="page11.htm">Feet</option>
<option value="page12.htm">Beauty Plus</option>
<option value="page11.htm">Line M</option>
<option value="page11.htm">Sun & Sport</option>
</select>

<input type=button value="Go" onclick='goto_export();'>
</form>

</body>
</html>
```

Creating pages via image frames

Application

Draw an image frame around your document. This effect, easily converted with HTML, gives your page an unusual appearance and a stronger visual impact than many other pages. A graphic image frame is drawn around the document content.

Implementation

Implementation using HTML is made easy by inserting a large table. The construction of the frame or a single graphic is relatively time-consuming. This therefore depends on how detailed your frame should be.

A complete frame should be drawn and divided into the single parts listed below. Precision is required. First cut the four outer corners of the frame and store these as separate files. Then cut out the frame pages below and above and the left and on right, and store these as graphics.

Example

```
<html>
<head>
<title>Page title</title>
</head>
```

```
<body>
<table cellpadding="0" cellspacing="0" border="0">

<tr>
      <td>
      <img src=" Frame_above_left.gif">
      </td>

      <td>
      <img src="Frame_above.gif">
      </td>

      <td>
      <img src="Frame_above_right.gif">
      </td>
</tr>

<tr>
      <td>
      <img src="Frame_left.gif">
      </td>

      <td valign="top" rowspan="2">
      "Here is your text"
      </td>

      <td align="right">
      <img src="Frame_right.gif">
      </td>
</tr>

<tr>
      <td>
      <img src="Frame_left.gif">
      </td>

      <td align="right">
      <img src="Frame_right.gif">
      </td>
</tr>

<tr>
      <td>
      <img src="Frame_above_left.gif">
      </td>

      <td>
      <img src="Frame_above.gif">
```

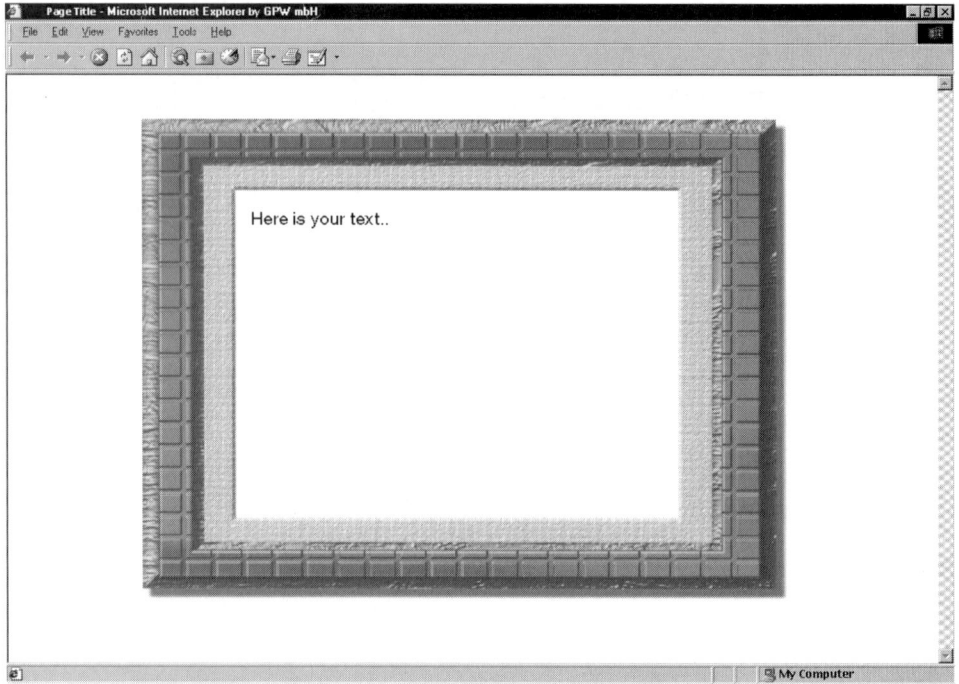

Image frames in your document

```
        </td>

        <td>
        <img SRC="Frame_above_right.gif">
        </td>
</tr>
</table>

</body>
</html>
```

Category: Good HTML Style

Embedding graphics

Application

When embedding graphics use all available parameters if possible, and indicate these in full. The alternative text as well as size information of the image are especially important.

Implementation

If possible, images should only be used in their original size, and scaling down or up of images should be avoided. The advantage of the size detail is that large dummies can immediately be inserted when constructing pages. If these parameters are not indicated, then the entire page must be calculated again once the images have arrived.

It is best to indicate a description of the image as text, which also makes sense if the image has not been downloaded correctly or the user has deactivated the graphics transfer. Mentioning the file size is useful so that the visitor can estimate how long the download will take.

Example

```
<img scr="image.jpg" width="100" length="200"
     alt="This image displays...">
```

Tips

In HTML 4.0 the alternative text is a recommended command.

Commenting documents

Application

To structure your document more efficiently and to make data processing easier for other people (e.g. in environments where several administrators handle the same document comment blocks can be inserted. These comments are not displayed and are only visible in the source text. However, remember that every visitor to your site can a view the source text. On the one hand, you can learn from other pages through doing this; on the other hand somebody may steal a good idea from you.

Implementation

Comments can easily be inserted using of the comment tags. Only use comments if they make sense because they waste down-loading time.

Example

```
<!--
You need a browser version 4 for the complete representation of this
document
-->
```

Tips

By inputting JavaScript it is recommended that the program code be indicated as a comment. Non-JavaScript supporting browsers recognise the script as a comment, so no error is reported.

Changing download sequence

Application

HTML has no control over the sequence in which elements of the Web site are download. At first, the browser transfers the HTML document and then starts to transfer the single embedded elements of the sequence from beginning to end. Depending on how many simultaneous downloads have been assigned to the browser, it can happen that three or four elements are simultaneously rebuilt.

It is sometimes preferable and perhaps sensible to change this sequence.

Implementation

Any image embedded in HTML also enables an image with correct resolution to be indicated, which is loaded before the real graphic. The browser goes through the HTML source code, and first loads the lower resolution image provided, and then passes on to the next image.

The image is also reloaded in a higher resolution in the next run. Should an image only be indicated in a higher resolution, it can immediately pass to the next image.

If this image is chosen in a lower resolution and with a low file size, this event will be completed very quickly. A transparent GIF image offers a minimal size of 1 x 1 pixels. The actual size of the image must then of course be indicated.

Consequently, a "blind" image is inserted into all images provided with an alternative graphic with a lower resolution. The browser immediately passes to the next graphic. If no alternative graphic is indicated, the original image will immediately be downloaded. In this way, important images appear more quickly than "less important" graphics in 1 x 1 GIF format.

Example

```
<!--unimportant image-->
<img scr="image.jpg" lowscr="empty.gif"
                width="100"length="200">
<!--Essential image-->
<img scr="image.jpg">
```

Tip

This method works exclusively with images of the same graphic type. For example, JPG images may not be selected in a high resolution, and GIF images in a low resolution.

Use of META tags

Application

By automatically registering pages, many Internet search engines only read the first 200 characters of a file and transfer these into their database.

For this reason one should ensure that as many important keywords as possible are displayed in the first 200 characters of the HTML document. This is almost impossible with pages containing frames. Many search engines also therefore have considerable problems with frames technology.

Some criteria to register with search engines are formulated using META information. Of course, these are not handled in the same way by every search engine. Rather it is better to consider the construction of the META information every time.

Implementation

Submit indications for registration in the index of the search engine by using the META tags so as to achieve better search results.

Indicate a short description of the content of the pages in two or three sentences with the `Description` keyword. With `Keywords`, you can indicate the keywords with which you would like your site to be found. This detail should be a maximum of 1000 characters.

Example

```
<meta name="description"content="Description">
<meta name="keywords"content="Keyword1, Keyword2">
<meta http-equiv="pragma"content="no-cache">
<meta http-equiv="robots"content="index,follow">
<meta name="resource-type"content="document">
<meta http-equiv="language"content="de">
```

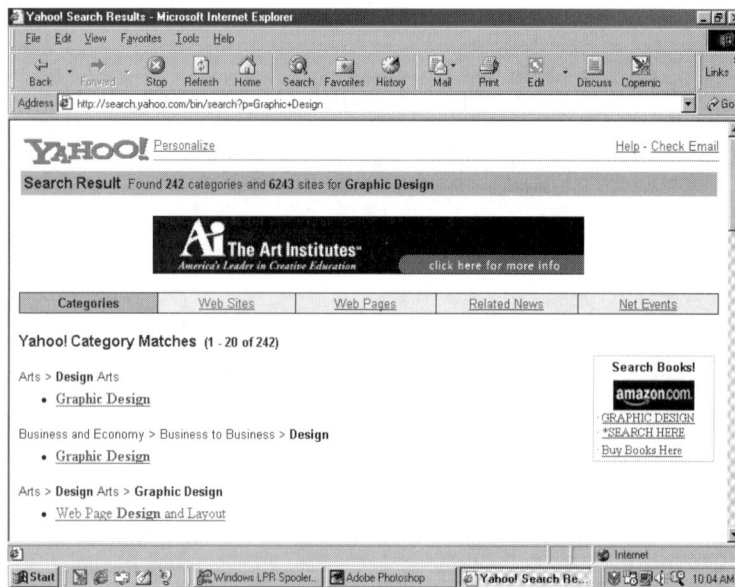

If you are lucky, a search engine shows your site as a result of a search on a relevant keyword

Tips

Do not try to influence the search engine by repeatedly using the same keywords. Nowadays, most search machines acknowledge if somebody is cheating by using algorithms, and many react by giving those sites a lower rating in the index.

Typography

Application

It is currently possible to choose the font size of the character type with the progressive browser version, provided that the set font is available on the user's computer. One only need use the following three fonts, which can be found on almost every Windows and Macintosh computer:

- Arial
- Courier New
- Times New Roman

Implementation

Windows displays the Arial font. The corresponding Macintosh font is Helvetica. This command works with both Explorer and Navigator from version 3.0 onwards.

Example

```
<font face="Arial,helv,Helvetia"></div>

<div style="font-family:Arial,Helvetica"></div>
```

Tips

You should ideally use style sheets to select the font, and avoid the command FONT where possible.

Hyperlink colours

Application

Every browser user can define in which colour hyperlinks he wants to be represented. If this setting is not executed, the standard colours or the colours provided by the author of the page will be used.

Even if this choice should be left to the discretion of the user, there is a useful range of applications for this option.

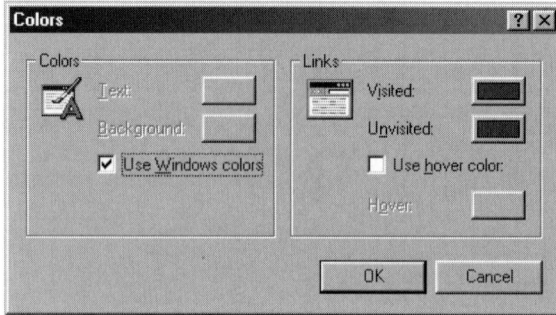

You find the settings in Internet Explorer under Tools/Internet Options/General/Colors

The default setting is as follows on most computers:

- Hyperlink
  General link, not yet clicked
  Blue

- Frequented hyperlink
  Previously clicked link whose pages can be found in the cache memory
  Violet

- Active hyperlink
  A previously selected hyperlink
  Red

Implementation

If one looks at the previously used colours and checks with what they are associated, the following changes are actually implemented:

- Hyperlink
  This link is still new to the user, and must be drawn to his attention with a bright red.
  Red

- Frequented hyperlink
  The pages in this link are already known to the user, and can be entered via a calm blue colour in the background.
  Blue.

- Active hyperlink
  This colour only plays a subordinate role since it is only displayed for a short time.
  Violet

Example

```
<body alink="black">
<body vlink="red">
<body link="#00FFFF">
```

Tips

Avoid using too many hyperlinks on your pages. A page with too many cross-references is confusing.

Deleting lines behind images

Application

Sometimes a small line disturbs the general impression of the page behind the graphics. The origin of the line stems from text being marked blue to indicate a link. How can it appear like this? It means that there has been a mistake in the programming of the link.

Implementation

This error lies in the blank space indicated in the link. This blank space should be deleted or placed behind the link so this line disappears.

Example

Incorrect

```
<html>
<body>
<a href="page2.htm">
<img border="0" src="vwlogo.gif"> </a>
Click here
</body>
</html>
```

Correct

```
<html>
<body>
<a href="page2.htm">
<img border="0" src="vwlogo.gif"></a>
Click here
</body>
</html>
```

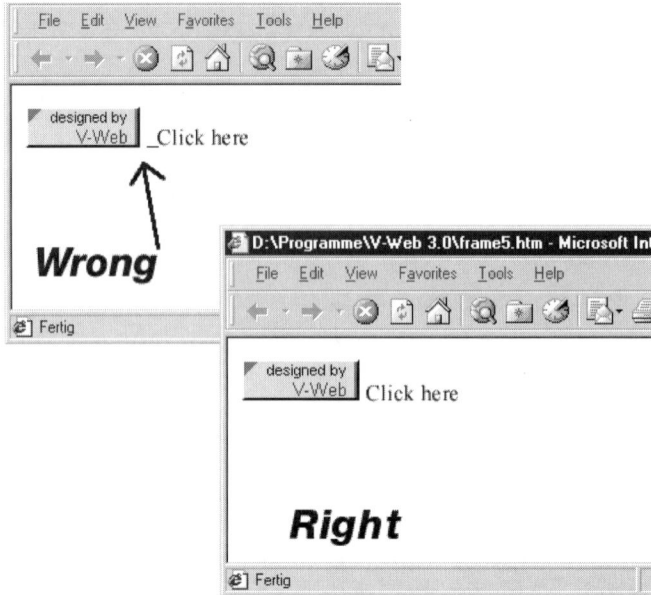

Inserting the correct colour value

Application

As soon as you wish to insert HTML colours directly, for example for the background or a text, you must know the corresponding colour code. On the one hand the universal hexadecimal values can be entered to display these colours, or alternatively the common English colour names may be entered instead.

Implementation

The hexadecimal value gives the colour components red, green and blue in the RGB colour system (#RRGGBB). Each of these three colours ranges from 0 to 256 in other colour. The respective shares are indicated as two-digit hexadecimal numbers. Every arbitrary colour is formed in this way.

Most browsers also understand common English colour names. For these an RGB value is already saved in the browser and needs only be called. Alternatively, the colour notation can be used.

As there are no uniform standard colour names, take care when using the Browser. However, the 16 most commonly used colours are understood by both the Netscape browser and by Internet Explorer.

Colour name	Hexadecimal value
aqua	#00FFFF
black	#000000
blue	#0000FF
fuchsia	#FF00FF
grey	#808080
green	#008000
lime	#00FF00
maroon	#800000
navy	#000080
olive	#808000
purple	#800080
red	#FF0000
silver	#C0C0C0
teal	#008080
white	#FFFFFF
yellow	#FFFF00

The following 216 colour names were introduced by Netscape:

Colour name	Hexadecimal value
aliceblue	#F0F8FF
antiquewhite	#FAEBD7
aquamarine	#7FFFD4
azure	#F0FFFF
beige	#F5F5DC
blueviolet	#8A2BE2
brown	#A52A2A
burlywood	#DEB887
cadetblue	#5F9EA0
chartreuse	#7FFF00
chocolate	#D2691E
coral	#FF7F50
cornflowerblue	#6495ED
cornsilk	#FFF8DC
crimson	#DC143C
darkblue	#00008B

Colour name	Hexadecimal value
darkcyan	#008B8B
darkgoldenrod	#B8860B
darkgrey	#A9A9A9
darkgreen	#006400
darkkhaki	#BDB76B
darkmagenta	#8B008B
darkolivegreen	#556B2F
darkorange	#FF8C00
darkorchid	#9932CC
darkred	#8B0000
darksalmon	#E9967A
darkseagreen	#8FBC8F
darkslateblue	#483D8B
darkslategrey	#2F4F4F
darkturquoise	#00CED1
darkviolet	#9400D3
deeppink	#FF1493
deepskyblue	#00BFFF
dimgray	#696969
dodgerblue	#1E90FF
firebrick	#B22222
floralwhite	#FFFAF0
forestgreen	#228B22
gainsboro	#DCDCDC
ghostwhite	#F8F8FF
gold	#FFD700
goldenrod	#DAA520
greenyellow	#ADFF2F
honeydew	#F0FFF0
hotpink	#FF69B4
indianred	#CD5C5C
indigo	#4B0082
ivory	#FFFFF0
khaki	#F0E68C
lavender	#E6E6FA

Colour name	Hexadecimal value
lavenderblush	#FFF0F5
lawngreen	#7CFC00
lemonchiffon	#FFFACD
lightblue	#ADD8E6
lightcoral	#F08080
lightcyan	#E0FFFF
lightgoldenrodyel-low	#FAFAD2
lightgreen	#90EE90
lightgrey	#D3D3D3
lightpink	#FFB6C1
lightsalmon	#FFA07A
lightseagreen	#20B2AA
lightskyblue	#87CEFA
lightslategray	#778899
lightsteelblue	#B0C4DE
lightyellow	#FFFFE0
limegreen	#32CD32
linen	#FAF0E6
mediumaquamarine	#66CDAA
mediumblue	#0000CD
mediumorchid	#BA55D3
mediumpurple	#9370D
mediumseagreen	#3CB371
mediumslateblue	#7B68EE
mediumspringgreen	#00FA9A
mediumturquoise	#48D1CC
mediumvioletred	#C71585
midnightblue	#191970
mintcream	#F5FFFA
mistyrose	#FFE4E1
moccasin	#FFE4B5
navajowhite	#FFDEAD
oldlace	#FDF5E6
olivedrab	#6B8E23

Colour name	Hexadecimal value
orange	#FFA500
orangered	#FF4500
orchid	#DA70D6
palegoldenrod	#EEE8AA
palegreen	#98FB98
paleturquoise	#AFEEEE
palevioletred	#DB7093
papayawhip	#FFEFD5
peachpuff	#FFDAB9
peru	#CD853F
pink	#FFC0CB
plum	#DDA0DD
powderblue	#B0E0E6
rosybrown	#BC8F8F
royalblue	#4169E1
saddlebrown	#8B4513
salmon	#FA8072
sandybrown	#F4A460
seagreen	#2E8B57
seashell	#FFF5EE
sienna	#A0522D
skyblue	#87CEEB
slateblue	#6A5ACD
slategrey	#708090
snow	#FFFAFA
springgreen	#00FF7F
steelblue	#4682B4
tan	#D2B48C
thistle	#D8BFD8
tomato	#FF6347
turquoise	#40E0D0
violet	#EE82EE
wheat	#F5DEB3
whitesmoke	#F5F5F5
yellowgreen	#9ACD32

Example

```
<body alink="black">
<body vlink="red">
<body link="#00FFFF">
<body bgcolor="blue">
<body bgcolor="#FFFF00">

<font face="Arial" color="blue">
Now it changes to blue...
</font>
<font color="#000000">
... and now black!
</font>
```

Category: Faster Downloading

Loading background graphics

Application

Nowadays, there are often single pages on the Internet on which visitors spend a long time, as they probably read the text without the pages being accompanied by extensive graphics. These pages are therefore downloaded very quickly. It may happen occasionally that no data will be downloaded and the server will wait for user input.

This time could be put to good use by loading graphics for the next page in advance. These are then displayed considerably faster on the users screen.

Implementation

This trick makes use of images being downloaded to the visitor once and being quickly renewed on other pages through the fast cache memory of the browser. Of course it makes little sense to load an image which is already available on the previous page. These images must be downloaded invisibly and in the background. The same images are then reinstated on the following page. The browser already "knows" these and fetches them from its cache memory.

To make images invisible, there is a small but effective trick. Simply submit 0 as a value for the height and width of the image. The image is then transferred in its entirety, but not displayed.

Example

Page1:

```
<img src="image.gif" width="0" height="0">
```

Page2:

```
<img src="image.gif">
```

Tips

This trick is ineffective if the user has turned off the browsers cache memory. In this case, it may even lead to the images being downloaded twice.

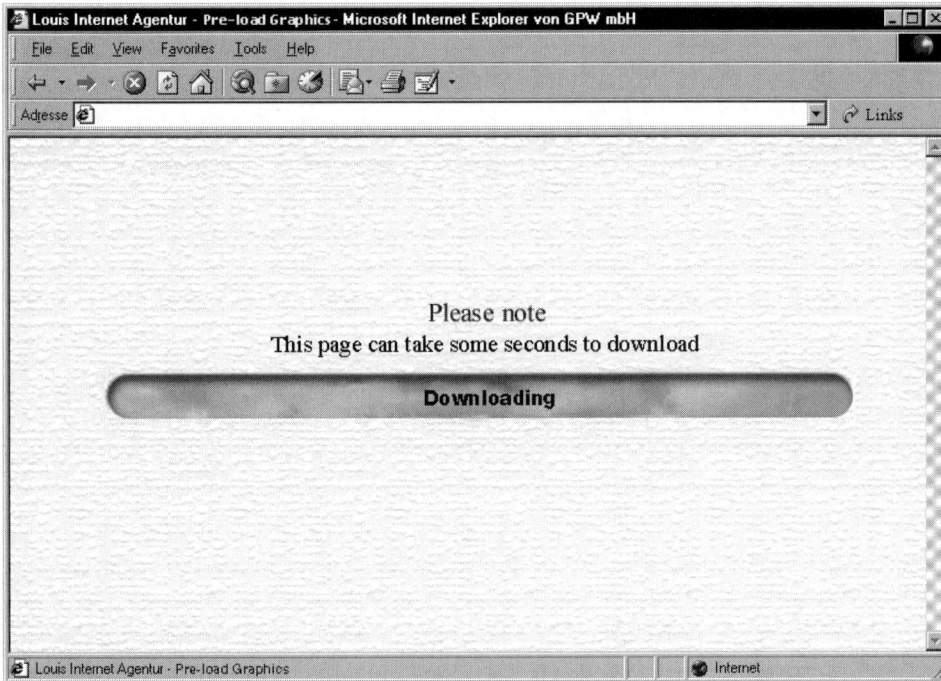

The user will frequently be notified that a download is taking place in the background

Tiling large tables

Application

Most browsers encounter problems with displaying large tables. The browser can then build up the table if it knows the exact measurements of the single cells. It will often only recognise this if all contents and embedded graphics are completely downloaded.

The user may wait for several minutes without seeing either the table or any action during this time. The visitor will frequently give up and surf to the next page.

Implementation

The tables should be divided into many small tables. It will build up slowly and the visitor can follow its progress.

Example

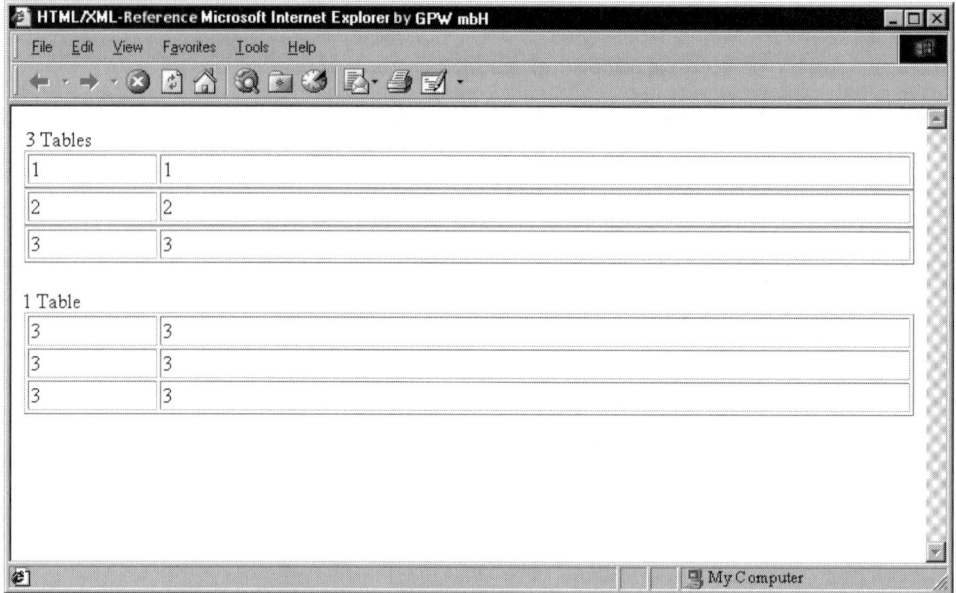

There is hardly any difference between the two solutions

```
<html>
<head>
<title>HTML/XML-Reference</title>
</head>
<body>

3 tables
<table width="100%" border="1">
<tr>
    <td width="100">1</td>
    <td>1</td>
</tr>
</table>

<table width="100%" border="1">
<tr>
    <td width="100">2</td>
    <td>2</td>
</tr>
</table>

<table width="100%" border="1">
<tr>
    <td width="100">3</td>
    <td>3</td>
```

```
</tr>
</table>

<br>
1 table
<table width="100%" border="1">
<tr>
     <td width="100">3</td>
     <td>3</td>
</tr>
<tr>
     <td width="100">3</td>
     <td>3</td>
</tr>
<tr>
     <td width="100">3</td>
     <td>3</td>
</tr>
</table>

</body>
</html>
```

Tip

Ensure that tables are created with the same measurements by stating their size. In this way the small tables will work just like one single large table.

Accelerating hyperlinks

Application

When you install external hyperlinks into your pages, it goes without saying that their functionality should be checked on a regular basis.

However, did you know that links functioning correctly can be accelerated in their execution? If possible, you should always indicate the whole address of hyperlinks, including the name of the page. Even if you indicate the domain, the server will not necessarily recognise this immediately. The server must first respond with the name of the home page. Only then can this be downloading.

Implementation

Instead of a domain, simply indicate the complete URL of the hyperlink, including the name of the HTML document.

Example

Poor:
```
<a href="http://www.yahoo.com">
Search engine Yahoo
</a>
```

Better:
```
<a href="http://www.yahoo.com/">
Search engine Yahoo
</a>
```

Best:
```
<a href="http://www.yahoo.com/index.html">
Search engine Yahoo
</a>
```

Tips

You should also ensure that spelling is correct. In this way you ensure that the browser can immediately obtain the page from its cache memory.

Accelerating JavaScript execution

Application

Provided that a script does not execute any changes in screen contents, this execution can be accelerated. The browser should immediately speed up.

Implementation

The DEFER attribute is executed if no changes are made by the script to an HTML document. In this way the browser can continue to construct the page without further modifications. You could insert this attribute into the SCRIPT command.

Example

```
<!--
<script type="JavaScript" defer>


...

</script>
--/>
```

Table Index

Table Index

7

Function / Command	Reference	Practice
displaying a margin line	64	
distance from bottom	287	
distance from first character	79	
distance from left	286	
distance from margin	245	
distance from right	286	
distance from top	287	
DIV	130	
DL	133	
DM	80	
DOCTYPE		436
— XML	136	
document alignment	21	
document directory	94	
document features	253	
document head	185	
document type		436
document type definition	136	436
dotted (border style)	66	
double (border style)	66	
drop-down field		534
DT	136	
DTD	136, 139	436
dur	288	
DURATION		515
Dutch	221	
EBN-Form		483
electronic mail address	94	
electronic speech synthesizer	249	
element	141	
— XSL	141	
ELEMENT	141	
element activated	70	
element of group activated	81	
element title	395	
EM	142	
e-mail	19	
e-mail reference	9	
embed	145	
EMBED	145	
embedded frames	192	

Function / Command	Reference	Practice
fixed	43	512
flow text	113	
font family	155	
font size	156	
font width	156	
FONT	152	458
font-family	155	471
font-size	156	
font-stretch	156	
font-style	157	
font-weight	158	
FOR	158	
FORM	159	
form data format	147	
form data	18	
form field	14	
FORM	159	
forms	159	524
FR	221	
frame	164	437
FRAME	164, 165	487
frame definition		487
FRAMEBORDER	168, 169	487
frames		486
— as margin		487
— invisible		487
FRAMESET	169	437
FRAMESIZE		487
FRAMESPACING	170	
French	221	
ftp	339	
FUCHSIA	375	
functional expressions	148	
General entity	171	
generic family	155	
German	221	
GET	161	
gif		489
GIF image		541
glossary	113	574
GLOSSARY	305	

Function / Command	Reference	Practice
table footer	22, 73	
table header	10, 23, 73	
target document language	183	
target window	362	
TARGET	362	443, 497, 498
target-element	363	
TBODY	364	
td		473
TD	368	
TEAL	375	
television	249	
telnet	339	
text body	61, 185	
text color	105, 374	
text conversion	382	
text-decoration	380	517
text direction	50	
text paragraph	24	
text section	130	
text with shades	381	
TEXT	374	
— SMIL	373	
text-align	375	
TEXTAREA	376	
text-decoration	380	
text-indent	381	
text-shadow	381	
text-transform	381	
TFOOT	382	
TH	386	
THEAD	391	
three-dimensional margin	168	
tiff		471
tile effect	45	
Time Zone Designator	113, 119	
time zone	113	
title		504
TITLE	396	
— html attribute	395	
token	261, 398	
tool tips		533